A History of Economic Thought

LIONEL ROBBINS

A History of Economic Thought

THE LSE LECTURES

EDITED BY
STEVEN G. MEDEMA
AND
WARREN J. SAMUELS

PRINCETON UNIVERSITY PRESS

PRINCETON AND OXFORD

Copyright © 1998 by Princeton University Press
Published by Princeton University Press, 41 William Street, Princeton, New Jersey 08540
In the United Kingdom: Princeton University Press, 3 Market Place,
Woodstock, Oxfordshire, OX20 1SY
All Rights Reserved

Fifth printing, and first paperback printing, 2000
Paperback ISBN 0-691-07014-8

The Library of Congress has cataloged the cloth edition of this book as follows

Robbins, Lionel Robbins, Baron, 1898–1984.
A history of economic thought : the LSE lectures / Lionel Robbins;
edited by Steven G. Medema and Warren J. Samuels.
p.   cm.
Includes bibliographical references (p.   ) and index.
ISBN 0-691-01244-X (cloth : alk. paper)
1. Economics—History. I. Medema, Steven G. II. Samuels, Warren J., 1933–.
III. London School of Economics and Political Science. IV. Title.
HB75.R526 1998   330.1—dc21   97–51808

This book has been composed in Galliard

Printed on acid-free paper. ∞

www.pup.princeton.edu

Printed in the United States of America

7   9   10   8

TO THE MEMORY OF

• *LADY ROBBINS* •

(1 8 9 6 – 1 9 9 7)

CONTENTS

WILLIAM J. BAUMOL, NEW YORK UNIVERSITY

THESE ELOQUENT lectures speak for themselves, and so does the careful and scholarly accomplishment of the editors. What, then, can I hope to add in a foreword? The answer is that I was there. I, like so many before and after me, had the unduplicable experience of hearing these illuminating lectures delivered by this remarkable man, my teacher, who became my close friend. Anyone reading these lectures can, and surely will, admire their style, the range of material they cover, the dazzling intellectual brilliance, and the stimulation they provide. I can only attempt to convey, although inadequately, the flavor of the unforgettable experience.

Central to that experience was the man himself. Tall, massive, stately, with a sonorous voice and a leonine mane that made all his students marvel at his parents' perspicacity in providing such felicitous genes. It is sheer understatement to describe him as a man with a powerful personality. His students would find themselves unconsciously mimicking his style, the personal attributes and speech patterns which recalled an earlier, less mechanized age. Yet one soon learned that his was not a domineering personality. His sense of humor was profound, and his anecdotes riveting. He was invariably considerate and kind, particularly to younger people and particularly when few others were present to observe his acts. But even more striking were his command of the language, his clarity of mind, and his incredible erudition assisted by an incredible memory.

An anecdote will illustrate two of these attributes, though I can tell many more. As sometimes happened, I found myself at lunch with Lionel, this time joined by Harold Laski. I was then an assistant lecturer, a rank so low that it has no U.S. equivalent. Soon the conversation became a heated discussion of some obscure eighteenth-century authors and their even more obscure nineteenth-century critics, none of whom I had heard of before. Still, I was not condemned to be left out of the conversation. From time to time as it progressed, after some thought had been expressed, Lionel would turn to me: "Don't you agree, my dear William?" with a pause long enough for me to add a comment if I wished, but not so long as to embarrass me if I had nothing to say.

He knew incredible amounts about the visual arts, opera, literature and history besides economics, but it was the magnitude of the information he had about economics that was really overwhelming, and much of that came out in the lectures. They were delivered in the large auditorium called "the old theatre," a dark paneled room, poorly lit and very poorly heated. I attended the London School of Economics from 1946 to 1949, immediately after World War II. London still bore the ugly signs of the brutal bombing it had undergone. Fuel and food were scarce and closely rationed. The student body, clothed in the durable, well-worn garments that were hoarded from an ungenerous clothing ration, were as scruffy a lot as can be imagined just this side of gentility. Yet all that was forgotten as graduate students joined undergraduates to listen, spellbound, as that sonorous voice recreated for us not only the ideas but the very frame of mind of our predecessors in economic analysis.

On later visits to London, he would generally take his delightful wife, a powerful personality in her own right, and mine along with me to the National Gallery on a Sunday morning when it was closed to the public but open to him as a member of the board. On one of the last of these visits he complained to me that his memory was no longer what it had been. Then, as we strode through the galleries, whenever I showed particular interest in some painting he would unfailingly report how it had been acquired by the gallery, whether its first owner was known and who it was, the condition of the painting, and what the X rays showed to lie beneath its surface.

After receiving my degree from the LSE I went on to teach my own seminar on the history of economic ideas at Princeton University for some twenty years. When I first received this manuscript from the Robbins family, who continue to be our dear friends, I wondered how much I would now get out of it. To begin with a sampling, I happened to turn to the chapter on Mandeville and came across Lionel's praise of the style and wisdom of this migrant from another country (the Netherlands) and another discipline (medicine). The urge to rush to my own copy of Mandeville could not be resisted, and the next few weeks included the delight of discovery for myself of these observations of one great mind about another.

In the last years, all the correspondence between us and Lionel and his wife Iris were invariably signed "with love." I trust this preface communicates some of that feeling.

THESE LECTURES, which are published here for the first time, were given by Lionel Robbins at the London School of Economics during 1979–1980 and 1980–1981.

Lionel Robbins was one of the giants of university education in general and of economics in particular in the United Kingdom in the twentieth century. He had a distinguished career in public life, as an economic advisor to government, in the management of the arts, in journalism, and in the reform of higher education.[1] Although perhaps best known in economics for his work in economic theory and methodology (notably *An Essay on the Nature and Significance of Economic Science* [London: Macmillan, 1932]) and on the theory of economic policy, Robbins was the leading historian of economic thought in the United Kingdom during his professional life. He produced seminal works on a number of subjects, including *The Theory of Economic Policy in English Classical Political Economy* (London: Macmillan, 1952), *Robert Torrens and the Evolution of Classical Economics* (London: Macmillan, 1958), *The Theory of Economic Development in the History of Economic Thought* (London: Macmillan, 1968), and *The Evolution of Modern Economic Theory* (Chicago: Aldine, 1970).

There have been several magisterial and duly celebrated lecture courses on the history of economic thought. Those given by Wesley C. Mitchell at Columbia, Jacob Viner at Chicago and Princeton, Joseph Schumpeter at Harvard, and Edwin R. A. Seligman at Columbia are among the best known and most revered. Included in that class in the United Kingdom was the course given by Lionel Robbins at the LSE. In that course and through his published work, Robbins either taught or greatly influenced many if not all of the leading historians of economic thought of the next generation in England and elsewhere.

The lectures transcribed here, delivered when Robbins was in his eighties, were truly magisterial. Robbins had the erudition and rhetorical capacity, as well as the motivation and loving care, to teach his subject interestingly and well. The lectures, given their varying levels of specificity, are masterly examples of concision, clarity, and brilliance of exposition. But these are only lectures, subject to the limitations of the mode of presentation, constraints of time, style of language and exclusion of both relevant content and detail. The text is not that of the treatise Robbins might have written. But the lectures do present Robbins' major themes on the subjects covered.

One can learn a good deal about the history of economic thought from these lectures. Although they probably are not the best initial reading for someone just getting started in the field, the reader will not go wrong in perusing them. The greatest value in these lectures will be for those interested in Robbins himself or in the teaching of the subject, as well as in how he handled numerous interpretive matters.

The history of economics does not write itself. The economy, the development of economic thought and of economics as a professional discipline, and the historical account of that development are artifacts, each socially constructed. Accordingly, the reader will be interested in Robbins' construction of the history of economic thought.

In his first lecture, Robbins justifies his subject and identifies his mode of expounding it. Paraphrasing, Robbins regards the history of economic thought as of some use in understanding what goes on in both the contemporary world and intelligent conversation about economic topics. Whereas the history of natural science is not necessary for understanding contemporary physics and biology, that is not true of economics. "Contemporary institutions and contemporary thoughts are shot through with the heritage of the past, and to know how various ideas originated, what their vicissitudes have been, intrinsically in the development of the subject, extrinsically in their influence on general thought about society, how they have become transformed, their implications in everyday speech"—all this is important if one is to have a sophisticated rather than a naive view of what is going on. In this connection he puts to good use quotations from Mark Pattison and John Maynard Keynes. It is "difficult to understand contemporary developments without some knowledge of the way in which they developed." One of Robbins' examples is "laissez faire," and in several of his aforementioned publications, especially *The Theory of Economic Policy in English Classical Political Economy*, he made essential contributions to our understanding of the fundamentals of the economic role of government. If contemporary discourse on the subject were seriously informed along the lines Robbins identifies, that discourse would indeed be far more sophisticated, and less amenable to ideological manipulation, than it presently is. The reader should understand that such sophistication would not involve antecedent assumptions as to whose interest should count in government policy; it would make both the fundamental involvement and the nature of policy changes much clearer.

Robbins next considers how his subject will be expounded. He argues in favor of using a catholic approach, which avoids the extremes of considering economic ideas to be only by-products of contemporary socioeconomic conditions and of treating economic ideas as only examples of pure thought. He aptly illustrates this position with the work of David Ricardo, whose thought was stimulated by the great issues of his day but which was conducted on terms of pure abstract reasoning "in greater remoteness from contemporary conditions than any but modern mathematical economists." He also takes a catholic, or eclectic, approach to how he will arrange his subject: "I shall go my own sweet way," he says, and will "sometimes talk about doctrine, sometimes talk about persons, sometimes talk about periods." And, apropos of the problem of taking "an impartial view

of matters so intimately concerned with one's interests and one's daily
life," Robbins adopts Gunnar Myrdal's position of "revealing one's bias
whenever one is conscious of it."

The design and content of the lectures reflect Robbins' conception of
what economics, as well as the economy, is all about. Like most mainstream economists, Robbins concentrated on exchange, pricing (value),
and the allocation of resources and therefore on the price mechanism and
the operation of pure conceptual markets. Broader considerations—such as
the organization and control of the economic system, the relationships between the theory of knowledge and social policy, and the problem of order
(considerations of freedom versus control, continuity versus change, and
hierarchy versus equality), considerations which were central to the work of
such mainstream economists as Frank H. Knight and Joseph J. Spengler—
often receive only tangential attention. In the case of Plato and Aristotle,
for example, Robbins concentrates on the issues of communism for the
ruler-guardians and of slavery—though larger implications of the division
of labor are considered—and in the case of Rome presents the conventional
view that there was no significant economic theorizing. Yet questions of
justice (which he acknowledges) and of systemic organization and control
were rampant in both Athens and Rome, and the two Greeks are known for
their different attitudes toward the problem of knowledge as the basis of
policy (idealism versus realism).

The treatment of the history of economic thought thus depends on the
lecturer's conception of the scope of economics. When Robbins treats
premodern economic thought as a matter of "anticipations" of economic
thought or of economics in the historic literature of moral philosophy,
rather than considering early thought in its own context and within larger
concerns, he clearly intends to identify economic thought with the modern
mainstream, even though post-eighteenth-century economics has always
been diverse, comprised of varieties of orthodox and heterodox schools
and individual thinkers. Thus, his "anticipations" theme is a solidly Whig
history of economic thought.[2] The meaning of past ideas is considered
largely only in relation to modern economics, for example, exchange, interest, price—and to more or less only one version of it. The economics of
earlier periods dealt with problems not significantly covered qua economics
by neoclassical theorists—though they constituted major topics for Marxian, Austrian, and Institutional economists, and even for Robbins himself
in certain of his works (*The Theory of Economic Policy in English Classical
Political Economy* [1952]; *Robert Torrens and the Evolution of Classical
Economics* [1958]; *Politics and Economics: Papers in Political Economy*
(London: Macmillan, 1963); *The Theory of Economic Development in the
History of Economic Thought* [1968]; *The Evolution of Modern Economic
Theory* [1970]; and *Political Economy: Past and Present* [1976]). Such
considerations notwithstanding, Robbins does acknowledge that "Eco-
nomics and what I call political economy have taken different paths" and

affirms his greater interest (than in Samuelson's book *Economics* [1948]) in the questions dealt with so profoundly in John Stuart Mill's *Principles of Political Economy*—though he also notes that Mill's *Some Unsettled Questions of Political Economy* is "economics in the strict sense of the word," "the narrow sense of the word."

Robbins' view of these matters is suggested by his language in going from Hume's theory of property to his theory of money. Having spoken at some length about Locke's theory of property and in even greater detail (in part through extended quotations) about Hume's theory of property, he says, "you'll find Hume's contribution, not to the background of political economy, which is what I have been talking about now, but to analytical economics." A stronger version of the statement comes earlier, just before his discussion of Locke, wherein Robbins says that he will "deal first with his [Hume's] reflections on property and then . . . proceed to the more analytical part of [Hume's] essays which deal with economics." Such a reiterated, and strongly expressed, point is not incidental. Some would say that the theory of property, so fundamental to the organization and control of the economy and to the determination of putatively "market" outcomes, is indeed part of economics, even of "analytical" economics, and not just so much "background." At any rate, all this is in aid of understanding Robbins' notion of economics as it affected what he covered and what he said in the lectures. Robbins seemed to have exhibited some tension in these matters.

What is one to make of the following statement: "And make no mistake, that although Jevons is very high up in the history of economic analysis, he is higher still as an all-round intellect in the social sciences"? The answer is suggested by a distinction coming shortly thereafter: "His important works, from your point of view—not from the point of view of these lectures. . . ." One surmises that Robbins had difficulty in pursuing a strategy for making his course coverage manageable; that the distinction between analytical economics (sometimes seemingly equated with economics) and political economy, applied economics, social science, and so on, was in aid thereof; and that one should not make too much of narrowing statements from a disciplinary point of view. Apropos of making the course manageable, one finds Robbins saying at one point (and implying at numerous other points) that "I shall ignore all that as not being, so to speak, within the limits of the subject which I am engaged to lecture on." Of course, the solution to the problem of manageability gives effect to some principle(s) of design and thereby to some notion of the subject matter. Still, in discussing Wieser's theory of imputation, Robbins argues that "the sociological and moral influences—boring subjects . . . are relevant"; they "form part of a conception of . . . causation." A similar point is made in his lecture on marginal productivity theory:

> Imagine putting to a very intelligent but very low-paid wage earner the proposition that "Your wages are determined by marginal productivity and therefore

are just." And this very intelligent but low-paid man might reply saying, "I agree that I am rewarded according to marginal value of my product to the employer, but you haven't dealt with the reasons why my marginal productivity is so low—the failure of my parents to obtain access to capital which would have made my marginal productivity higher, not to mention all the institutional obstacles which prevent my mobility being greater, and having a wider range of choice, and having access to places where the wages as determined by marginal productivity are higher." I think that that puts paid to J. B. Clark's simple proposition.[3]

The reader is cautioned against drawing hard and fast distinctions on the basis of statements made in lectures which may have been made to establish minor points. For example, in discussing Smith's attention to the increased costs of defence since the invention of gunpowder and the greater specialization of defence, Robbins concludes by saying, "that doesn't involve economic analysis, and I pass on"—which is strange coming from an author who had published books on *The Economic Causes of War* (London: Jonathan Cape, 1939) and *The Economic Problem in Peace and War* (London: Macmillan, 1947). On another occasion, having discussed Malthus' theory of population and its reverberations, he says that "that's the history of political economy rather than the history of economics," by the latter of which he apparently means theoretical economics; and shortly thereafter he emphasizes that the theory of population "provided, together with Adam Smith, the essential background" to nineteenth-century classical economics. One is not certain if anything analytical or historiographical is to be conclusively read into such passages. At any rate, the course was on the history of economic *thought*, not *theory*.

Also noteworthy—for its admiration of an American classic and for its implications regarding political economy (rather than economics, despite his occasional narrowing statements)—is Robbins' statement about *The Federalist*, "which in my judgement is the best book on political science and its broad practical aspects, written in the last thousand years." He goes on to say that Alexander Hamilton "perhaps doesn't enter into the textbooks on the history of economic thought as he deserves to."

Also revealing—that one should go beyond seemingly narrowing statements—is Robbins' injunction that "You oughtn't to be mere economists; you ought to take a broader view of social studies than that. And anybody who takes social science seriously, even if you disagree with a good deal of it, should make the acquaintance of Max Weber."[4]

Interestingly, early in Lecture 3 Robbins seems to imply that the development of economics as we know it had to await the development of a primarily money economy characterized by commerce and industry; also pertinent in this connection is his treatment of certain aspects of the just price in terms of isolated versus organized social exchange.

One has to be impressed with Robbins' civility and open-mindedness in the lectures. This is illustrated by the several occasions in which he remarks that a commentary or statement of his own or by someone else is "tendentious." His candor is illustrated by his acknowledgment that in his lectures on economic thought in the Middle Ages he is "relying very largely" on secondary authorities. Otherwise he reports on his own work; even here he is not hesitant to offer interpretive judgments, though he does not present them as definitive. He also notes that he gets a small royalty from his preface to a book but nonetheless does not recommend student purchase.

A function of courses in the history of economic thought is to expand the mind of the students.[5] Robbins attempts this admirably. The following come readily to mind: His catholicity, rather than doctrinaire exclusivism, in his approach to the history of thought. His calling to his auditors' attention the word, and thereby the concept, "natural" creeping, as he puts it, into economics, thus providing a basis for the student's recognizing its problematicity and not taking for granted some pet attribution of his or her own. His distinction between mercantilism in the narrower and wider senses. His emphasis that what a writer said can be historically important, "whether you agree with him or not." His distinction between arguments "advanced with reference to contemporary circumstances" and those that are doctrinaire and absolute. His emphasis on the distinctions between quantitative and nonquantitative versions of utilitarianism and between simplistic and sophisticated interpretations of natural law. His caveat, apropos of Locke's contract theory of money, that it "doesn't make particularly convincing sense to me, but it's certainly an apologia which was bandied about in the political discussion of the eighteenth century, and you ought to know about it." His critique of modeling: "models in the pretentious way in which we envelope, very often, pure banalities in this jargon. . . ." His drawing attention to the importance of definitional differences in comparing different authors. His defense of J. B. Say: "But there it is: give a dog a bad name and it will stay with him. And so I suppose this will go on being called Say's Law even though the history of economic thought shows that Say was not so guilty as other people." His defense of the combination of natural endowment with circumstance and education, saying that "I wouldn't have been an academic for so long if I didn't think that education was sometimes good to some of you." His lament of certain interpretations, saying, "You have to go back to the original texts, you know, to get the truth." His indicating that issues of continuity and discontinuity in the history of economic thought are a function of how one formulates fundamental concepts, and his indicating that a particular matter "is open to controversy, and reasonable people, provided that they define their terms, are entitled to claim him [J. S. Mill] on one side or the other."

Of many splendid linguistic constructions, the following may be cited: Speaking of Oresme's *De Moneta*: "It is not tinged with the vices of pamphleteering. It is tinged, rather, with the virtues of pamphleteering." Speaking about Malynes: "There is some continuity between the history of economic thought and even the history of economic error." Speaking about a nonquantitative prediction by Petty: "Predictions in economics, you know, are not to be relied upon. If anybody tells you what will happen next year in quantitative terms, write him down as being either simple or talking without justification." Discussing investment in human capital and its assumption "that lectures didn't perish in the moment of their production," he remarks that "Having been a lecturer for nearly sixty years of my life, I am not quite so sure." Discussing increasing returns, he notes "the history of the automobile industry, the pioneers of this mode of travel, which takes us about quickly on Sundays but which hampers progress nowadays on weekdays."

A few oddities are present. In one, Robbins defends Adam Smith against Terence Hutchison's charge that his failure to acknowledge James Steuart's work was shabby, saying that "it was perfectly legitimate for Smith" to refrain "from giving his opponent, who was by that time returned to Scotland and who was mixing in much the same circles as Adam Smith, a free advertisement."

Robbins also indicates that one function of work in the history of economic thought is to correct wrong-headed attributions to, and interpretations of, past writings. Nowhere was this more important than in the case of the classical economists:

> As time went on, I had been increasingly disturbed by the crudity and wrong-headedness of many contemporary conceptions [of the origins of contemporary controversy], particularly in regard to the famous classical system. At a very early stage I remember Cannan drawing my attention to an allegation by the then Master of Balliol that the classical economists had "*defended*" subsistence wages—as unscholarly and misleading a proposition as it is easy to imagine; and, as the contemporary debate on theories of policy proceeded, I felt more and more that the classical system in general, misrepresented almost beyond belief, was being used as a convenient Aunt Sally by any writer or speaker who wished to set his *soi-disant* enlightened views against a background of black reaction. I felt this to be quite deplorable. I was far from thinking that the classical outlook was always correct; still less that it contained any degree of finality in its treatment of the questions with which it dealt. But it seemed to me that current conceptions thereof not only falsified history, but also lowered the quality of what should be a serious and important argument—made it much less *interesting* than it should have been—by this degree of inaccuracy and superficiality. (Robbins 1971, p. 226; see n.1)

This led directly to *The Theory of Economic Policy in English Classical Political Economy*.

If one theme of the lectures is that students and scholars should aim at correct, rather than distorted, understandings of what authors had to say, another theme is that particular economic theories—for example, the theory of interest, value theory, the quantity theory—have been given varied specifications, and that one role of the history of economic thought course is to alert students to the richness of a theory beyond its contemporaneously taught formulation. Moreover, his treatments of value, capital, money, and interest suggest that each particular theory of each subject covers only one aspect and that full understanding requires both the existence and comprehension of multiple theories. Economic nationalism was but one topic to which apply his admonition that "all simple generalisations in this sphere are liable to be misleading."

On the subject of the mathematization of economics, Robbins makes a number of interesting statements. Speaking of Jevons' *Theory of Political Economy*, he says that "it's fiddling mathematics, and indeed I think Marshall was probably right when he said that Jevons would have done well to leave mathematics out." In discussing Fisher, Robbins notes that "of course he doesn't confine himself to geometrical representation. He goes on with the chaste use of mathematics. (The great mathematical economists, you know, always use mathematics rather chastely. They don't end up with conclusions which can't be put into economic terms.)" As for the device of indifference curves, he remarks that "God knows what observations you would have to make in order to find any large set of indifference curves." This may be strange, coming from a theorist.

Robbins relates in his *Autobiography* his preparation and delivery procedure in lecturing, at least in his early years: "I wrote out my lectures in full and spent much time conning them over. I hasten to say that, when they had to be delivered, I never read them. I used as a reminder only brief summaries inscribed in broad margins" (Robbins 1971, p. 104). Not only was Robbins both learned and on top of his materials, he clearly carefully planned his lectures in advance. In the lectures he remarks that "Following my unswerving rule of refreshing my memory on things that I am going to talk about, I read it [Locke's second essay on government] myself in half an hour." This is also attested to by his bringing to class copies of the works he was discussing, which must have had the effect of helping bring the works alive.

Both graduate (doctoral and master's) and undergraduate students, and both foreign and U.K. students, constituted Robbins' audience in the course. Robbins expected a high level of interest on the part of his students, including some considerable (however uneven) background work, especially on the part of the graduate students. Yet he was obviously prepared to distinguish between the "serious-minded" among his audience and those who were not.

Robbins is not inappropriately held in reverent awe by many of his former students and is typically spoken of with enormous respect by others. But he did not appeal to all, though the fault may well have been with the others than with him. Thus, Herbert Simons writes of meeting Robbins for the first time in 1974 in Nafplion, Greece: "Lord Robbins reminded me of all the things I disliked in the arrogance of economics and its detachment from facts. Irritated by his pomposity, I replied to one of his discussion comments in a distinctly insulting way, for which I was later scolded (privately) by John Hicks."[6] On the other hand, Mark Perlman, more positively impressed with Robbins, refers to his "patrician lordliness,"[7] and

James Meade to "[h]is good companionship, his infectious enjoyment of all that was around him, his marvellous sense of the ridiculous, [and] his gift as a kind-hearted raconteur of the foibles of oneself, of himself and of others."[8] In the words of William Baumol, "Lord Robbins was the embodiment of all the virtues of civilized behaviour and scholarship."[9]

What do these lectures suggest as to Robbins' demeanor? He clearly projected a tone of seriousness, self-confidence, and authority. Yet he is clearly also modest and restrained. He calls attention to his reliance on other authorities, to interpretive problems on which he is unable to reach a conclusive position, to limitations of his knowledge, and to necessarily abbreviated, even crude (the word is his, as is "odious in its superficiality") summaries of ideas compelled by the pressure of time. He displays a considerable mastery of the materials of the field, especially of those materials he considered important and that his expertise enabled him to master. His interpretive judgments are typically sensible, though, as he often notes, not without controversy. Like all courses on the history of economic thought, his was not given for intended specialists alone. But it was one on which, thanks largely to his magisterial treatment, a specialist could begin to erect a career in a field clearly laden with adventure and meaningfulness.

Otherwise, he was an impressive man and intellect who, like most other people, did not appeal to everyone. He had perhaps more of an appeal to the layman and the ordinary person than have most academic economists. For us, the lectures—which, among other qualities, exude charm and are sensitive lest they give offense to any student—speak for themselves. The lectures reveal not only a theoretician's mastery of his subject but also a large mind, perceptive and sensitive, going out of its way, as it were, to avoid doctrinaire statements. The course had more or less conventional coverage and was rich and deep, laden with sophisticated interpretive commentary. As for his students, even though he occasionally chides them for their limited or narrow reading (at one point he says, "I know that you don't like me to recommend the reading of whole books"),[10] they apparently had great affection for him, giving him a card celebrating his birthday, surely an unusual event in academia. William Baumol has written of "the powerful impression [Robbins] made upon us students," particularly through "his incredible erudition, his deep and genuine modesty and his abilities as a teacher."[11] No doubt the generation of students to whom these lectures were addressed was similarly impressed, as will be the reader.

Among the several leitmotifs running through the lectures is Robbins' assumption that his students will be interested in building up a personal professional library. Indeed, Robbins' personal library, much of which is now held by the Banca d'Italia, included some three thousand volumes, spanning the range of economic thought from the ancient Greeks to the late twentieth century. In this connection, it is interesting to note his role in having Torrens' *Letters on Commercial Policy* reprinted: "It's [the original edition] an extremely rare book, and I coaxed the London School of Economics to reprint it, partly because I had never been able to find a copy of it myself except in museums."[12] We sympathize with Robbins here: One of the motives behind the Transaction Books series of reissues—*Classics in Economics*—which we now co-edit, is the same.

The reader has to be taken with Robbins' charming defense of his use of quotations: "Adam Smith said of the professors at Oxford, who had long ago abandoned 'the pretence of teaching,' that they sometimes saved their self-respect by reading aloud boring books. Well now, I hope I don't read aloud to you boring books. I only read aloud to you, rather than depend on my own improvisation, because I think that the passages are more vivid than anything I can make them." Anyone who has lectured, perhaps especially on the history of economic thought, can appreciate his sentiment.

Two comments in particular manifest Robbins' decency and charm. One is his comment on J. S. Mill's review of William Thornton's *On Labour*: "cordial and friendly, as befitted a review written by one of one's friends (and should be of most of one's enemies)." The other has to do with Marx: "Marx, I ought to say, whether you agree with him or disagree with him, was probably the best historian of economic thought of his time, although I personally think—and this is a value judgement—that Marx was *frightfully* unfair to some of the people he criticised."

Also charming, and instructive, is Robbins' example to illustrate the possibility of exchange given different comparative costs. Whereas a common American teaching example is the employer who can type better than his secretary, Robbins' is the gentleman academic who is "superior to his gentleman's personal gentleman." As Jeff Biddle said, on being told of this, both examples reflect not only comparative cost but hierarchy (and, in the American example, sexual division of labor): one could use a carpenter and plumber as an example; the difference is that the former examples capture the imagination.

Something of the nature of the origins of interpretive fads in the history of economic thought is suggested by Robbins in his handling of John Stuart Mill's reputation: "When I was a young man there was a tradition in this school—clearly created by Cannan—of rather looking down one's nose at John Stuart Mill. And I have no doubt that this arose in Cannan's mind when he was a young man, and when John Stuart Mill was probably rammed down his neck at Oxford as having uttered more or less the last word on the subject." Not inappropriately, Robbins summarizes George Stigler's list of Mill's important contributions to theory. Much earlier Robbins wrote about Cannan's course at LSE that it was "a safeguard against immersion in the doctrines of any particular School and neglect of doctrines which already had been discovered."[13]

•

The lectures were tape-recorded by Robbins' grandson, Philip Robbins, who was then a student at LSE.[14] The original transcription of the tape recordings was done by Rosemary Pedder of Surrey. This typescript, with handwritten edits by Lady Robbins and Christopher Johnson, Robbins' son-in-law, is on file in the archives at the London School of Economics, where it was deposited by the Robbins family in 1989. When Medema ran across this manuscript while doing some research at the LSE archives in the summer of 1995, it was immediately apparent to him that this was something special, and that a wider circulation was in order. When we contacted the Robbins family about the possibility of publishing the lectures, we were informed that the original tape recordings were available, and, armed with these, we began the lengthy process of editing the lectures for publication.

The original typescript contains innumerable errors and omissions, most of which owe, understandably, to the typist's lack of familiarity with the history of economic thought. A photocopy of the original typescript was scanned into a computer and edited against the tape recordings by Medema, and the text was then edited by the two of us. The lectures are reproduced as they were given, with only stylistic and other minor corrections. No attempt has been made to correct putative "errors." With the exception of bracketed insertions within quotations, all annotations (in square brackets) are by the editors. All of the endnotes are also editorial insertions. With the exception of quotations (unless otherwise indicated), words appearing in italics are words which were emphasized by Robbins in his lectures.

The copy of Robbins' reading list, reprinted here as appendix A, includes an outline of the lectures. However, as some of these lectures were not given and two of those given were not recorded, we have decided to number the lectures sequentially rather than according to Robbins' numbering scheme. Because material treated in one lecture sometimes carries over into the next lecture, we have also renamed certain of the lecture titles (vis-à-vis the titles given in Robbins' outline) so that the titles more appropriately reflect the contents of the lectures. In doing so, however, we have attempted to remain as close as possible to Robbins' own titles.

Christopher Johnson supplied a number of citations to the works referred to or quoted by Robbins in the original typescript copy, and we have completed the citation process here, including providing page citations for the quotations and a complete list of references. Wherever possible (and there are only a handful of exceptions), the citations given are to the works from Robbins' own library or editions identical to those Robbins owned—and thus to the exact works from which Robbins was quoting during the lectures.

The process of preparing these lectures for publication has left us indebted to numerous organizations and individuals who have assisted us in this work. Generous financial support was provided by the American Philosophical Society, which funded the visit to the LSE during which Medema initially ran across the manuscript copy of the lectures as well as a subsequent visit to Rome to check quotations and citations against Robbins' own library, now in the possession of the Banca d'Italia. We would particularly like to thank Eleanor Roach and Mildred Cohn, Chair of the A.P.S. Committee on Research, for their efforts in making this funding possible. Additional funding was provided by the University of Colorado at Denver Office of Sponsored Programs.

We are also grateful to Dr. Angela Raspin and the staff at the LSE archives—Sue Donnelly and Brenda Lees in particular—for their invaluable assistance during Medema's visit to the LSE.

We would also like to thank the Banca d'Italia and the staff of the Servizio Studi, Divisione Biblioteca e Pubblicazioni, who went out of their way to facilitate the process of quotation and citation checking during Medema's visit. Maria Teresa Pandolfi, Head Librarian, Patrizia Pagliano, Antonio Rubiu, Pierino D'Armi, Roberto Pisani, Romano Mancinelli, Roberto Marzinotto, and Renzo De Francesco bent over backwards to assist us in tracking down all manner of materials. All of this was done with cheerful enthusiasm and efficiency, which helped to overcome both the tight time constraints on the visit and Medema's almost complete lack of knowledge of the Italian language. A special thank you is due to Patrizia and Antonio, who came to feel like friends within two weeks' time.

The staff of the Auraria Library at the University of Colorado at Denver, and, in particular, the people in the office of Inter-Library Loans, provided ongoing assistance in tracking down various works quoted or referenced.

Numerous individuals assisted us in various ways throughout this process. Kate Denning ably handled the scanning of the transcript and the conversion and cleaning of the scanned files. Therese Cogeos did yeoman's work in cleaning scanned files, compiling the citation list, tracking down references, and assembling the bibliography of Robbins' writings in the history of economic thought, which is included as an appendix to this volume. All of this was done with her usual efficiency and enthusiasm. The figures were prepared by Timothy Potter, and Lynn Ferguson provided her usual efficient secretarial support. Debra Medema provided extremely valuable assistance in tracking down quotations and citations during our visit to the Banca d'Italia, taking upon herself the not-too-inspiring task of wading through book after book in search of extracts as short as a couple of words. And, as always, she was an inspiration throughout.

William Barber was kind enough to help us pin down the Irving Fisher story to which Robbins refers in lecture 30, Donald Moggridge assisted us in tracking down some material on Keynes, and Donald Walker did likewise for Walras. Andrea Salanti provided a translation from the Italian of Barone's trade theory diagram and analysis. Susan Howson, Robbins' official biographer, assisted us in the preparation of the bibliography of Robbins' writings in the history of economic thought, as did Denis O'Brien, whose biography of Robbins was most helpful in this regard. Special thanks are also due to William Baumol and Mark Perlman, both for their support for this project and their suggestions regarding the editing of the manuscript.

As always, Peter Dougherty and the folks at Princeton University Press were incredibly supportive throughout the process of bringing these lectures to publication. We are grateful to them for their willingness to undertake the publication of these lectures and for their assistance in seeing this project through to completion.

Finally, and most importantly, we would like to thank the Robbins family for granting us permission to undertake this project, for providing us with the tape recordings of the lectures, and for all the assistance that they have given along the way. Christopher and Anne Johnson have provided an enormous amount of information throughout this process and have opened many doors for us.

One of the many highlights associated with this project was learning how thrilled Lady Robbins was that the lectures were going to be published. In January 1997, at the age of 100, Lady Robbins passed away. She was, for Robbins, "a sensitive, spirited, and intelligent companion."[15] It is to her memory that this book is dedicated.

Steven G. Medema
and
Warren J. Samuels

NOTES

1. See Lionel Robbins, *Autobiography of an Economist* (London: Macmillan, 1971), and biographical and other materials in D. P. O'Brien, *Lionel Robbins* (New York: St. Martin's Press, 1988), and "Lionel Charles Robbins, 1898–1984," *Economic Journal* 98 (March 1988): 104–25; Mark Blaug, *Great Economists since Keynes* (Totowa, N.J.: Barnes & Noble Books, 1985); T. W. Hutchison, "Robbins, Lionel," in D. L. Sills, ed., *International Encyclopedia of the Social Sciences*, vol. 18 (New York: Free Press, 1979); M. Peston, "Lionel Robbins: Methodology, Policy and Modern Theory," in J. R. Shackleton and G. Locksley, eds., *Twelve Contemporary Economists* (London: Macmillan, 1981); and B. A. Corry, "Robbins, Lionel Charles," in J. Eatwell, M. Milgate, and P. Newman, *The New Palgrave: A Dictionary of Economics*, vol. 4 (London: Macmillan, 1987).

2. The "Whig" approach analyzes the history of economic thought in terms of a progression from error to truth, with the discipline's history being important only or largely as measured against the ideas of the present, rather than on its own terms or within the context in which the ideas were developed.

3. This presentation parallels that given in *The Evolution of Modern Economic Theory* (1970, pp. 19–20), in which Robbins wrote that "In this connection, I would like to go out of my way, here and now, to repudiate certain uses to which this analysis has been put. It has sometimes been argued—J. B. Clark is perhaps the chief culprit—that a proof that, under competitive conditions, productive agents are paid according to the value of their marginal physical product is a proof that such a system is just. This of course is a complete non sequitur, and one that is a

temptation to tendentious usage. Before we can begin to discuss distributive justice in this connection, we must investigate the arrangements—the distribution of property, the accessibility to appropriate training, the availability of appropriate information and so on—which bring it about that a man's marginal product is what it is and not otherwise, and that involves many considerations quite outside the range of the kind of analysis I am discussing. It is to be noted, however, that the leading exponents of this idea, with the exception of von Thünen, have made no such claims. If we take Marshall as providing the locus classicus of its prudent application, we find that he definitely goes out of his way to deny that it affords a complete theory of distribution, even in the narrow sense, and throughout puts it in its proper place as a partial explanation of derived demand and as an essential ingredient of the idea of substitution." Robbins twice notes the relevance of the criticism of the use of "abstinence" by Senior in explaining interest, a criticism of naïveté about rich people suffering austerity. Further apropos of partial theories, see below.

4. Apropos of the history of economics—in contradistinction to the history of economic thought and theory—Robbins interestingly remarks that "Economics, as it developed in the nineteenth century, was *not* a subject which was a part of the obligatory reading of a well-educated gentleman."

5. Perhaps that explains Robbins' saying that "I have been told that meetings of the American Economic Association . . . in which *trainloads* of Americans go to the skyscrapers in different capital cities of different states in the United States, and there you have learned papers read, and there is a sort of cattle market for junior economists being bid for by senior economists to improve their own departments. It does not work badly, you know. Let us not look down our noses at this system. There are two ways of looking at it, but it hasn't turned out awfully badly as regards the production of economists in the United States this century." Of course, his description of academic labor markets is incomplete.

6. Herbert A. Simon, *Models of My Life* (New York: Basic Books, 1991), p. 321.

7. Mark Perlman, "What Makes My Mind Tick," *American Economist* 39, no. 2 (fall 1995): 12.

8. Meade's obituary tribute to Robbins, *Economica* 52 (February 1985): 3–5 at 5.

9. Baumol's obituary tribute to Robbins, *Economica* 52 (February 1985): 5–7 at 5.

10. He himself points to the impossibility of reading everything. Speaking of Böhm-Bawerk's theory of roundabout methods of production, he says that it "was the famous ground which has occupied so many articles in my middle age that I can't bear to think of the ones that I have left unread."

11. Baumol's obituary tribute to Robbins, *Economica* 52 (February 1985): 5–7 at 5.

12. Speaking about the rarity of John Rae's *New Principles of Political Economy*, Robbins confesses that "I have often seen a copy at a club that I used to belong to, and have felt fantastically inclined to theft. Nobody had read it since it was published, but, being well brought up, I refrained."

13. Lionel Robbins, "A Student's Recollections of Edwin Cannan," *Economic Journal* 45 (June 1935): 396.

14. Most of the lectures were recorded in 1979–1980. However, certain of the gaps were filled in 1980–1981.

15. Lionel Robbins, *Autobiography of an Economist* (London: Macmillan, 1971), p. 97.

The Robbins Lectures

A. Anticipations

Introduction—Plato

IN GENERAL, I don't intend to begin lecturing until six past the hour. This is partly by reason of the difficulty of passing from one lecture room to another, which some of you have to do, partly by reason of the fact that I think that fifty-five minutes on the history of economic thought is as much as most of you can take at a time, so, if I start just a little early at this moment, it is that I think that sufficient of you are gathered together, and I want to make some preliminary remarks.

First of all, about these things that I've passed around [see appendix A]. Don't let them strike terror into your hearts. If you've read the first paragraph, you will realise that they are *not*, underline *not*, in the American sense a reading list—a list of the things which you are expected to read. On the contrary, I don't expect you to read one-twentieth, or even less, of the books and articles which are enumerated there. The reason for the circulation of this list is simply to save a certain amount of trouble. In my young days, when the literature of the subject was much less extensive, the first professor of economics at LSE—the famous Edwin Cannan—used to refuse to give any injunctions with regard to reading at all. His maxim was: "Let them plunge in at the deep end of the library and learn to swim for themselves." And doubtless in those days that was very good advice indeed, because the economics books in the library on the open shelves consisted of two stacks such as one might accumulate in the first few years of one's work as a professional economist, and it was interesting and illuminating to take down the books to get the smell of them and to decide which one was worth reading as part of the educational process in those days. But now the literature of the subject has multiplied so much. I've been told in the Economist Bookshop that one book on economics is published every three minutes in the world, and it really would be a matter for the society for the prevention of cruelty to young adults if I were to leave you without any guidance. So, this list, which I revise every year according to my presentation of the valuable literature and what's appeared in the last twelve months, is simply, so to speak, to reproduce the conditions which used to prevail in the collection of books in the library. It is a list of works covering the subject to which you're going to devote—if you hang it out—thirty-five attendances at these lectures, a list of books which you can read without wasting your time.

But I fancy I see before me a mixture of high-brow graduates and equally high-brow third-year undergraduates. The requirements as regards reading must of course be different. As regards undergraduates, you are so overworked in so many ways that it would be cruelty to expect you to read all but the most notable books, and even in such cases there are things which you needn't read. I can indicate that as we go along. As regards graduates, of course if you aspire to be dons or expert economists in some way in which the history of economic thought may be useful to you—I shall touch on that in a moment—then in the next ten years you ought to read most of the books that I recommend. But since the master's degree takes one or two years, you too are not expected to read *nearly* all the things that are enumerated there. Well, I think I've said enough about that.

Now, I want to devote this lecture first of all to some general observations about the subject matter, and then, unless I've lost my sense of timing during August, I shall want to begin with the first of the great names which you need to study in this connection—namely, the name of Plato. But first of all, some general observations.

The question may have arisen in your minds, Why do reasonable people studying economics attach some importance to the history of the subject? Well, the history of the subject is not necessarily important to you in professional life, unless you aspire to teach the subject matter later on. Be under no delusion in that respect. But as regards *understanding* of what goes on in the contemporary world, of what goes on in intelligent conversation about our subject, the answer is different. The answer is, I think, that the subject *is* of some use. It's a subject which, strange as it may seem, has the property of being described—to use the fashionable word—as relevant to your interest in the world around you.

Well, now, first of all let me state the case against this which you will find in all sorts of superficial books and in the course of all sorts of superficial observations. Why should we pay attention to the history of social science study where we don't pay such attention to it as regards natural science? The history of natural science—as you will learn if you go, for instance, to lectures in the Department of Philosophy and Scientific Method—is an absorbingly interesting subject. But it's not necessary in the sense in which I shall argue that it is in our case, in the case of the conspicuous members of the group "natural sciences." Interesting as it may be to understand the astronomical systems of 1,000 or 500 years ago, it's not necessary in order to become a first-class astronomer that you should know all about Ptolemy or indeed all about Copernicus. What there is remaining of the Copernican system will be imparted to you in other lectures. And similarly with the history of biology, and so on. But when you come to those subjects which are dedicated to the interpretation of social life, I submit that the case is different.

Contemporary institutions and contemporary thoughts are shot through with the heritage of the past, and to know how various ideas originated, what their vicissitudes have been, intrinsically in the development of the subject, extrinsically in their influence on general thought about society, how they have become transformed, their implications in everyday speech—these are subjects with which, even though you don't become experts, I do think that those who aspire to call themselves economists in some way or another should have a nodding acquaintance. Indeed, I would say that unless you have some such knowledge you really lack a dimension of understanding the broad subject matter. Let me quote to you an eminent Victorian, the historian Mark Pattison. (Hands up, any of you who've read Mark Pattison's memoirs. I ask questions of this sort at an early stage of these lectures quite frequently in order that I know what to mention and what would be boring reiteration.) Mark Pattison is a very famous historian, and he wrote one of the three or four best autobiographies in nineteenth-century literature. And he said, rather portentously, "A man who does not know what has been thought by those who have gone before him is sure to set an undue value upon his own ideas" [Pattison, 1885, p. 78].

And if you come forward to the great intellectual of our own subject, of our own times (or nearly of our own times—he's been dead more than twenty years now), Keynes, the great intellectual revolutionary, said, "a study of the history of opinion is a necessary preliminary to the emancipation of the mind. I don't know which makes a man more conservative"— and he used that in a rather pejorative sense—"I don't know which makes a man more conservative, to know nothing but the present or nothing but the past" [Keynes, 1926, p. 277]. Or again, some of you at any rate have looked at *The General Theory* of Keynes; it concludes with the famous passage about "Madmen . . . who hear voices in the air" (he was writing at the time of Hitler): "Madmen . . . who hear voices in the air, are distilling their frenzy from some academic scribbler of a few years back" [ibid., p. 383]. And he goes on to say that he is convinced that it is ideas and not vested interests which are, *in the long run* (it would be silly to say that it was so in the short run), dangerous for good or evil.

But now, more particularly, apart from these vanities of knowing something about Petty, Locke, the physiocrats, Adam Smith, Ricardo, and so on, I would contend that, as regards the history of analysis in the rather narrow sense, it is difficult to understand contemporary developments without some knowledge of the way in which they developed. Take the pure theory of value, for instance. How many papers have I marked in my time—I get so upset over that now, I shan't read your papers; I shall simply suggest a series of questions—how many papers have I read dealing with the theory of quasi-rents which got things all wrong simply because they had not studied the history of the evolution of that technical term which was introduced by Marshall. If you widen your horizon a little bit and think not merely of the history of analysis but the history of economic *thought* as Schumpeter [1954] calls it—the history of the connection between analysis and one's appraisal of what goes on in the world and what is suitable policy and so on and so forth—how can you begin to understand contemporary thought, contemporary language about these matters, laissez faire, collectivism, and so on and so forth, unless you know something of what happened in the past?

Furthermore and finally—and I shall finish these preliminary remarks in a moment—the study of the development of theory in different social contexts gives you, so to speak, a new dimension for thought experiments. You know that in economics one of our difficulties is that we can't conduct very frequently laboratory experiments. We are therefore forced back upon thought experiments of one kind or another, and the thought experiments are much more difficult to carry through without mistake than laboratory experiments. The history of the subject affords you concrete cases of thought experiment about which one already knows a good deal by way of history. For instance—not to dwell on this subject longer—in the theory of money, if you study the so-called bullionist controversy of, roughly speaking, the wars between England and France at the time of Napoleon, you have the opportunity of verifying thought experiments on the explanation of the inflation which took place in those days and the deflation which followed. If you come forward into the middle of the nineteenth century and study the so-called controversy between the banking and the currency schools (I won't go into the personalities involved here), you find yourself in the midst of controversies which are not settled even to this day. But you find yourself in the midst of the origins of these controversies which make clearer to you the issues fundamentally involved.

Well, so much by way of justification of the subject. Now, how do I propose to expound it? I see two extremes to avoid. Firstly, to confine oneself to the history of pure thought in this subject with no explanation whatever in terms of context. History of that sort is very apt to mislead. You get very wrong ideas, for instance, of the history of the evolution of the theological thought bearing on the economics of the Middle Ages unless you study successive stages of the evolution of that thought. The second mistake to make—and it's one which you are much more likely to fall into because you will hear as you go about daily life all sorts of nonsensical versions of this—is to discuss the evolution of theory as being merely the by-product of contemporary, or the then contemporary, sociological conditions—an epiphenomenon, so to speak, of the circumstances of the time. That's a classic case of overdoing a good idea. There is no doubt at all, as you will see at an early stage, that the economic thought of our history has unquestionably been influenced by the social and economic conditions of the time. No doubt about that at all, and no doubt that I shall omit considerations of that sort as I proceed. But if you study the subject at all clearly and at all carefully you will realise that very often in this sociological process there comes a stage at which the contemporary social conditions become unimportant and pure thought—logic and testing—takes charge.

Let me give you an example, the most conspicuous example in many respects: the case of Ricardo, whose *Principles* [1817], some of the chapters of which you all ought to read—some of the difficult chapters of which you all ought to read—presents in some ways thought in greater purity, in greater remoteness from contemporary conditions, than any but modern mathematical economists. But there can equally be no doubt at all that Ricardo's thought was stimulated by the monetary disorders of his time, the inflation after the inflation phase of the bullionist controversy and the dispute with regard to whether the Corn Laws should be restored at the end of the Napoleonic Wars or not. No doubt at all that he was influenced that way. Equally no doubt that once he had been forced by his friends into writing a principles of economics, logical thought took charge and carried him far away from these local circumstances. And the conclusions that he reached, whether right or wrong, were conclusions that he had reached by the application of logic and from time to time testing the logic by what was all around him. I choose Ricardo because there is one change in his thought in his *Principles* between the first edition and the third edition [1821] which has been praised even by Karl Marx[1]— namely, in his first edition he argued that the introduction of machinery could *never* be anything but beneficial to the wage earner. Having meditated further on this subject, in the third edition he developed a very complicated argument to show that in some circumstances—at any rate in the middle period—it *might be*. And he wrote it down rather to the dismay of some of his friends who had preferred the simplicity of the first edition of the *Principles*. But he persisted; he had seen what he believed to be the truth. Hence, and the moral of all this is that, you should adopt a rather catholic approach to the history of thought, avoiding pure analysis or pure sociological explanation.

Finally, the question is: Can one take an impartial view of matters so intimately concerned with one's interests and one's daily life? And the answer probably is that one can't. But that is no argument whatever for not trying. It is, however, an argument for the view, which I shall certainly try to observe in these lectures, of revealing one's bias whenever one is conscious of it. And then, after all, it is up to you to decide whether the bias is mistaken or whether it adds force to the argument. In any case, however far back you go, you must, in this subject as in all social studies, hold yourself open to criticism and debate. If there is one thing that universities should teach you, and not all universities have taught that in the past or the present, it is open-mindedness and continual criticism of your own ideas.

Well, then, I can just enumerate three ways in which one can actually arrange the subject. First of all you can discuss individual theories and their history. Viner's *Studies in the Theory of International Trade* [1937] is a classic example of that. Cannan's *Production and Distribution* [1924] is another good example. Secondly, you can study the evolution of individual thought as, for instance, you will have, par excellence I would say, in the work of an ex-student of this School, Professor Samuel Hollander, now of the University of Toronto, whose book on Adam Smith [1973] is the answer to a prayer to anyone who is bewildered by Adam Smith's *Wealth of Nations* and whose forthcoming book on Ricardo [1979] is an answer, so to speak, to collective prayer. It is almost a book to put an end to prayer about Ricardo it's so good. Or, for instance, another very good book on classical economics, Professor O'Brien of Durham's book on McCulloch [1970], and so on and so forth. Or you can study particular periods. You can study, for instance, the thought of the Middle Ages, which I shall do in the next lecture but one. Or, you can study the period some people call the period of mercantilism, ambiguously so-called because mercantilism has more than one meaning—as for instance in the work of Ashley [1901] or Heckscher [1935].

Well, I shan't stick to any of these methods; I shall go my own sweet way—sometimes talk about doctrine, sometimes talk about persons, sometimes talk about periods. And my plan will fall into four or five parts. I shall deal in the first six or seven lectures with the anticipation of economics in historic literature. I shall then deal in greater detail with the emergence of economics in the eighteenth century. I shall deal at some length with nineteenth-century classical economics and—another division—with the beginnings, the anticipations of modern analysis, and then finally I shall in five or six lectures trace the beginnings up, let us say, to 1914, of the analysis which you study in detail from superior personalities in other lectures.

Now, anticipations. The anticipations of economic thought in the past spring from two rather different sources: On the one hand you have anticipations in moral philosophy from the Greeks, through the Scholastics, through the early modern lawyers and philosophers. And then secondly, you have anticipations in ad hoc pamphlets—pamphlets or monographs or sometimes rather heavy books written by government officials, by merchants, by theologians, anxious to argue a particular case, a particular abuse—the debasement of a currency for instance, or protection for a certain group of industries, or, in a wider sense, particular measures to safeguard the balance of payments. There's an enormous literature there; all I can do in two or three lectures is to dip a pail into the ocean and produce representative specimens. The line is not absolute. For instance, in the Middle Ages you find the theologians who are chiefly the authors of anticipations of general economics in moral philosophy turning aside to discuss particular problems. Thus, in a lecture or two from now I shall be discussing the famous treatise on money of Nicholas Oresme [1360/1956], who was the head of a monastic community and who also wrote on moral philosophy. The thing is a bit mixed, but the division I think is a useful one, and I proceed to the first stage thereof.

And the first stage of the first division is occupied by two famous Greek philosophers: Plato and Aristotle. Later on you get the Scholastics and you get other philosophers influenced by Aristotle. But today and next time I want to devote most attention to the Greeks, and nearly exclusive attention to Plato and Aristotle.

Now, both Plato and Aristotle were more famous as general philosophers, moral philosophers and as philosophers concerned with metaphysics, the nature of the world, epistemology and so on and so forth. And their anticipations of economics—and in the case of Aristotle it is extremely important and in the case of Plato it is outstanding but not so influential—their concern as moral philosophers with questions of an economic nature arose essentially with their concern with the good State. What was the good State? This was the *urgent* preoccupation of Plato in his famous *Republic* [1953b] and later on in his infamous *Laws* [1953a], which I don't particularly recommend you to read (I shall quote a section from it in a moment). And approaching the good State from the question What is justice in a good State? they were led to consider, in some sense or other, the economic relationships prevailing in *actual* States and contrasting them with what they hoped to find prevailing in the good State.

Now, you must not expect too much of Plato and Aristotle. In a sense, without disrespect, they were backward looking. At the time they wrote, Athens was the centre of a not inconsiderable empire and certainly the centre of flourishing commerce and trade. If you look at the short extract in Monroe's book, which I recommend in my reading list on early economic thought—which, I'm sorry to say, is now rather difficult to get hold of—if you look at Xenophon's [1948] discussion of the conditions in Athens, you get an example of the view of a contemporary or even someone who slightly preceded Aristotle. But both Plato and Aristotle were backward looking. Plato positively hated democracy. Professor Popper, in his marvelous book *The Open Society and Its Enemies* [1952] (which is not in my list, I fancy, but which should be read by all students, whatever subject, in this institution), accuses Plato of an ingrained dislike of change. His admiration of Sparta rather than Athens shows that. Aristotle is not so extreme, but you can detect some inclinations that way, as I shall show in the next lecture. And after all, it is the most remarkable thing about Aristotle's *Politics* [1948]. Anybody here who's read Aristotle's *Politics*? Those of you who have read Aristotle's *Politics* will remember that although he was tutor to Alexander the Great, there is nothing in Aristotle's *Politics* suggesting that the world could change, and that the conquests of Alexander had created a new world, of which the centre was no longer Greece. But while what I am going to say in a sense may be regarded as being slightly derogatory of both Plato and to some extent of Aristotle, I wouldn't have you think that my general estimate of these great men is derogatory. Both Plato and Aristotle were among the most superior minds that have ever existed on this

planet, and their contribution and their influence on subsequent thought
has been tremendous.

But now let us start with Plato, who lived, incidently, from 428 to 348
B.C. And we can concentrate our attention on a very narrow part of the
Republic. Plato's *Republic* is descriptive of his ideal State as a comparatively
young man. It's in the form of a dialogue between Socrates and his followers. Plato's *Republic* can be called, in a way, the most eloquent plea for a
certain kind of communism that has ever been written. Plato's *Laws* was
written when he was disillusioned of man and had tried his hand at advising
various politicians and had not been altogether successful, and it is much
less attractive as a book. And if Plato's *Republic* can be called communist,
Plato's *Laws* can be called fascist; but more of that in a moment.

The important thing from our point of view is that Plato is the first man,
or first famous writer (and if the professor had read all of the books that
may have been written), to enunciate the principle of the division of
labour. He gets to this in the course of this absolutely fascinating discussion of justice in the first book of the *Republic*. They talk in a very high-
brow and elevated way about justice, and the conversation is then interrupted by a Sophist who says, roughly speaking, that all this talk about
justice in an idealistic sense is nonsense and that justice is what works,
roughly speaking. Then, Socrates in book 2 suggests that perhaps they will
get closer to reality—not very close, but closer to reality—if they discuss
justice in a *State*, and this leads him to construct hints as to the foundations
of States and the foundations of justice in his ideal State. Let me read you
the critical passage here—you'll find that in the Platonic dialogues, and
many of them are pure poetry, but Socrates, or the leading speaker, usually
gets the best of it. The replies which I will read aloud are rather banal in
this particular case:

A State, I said,

—that's Socrates—

arises, as I conceive, out of the needs of mankind; no one is self-sufficing, but
all of us have many wants. Can any other origin of a State be imagined?

The reply:

There can be no other.
Then as we have many wants, and many persons are needed to supply them,
one takes a helper for one purpose and another for another. . . .
True, he said.

Now we get to the economics.

And it is in the belief that it is for his own good, that one man gives to
another or receives from him in exchange.
Very true.

Then, I said, let us construct a State in theory from the beginning; and yet the true creator, it seems, will be necessity

—who is the mother of our invention.

Of course, he replied.

Now, the first and greatest of necessities is food, which is the condition of life and existence.

Certainly.

The second is a dwelling, and the third clothing and the like.

True.

And now let us see what must be the size of a city able to supply such a demand: We may suppose that one man is a husbandman, another a builder, someone else a weaver—shall we add to them a shoemaker, or perhaps some other purveyor to our bodily wants?

By all means.

The simplest possible State must include four or five men.

Clearly.

And how will they proceed? Will each bring the results of his labours into a common stock?—the individual husbandman, for example, producing for four, and labouring four times as long and as much as he need in the provision of food with which he supplies others as well as himself; or will he have nothing to do with others and not be at the trouble of producing for them, but provide for himself alone a fourth of the food in a fourth of the time, and in the remaining three-fourths of his time be employed in making a house or a coat or a pair of shoes, not bothering to form a partnership with others, but supplying himself all his own wants?

Adeimantus

—that was one of his followers—

thought that he should aim at producing food only and not at producing everything.

Probably, I replied, that would be the better way; and when I hear you say this, I am myself reminded that we are not all alike; there are diversities of natures among us which are adapted to different occupations.

Very true.

And will you have work better done when every workman tries his hand at many occupations, or when each has only one?

When he has only one.

Further, there can be no doubt that a work is spoilt when not done at the right time?

No doubt.

For business is not disposed to wait until the doer of the business is at leisure; but the doer must follow up his opportunity, and make the business his first object.

He must.

> And if so, we must infer that all things are produced more plentifully and
> easily and of a better quality when one man does one thing which is natural to
> him and does it at the right time, leaving other crafts alone. [Plato, 1953b, pp.
> 211–12]

Well, there you are. There are the sum of the principles, more or less correctly stated, of the division of labour.

He then goes on—and I won't read you this—to explain how in fact this
was a very small example and there will be other people doing other things,
but the number of things that he mentions is so small that Glaucon—one
of his other disciples—actually ventures to contradict his teacher, and he
says, roughly speaking (and this is the famous term), "you are producing a
city of pigs, people who live in an extremely primitive way." And Socrates
says, "Oh well, if you want to produce a society in a state of high fever, I
don't object at this moment of my argument, but I myself believe that living in a more primitive way is the healthier way for a society to be constituted." And then he goes on to moralize.

Now, you will notice that there is a great difference between the principles of the division of labour and the principles of the division of labour
here in the famous first chapter of Adam Smith's *Wealth of Nations* [1776].
Adam Smith's *Wealth of Nations* dwells all, or nearly all, upon education.
He says that at birth the difference between a philosopher and a porter is
negligible. It's all what happens afterwards that makes the division of
labour possible. Plato, on the other hand, doesn't talk about education
here (he talks about the education of the Guardians later on), he talks
about differences of nature. Now, we know that allegations of differences
of nature are, from my point of view at any rate, very often used for immoral and cruel purposes. As we shall see in the next lecture, Aristotle justified slavery by differences of nature. But although nearly everybody who
talks about differences of nature, including professional natural scientists,
talks nonsense, and nonsense which can very easily be converted into immoral acts, it is quite important to realise that Socrates had hit on something. It really is true that if all the best tutors in the world were to concentrate (I won't be insulting and say on any of you) on most people, they
couldn't produce an Einstein, they couldn't produce a Mozart. There are
differences of nature, although we don't at this moment know awfully
much about them.

Well, this leads Socrates to go on to talk about the morality of having
each person in his proper place in society according to his nature. And as
you would find out if you read the whole of the *Republic*, the Guardians—
very superior people indeed—are to discover what the differences of nature
are and to fit the people into their places in that ideal republic, which some
of you may think would be not so ideal. Well, so much for Plato and the
division of labour. At the beginning of my lecture tomorrow I will say just

a word about the nature of the *Laws*. I shall be spending most of the time discussing Aristotle, who is much more germane to technical analysis than Plato's remarks on the division of labour.

NOTE

1. See Marx, "David Ricardo," in Marx (1952, pp. 199–427).

Plato and Aristotle

I NEEDN'T spend time reminding you of what I said yesterday, at any rate at any length. The first half of the lecture was devoted to general instructions and a certain apologia to the subject. The second half of the lecture, roughly speaking, was devoted to the beginning of lectures on anticipations of economic thought in moral philosophy, beginning with the Greeks. I began in that connection with Plato, in whose *Republic* you find the outline of the role which division of labour plays in the constitution of any society. Plato was in fact outlining his ideal society with a view to examining the ideal society and discovering what constituted justice therein. But in order to sketch the outlines of society he gives a quite remarkable account, since it's the first time in conspicuous literature at any rate, of the advantages so far as productivity is concerned of the division of labour. But he stops there. He goes on to draw conclusions—moral and political conclusions with which we are not connected—with regard to the importance of each person being allotted his proper place, the proper place being determined by the Guardians.

Now, I don't want to follow Plato there. I do, however, want to read you a passage from the *Laws* which, as I said yesterday, was a rather more realistic account of his conception of the best society which could be obtained—the conditions of life being what they are—a fascist conception rather than a communist conception as the *Republic* was. Now, this passage is simply incidental, but it is very indicative. He is talking about a medium of exchange and the law relating thereto, and he says

> the law enjoins that no private man shall be allowed to possess gold and silver, but only coin for daily use. . . .

—and that coin for daily use was in his conception probably best composed of leather—

> Wherefore our citizens, as we say, should have coin passing current among themselves, but not accepted by the rest of mankind; with a view, however, to expeditions and journeys to other lands,—for embassies [etc.] the state must also possess a common Hellenic currency. If a private person is ever obliged to go abroad, let him have the consent of the magistrates and go; and if when he returns he has any foreign money remaining, let him give the surplus back to the treasury, and receive a corresponding sum in the local currency. And if he is discovered to appropriate it,

—to keep it to himself—

let it be confiscated, and let him who knows and does not inform be subject to curse and dishonour equally with him who brought the money. [Plato, 1953a, pp. 310–11]

Sounds a bit familiar doesn't it? Well, bear that in mind when we are dealing with Aristotle, to whom I intend to devote the greater part of this lecture.

Aristotle was in fact in his young days a pupil of Plato. He lived from 384 to 322 B.C., and, like many pupils, he didn't always agree with his teacher, and various works of his call in question various compositions and policies suggested by Plato.

Now, it's very difficult to overestimate the importance of Aristotle in the history of economic thought, as I hope to have convinced you by the end of this lecture. But I can't promise you the same delectation that you would enjoy if you were to read Plato, whether you agreed with him or not, because Plato was one of the most marvelous writers that ever lived. He incidentally was a poet of some standing, and, as I say, whether you agree with him or not Plato is a delight to read. Whereas, we don't possess the origin of Aristotle's lectures; we only possess student notes, and student notes are not always as veracious an account of what has been said, and they are not necessarily so enjoyable to read. But for all that, it is Aristotle rather than Plato among the Greeks to whom you should look for influence on subsequent thought. The medieval theologians used to refer to Aristotle simply as "*the* Philosopher." Before the Renaissance Plato was not at all well known, whereas "*the* Philosopher" was appealed to by most of the writers on moral philosophy from Thomas Aquinas downward. And even to this day you will find in the analysis which you are taught lingering remnants of propositions which Aristotle originally put forward, both in his *Politics* and in his work on *Ethics*.

There came a reaction against Aristotle. Up to the sixteenth-century and into the seventeenth-century he dominated philosophical thought, moral philosophy and so on. Then came a reaction. The poet Dryden echoed the reaction in very memorable terms. Aristotle, I ought to explain before I read you four lines from the poet Dryden, was born at a place called Stagira and he was commonly referred to as "the Stagirite." Dryden says:

> The longest Tyranny that ever sway'd,
> Was that wherein our Ancestors betray'd
> Their free-born *Reason* to the *Stagirite*,
> And made his Torch their universal Light.
>
> [Dryden, 1663/1961, p. 43]

Well, his torch—although I should hate for you to think that I follow Aristotle in all that he had to say—was no mean torch, especially at that time of history.

He touches on a variety of matters mentioned by Plato in the *Republic* but on which I don't intend to dilate at any length in this lecture. Plato had suggested that, among the Guardians at any rate (who were the most supe-rior people and who ruled the ideal community), there should be commu-nity of wives and children. No one should know who his child was nor necessarily by whom it was begotten nor by whom it was conceived. Aris-totle didn't think that was a frightfully good plan. Aristotle thought that it might lead—inadvertently—to incest, which apparently he thought to be a heinous offence. He thought that people would at any rate be tempted to guess who their children were and perhaps to favouritise them. On the whole, Aristotle favoured the more normal arrangement of the family and overt position of the children so begotten and conceived in the family.

As regards material property, which Plato had banished from, at any rate, the Guardians in his *Republic*, Aristotle questioned that, and if you read that part of Aristotle's *Politics* (I don't intend to dilate on it at any length), you will find anticipations of those philosophers and economists who have recommended the institution of private property as pertaining to the utility of the law and social arrangements. Aristotle thought that prop-erty would be more likely to be better looked after if someone owned it and profited from it than if it were all treated as common. He said, and of course this is a tendentious remark in the present day, "Such legislation"—he's referring to Plato—

> may have a specious appearance of benevolence; men readily listen to it, and are easily induced to believe that in some wonderful manner everybody will become everybody's friend, especially when some one is heard denouncing the evils now existing in states, suits about contracts, convictions for perjury, flat-teries of rich men and the like, which are said to arise out of the possession of private property. These evils, however, are due to a very different cause—the wickedness of human nature. Indeed, we have seen that there is much more quarrelling among those who have all things in common, though there are not many of them when compared with the vast numbers who have private prop-erty. [Aristotle, 1948, p. 25]

Well, that's a statement of a case which had considerable influence through history, but I don't intend to discuss it further.

From our point of view the important influence of Aristotle has not been so much in that sphere of economic *thought*, to use Schumpeter's [1954, pp. 38–40] phrase distinguishing general ideas about economic arrange-ments from economic analysis; it is in economic *analysis* that Aristotle's influence has been so long-lasting. But now, you must notice at once that Aristotle would not have called his remarks on this subject political econ-omy or economics in our sense of the term. For Aristotle, at any rate, the term *economy* related to household management, and it is in the course of his discussion of household management and its connection with the rest of society that his important remarks occur.

But before I get to the important remarks, I can't go on without draw-ing attention to the fact that, in his discussion of household management, he attempts a justification of slavery, and the justification of slavery for what it is worth—and my judgement is that it is highly misleading—is that some people are born to be slaves—to be dominated—and others are born to give orders. And he discusses this at length. Obviously the question had begun to be discussed in Athens. There were enlightened people—I use the word enlightened with a certain bias—who were beginning to question the institution of slavery, and Aristotle at any rate thought that as a moral philosopher he ought to give some justification thereof. Well, I am afraid I think that's all very lame and dull stuff, especially when it appears incidentally that most of the Greeks—and one's suspicion is that Aristotle himself—thought that most of them were born to give orders and the rest of the world, the barbarians as he calls them, were of the other nature, more fitted to receive orders than to give them.

There is, however, in the course of Aristotle's discussion one extremely clever remark: He discusses at some length, and without according to modern ideas being at all convincing, the necessity for people having not merely material possessions but human possessions who shall act as *instruments* for carrying out their will. But then the thought occurs to him that, supposing the material instruments should become sufficiently complicated to do the humble and banal tasks which were assigned to the slaves, supposing that the machines should really become clever as he quotes (I won't refer to the book) the tripods (obviously some ritual instruments) which entered self-moved the Temple of the Gods, if the machines were as clever as that and could move themselves, then there would be no need for slavery—which is one of his brighter remarks.

But our business is really with his remarks on value and on money, and this comes into his discussion on household management because he perceives that, while very humble households in primitive conditions can perhaps manage with barter and without money, the probability is that, as soon as things become at all complicated, barter will give rise to indirect exchange—exchanging commodities for money which in turn is exchanged for other commodities which the original chap wanted more than the commodities that he possessed. And he perceives too—and this is the raison d'être of his disquisition; he is speaking as a moral philosopher but is obliged to go into what we should call economics—that indirect exchange may serve not only household management—the acquisition of shoes, and meat, and clothes and so on—but it may give rise to commerce and trade and complicated arrangements which on the whole as we shall see he deprecated.

But he feels it necessary to go into it, and he says (he is discussing the art of acquisition in a household):

Of the art of acquisition then there is one kind which is natural

—you'll notice the word natural creeping into economics at a very, very early stage—

and is part of the management of a household. Either we must suppose the
necessaries of life to exist previously, or the art of household management
must provide a store of them for the common use of the family or state. They
are the elements of true wealth;

—a value judgement creeping in—

for the amount of property which is needed for a good life is not unlimited,
although Solon in one of his poems says that,—
    No bound to riches has been fixed for man. [Aristotle, 1948, p. 15]

But he goes on to say:

There is another variety

—unnatural—

of the art of acquisition which is commonly and rightly called the art of making money, and has in fact suggested the notion that wealth and property have
no limit.

—reference to Solon—

Being nearly connected with the preceding, it is often identified with it. But
though they are not very different, neither are they the same. The kind already
described is given by nature

—that is, the art of acquisition to the management of the household—

the other is gained by experience and art. [ibid., p. 16]

Well, then he says:

Let us begin our discussion of the question with the following considerations:

—I propose to read you a bit—

Of everything which we possess there are two uses: both belong to the thing
as such, but not in the same manner, for one is the proper, and the other the
improper or secondary use of it. For example, a shoe is used for wear, and is
used for exchange; both are uses of the shoe. He who gives a shoe in exchange
for money or food to him who wants one, does indeed use the shoe as a shoe,
but this is not its proper or primary purpose, for a shoe is not made to be an
object of barter. The same may be said of all possessions, for the art of exchange extends to all of them, and it arises at first in a natural manner from the
circumstance that some have too little, others too much. Hence we may infer
that retail trade is not a natural part of the art of money-making; had it been
so, men would have ceased to exchange when they had enough. And in the
first community, which is the family, this art is obviously of no use, but only
begins to be useful when the society increases. For the members of the family
originally had all things in common; in a more divided state of society they still
shared in many things, but they were different things which they had to give

in exchange for what they wanted, a kind of barter which is still practised among barbarous nations who exchange with one another the necessaries of life and nothing more; giving and receiving wine, for example, in exchange for corn and the like. This sort of barter is not part of the money-making art and is not contrary to nature, but is needed for the satisfaction of men's natural wants. The other or more complex form of exchange grew out of the simpler. When the inhabitants of one country became more dependent on those of another, and they imported what they needed, and exported the surplus, money necessarily came into use. For the various necessaries of life are not easily carried about, and hence men agreed to employ in their dealing with each other something which was intrinsically useful and easily applicable to the purposes of life, for example, iron, silver, and the like. Of this the value was at first measured by size and weight, but in the process of time they put a stamp upon it, to save the trouble of weighing and to mark the value. [ibid., pp. 16–17]

That's the first time there occurred in the literature, so far as is known to me, elementary propositions as regards the origin of money which you are still taught.

Well, he goes on:

When the use of coin had once been discovered, out of the barter of necessary articles arose the other art of money-making, namely, retail trade; which was at first probably a simple matter, but became more complicated as soon as men learned by experience whence and by what exchanges the greatest profit might be made. Originating in the use of coin, the art of money-making is generally thought to be chiefly concerned with it, and to be the art which produces wealth and money. . . . Indeed,

—he goes out of his way to say—

wealth is assumed by many to be only a quantity of coin, because the art of money-making and retail trade are concerned with coin. Others maintain that coined money is a mere sham, a thing not natural, but conventional only, which would have no value or use for any of the purposes of daily life, if another commodity were substituted by the users. [ibid., p. 17]

Obviously a reference to Plato's internally valueless material which was used as coin.

And he goes on to say: Well that's all wrong. "[H]e who is rich in coin may often be in want of necessary food" [ibid.]. And here you come upon one of the most famous examples in the history of economics: "But how can that be wealth of which a man may have a great abundance and yet perish with hunger, like Midas in the fable, whose insatiable prayer turned everything that was set before him into gold?" [ibid., pp. 17–18]. You all know the fable of Midas to whom the gods promised the fulfilment of whatever he asked for, and he asked that he should have the gift of turning anything into gold. And having received that gift he starved to death. He goes on to say that "Men seek after a better notion of wealth and of the art of making money than the mere acquisition of coin, and they are right. For natural wealth and the natural art of money-making are a different thing" [ibid., p. 18]. It is alright if you use money in order to procure the things that you need in the management of the household. But if you go into retail trade, which Aristotle obviously had some contempt for, and seek to make a profit out of it, then you pass out of what is natural and what is moral and you are indulging in an activity which is not intrinsically worthwhile like the art of household management:

> some persons are led to believe that making money is the object of household management, and the whole idea of their lives is that they ought either to increase their money without limit, or at any rate not to lose it. The origin of this disposition in men is that they are intent upon living only, and not upon living well; and, as their desires are unlimited, they also desire that the means of gratifying them should be without limit. [ibid.]

But this enjoyment, he goes on to say, can be "in excess":

> they seek an art which produces the excess of enjoyment; and, if they are not able to supply their pleasures by the art of money-making, they try other arts, using in turn every faculty in a manner contrary to nature. The quality of courage, for example, is not intended to make money, but to inspire confidence; neither is this the aim of the general's or of the physician's art; but the one aims at victory and the other at health. Nevertheless, some men turn every quality or art into a means of making money; this they conceive to be the end, and to the promotion of the end all things must contribute. [ibid., p. 19]

Well, he expatiates at some length on that, and then he sums up by a statement which is extraordinarily important in the subject that I want to go on to, namely, the history of economic thought in the Middle Ages. He says:

> Of the two sorts of money-making one, as I have just said, is a part of household management, the other is retail trade: the former necessary and honourable, the latter a kind of exchange which is justly censured; for it is unnatural, and a mode by which men gain from one another. The most hated sort, and with the greatest reason, is usury, which makes a gain out of money itself, and not from the natural use of it. For money was intended [originally] to be used in exchange, but not to increase at interest. And this term usury . . . , which means the birth of money from money, is applied to the breeding of money because the offspring resembles the parent. Wherefore of all modes of making money this is the most unnatural. [ibid., p. 20]

Now, if you go on into the history of medieval economic thought, however enlightened in other respects, you will find this dictum of Aristotle and

sundry texts—not all—from the Bible appealed to as justifying the fero-
cious laws against *any* interest on loaned capital. But on that, more later.

Now, so much for what Aristotle says in the *Politics*. But in *Ethics* he
goes on to define the functions of money and money-making rather as
though he has not issued this very stern warning about the limits of money-
making in the *Politics*, and there is a passage in the *Ethics*, which is quoted
in this work of Monroe's (and you'll find it in the translation of the *Ethics*
by Welldon [Aristotle, 1892], which, in the absence of Monroe in the
shops, you may find it more convenient to go into), and here you find a
truly profound economic analysis of money. In the *Ethics*, still as a moral
philosopher, Aristotle is talking about justice and justice in exchange—reciprocal exchange. And he says that, in order that exchange may be just, it
is necessary that the *values* exchanged may be equivalent, and in order that
the values exchanged may be equivalent there must be a common measure
of value.

This is the reason for the invention of money.

—I'm quoting here from Welldon's translation—

Money is a sort of medium or mean; for it measures everything and consequently measures among other things excess or defect, e.g., the number of
shoes which are equivalent to a house or a meal. As a builder then is to a
cobbler, so must so many shoes be to a house or a meal; for otherwise there
would be no exchange or association. But this will be impossible, unless the
shoes and the house or meal are in some sense equalized. Hence arises the
necessity of a single universal standard of measurement, as was said before.
This standard is in truth the demand for mutual services, which holds society
together. [Aristotle, 1948, p. 27]

The leading chapter in the introductory textbook which used to be used in
this institution when I was a student—Cannan's *Wealth* [1919]—is entitled "The Controlling Power of Demand." "Money," Aristotle goes on,
"is a sort of recognized representative of this demand" which holds society
together [Aristotle, 1948, p. 27]. Then he goes on, this remarkable man,
to say that money is serviceable not only for contemporary exchange, it is
also "serviceable with a view"—I'm quoting—

to future exchange; it is a sort of security which we possess that, if we do not
want a thing now, we shall be able to get it when we do want it; for if a person
brings money, it must be in his power to get what he wants. . . .
Money therefore is like a measure that equates things, by making them com-
mensurable; for association would be impossible without exchange, exchange
without equality, and equality without commensurability. [ibid., p. 28]

Now, all that has had a lasting influence throughout the history of economics. And it is not until Petty at the end of the eighteenth century or
Adam Smith or Hume that anybody said anything more concise about the

functions of money. Therefore, I think you must give Aristotle rather high marks for thinking of these—for all of you rather banal—propositions for the first time.

He is also attributed by some—it is in an obscure volume of his called the *Topics* [1960], which is quoted after the rise of the Austrian school by a German scholar in the name of Kraus [1905]—with some perception of the principle of diminishing marginal utility. But that I think is just a footnote. He obviously had some glimmering which may have communicated itself to subsequent writers, although in an obscure way. It's not in my judgement one of the things that you have to put to his supreme credit as you do the distinction between use value and exchange value, his condemnation of trade, and his condemnation of usury, which, whether they were right or wrong, had tremendous influence hereafter.

Now, there is no need, I think, in a course of this kind to go further into obscure references to economic matters among the Greeks. And there is very little in the Roman world. It is one of the extraordinary things that Rome, unlike Athens which lost its comparatively small empire, became the dominant empire of western civilization before its decline and fall. It ruled many races, many language areas; they all became in one shape or other Roman citizens or Roman slaves. It indulged in extensive operations of the state, building roads, bridges, and so on and so forth, and very considerable use was made of money and credit, but there is no further economic speculation among the Romans. What we get from the Romans as such is some very profound and influentially important discussion of the institution of property, and that derives specifically from the Roman lawyers, rather than from people who were speculating about the economic relationships in society.

Well, what about Christianity? Early Christianity provides no further speculation on economic matters, and for the very plain reason that the early Christians in the New Testament—they get it from the lips of the founder of Christianity—believed that the end of the world was at hand, and that there was no point in taking thought for the morrow and in taking any particular thought about the economic arrangements of society. There was some asceticism described in the early chapters of the Acts of the Apostles in which some Christians pooled their property. You all know the veritable story of Ananias and Sapphira, who pretended to pool all their property, but concealed some of it and were by some heavenly action struck dead for their untruth. But on the whole, there's no economic speculation in early Christianity.

Well, in subsequent centuries, commerce was almost extinguished, with money economy, with the overrunning of the Roman Empire by people from Asia, and the eventual overrunning of North Africa, closing the Mediterranean to seaborne trade, by the armies of Mohammed. But gradually, after the stabilisation of society centuries on, after the Dark Ages, by the tenth, eleventh, twelfth, thirteenth century, you had a revival of commerce and trade, and complicated economic speculation. But the Christian philosophers of those days started from a different point of view from the Greek philosophers. The Greek philosophers had been searching for the best state—Plato's *Republic* for the ideal state, and Aristotle for the best state that could be achieved. But, the Scholastic philosophers were much more concerned—states in those days having only begun to emerge in their modern form—with individual duty, with what it was, what it was not, the duty of a Christian man to do. If you look at the part of Saint Thomas Aquinas's great *Summa Theologica*, which is still regarded by many Catholics as containing almost the be-all and the end-all of theological wisdom, you come to a part which is devoted to economic questions, but it is devoted in a way which is very odd to us. The first sentence is: "We next have to consider the sins which have to do with voluntary exchanges . . ." [Aquinas, 1948, p. 53].

Well, I will consider the sins which have to do with voluntary exchanges in my lecture next Wednesday.

Aquinas and the Scholastics

AT THE close of my lecture last Thursday, after a brief discussion of the extraordinary absence of economic speculation in the secular literature of the Roman Empire, save insofar as it occurs in discussions of laws relating to property and contract, and the equal poverty of discussion among the early apostles of Christianity or the theologians of the centuries before the Dark Ages, I leapt forward to the period when the Dark Ages had become less dark, at the revival of the money economy and the development of flourishing commerce and small industry, conspicuously in Italy. And I continued my lecture by drawing your attention to the change in the objectives of the moral philosophers of that period. Whereas the Greeks had concentrated on discussing incidentally the economic characteristics of a good State, the Christian philosophers concentrated on the obligations of the individual: What ought a Christian man to do? And I think I concluded the lecture by quoting to you the opening sentence of that part of Saint Thomas Aquinas' *Summa Theologica* in which he says that he proposes to discuss the sins associated with the exchanges.

Now, I want to devote this hour to a thumbnail sketch of the broad perspectives of these incidental comments on value and distribution which are to be found in the works of the Christian theologians from the thirteenth century until the Reformation. And I should warn you that alone, I think, of the thirty-five lectures that I am delivering, I am relying very largely in this respect on secondary authorities. My immediate acquaintance with the miscellaneous writings of all the Catholic theologians of the Middle Ages is comparatively restricted. So, since this is a controversial subject, you must bear that in mind. Having said that, let me plunge at once into part, at least, of the controversy.

In earlier days, when the history of economic thought first became the subject of serious attention, the treatment of the relevant theological writings of the Middle Ages seems to have been very sketchy and, according to more recent lights, to some extent misleading. In my young days I was an enthusiastic Guild Socialist, a movement which flourished during the First World War and shortly before, and I remember reading a book by an admirable man called Mr A. J. Pentey [1917], who discussed the guild system of the Middle Ages and sought to apply the morals that he drew from this discussion to modern society as he desired that it should be changed. According to this view, the centre of gravity of the discussion on value and exchange in the medieval theologians was the just price. Now, that is not a controversial statement. What is controversial is the interpretation of the just price. According to very great authorities of the past, the just price had an intimate connection with hierarchical status in society. It was thought that the just price was a price which could be more or less objectively ascertained, that it depended, roughly speaking, on the cost of production, especially the labour cost of production, and this was linked to some idea of social hierarchy. The just price was a price which, taking account of the amount of labour and so on and so forth, enabled you to maintain your status in a system of hierarchy. And linked with this—and this brings me back to Mr A. J. Pentey—the organisation of industry was supposed to depend upon guilds, associations of producers whose activities were directed to securing that the just price was charged.

Now, you mustn't underestimate the authority which underlies that interpretation of the outlook of the moral philosophers of the Middle Ages. It certainly at one stage inspired no less a person than Max Weber, the greatest sociological mind of the twentieth century in this country, in my judgement. You will find that it inspires—what is still quite worth reading—the chapters on economics in the Middle Ages in Ashley's *Economic History* [1901]; Tawney's *Religion and the Rise of Capitalism* [1926], which has enjoyed a tremendous vogue in my lifetime and still commands great respect, if only for the magnificence of its prose style; and the authoritative Italian politician Fanfani [1961]. These writers have all given countenance to this view. Yet, so far as I am able to judge—let me refrain from being dogmatic in this connection—it is largely imaginary. If you read your Schumpeter [1954], which is very good on this period (remember that I do not recommend beginners to start on that thousand-page volume, but you can read the chapter which deals with the Scholastic philosopher, regardless of the rest), you will find that he argues the contrary—the position which I am going to develop shortly.

More valuable than Schumpeter, and I suspect inspiring at any rate some of Schumpeter's judgement, is the author of this monograph, which in my judgement is the best introduction to the subject that I know, by a lately deceased economic historian—who started, I believe, at the London School of Economics—called Raymond de Roover, and it is called *San Bernardino of Siena and Sant' Antonino of Florence: The Two Great Economic Thinkers of the Middle Ages* [1967]. It's published by the Kress Library of Harvard. I think that this is the best of de Roover's writings on this subject, but those of you who find it difficult to get access to a copy—it should be in the library—will find an earlier article on the just price and its determination by de Roover [1958] reprinted in that collection of essays which is enumerated on the last page of the bibliography which is all in your possession.

Now, de Roover's [1958, pp. 24–26] main contention in the article on just price, and incidentally in this article on San Bernardino and the others, is that the great authorities whose pronouncements I have drawn your attention to rely, almost all of them, on the utterance of a certain Heinrich von Langenstein, who lived from 1327 to '97. And Langenstein seems to have made a statement to the effect that if the authorities don't fix the price, then the producer should not charge more than would enable him to maintain his status. This utterance of Langenstein's was first cited by the great German economist and economic historian Roscher, in his history of German economics, 1874, and then all the others picked it up, according to de Roover, from Roscher. But—again according to de Roover and Schumpeter—Langenstein was a very minor figure, not carrying much weight in the great body of the literature of medieval moral philosophy. And again, according to de Roover, the main Scholastic authorities had different views.

Now, to start with Saint Thomas, extracts from which are in this valuable work of Monroe's on *Early Economic Thought*. Saint Thomas' disquisition on the sins which arise in the course of exchange is rather wooden and slightly pedantic, and it is very difficult to put an exact interpretation on what he is getting at at different times. From time to time, if you read the extracts in the *Summa*, he seems to be talking about isolated exchange, and this point is taken up by Ashley among the apologists for the view which de Roover poses, and of course isolated exchange does raise moral problems of quite a different order from a more organised social exchange.

Saint Thomas quotes no less a person than Saint Augustine, who praises the behaviour of someone who was offered a book below the price which it could presumably have obtained elsewhere and who refused to pay that price and offered a higher one. Well now, don't think that I do not agree with Saint Augustine in that particular context. If any one of you, or most of you at any rate—perhaps there may be very learned people in the literature of the history of economic thought among you—were to come to me, for instance, and offer me a copy of, what shall I say, Cantillon's *Essai sur la nature du commerce*, and say "Will you give me £5 for it?" I should be an utter cad if I gave you £5 for it, *knowing* that in fact among the booksellers who know their business, an original copy of a first edition of Cantillon's *Essai sur la nature du commerce* [1755]—on which I shall give you a whole lecture later on—would be worth anything up to £100 or its equivalent in francs. But that does not carry you very far—the discussion of individual relationships. If I go in, let us say, to Francis Edwards, which is one of the best antiquarian bookshops in London, located in Marylebone High Street, and were offered a copy of Cantillon's *Essai sur la nature du commerce* at that price, I would snap it up. It would be Francis Edwards' job to know his business, and if I knew the business better than Francis Edwards, I should not feel in the least ashamed of myself if I got a bargain that way. Many lecturers in the history of economic thought have built up quite respectable libraries from knowing rather more about it than the expert antiquarian booksellers.

But de Roover [1965, p. 28] argues that, when Saint Thomas is not discussing isolated exchange, by just price Saint Thomas means the price that is paid by common estimation in a more or less competitive market.

And he reinforces this point by saying that Saint Thomas says that if a merchant arriving at a place of dearth, knowing that there are merchants, let us say, a week behind him who are due to arrive at a place of dearth and who will bring the price down, he is not committing a mortal sin if he sells at the price prevailing in the place of dearth—although Saint Thomas adds that it might be more *virtuous* if he revealed that there were other chaps speeding along about a week behind.

On the whole Saint Thomas' thought has to be reconstructed from bits and pieces. He actually on one occasion seems to anticipate a utility theory of value, because he argues that otherwise a mouse, which has the principle of life in it, would be more highly argued than a pearl, which is dead matter—which seems to suggest that he had some idea of what modern economists talk about when they discuss the connection between utility and price.[1] But on the whole I think it's a great mistake, especially since Saint Thomas goes out of his way, following *the* philosopher, Aristotle, whom I was talking to you about last week, to disparage retail trade carried beyond the natural limit of acquisition for the household. It's, I think, better to go to the later Scholastic writers, particularly San Bernardino of Siena, who lived from 1380 to 1444, and his sermons, which, being translated, are entitled *The Eternal Gospel* [1484]. There are sixty-five of them, of which fourteen deal with matters of contract, and exchange, and price and so on.

If you look at the very full account which de Roover [1967] gives of San Bernardino's writings, which are not easily accessible, you notice at once a certain contrast with Saint Thomas. Saint Thomas, as I have just said, followed Aristotle as regards the disparagement of retail trade carried on as a profession—carried on beyond the means of natural acquisition for household management. San Bernardino recognises trade and manufacture as useful. He praises them. He praises the upright tradesman. He at once goes out of his way to disparage the tricks which nonupright tradesmen resort to. He passes very astringent comments on the iniquitous behaviour of travelling merchants. Very interesting that he should hit on travelling merchants. Adam Smith in the *Wealth of Nations* [1776] devotes some attention to the morality of commerce, and he thinks that where you have extensive markets, people discover iniquitous tricks which individual merchants may be up to and tend to avoid them, so that from that rather low point of view, honesty, where commerce is widely spread—according to Adam Smith—is the best policy. In that respect the points of view of Adam Smith and San Bernardino, I think, were not frightfully different. But San Bernardino comes down heavily against cheating, against unfair competition. Then he reverts to the fact that good entrepreneurship, good managerial ability, was rare, and he has no objection to them being rewarded.

He also follows Aristotle in his opposition to Plato, who preached Communism among the Guardians. He follows Aristotle in thinking that property will probably be better looked after by people who have a direct interest in its use and utilisation for profit than if it is commonly owned. It is interesting—this is a tendentious remark—it is very interesting to find that these people who, all of them—the medieval theologians—supported communistic, monastic institutions, followed Aristotle in deprecating common property outside the monastic institutions.

But San Bernardino is most interesting on the theory of value and price. Saint Thomas, as I have mentioned to you, had contrasted the value of mice and the value of pearls, and de Roover [1967, p. 17] points out that while Tawney goes out of his way to depict Karl Marx as the last of the schoolmen, basing price predominantly at any rate on its labour cost, according to de Roover, who declares that he has searched the literature, there is no trace of that sort of thing in Saint Thomas. Well, the opposite approach is clearly developed by San Bernardino, and San Bernardino argues that value is determined by three elements: first of all, the intrinsic usefulness of the object—intrinsic in the sense that it so to speak provides something which does good to the consumer; secondly, to the scarcity of the object—there creeps in the up-to-dateness; and, thirdly, its desirability. De Roover [ibid., p. 18] thinks that the distinction between the usefulness and desirability has some relevance. Well, it may have in moral philosophy; it certainly has no relevance when we talk about utility in the modern theory of value. And at this point I think I part company just a little bit in de Roover's reservation on modern developments. De Roover thinks that possibly it might have been a good thing if San Bernardino's classification had been retained.

Now, what about San Bernardino's originality in this respect? De Roover, in his early articles, thought that San Bernardino's exposition was not only the most powerful among the Scholastic philosophers, but it was also the most original. But he has now discovered, and he expounds it in his book [ibid., pp. 19–20], that there are traces—more than traces—of San Bernardino's discussion of value and utility in the work of a man of the century before, 1248–1298, called Pierre Olivi. And the odd thing is that San Bernardino, who obviously was an extremely virtuous and meticulous man, and always cites—or nearly always cites—his quotations, does not cite Olivi, who anticipated him at this particular point. Was this a mortal sin in San Bernardino? No, says de Roover, because it so happens that after Olivi's death he was accused of heresy—of mortal heresy—and his bones were dug up and scattered to the four winds. Well naturally, San Bernardino, with his authority in the Italian church, would not cite as his authority a man who had been accused of heresy and his bones dug up and the ashes scattered to the four winds.

Well, to continue with San Bernardino, the usefulness or the desirability as a deciding factor is not absolute. "Otherwise," he says, "a glass of water would be almost priceless," but it's "abundant" [ibid., p. 20]. He doesn't actually solve the so-called paradox of value as you get it in Adam Smith and some of the classical economists, but he gets pretty near to it. And Dr

Bowley [1973], in quite an interesting essay, in a collected book of essays, on "Utility . . . and 'all that' . . . ," has discovered various other people writing long before Adam Smith, and passages in Adam Smith himself, which suggest that perhaps the paradox of value was not so acute a paradox as certainly Ricardo and others represented it to be.

According to San Bernardino, price is determined by collective estimation—that is, market valuation. The seller may have to sell something for less than he gave for it, and he may sell for more than he gave for it. It depends upon the contemporary market estimation. San Bernardino admits exceptions to this. He can conceive positions—positions presumably of extreme dearth—in which prices may have to be fixed by authority. As far as I know he doesn't mention that, if prices are fixed by authority, which I don't disapprove of in circumstances of extreme dearth, you have to have rationing as well, otherwise the scarcity becomes more intense. That's a modern perception.

San Bernardino goes on to condemn, in all its manifestations, monopolistic collaring of the market. He thinks that the practice of monopoly is so wicked that it deserves perpetual exile in this world and perpetual punishment in the flames of hell in the next. So much for the prices of ordinary commodities.

On wages, San Bernardino only says that the same rules that apply to the prices of goods apply also to the prices of services. This side of the matter is developed much better in the other great economist of the Middle Ages—according to de Roover [1967, pp. 24–27]—Sant' Antonino of Florence, who lived from 1389 to 1459, in his work which was also called *Summa Theologica* [1511]. He adopts San Bernardino's value theory, and he is very much against bad employers and very much against employers who pay in kind rather than in cash, or, as some employers were apt to do in Florence of his period, who paid in clipped money rather than in money of full metallic value. He's against workers who spoil the materials. And while on the whole, according to de Roover, there is very, very little discussion of guilds among the moral Scholastic philosophers, Sant' Antonino mentions the clothiers' guild, but he denounces the guild for paying the workers in truck or debased coin. And so I could go on.

But now we come to an analytically more interesting subject. Whatever the opinion of the later Scholastics—and the later Scholastics certainly followed San Bernardino and Sant' Antonino, rather than Langenstein and anybody else who held his views—they all held at first to Aristotle's condemnation of usury. And on this you certainly should consult, if you can get access to it, Saint Thomas's discussion, because Saint Thomas is very active on this and very downright, and he is followed in this respect by many of the moral philosophers.

Question 78 in the *Summa* is "Of the Sin of Usury Which Is Committed in Loans." Now, you should all be aware that usury, as discussed by the medieval philosophers, was interest on loans. They were *not* opposed to the profit of partnerships. They *were*, at any rate at the beginning, inflexibly opposed—as Aristotle had been—to interest on money advanced by way of a loan.

Saint Thomas starts by the familiar citation of texts. I am bound to say that he cites texts from the Old and New Testaments which don't all sustain the attitude which he eventually adopts. He starts by stating the arguments in favour: "It seems that it is not sinful to receive usury on money loans. For no one sins in following the example of Christ. But the Lord says of himself (Luke xix, 23) . . ."—Are you all acquainted with the Holy Scriptures nowadays? I do not speak as a profound believer, but you miss quite a lot if you do not read this wonderful heritage of literature. In the parable of the unjust steward, which I shall not insult those of you who know it by repeating, Christ actually put into the mouth of the employer of the unjust steward the reproach (the unjust steward had buried the money that he was entrusted with)—"At my coming I might have exacted it [if he had let it out] with usury" [Aquinas, 1948, p. 65]. And then Saint Thomas cites the passage in Deuteronomy [23:19] which says to the followers of Moses: " 'Thou shalt not lend money to thy brother on usury, nor corn nor any other thing, but to the stranger' " [ibid.]. And so on and so forth.

"*But opposed to this*"—and this is relied upon by Saint Thomas very, very heavily—"is the saying of Exodus xxii, 25: 'If thou lend money to any of my people that is poor, that dwelleth with thee, thou shalt not be hard upon them as an extortioner, nor oppress them with usuries' " [ibid., p. 66], which might, you see, be interpreted—as Saint Thomas does not go on to interpret it—as being a case of isolated loans between someone who is long on cash and someone who happens to be short on cash, in which case, as in the case of the isolated exchange, there may easily be two opinions as to what is right and proper. It certainly would not be regarded by a modern economist as absurd to say that a rich man lending to a very poor man, who is in need or difficulties, should not charge interest.

But Saint Thomas—and this is why I am dwelling on Saint Thomas—then goes on to advance an analytical argument. Now, listen carefully; I'm going to read you the analytical argument because it contains what I am prepared to argue is an analytical fallacy: "In proof of this," he says,

> it should be noticed that there are some things the use of which is the consumption of the things themselves; as we consume wine by using it to drink, and consume wheat by using it for food. Hence, in the case of such things, the use should not be reckoned apart from the thing itself; but when the use has been granted to a man, the thing is granted by this very fact; and therefore, in such cases, the act of lending involves the transfer of ownership (*dominum*). Therefore, if a man wished to sell wine and the use of the wine separately, he would be selling the same thing twice, or selling what does not exist; hence he would obviously be guilty of a sin of injustice. For analogous reasons, a man

commits injustice who lends wine or wheat expecting to receive two compensations. [ibid.]

A *fortiori*, according to his classification of money—he classifies it as a consumable—the charging of money on loans is sinful.

And then he goes out of the way in the next paragraph to recite what is in effect—I think it would be commonly agreed—the refutations of his argument:

> There are some things, however, the use of which is not the consumption of the thing itself; thus the use of a house is living in it, not destroying it. Hence, in such cases, both may be granted separately, as in the case of a man who transfers the ownership of a house to another, reserving the use of it for himself for a time; or, conversely, when a man grants someone the use of a house, while retaining the ownership. Therefore a man may lawfully receive a price for the use of a house, and in addition expect to receive back the house lent. [ibid., p. 67]

Well, it is astonishing that a masterly philosopher, like Saint Thomas is, should have provided the refutation of his own logic in the preceding paragraph, because if you pay for the wine at once when you drink it, you don't pay interest. You just pay the price of the wine. But if you drink the wine and you don't pay for a year, your position is exactly the same as the man who accepts the loan of a house for a year and does not pay rent until the end of the year. Moreover, Saint Thomas and the medieval scholastics who went with him permitted the sale of rent charges. Now, the sale of rent charges—that is, the capital value of rents stretching into the future—implies a rate of interest; otherwise the capital value of perpetual rents would be infinite. You have to discount the more distant rents in order to get the capital value. So while permitting the sale of rent charges, they were implicitly permitting an implicit rate of interest.

Well, were there not exceptions? There was an exception which was called *damnum emergens*. If a man actually suffered a loss in respect of the repayment of capital, then he charged the loss, but that isn't any real concession. The real question arose whether he could charge, in addition to the return of his loan, what he might have got himself if he had employed the money profitably. That was called in Latin *lucrum cessans*. And Saint Thomas forbade that. But by the time Sant' Antonino came to write, Florence had developed quite a flourishing banking business, and loans—cash loans—were becoming part of the commerce of Florence, and, rather grudgingly, Sant' Antonino does begin to permit it.

And thenceforward doubts begin to creep into the minds of a certain number of thinkers on this subject. These thinkers were of different schools theologically. We are coming forward to the Reformation. Luther was as emphatically against interest as the followers of Saint Thomas Aquinas. Calvin saw no objection to the charging of reasonable interest, and eventually it was a Catholic theologian of the name of Dumoulin [1546], whose work is reproduced in Monroe's *Early Economic Thought*,[2] who really made hay of the argument against the charging of *any* interest. Henceforward, although you get people lingering into the Elizabethan period here— some, theologians—the prohibition of interest in general was maintained. But it was a losing cause. Henceforward, the argument about interest— which is still a very interesting argument—was whether interest should be regulated and whether the legal rate of interest should be lower than the rate charged in certain departments of commerce and so on and so forth.

But I see my time is up. I recommend you to read Dumoulin who really is, in my judgement, slightly tendentious. I recommend in my bibliography a book by a man called Father Divine [1959]—not that rather brash man who used to make terrific broadcasts in the interwar period, but a man who studied for a Ph.D. at the London School of Economics in the interwar period. His doctoral dissertation is of interest, and I commend it to you. Lest you think that as a non-Catholic I have been weighting the scales in this lecture, I commend to you Father Divine's treatment of the history of interest.

NOTES

1. See De Roover (1967, p. 17).
2. Charles Dumoulin, Latinized as Carolus Molinaeus, *Tractus Contractuum Et Usurarum Redituumque Pecunia Constitutorum* (1546), reprinted in Monroe (1948, pp. 103–20).

Pamphleteers—Money (Oresme, Bodin, "W.S.")

I HAVE finished, in a disgracefully hurried way, the remarks that I want to make in this course of lectures on the anticipations of economics springing from moral philosophy. At the end of my last lecture I was dilating on the fascinating subject of the French revolution of thought regarding usury. We shall be returning to the development of analysis regarding the rate of interest at a later stage, and it may be possible to link up with the parts that I scamped at that stage. I must not get too behind, and the hints I gave, I think, were sufficient to indicate a broad perspective of the subject.

Now I want to turn to anticipations in the realm of ad hoc pamphleteering, of which the coverage is simply enormous and quite impossible to compress in a couple or more lectures—money, trade regulation, poor relief, employment, emigration, population, learning and so on and so forth. But as I was saying, it is possible to dip the bucket in the ocean and then direct attention on what it contains.

But first of all, let me say just a word about the background of all this. We are moving somewhat beyond the Middle Ages in this respect. The background of the great part of this pamphleteering literature—which, of course, is continuous up to the present day, but that is another matter—takes its rise, very largely, contemporaneously with the rise of the nation state. For good or bad, as the Dark Ages came to an end, and as the rate of restoration of order and commerce and trade developed in different parts of the western world, so nationality—the feeling of nationality—for good or for bad, and it has both sides, began to develop. Those of you who have seen Bernard Shaw's play *Saint Joan* will get a very vivid idea of the beginnings of national feeling across the Channel. The ordinary people were beginning to feel that their language was *the* language, rather than the Latin in which the more lettered classes communicated with one another, irrespective of national frontiers. Moreover, gunpowder, a material circumstance, was making the feudal system, in which any tinpot baron could have an area in which he could more or less tyrannise over himself. According to the time and place, he might, or might not, have allegiance to someone above him, and in the end the allegiance of the feudal barons was supposed to be to the supreme feudal lord, the King.

And then on the other side you have the disintegration of the more or less uniform version of Christian religion, which took place with the Reformation and which gave rise in the sixteenth and the seventeenth centuries to a good deal of shedding of blood. And then, of course, there was Christopher Columbus, who discovered the New World and, with the New

World, more abundant supplies of the precious metals, which, in the course of two centuries brought about, at only something like 2 percent compound interest per annum, a very serious fall in the purchasing power of money.

All this led to new administrative problems. In the early part of the period, the King, as supreme feudal lord, lived, as the saying was, on his own. He had extensive estates, he had extensive servants and slaves, and the part which taxation played in his household management was relatively minor. But with the emergence of nationality and the emergence of the superior power of the monarch in such States, taxation became more important, and how to make great the revenue of the State became a subject of urgent preoccupation on the part of ambitious civil servants. There were also matters of which the King couldn't rid himself of responsibility, and many of them snatched at the occasion for irresponsibility which that power conferred—there were matters relating to money and the exchanges.

Well, a good deal of this ad hoc pamphleteering by civil servants is rather dull stuff. The Germans call it *Kameralism*. *Kamer* in German means chamber, and you will remember the nursery rhyme:

> The King was in his chamber counting out his money,
> The queen was somewhere or something eating bread and honey.[1]

For the most part the literature of taxation at that early stage is for specialists. There is some superior writing there. Monroe gives extracts from a German eighteenth-century man called Justin—worth looking at. In England it links up with what Adam Smith called "political arithmetic"—the beginnings of statistics, beginnings in which Adam Smith [1776, 2:36] declared that he had pretty little confidence.

And then secondly, against this background you have polemical literature written on behalf of different groups in the emerging national States: merchants with an axe to grind, subsidies to be demanded, protective tariffs to be urged—always in the general interest, doubtless—and so on and so forth—the whole literature of what is sometimes called mercantilism. But don't take that too seriously because mercantilism is an ambiguous term, and in my next lecture I shall be dilating on the ambiguities thereof.

Well, I am going to cover all this ad hoc pamphleteering by taking two principal groups. I am going to take the development of monetary analysis in this lecture, and in the next lecture I am going to talk about mercantilism in the narrow sense of the word—having warned you that there is a wider sense of the word.

Now, money. I want to touch on two main questions this morning. I want to touch on the literature regarding debasement, and I want to touch on the early literature regarding the influence of changes in the volume of money. And this is quite convenient from my point of view because the first work I want to discuss was not written by a Government servant and was not written by a merchant anxious to fill his and his group's pockets; it was written by a disinterested monk. And this is, so to speak, one of the links with the literature that I've been discussing—the literature of moral philosophy. And the work to which I want to draw your attention is a work of which some extracts are reproduced in Monroe, but there is a full Latin and English version of this work which is called, in Latin, *De Moneta* [1360; 1956] and is translated by the author of this Nelson edition, which I should imagine is still in print. I cannot believe that it has gone like hotcakes. It is called *The Mint*.

Now, the author of *De Moneta* was a Frenchman of the name of Nicholas Oresme, whose general frame of mind is very representative of the Scholastic philosophy of which we've been talking already. But this book, *De Moneta*, is Scholasticism ad hoc. It is not tinged with the vices of pamphleteering. It is tinged, rather, with the virtues of pamphleteering. Well now, Oresme is a fascinating figure, and it would be nice to talk about him at length. He lived from 1320 to 1382. Don't think, any of you, that I attach enormous importance to dates; I just throw them out in order to give you some sort of general perspective. The expectation of universities in my conception is not that you should remember trifling details of this sort— although of course you ought get your dates right if you mention them— but that you should have broader perspectives at this stage. He was a French cleric. He wrote on theology; he wrote on mathematics; he translated *the* philosopher, Aristotle; he became master of a College of Navarre in the south of France; and then in 1377 he was made a bishop of Lisieux. And he wrote *De Moneta* probably—we're not sure—about 1360. Now, it is in the form of a treatise, and it is indeed the subtitle of the treatise. It's *A Treatise*—I'm quoting the right-hand pages; I am not going to read you the Latin—*on the Origin, Nature, Law and Alterations of Money* by Master Nicholas Oresme, STP [Sacre Theologie Professorem], which means "of the Holy Theology, a Professor."

But while it is a treatise in shape, it is also a polemic, and you can see that if you read the preface. And I'll read you the whole of the preface, which is short:

> Some men hold that any king or prince may, of his own authority, by right or prerogative, freely alter the money current in his realm, regulate it as he will, and take whatever gain or profit may result: but other men are of the contrary opinion. I have therefore determined to write down in this treatise what seems to me from a philosophical and Aristotelian point of view, essentially proper to be said, beginning with the origin of money. I make no rash assertions, but submit everything to the judgment of my seniors. Perhaps my words will rouse them finally to settle the truth of this matter

—what a beautiful humility—Keynes!—

> so that the experts may all be of one mind, and come to a conclusion which shall be profitable both to princes and subjects, and indeed to the State as a whole.

That, conjecturally, was written in 1360, and we have not yet established one mind on the subjects that we are about to discuss.

Well now, this is an interesting book to read, and graduate students should certainly have a sniff at it. I won't say that it is incumbent on undergraduates. But you can get a very good idea of it by just looking at the contents table. And let me read it to you, or read some of it.

1. Why money was invented
2. The material of money
3. Of the variety of materials and of alloys
4. Of the form or shape of money
5. [beginning to get near the point] Who has the duty of coining?
6. Who owns the money?
7. Who bears the expense of coining?

And then, in 8, you plunge to the raison d'être of his pseudo-Aristotelian treatise:

8. On alterations in coinage in general

Now, I pause perhaps and say that if you don't realise, if you are not expert—which I am not—in medieval economic history, debasement of the coinage was a quite frequent recourse of the heads of States. If they were able, for instance, to diminish the amount of precious metal in the coin and still call it by the same name—sterling bears the name which it has borne historically for a very, very long time, but doesn't represent the same purchasing power—but if you were able to do that to metallic money, either by changing the weight or by changing the alloy and keeping the name, then, pro tem, the prince could make profit, and only those who were alive to what was happening—money changers, who speedily twigged that they were being made suckers of—escaped the *tax* on the people which is the real name for debasement of money.

So, chapter 8 deals with alterations in coinage in general. And then the next chapters deal with "Changes of form," "Changes of ratio," "Change of name," "Change of weight," "Change of materials," "Compound change[s]."[2] And then, in chapter 15, warming up to his task, Nicholas says, "That the profit accruing to the Prince from alteration of the coinage is unjust."

16. That such profit is unnatural
17. That profit from the change of money is worse than usury

Now, you remember that those who believed in the prohibition of usury thought that it deserved among merchants exile in this world and the flames of hell in the next.

18. That such alterations of money are essentially not permissible

And then, cunning man that he was,

19. Of certain disadvantages to the Prince resulting from alterations of the coinage

20. Of other disadvantages to the community as a whole

21. Of disadvantages to part of the community

And then—I'll read you the whole—

22. Whether the community can make such alterations

23. An argument that the Prince may alter the coinage

24. Reply to the previous chapter and main conclusion

And then

25. That a tyrant cannot be lasting

And

26. That the taking of profit from alteration of the coinage injures the whole Royal Succession

Well, so much for Nicholas Oresme. The burden of his argument is that it is immoral—debasement. He touches on the confusions and so on and so forth, but the burden of his argument is that it is immoral, that it is unjust and that it is worse than usury. Hence, in one [inaudible words] of, so to speak, the sense of our subject—this is a value judgement—I personally would give a high mark to Nicholas.

Now, I wonder if any of you have looked at that collection of tracts in French which is recommended in my bibliography—Le Branchu's [1934] collection. If you have, you will find something which I didn't know about before I read Le Branchu some twenty years ago—I bought it since the war. He actually prints a disquisition on debasement and on changes in the purchasing power of money—by whom? Intelligence test. Who changed our whole idea of the nature of the starry universe? Come on. [Students call out the name of Galileo.] Nearly. He had a distinguished predecessor. We must not waste time. Copernicus.

Now, one can't say that Copernicus had a widespread influence on thought because his disquisition is in manuscript. There is reason to suppose that his document, which was written probably about 1538, was in the hands of the administrator of that part of Northern Europe where he lived. Well, it wasn't published in print until 1810. So one need not linger on it, and it's not essential reading for you. His emphasis is much more than the emphasis two centuries before of Nicholas Oresme on the economic effects of debasement, but he dwells on debasement and argues strongly against it—the distributive alterations which he thinks are not only unjust but economically embarrassing. And he does actually—on page 9 of Le Branchu's reproduction of his manuscript—he actually does formulate a primitive version of Gresham's law—namely, that bad money drives out good.

Well, now, we mustn't linger on debasement, although debasement continued to take place. Henry VIII debased the currency and caused all sorts of upsets which I shall be talking about in the last five minutes of my lecture if I get through to that.

But we are now at the point at which the world is enjoying the effects of the discovery of North America and the Caribbean by Columbus, and precious metals were beginning to pour into Spain. And there's an obscure man who is mentioned in this splendid book by Miss Grice-Hutchinson on *Early Economic Thought in Spain* [1978]—an obscure man called Azpilcueta de Navarro. And he actually more or less is the first person to enunciate the quantity theory of money. He says—let me read it to you—

> other things being equal, in countries where there is great scarcity of money, all other saleable goods, and even the hands and labour of men, are given for less money than where it is abundant. Thus we see by experience that in France, where money is scarcer than in Spain, bread, wine, cloth and labour are worth much less. [Grice-Hutchinson, 1978, p. 104]

And so on and so forth.

Well, in a way this chap is a curiosum. Although dealt with in the writings of Miss Grice-Hutchinson on the School of Salamanca and this book that I know is in print, because it only came out last year, it hasn't crept into the textbooks that you are supposed to have read. And so I will just draw your attention to it, and to Miss Grice-Hutchinson in general, and proceed to something which is much more important in the history of thought, namely the famous *Paradoxes du Seigneur de Malestroict*, of which the first edition was published in 1566.

Well, not much is known about Malestroict. Those of you who want to know more about him will find that his work, his *Paradox on the Course of the Value of Money* [1566], which was deteriorating in his day in France, has been edited in our own day by no less a person than the first President of Italy—Luigi Einaudi—who was, you know, before he became President—he is now dead—a very, very splendid man who was a famous economist who had to go into hiding during the Mussolini days.

Einaudi can tell you all about Malestroict if you want to find out about him. Not much is known about him, he was an official of the so-called *Cour des Monnaies*, and he seems to have been charged with investigating the cause of the rise of prices. And he produced a curious document, a very curious document in a way—not without ingenuity. He argues first that if you take the *real* value of gold and silver, as distinct from the value of the coins which have been debased, the real values of exchange between gold and silver and other commodities had not changed. It was just the debasement which had caused the rise in prices, but the real value of gold and silver had not changed. And then he goes on to say that what had happened was debasement, and his book is an indication of the official thought of the time. But one wouldn't trouble to mention, even to such a select class as this, Malestroict at great length if it were only for the substance of his paradox. The point is that he provoked a reply from someone whom some of you ought to have heard of, namely the *very* famous jurist Jean Bodin.

Bodin's reply is reprinted in this thing of Monroe [1948]. Since Monroe is rather difficult to get at, I was looking at the English translation of Bodin, which was published by Blackwells just after the war—the English translation of Bodin's [1576] great book on the *Republic*. I ought to say for those of you who don't know about Bodin—and I was looking round to see those of you with whom the name struck a bell—that he was the author of the famous doctrine of State sovereignty. Multitudinous are the books that have been written on State sovereignty since the sixteenth century. Bodin is the author of the great work on the *Republic* which enunciated this doctrine which many of us think has done so much harm in the world, but that is not its fame. Its fame is that it has provided the background of constitutional jurisprudence from that day until it began to be questioned in the last hundred years, although it was not without opposition before that.

And he wrote a pamphlet, which is reproduced in *Early Economic Thought* by Monroe [1948], called—well, let me translate—*The Response of Jean Bodin to the Paradoxes of Monsieur de Malestroict touching the increasing dearness of everything and the means of remedying it*. And this was published in 1568. And this is quite important, and you should look it up in Monroe when you get hold of a copy. He begins by casting doubt on Malestroict's assertion that there was no change in the relation between commodities in general and gold and silver measured by weight and by the alloy that they contained. Bodin doesn't deny Malestroict's judgement that there has been debasement of the currency—that was wide knowledge—but he does deny that there have been changes in the relative prices of some goods and some bits of land which are not capable of explanation only in terms of debasement of the content and alloy of the French money.

And he then goes on to give the causes of the rise in prices other than the debasement. And he gives all sorts of causes, and no doubt some of them are valid—monopolies and the evil influence thereof, waste on the part of various people, lavish expenditure on particular commodities or particular bits of land and so on and so forth. But, he says, "The principal reason," and this is on page 127 of Monroe's book if you can get hold of it,

> The principal reason which raises the price of everything, wherever one may be, is the abundance of that which governs the appraisal & price of things. Plutarch & Pliny testify that, after the conquest of the Kingdom of Macedonia, under the King of Persia, the Captain Paulus Æmilius brought so much gold & silver to Rome that the people were freed from paying taxes, & the price of lands in the Romagna rose by two thirds in a moment.

I do not believe that they rose by two-thirds in a moment, but it was pretty quick.

And Suetonius

—he's mustering his big guns—

Suetonius says that the Emperor Augustus brought so much wealth from Egypt that usury fell, & the price of lands was a good deal higher than formerly. Now it was not the scarcity of lands, which can neither increase nor diminish, or monopoly, which cannot exist in such a case: but it was the abundance of gold & silver, which causes the depreciation . . . of these & the dearness of the things priced . . . ; as happened

—going back into history—

at the coming of the Queen of Candace, whom holy Scripture calls the Queen of Sheba,

—you've all heard of the Queen of Sheba surely—

into the city of Jerusalem,

—when she was paying a visit to King Solomon, whom you've also heard of, I hope—

whither she brought so many precious stones that people trampled them under foot.

—I don't believe that—

And when

—now he is coming to the point—

And when the Spaniard made himself master of the new world, hatchets & knives were sold for much more than pearls & precious stones: for there were only knives of wood & stone, & many pearls. It is therefore abundance which causes depreciation. Wherein the Emperor Tiberius was much mistaken, when he had a man beheaded who had made glass soft & pliable, fearing, as Pliny says, that if the news got out, gold would lose its vogue; for the abundance of glass, which is made of almost all stones & of several plants, would have caused its depreciation anyway. Thus it is with everything.

It is therefore necessary to demonstrate that there was not as much gold & silver in this Kingdom three hundred years ago, the time of which Malestroict speaks, as there is now: which is evident at a glance. [Bodin, 1568/1948, pp. 127–28]

And so on and so forth.

Now, I want to draw your attention to something which is accessible— at least I hope that it is; you never can tell what books are missing from the library—and which is highly readable. I won't say that these chaps to whose books I have been drawing your attention this morning are *highly* readable, although serious-minded people will get caught up in them, but the book that I am holding in my hand now is a very famous work in English literature. It's called—and I don't expect many of you have heard of it unless you are economic historians, which some of you are—*A Discourse of the Common Weal of this Realm of England* [1581]. And it was reprinted by a very learned lady called Miss Lamond at the University Press, first of all in 1893, but it was reprinted in 1929, and there should be copies of it lying about in the history section of any self-respecting library.

It was first printed in 1581, and it was edited in 1581 by someone who signed himself "W.S." Now, what does that raise in your mind? Well, I see you've taken the point. Well, the point was taken by a printer in the middle of the eighteenth century who did reprint it as attributed to William Shakespeare. But Shakespeare was in his teens when this was written—he was only seventeen. There is no reason at all to believe that Shakespeare wrote *A Discourse of the Common Weal of this Realm of England.*

Now, I dwell on this because Miss Lamond has a very learned introduction, which she wrote under the supervision of Archdeacon Cunningham, who was or was not a famous economic historian of the 1890s and the early years of this century. And she attributed it to a public man of the name of John Hales, and she was followed by most historians. But Le Branchu, who took the trouble to translate it into French, and who scrutinised Miss Lamond's sources, disputed the attribution to Hales and said that it was much more plausibly to be attributed to the famous—are there any political scientists among you here?—the famous Sir Thomas Smith, whose chief book is a book on the constitution of England. And in *Economic History*— which is a journal which is extremely well worth reading by all of you who are economists and who want to be something more than mere economists—in the *Economic History Review* for August 1966, there is an article by Miss Mary Dewar, who lived in Texas in those days, in my judgement fully establishing the case for Sir Thomas Smith. And "W.S." was probably his not frightfully literate nephew William Smith, who, on Thomas Smith's death in the seventies, found this and other papers bearing on it among his uncle's papers and gave it to the world.

Well, I commend *A Discourse of the Common Weal of this Realm of England* to you, not only because it contains the first statement—in the note, added probably by Sir Thomas Smith (it was published in 1581)—of the quantity theory of money. But it's not only that; it is a thrilling discussion, in the form of a Platonic dialogue, between a group of citizens: a professor of theology, a husbandman—that is, a farmer—a craftsman, a man who makes caps, and a public man who called himself a knight. And they met and they all started grumbling about the increasing dearness of things. And some blamed it on enclosure, and some blamed it on monopoly, and some blamed it on—eventually the theologian in the body of the book leads them to the conclusion, after much argument about the nature of money, a very good discussion about the nature of money going a bit beyond Aristotle in the earlier part of the dialogues—and some blamed it on debasement. Well, all that is extremely good reading—extremely good bedside reading.

Sir Thomas Smith, or whoever wrote it, knew how to write on contemporary issues in an extremely fascinating way, and you become interested in the personality of the knight, the capper, the husbandman, and still more of the professor of theology who makes an apologia for the existence of universities which warms the hearts of anybody who is associated with them. But there is a note which is probably written by Sir Thomas Smith himself, because it is thought by Miss Dewar that "W.S." hadn't got it in him to write it, and this note I can read to you. It occurs in a part of the dialogue which is omitted from Miss Lamond's text but is in her appendix. The doctor finds debasement to be the cause of the main dearness of things.

The doctor admitted all sorts of other evils in the course of these three rather thrilling dialogues, and he then, in the last dialogue, advocates a revaluation: let the government of the day do the honest thing and reverse the dishonest thing that was done by Henry VIII and so on. But at the end of this interpolation he says:

> Another reason I conceiue in this matter, to be the great store & plenty of treasure, which is walking in these partes of the world, far more in these our dayes, than euer our forefathers haue sene in times past. Who doth not vnderstand of the infinite sums of gold & siluer, whych are gathered from the Indies & other countries, and so yearely transported vnto these costes? As this is otherwise most certain, so doth it euidently appeare by the common report of all auncient men liuing in these dais."

—men over eighty—

> It is their constant report, that in times past, & within the memory of man, he hath beene accoumpted a rich & wealthy man, & well able to keepe house among his neighbors, which (all things discharged) was clearely worth [£30, £40, £50 or £60]; but in these our dayes the man of that estimation, is so far (in the common opinion) from a good housekeeper, or a man of wealth, that he is reputed the next neighbor to a beggar. Wherefore these ii. reasons seemed vnto me to contain in them sufficient probability for causes of the continuaunce of this generall dearth. [W.S., 1581, p. 187]

So ends the first statement that I know of in English of the quantity theory of money.

Don't go away thinking that I am trying to sell you a crude version of monetarism or something of that sort. I am not a true monetarist. I do happen, however, to believe that the quantity of money in relation to gross national product—whether the money be metallic or whether it be paper—has something to do with the purchasing power of money, and that is sometimes forgotten by people who are otherwise high in public esteem.

Notes

1. "The queen was in the garden eating bread and honey."
2. The actual title of this last chapter—chapter 14—is "Compound Change of Money."

Pamphleteers—Mercantilism
(Malynes, Misselden, Mun)

I WON'T waste your time recapitulating the subject of my last lecture last week. Suffice it to say that I have passed from general considerations of moral philosophy involving some glance at the main economic relationships of exchange and interest to the contribution made to the anticipations of systematic economic thought by miscellaneous pamphleteers. I explained to you how *legion* this literature is and announced my intention simply of dipping the bucket in the ocean in two respects. And I devoted that lecture to discussing early contributions to the theory of money, debasement, and expositions of the quantity theory of money, and now today I want to discuss in the narrow sense of the word—on which I shall expatiate in a moment—the literature of mercantilism.

Now, let me warn you straightaway that this is a highly complex and controversial subject. I don't think that anything that I said about Nicholas Oresme, Copernicus, Bodin, or the author of the *Discourse on the Common Weal* last Thursday needed a warning of that sort. But the very meaning of the word "mercantilism" is still the subject of learned debate, although it has been in vogue since 1776, when it was first exploited by no less a person than Adam Smith.

So perhaps I ought to begin by asking what is meant by mercantilism—what is meant by the mercantile system of policy. The term, so far as I know, was first used by a rather picturesque man—the leading disciple of Quesnay, the leader of the physiocrats on whom I shall be talking to you about in a week or two's time—Mirabeau, the father of the famous French statesman, who published a book by which he was usually called, entitled *L'ami des hommes* [1883]—the friend of man, and, some wag at the time, having regard to his domestic circumstances, added "the enemy of his wife and family"! Well, Mirabeau, in a book which he wrote jointly with Quesnay, the leader of the physiocrats, the *Philosophie rurale* [1764], does incidentally mention the mercantile system. But I don't think that you need to worry much about that. The term was exploited and made the subject matter of the longest book in *The Wealth of Nations*—namely, book 4—by Adam Smith. And Adam Smith and, I suspect, Mirabeau—but Adam Smith certainly—gave it an unequivocal meaning—namely, any policy prescription tending to a favourable balance of trade—or rather, if you like, payments—encouraging exports, discouraging imports, imposing regulations on colonial trade and so on and so forth. He called this "the Mercantile System" [Smith, 1776, 1:396], and it fell under his severe condemnation, and it influenced for at least a hundred years talk regarding policy in these connections.

Now, the problem arises in this way. Adam Smith's practice was followed through the period of nineteenth-century classicism. Some of the classical economists, notably Senior and McCulloch, were apt to regard the *essence* of mercantilism as the belief that wealth consisted in the precious metals. But it's very difficult for me to believe that they believed in their hearts that this was the persuasion of most of the writers whom they described as mercantilists. After all, the so-called Midas fallacy—the fallacy of supposing that wealth consists only in gold and silver—had been exposed by no less a person than Aristotle. It is difficult to believe that the authors of these pamphlets forgot all about that. In the main, I think one can assume that the classical economists following Smith regarded mercantilism as being that system of thought or recommendations concerned with the balance of payments. Well, that was all right. It may not have done justice to all the writers concerned, but it was unequivocal, I think. I don't really attach very much importance to the accusation that wealth consisted in the precious metals.

The complication here arises with the development in the latter half of the nineteenth century of the famous German historical school, of which the leader in this respect was the famous, or infamous, von Schmoller. Now, von Schmoller was nothing if not authoritative. It was said at one time that you couldn't get a job in a university faculty covering economics unless you had the approval of von Schmoller, whose headquarters was the University of Berlin, the centre of the ascendency of Prussia. And Schmoller certainly, like so many of his contemporaries in that part of the world, was all out for deep teeth—profound explanations—and in his discussion of mercantilism, which was very influential, he reached out for something which was far more wide-embracing than recommendations with regard to the regulation of the balance of payments.

And in his essay on *The Mercantile System and Its Historical Significance*, which originally appeared in 1884, and which is accessible in the Harvard series of reprints—now, I suspect, out of print, but not at all rare, and certainly it ought be in the library—listen to von Schmoller:

> The essence of the system lies not in some doctrine of money, or the balance of trade;

—a flat contradiction, you see—

> not in tariff barriers, protected duties, or navigation laws; but in something far greater:—namely in the total transformation of society and its organisation, as well as of the state and its institutions, in the replacing of a local and territorial economic policy by that of the national state. [Schmoller, 1902, p. 51]

Well, this certainly widens it, and this practice was followed by the influential economic historian Archdeacon Cunningham, who was the leader of systematic economic history in the 1890s and in the first ten years of the twentieth century. It was followed also by a much more well-worth-reading man, Ashley, who was Professor of Commerce at Birmingham, and whose introduction to economic history [1901] is still worth reading.

But the practice was followed by a much greater man than Schmoller, Cunningham or Ashley, or any of their followers—namely, the only comparatively recently deceased Scandinavian economist, Eli Heckscher, who wrote a great work in two volumes, translated into English and easily accessible in any self-respecting library, entitled *Mercantilism* [1935]. And following von Schmoller in terminology and in width and perspective, he regarded the term *mercantilism* as being that body of thought which was concerned with nation-building—the transformation of the system of the Middle Ages into the system of national States.

Now, you will have judged, I think, perhaps by the way of which I spoke of Schmoller that he's not one of my favourites, and I may be perhaps a little unfair to him in comparison with Heckscher, who was a most delightful man and who, in my judgement, was a great historian of economic thought and a great member of that very distinguished senior generation of Scandinavian economists who have done so much to bring sweetness and light into the practice of our subject in the twentieth century.

Nonetheless, in making respectable this practice, I am inclined to think that Heckscher did some disservice. It is not at all clear that the various actions of national States as they emerged necessarily resembled one another, necessarily were influenced to any great extent by systematic thought. This is indeed said by more recent scholars than Heckscher, among whom was Professor Coleman, lately of this institution and now Professor of Economics at Cambridge, whose book—whose collection of articles—*Revisions in Mercantilism* [1969], you should all glance at. Coleman wonders whether there was such a system and whether we have not got simply to go back to the beginning, so to speak—the beginning of economic history—and discover to what extent thought in all these various directions influenced the policy of different national States at different times. Certainly this wider process is inconvenient compared with the simplicity of the Mirabeau-Smith conception. The Smith-Mirabeau conception related essentially to the regulation of commerce and money. It begins to be inconvenient if you extend the term *mercantilism* to cover the regulation of industry, save as a by-product of recommendations designed to affect directly—whether they are successful or not is another matter—the balance of payments. To talk of industrial mercantilism or even agrarian mercantilism, I think, is not conducive to clarity of thought.

At any rate, in the observations that I am going to make this morning, my intention is to go back to the Smithian narrow definition and to try to make this a little plainer. And it is not at all plain, and opinions concerning the Smithian analysis of mercantilism and the thoughts of mercantilists in that narrow strait is still, I warn you, controversial.

But certainly literature of that subject was widespread. You see this conception of operations designed to secure a favourable balance of payments in one of the most famous international tracts reproduced in Monroe [1948, pp. 143–67]—the tract of Antonio Serra, a Neapolitan, who wrote when he was in prison in Naples in 1613 a tract entitled *A Brief Treatise on the Causes which can make Gold and Silver plentiful in Kingdoms where there are no Mines*. I have read you that long title; I'm not going to reproduce Serra, whom you can read in your Monroe if you can find them. I read it because it does so exactly mirror the Smithian conception in the use of the term *mercantilism*. You'll find in Monroe [pp. 221–43] a much less subtle, a much less intellectual, more explosive and abusive and vulgar example of continental mercantilism in a tract by a man called von Hornick entitled *Oesterreich über alles—Austria over all—wann es nur will* [1684]— if only she has the guts to do it, so to speak. And this is a case for—an extreme case of—provision for autarchy as regards contacts with other nations, even at the expense of some temporary sacrifice.

Well, I propose to stick to representative English specimens. In particular, I want to talk to you about Gerrard Malynes, Misselden and Mun— Thomas Mun. You'll find plenty of others in the collection edited by McCulloch [1859], which you will find in my bibliography.

We do not know the dates of Malynes, to plunge straightaway into the middle of things. He was an Englishman who was probably born in Belgium, and in 1586 he held the post of Commissioner of Trade in the Low Countries. But he was back in this country at the beginning of the seventeenth century, and he published in 1601 a quite considerable work entitled *A treatise of the Canker of England's Common wealth*. You will find this reproduced in volume 3 of *Tudor Economic Documents*, edited by Tawney and Power [1951, pp. 386–404]. He published many other things: *Lex Mercatoria* [1686], which was a compilation of international commercial law, and a controversial tract called *The Maintenance of Free Trade*, which has, I think, been reproduced by Kelley in quite recent times, in 1622.

Well now, Malynes was first and foremost an advocate of exchange control, and some people had thought that he advocated exchange control because he thought that if the office of King's Exchanger, which had prevailed in earlier times, was revived, it might be a post for which he would be considered to be suitable. But although Malynes stands out in the history of economic thought as the leading exponent of the case for exchange control—the case for the prohibition of speculation in the exchanges, which caused the foreign exchanges to deviate from a fixed norm—in his book *The Canker of England's Common wealth*, he spreads the net pretty widely, and he recognises that "plentie of money maketh generally things deare, and scarcitie of money maketh likewise generally things good cheape." "Whereas," he goes on to say, "things particularly are also deare or good cheape according to plentie or scarcitie of the things themselves, or the use of them" [Malynes, 1601, p. 387].

And he did recognise to some extent—he made some remarks on Bodin, whom I mentioned in the last lecture—he recognised the effect of abundance or scarcity of the precious metals, but he thought that the national position in regard to the limited stock of precious metal depended essentially on the position created by speculation in the foreign exchanges. He thought that the ideal would be some inflow which would make the exchanges slightly favourable, which might—he doesn't use this term—improve the terms of trade and increase the yield of industry and increase employment.

There is no doubt that at the time that Malynes wrote, and earlier, there was a local fear, in the more advanced countries of the West, of scarcity of money. And hence, in the period before the writers I'm talking about flourished, there were very, very strict regulations of the movement of gold and silver. There was in this country legislation prohibiting people from taking gold and silver out of the country. There was legislation focussing attention on the trade done with other particular countries, and, if the balance of payments was not favourable with those countries, then there were regulations hampering trade with those countries.

It was Malynes' chief contention that the insufficiency of the inflow was due to the manipulation of bankers, who gained by rigging the exchange market. (Has anybody ever heard the phrase "The Gnomes of Zurich"? These things crop up, you know, from time to time. There is some continuity between the history of economic thought and even the history of economic error.) He blamed the manipulations of bankers, and he said that they made their profit by just putting their money anywhere where they thought they could make a profit without regard to the national interest. And so he advocated the resuscitation of the King's Exchanger to maintain a rigid path, and the enforcement of the Statutes of Employment compelling payments by foreigners for our exports in specie.

Well, needless to say, this attitude of Malynes, whether it was right or wrong, was very distasteful to the merchants, and in the late teens of the seventeenth century there were various inquiries concerning the difficulties under which trade was supposed to labour, and, in 1621, there was a Commission on Exchanges set up which included certain notable people who were critics of Malynes—namely, Misselden and Mun, both of whom had commercial connections with the East India Company, which figures very largely, in one way or another, in the discussion of policies relating to commerce for the next 200 years.

Now, the East India Company sent far more gold and silver to India and to the East than it brought back by way of payments in gold and silver for the exports which their ships took with them to India. And there therefore was a school of thought which argued that for that, and because it was a close monopoly—a separate question—the East India Company's operations should be limited, as tending to the scarcity of inflow of money into this country. Well, Misselden [1622; 1623] wrote tracts against Malynes, which I don't think you need bother about very much. There's quite a good account of this phase of the controversy about mercantilism in the introduction to a book written in 1892 by Hewins, who was first Director of the London School of Economics and eventually left the position to be a political adviser to Joseph Chamberlain, who was promulgating the doctrine of imperial preference in the early years of this century. But that political affiliation ought not to prevent you from having a look at Hewins' economic history and particularly at the introduction, which deals with this matter that I'm dealing with in this question.

Misselden emphasised the desirability of an increased supply of money and was, frankly, an inflationist. He advocated debasement from time to time as stimulating exports. He agreed that debasement made things dear, but he went on to say:

> That will be abundantly recompensated unto all in the plenty of *Money*, and quickening of Trade in every mans hand. . . . And it is much better for the *Kingdome*, to have things deare with plenty of *Money*, whereby men may live in their several callings: then to have things cheape with want of *Money*, which now makes every man complaine. [Misselden, 1622, pp. 106–7; emphasis in original]

I don't think you need to worry much about Misselden—graduates can have a look at his book—but you should worry, all of you, a little bit about Thomas Mun, whose book I hold in my hands now and which is reasonably accessible in various reprints. This one that I hold in my hands is republished by the Economic History Society by Blackwells [Mun, 1664].

Mun's book is of exceptional importance, partly by reason of its intellectual quality, partly by reason of the fact that it was singled out by Adam Smith as being the bible of mercantilism. He says in Cannan's edition of *The Wealth of Nations*: "The title of Mun's book, *England's Treasure [by] Foreign Trade*, became a fundamental maxim in the political œconomy, not of England only, but of all other commercial countries" [Smith, 1776, 1:401]. Now, that may be an exaggeration, but that is Adam Smith's view on the subject. And I think that if you look at Mun's book, you may or may not agree with him, but you will agree that the quality of argument is certainly superior to that of many contemporary writings on the subject. Indeed, I would be inclined to say that in his critique of mercantilism, Adam Smith himself missed some of the more telling points in Mun's book.

You need to know just a little bit about Mun's background. I'll give it to you very briefly. He was born in 1571, and he died in 1641. And he entered the service of the East India Company, and he became a director of it. In 1621, at the time when that commission was talked of, he wrote a pamphlet which has also been reprinted by the Economic History Society—*A Discourse of Trade from England into the East Indies*. And here his object was quite definitely to say that England *gained* from the operations of the East India Company, despite the fact that its payments to India in gold and silver vastly outnumbered the payments of India to the East India Company, on the grounds—which we see developed in his book—on the ground that the East India Company brought back from India and from the Indies spice and cloth of various kinds, which they were able to sell at a great profit in continental Europe and in the Mediterranean area, so that on balance the flow of money into this country was enhanced.

Now, *England's Treasure by Forraign Trade* was probably written about the end of the 1620s or the 1630s, but it was not published until *years* later when Mun was dead, and his son, having regard to contemporary discussion of these matters, thought it a pious duty to publish this "*England's Treasure by Forraign Trade. Or, the Ballance of our Forraign Trade is The Rule of our Treasure*. Written by Thomas Mun of Lond. Merchant, And now published for the Common good."

Well now, let me give you a very brief account of the content. I ought to say that the book is academically much more formidable than the earlier tract, which I haven't troubled to recapitulate, although I have given you the purport of it. This is obviously an old man's book, written at leisure, deriving doubtless from his experience and his loyalty to the East India Company, but seeking to sustain the various arguments that he puts forward by reason. And the first chapter deals with "The [knowledge and] Qualities which are [to be] required in a perfect Merchant of Forraign Trade" [Mun, 1664, p. 3]. And I guess that if you read that chapter—which I am not going to read to you—that most of you would be inflicted with the thought that if you yourself were contemplating going into foreign commerce, you would be lacking in many of the qualities that Mun enumerates. But that is by the way.

The burden of his arguments starts in chapter 2, and the title of the chapter is "The means to enrich this Kingdom, and to encrease our Treasure." And he says:

> Although a Kingdom may be enriched by gifts received, or by purchase taken from some other Nations, yet these are things uncertain and of small consideration when they happen. The ordinary means therefore to encrease our wealth and treasure is by Forraign Trade, wherein wee must ever observe this rule; to sell more to strangers yearly than wee consume of theirs in value. [ibid., p. 5]

And he expatiates on that. He compares the situation of a country to the situation of a private individual: A private individual enriches himself by not spending as much as he gains, and so too should be the maxim of a great country.

Then, chapter 3 contains "ways and means" of policy [ibid., p. 7], in which he recommends the development of natural resources so that we don't have to import so much, the development of national industries, and so on and so forth—all of which is going to be pretty familiar to any of you acquainted with the economic history of the time, and is pretty self-evident, having regard to Mun's fundamental position.

But he then warms up to the subject in chapter 4, and he says that "The Exportation of our Moneys in Trade of Merchandise is a means to encrease our Treasure" [ibid., p. 14]. And he takes the example of the East India trade and argues, as he argued in his earlier tract, that although the East India Company would spend more gold and silver in India, the things that it brought back could be sold at a profit elsewhere, and the inflow—the increase—of treasure would thereby be increased. And it winds up with a very weighty analogy:

> Thus we may plainly see, that when this weighty business is duly considered . . . , as all our human actions ought to be well weighed, it is found much contrary to that which most men esteem thereof, because they search no further than the beginning of the work,

—that is, the exportation of gold and silver by the East India Company—

> which mis-informs their judgments, and leads them into error: For if we only behold the actions of the husbandman in the seed-time when he casteth away much good corn into the ground, we will rather accompt him a mad man than a husbandman: but when we consider his labours in the harvest which is the end of his endeavours, we find the worth and plentiful encrease of his actions. [ibid., p. 19]

And so he goes on in the rest of the book to attack the policy involving the regulation of expenditure abroad, either in particular balances with particular countries or the balance in general.

He goes on to argue against keeping money at home on grounds which almost anticipate the idea of the quantity theory. At this moment you will ask yourself: Why did Thomas Mun not anticipate the idea of the self-righting mechanism of purely specie currencies, as developed by David Hume in the latter part of the century? He doesn't get as far as that, but he does go on to argue in the latter part of the book [ibid., chaps. 16–18, pp. 62–70] that of course the Prince will be increased by the inflow of money, and he may put aside a certain amount if the inflow is liberal, but he must be careful not to put aside too much, otherwise there would be deflationary influences—he doesn't use that term—embarrassment of trade. And he mustn't spend too much of it; otherwise, the reverse situation would follow.

And then you get a series of polemical chapters as against the prohibition of the export of gold and silver as in Spain [ibid., chap. 6, pp. 22–24], against the debasement [ibid., chap. 8, pp. 28–31], and a long chapter—a very sarcastic chapter—against Malynes on "The admirable feats which are supposed to be performed by bankers" [ibid., chap. 14, pp. 45–57].[1] And he thinks that that's all nonsense—that Malynes is on a false scent.

Well now, Mun, in many ways, as you read him, is an exceptional person. What did it all amount to? Mercantilism in this narrow sense was not the narrow view that gold and silver were the only forms of wealth—I don't think that—although occasionally you find in the literature suggestions that convey that the thought was passing through the writer's mind that certain protective measures might conceivably and—and we know theoretically that they may conceivably—turn the "factorial terms of trade" in favour of this country. They certainly attached importance to the accumulation of a war chest. The nation States, then as now, were actuated in their policy not only by considerations of plenty—industry and employment and so on—they were also actuated by the necessity of, say, covering themselves against attack or possibly of pursuing aggressive wars. For both of those, immediate finance was needed. Indeed, up to 1914 there was a special fund, a war chest, in imperial Germany. The idea of the war chest dies very hard. But chiefly, I think, if you are to rationalise mercantilism—if you are not to regard it in this narrow sense as all a muddle—it was actuated by the fear of the downward pressure on employment caused by an outflow of precious metals.

Whether that was right or wrong is another question which I shall return to when I discuss the eighteenth-century theory of the self-righting mechanism. It was thought absurd that when there was an inflow, a favourable balance of payments, there was greater prosperity than when there was an outflow. Mun was very careful about this, but you will find in the writings of no lesser a person than John Law—a seventeenth- and eighteenth-century writer of whom I shall speak later, a fear that trade was increasing more rapidly than money, and, consequently, that money should be based upon something other than precious metals—which led eventually from the land banks to the great catastrophe of the Mississippi boom and the collapse of France in the eighteenth century.

I think that Smith and the classicists were a little too critical, but in their detailed criticism of the measures recommended—the high protectionism of some and the colonial exploitation of others, and so on—they may have been right in general, but a little too hard on the more enlightened of the mercantilists in this narrow sense. And if you doubt that, I recommend you to read Mun's book. Do not think for a moment that I agree with Mun, even in his context, but I want to do justice to something which at the end I slightly misquoted.

Tomorrow I shall be going on to the influence of more scientific thought on the development of economics, and I shall concentrate nearly the whole of the lecture on the writings of that very conspicuous man Sir William Petty.

NOTE

1. The actual title of this chapter is "The admirable feats supposed to be done by Bankers and the Merchants Exchange" (Mun, 1664, p. 45).

Sir William Petty

THIS lecture, although I personally find the subject matter of it more interesting than anything that I've talked about so far, is betwixt and between. It still falls under the heading "Anticipations," but is different from anything that I have talked about before and much more high grade. Up to now, in talking about the moral philosophers and the pamphleteers, in a sense one has been trying to get under the skin of the personalities of another age. In some respects their thoughts resemble our thoughts, but their mode is different.

Now, the seventeenth century is one of the great centuries of the human race. It not only saw the most terrible slaughter in the Thirty Years' War, which put Central Europe back fifty or 100 years, but it is also the century of the most amazing developments in natural science. And it's, of course, with that influence that I am concerned. In the last half of the seventeenth century, by the time of Charles II, natural science had become the mode. It was patronised by the monarch himself, and its respectability was signalised by the formation of the Royal Society. But it is not only the emergence of natural science in the sense in which we understand it now which characterises the seventeenth century, it's also a break with *the* Philosopher. Descartes in France, Hobbes in this country, inaugurated a revulsion from the domination of Aristotle, and that we shall see in various ways as we go along.

But much more intimately connected with what I am going to talk about today is a change in style. We don't know exactly how the people of the sixteenth and seventeenth century talked. There is still dispute among literateurs as to whether Shakespeare talked Cockney, in which case the clown's wonderful song at the end of "Twelfth Night" would have as its refrain, "The rine it rineth every die," or whether he talked the language of southern Kentucky, a language which in many respects rests more softly on the ear. It may be that he talked something else. We simply don't know. We can reconstruct from the rhymes of poetry some of the changes which have taken place. In, for instance, the poet Pope, there occurs a couplet addressed to Queen Anne which runs

> Here thou, great Anna! whom three realms obey,
> Dost sometimes counsel take—and sometimes tea.
> [Pope, 1792/1967, canto 3, p. 158]

—which we should translate "tay." And Pope was very particular about his rhymes.

Well, it's the change in written style—this is what I want to bring home to you—which takes place at roughly the same time in France and in this country. In France you have the immortal writings of Pascal, which set the image for the beautiful French style which has prevailed up to this day, and in this country you have preeminently the prefaces to the plays of Dryden—splendid, lucid, comparatively short sentences. He talked, roughly speaking, our language—although he talked and he wrote it better—and, of course, Addison, Steel, Swift and so on.

Well now, this shows itself in certain economic writings of that stage. It's conspicuous in Sir William Petty, who is the subject of today's remarks, and in the philosopher Locke. Petty was conspicuous for his connection with science, as we shall see in a moment; Locke is conspicuous for his writing on epistemology and on political philosophy. On all this movement—not the change of style, but the movement of thought that I'm going to talk about—you might do worse than have a look at Professor Letwin's *Origins of Scientific Economics* [1963], which is a first-class scholarly work throwing a tremendous light on the various people who will be cropping up in the next two lectures.

Now, I want to talk to you about Petty today—Sir William Petty—who lived from 1623 to 1687. And since he was a very conspicuous man, it is worthwhile your knowing just something about his life, which is not un-eventful. He was the son of a poor clothier in the south of England. At a very early age he went to sea, and while he was in the English Channel his leg was broken and the ship put him ashore at Caen, where you know, just before you were born, there were notable battles in the Second World War, and in those days there existed a Jesuit college. They fattened him up intel-lectually—he obviously was a very brilliant boy—at Caen for some years, and then he joined the refugees from the Civil War in Holland in 1643, and he read with the great philosopher Thomas Hobbes. And then he returned to England in the latter half of the 1640s with an idea for double writing in his head. Remember that in those days there were no carbon copies. There were no typewriters. All manuscripts had to be laboriously copied, and Petty invented a machine whereby you could write two lines simultaneously.

Well, this and his association with Hobbes and his general intellectual brilliance got him into the intellectual society of that time, and in 1648 we find him appointed to a teaching post in medicine in the University of Ox-ford. And there in 1650—I must give you a little comic relief—I am read-ing now from Fitzmaurice's *Life of Sir William Petty* [1895], which those of you who have any biographical inclinations do well to glance at. Fitzmaurice said:

> In 1650 an event occurred which made his name known in the whole country and opened up the way to a larger career. One Ann Green had been tried, convicted, and executed at Oxford on December 14, 1651, for the murder of her illegitimate child. Her execution seems to have been carried out with a

combination of clumsiness and brutality characteristic of the times. It was observed "by the spectators that she seemed to take an unconscionable time in dying, so her friends went to assist her in getting out of this world, some of them thumping her on the breast, others hanging with all their weight upon her legs, sometimes lifting her up and then pulling her down again with a sudden jerk." At length the Sheriff was satisfied, and the unfortunate woman was certified to be dead. The body was then cut down, put into a coffin, and taken to the dissecting room.

This ends happily, for those of you who've got soft hearts.

When, however, the coffin lid was opened she was seen to be still breathing and to "rattle," "which being observed by a lusty fellow who stood by, he, thinking to do an act of charity in ridding her out of the reliques of a painful life, stamped several times on her breast and stomach with all the force he could." Just at this moment, however, Dr. Petty and Dr. Wilkins appeared on the scene, and recognising distinct signs of life, decided to attempt to revive the supposed corpse. They wrenched open Ann Green's teeth, poured cordials down her throat, and persuaded a woman to go to bed with her to restore warmth. Signs of life soon began to appear; The doctors bled her,

—I don't think that that did her much good—

ordered her a julep, and so left her for the night. In two hours she began to talk. The dead had come to life. Though legally defunct, she is said to have survived to marry and become the mother of children, in spite of the Sheriff and to the confusion of the hangman. [Fitzmaurice, 1895, p. 19]

So, you see, some economists have a varied life.

Well, in his capacity as physician, Petty was appointed physician to Cromwell's army in Ireland, and Cromwell had tempted a good many of the army by promising that if they were victorious they should have patches of land. And then when victory came it was discovered that there was no proper survey of the conquered land of Ireland, so Petty, who was a versatile man, offered to supervise the survey. He recruited various people whom he thought to be competent, and he gave them tutorials, and off they went. And arising from that, Petty became Commissioner for the distribution of the land which his people had surveyed, which got him into endless disputes which went on throughout his life concerning the justice of the distribution. In 1660, after a lecture by no less a person than Sir Christopher Wren, he was one of the founders of the famous Royal Society—a society which, many of you know, persists to this day and is one of the glories of British intellectual history.

Petty died worth £15,000, which was quite a lot of money in those days. His son became Lord Shelburne, and eventually the Shelburnes were changed into Lansdownes, who persist to this day. So Petty was the founder of the famous Lansdowne family.

His works on our subject are reprinted, conveniently, in *The Economic Writings of Sir William Petty*, edited by a learned American called Hull, and published by the Cambridge University Press in 1899. And it did achieve a rather high price in the secondhand market before it was reprinted, with or without the permission of the Cambridge University Press, by a Japanese publisher, and I imagine that it is pretty easy to get hold of if you are interested in his various works.

Now, Petty's fame in his own day was not so much as an analytical economist, but as one of the founders of systematic statistics, which in those days was called political arithmetic. He was associated with a man called Graunt, who shared with him—and probably took the predominant part—in a survey of mortality in London. On his own he attempted various surveys of economic conditions in this country and in Ireland, and whatever you think of his statistical methods, they are interesting as rough indications of the economic history of the time, and in this respect I think that Professor Letwin is just a little hard on Petty. After all, he was a pioneer, and his statistical method was not particularly reliable. He didn't impress Adam Smith either. Adam Smith said that he had pretty little faith in political arithmetic [1776, 2:36]. But I'm not going to talk to you about that.

Petty obviously attached very great importance to quantitative measurement. Petty subscribed to the Baconian philosophy—or thought he subscribed to the Baconian philosophy—which expressly said that if you collect enough facts they then suggest to you a series, and hence systematic science—which we know since the times of Whewell and Popper and other distinguished writers is standing scientific method on its head. You invent in science hypotheses, you test them for their logic, and then you test them—you try to falsify them or you try to verify them, it is a matter of words—by collecting relevant facts.

But from my point of view the important thing is his occasional economic insights, and they are on quite a different plane as regards modernity and analytical method than his political arithmetic. And very fortunately, from your point of view, his main achievement in this respect was a book which he wasn't frightfully proud of because I think it had been somewhat neglected, called *A Treatise of Taxes and Contributions*, and it was published in 1662. And I want to spend this lecture taking you through the relevant points that he makes.

He begins in chapter 1, as you might expect with a modern textbook, with a chapter on the objects of expenditure. He mentions expenditure on defence, expenditure on justice, and then he mentions "A third branch of the Publick Charge"—that is, "the *Pastorage of mens Souls*, and the guidance of their Consciences" [Petty, 1662, p. 19]. It is difficult to tell whether he wrote this with his tongue in his cheek or not. On the whole I am inclined not, because his writings just before his death suggest that he was a believer. He says:

if we consider how easie it is to elude the Laws of man, to commit unproveable crimes, to corrupt and divert Testimonies, . . . there follows a necessity of contributing towards a publick Charge, wherewith to have men instructed in the Laws of God, that take notice of evil thoughts and designs, and much more of secret deeds, and that punisheth eternally in another world, what man can but slightly chastise in this. [ibid.]

He also suggests—he had a very wide perspective in this respect—the charge of schools and universities, the maintenance of orphans and the maintenance of the poor: If "we think it just to limit the wages of the poor"—which obviously he had reservations about—"so as they can lay up nothing against the time of their impotency and want of work" [ibid., p. 20]. So that the law of nature obliges States not to let people starve. And he goes on to mention the charge of highways, navigable rivers, aqueducts, bridges, havens and so on.

And then in chapter 2, he discusses "the causes which encrease and aggravate the several sorts of Publick Charges" [ibid., p. 21]. And "the unwillingness of people to pay them" is not confined, as you will see, to the twentieth century, "arising from an opinion, that by delay and reluctancy they may wholly avoid them. . . . Another Cause which aggravates Taxes is, the force of paying them in money at a certain time." And then there are "Obscurities and doubts concerning the right of imposing" [ibid.]. And so on and so forth.

As for causes, "The Causes of encreasing the Military Charge are the same with those that encrease Wars, or fear of Wars, which are Forreign or Civil" [ibid.], and he distinguishes between offensive wars, of which he obviously thinks very poorly, and defensive wars, which he thinks are forced upon one by the nature of the world as he saw it. And he goes out of his way to say that "The causes of Civil Wars here in *Europe*"—and this is at the time of the terrible Thirty Years' War—"proceed very much from Religion," namely, "the punishing of Believers heterodox from the Authorized way" [ibid., p. 22]—and so on.

And he thinks that there are rather too many people in the Church, and he suggests that there should be national planning of these people instructed to teach the laws of God, and in that way various curacies could be amalgamated and there could be some saving of public expenditure. And then at the end of the chapter he recommends employment for the unemployed, and he thinks that it's better to be employed, even "if it be employed to build a useless Pyramid upon *Salisbury Plain*, bring the Stones at *Stonehenge* to *Tower Hill*, or the like; for at worst this would keep their mindes to discipline and obedience, and their bodies to a patience of more profitable labours when need shall require it" [ibid., p. 31].

And then, in chapter 3, he suggests various ways of lessening the disquiet of paying taxes, including political arithmetic. If people really understood the magnitude of the value of products and so on and so forth, then they might be less disinclined to pay their taxes. Well, we needn't linger on that chapter save that he does point out there how small a part of wealth money is—metallic money. There was no Midas fallacy in Petty's mind.

But now we come to chapter 4, which is critically important by all standards. He is not only admired only by neoclassical economists; Karl Marx goes out of his way to give him praise for his intuition.[1] Chapter 4 is called "Of the several wayes of Taxe," and he first of all discusses—which we need not discuss—a question of putting aside "a proportion of the whole Territory for Publick uses" [ibid., p. 38]. According to some modern ideas, he was quite enlightened on that point of view. But then he proceeds to the necessity of taxation, and he pitches on the taxation of real property—particularly land—in this connection. And it's in this connection that he makes his *startling* suggestions with regard to economic analysis, which lifts his anticipations of economic analysis on to a plane quite different from the planes on which I have been conducting you in a superficial way in the last lectures.

Well, he starts with some observations about house taxing, and he says that it's of a much more uncertain nature than that of land. And he sometimes thinks that houses are taxed disproportionately in order to discourage building, especially on new foundations. And then there comes one of the most extraordinary predictions in the range of economics. Predictions in economics, you know, are not to be relied upon. If anybody tells you what will happen next year in quantitative terms, write him down as being either simple or talking without justification. But his prediction is not quantitative here: He talks about London and its future movements. And remember, by London he was talking about the City. Westminster was separated from London in those days, although some linkage was beginning to take place:

> Now if great Cities are naturally apt to remove their Seats, I ask which way? I say in the case of *London*, it must be Westward, because the Windes blowing near 3/4 of the year from the West, the dwellings of the West end are so much the more free from the fumes, steams, and stinks of the whole Easterly Pyle. [ibid., p. 41]

Coal was beginning to come into vogue in those days.

> Now if it follow from hence, that the Pallaces of the greatest men will remove Westward, it will also naturally follow, that the dwellings of others who depend upon them will creep after them. This we see in *London*, where Noblemens ancient houses are now become Halls for Companies, or turned into Tenements, and all the Pallaces are gotten Westward; Insomuch, as I do not doubt but that five hundred years hence, the King's Pallace will be near *Chelsey*, and the old building of *Whitehall* converted to uses more answerable to their quality. [ibid., pp. 41–42]

He goes on for a bit and then he says:

> This digression I confess to be both impertinent to the business of Taxes, and
> in it self almost needless; for why should we trouble our selves what shall be
> five hundred years hence, not knowing what a day may bring forth; and since
> 'tis not unlikely, but that before that time we may be all transplanted from
> hence into *America*, these Countreys being overrun with Turks, and made
> waste, as the Seats of the famous Eastern Empires at this day are. [ibid., p. 42]

But now we get to economic analysis:

> before we talk too much of Rents, we should endeavour to explain the myste-
> rious nature of them, with reference as well to Money, the rent of which we
> call usury; as to that of Lands and Houses afore-mentioned. [ibid.]

Now, on page 43 of volume 1 of the *Economic Works* is something which
you should all have a look at. First of all, he discusses rents as a surplus. I'm
going to read it to you.

> Suppose a man could with his own hands plant a certain scope of Land with
> Corn, that is could Digg, or Plough, Harrow, Weed, Reap, Carry home,
> Thresh, and Winnow so much as the Husbandry of this Land requires; and
> had withal Seed wherewith to sowe the same. I say, that when this man hath
> subducted his seed out of the proceed of his Harvest, and also, what himself
> hath both eaten and given to others in exchange for Clothes, and other Natu-
> ral necessaries; that the remainder of Corn is the natural and true Rent of the
> Land for that year; and the *medium* of seven years, or rather of so many years
> as makes up the Cycle, within which Dearths and Plenties make their revolu-
> tion, doth give the ordinary Rent of the Land in *Corn*. [ibid., p. 43, final
> emphasis added by Robbins]

Well, you're pretty near Ricardo there, are you not? But then, he goes on
to say,

> a . . . collaterall question may be, how much English money this Corn or Rent
> is worth? I answer,

—listen carefully—

> so much as the money, which another single man can save, within the same
> time, over and above his expence, if he imployed himself wholly to produce
> and make it; *viz.* Let another man go travel into a Countrey where is Silver,
> there Dig it, Refine it, bring it to the same place where the other man planted
> his Corn; Coyne it, &c. the same person, all the while of his working for Silver,
> gathering also food for his necessary livelihood, and procuring himself cover-
> ing, &c. I say, the Silver of the one, must be esteemed of equal value with the
> Corn of the other: the one being perhaps twenty Ounces and the other twenty
> Bushels. From whence it follows, that the price of a Bushel of this Corn to be
> an Ounce of Silver. [ibid.]

What is this but a premonition of a labour theory of value? No wonder Karl Marx thought that he had insight.

Well, he goes on to talk about the risks of digging and refining silver, and

> the true proportion, between the values of Gold and Silver, which many times is set but by popular errour, sometimes more, sometimes less, diffused in the world; which errour (by the way) is the cause of our having been pestred with too much Gold heretofore, and wanting it now. [ibid., p. 44]

And then he goes on—you can't get to the end of these vital two pages here:

> The world measures things by gold and silver, but principally the latter

—you see, gold was less important than silver as a measure of value in those days—

> and consequently the better of many must be the onely of all; that is, by fine silver of a certain weight: but now [it's] hard to measure the weight and fineness of silver.

And he goes on to expatiate on correctly valuing the silver and goes on to say:

> that which I would say upon this matter

—and this is frightfully important when we come to the eighteenth century—

> is, that all things ought to be valued by two natural Denominations, which is Land and Labour.

There it is.

> [W]e ought to say, a Ship or garment is worth such a measure of Land, with such another measure of Labour; forasmuch as both Ships and Garments were the creatures of Lands and mens Labours thereupon: This being true,

he says—a true scientific spirit,

> we should be glad to finde out a natural Par between Land and Labour, so as we might express the value by either of them alone

—saying it was worth so much units of labour or so much units of land, the par between land and labour having been discovered.

> Wherefore we would be glad to finde the natural values of the Fee simple of Land, though but no better then we have done that of the *usus fructus* above-mentioned. [ibid., pp. 44–45]

But now, you see, he is leading up to the capital value of land, the value of the fee simple of land. And the next paragraph starts:

> Having found the Rent or value of the *usus fructus per annum* [of land], the question is, how many years purchase (as we usually say) is the Fee simple naturally worth? [ibid., p. 45]

You see, he has moved—as Walras did—from the exchange value of commodities, and he has tried to find the value of the services of land and labour and find a natural path between them, and he is now moving on to the capitalisation problem—the value of rents stretching indefinitely into the future. He twigs the problem here, the problem which you I think asked me about the other day. He actually tumbles to the fact that, if there is no discounting of the future rents of land—and it is assumed that the land continued to be kept up at its usual rate of fertility—then, if there were no discounting, he says, if there were an infinite number of rents,

> then an Acre of Land would be equal in value to a thousand Acres of the same Land; which is absurd, an infinity of unites being equal to an infinity of thousands. Wherefore,

he says,

> we must pitch upon some limited number, and that I apprehend

—and this I find to be the most astonishing of Petty's discoveries here—

> to be the number of years, which I conceive one man of fifty years old, another of twenty eight, and another of seven years old, all being alive together may be thought to live; that is to say, of a Grandfather, Father and Childe; . . . for if a man be a great Grandfather, he himself is so much the nearer his end, so as there are but three in a continual line of descent usually co-existing together; and as some are Grandfathers at forty years, yet as many are not till above sixty

—and so on and so forth.

> Wherefore I pitch the number of years purchase, that any Land is naturally worth, to be the ordinary extent of three such persons their lives. [ibid.]

Now, if any of you in your analytical economics have had a look at that excellent book, Cassel's *Nature and Necessity of Interest* [1903], you will find that, as regards the downward limit of real interest, Cassel fixes it at something round about 2 percent.[2] And why? Because if it were to fall below that figure very much, then instead of turning income into capital it would be worthwhile turning capital into income and living on one's capital, provided that one were taking into account three generations. There is no reason for me to believe that Cassel got this from Petty, and there is no reason at all to believe that Petty got it from Cassel, who lived 200 years afterwards.

And so he goes on, and then he approaches the usury problem. And he dismisses the problem of usury—the problem of interest in the sense in which it used to be regarded as a sin, as an offence against something that was laid down in the book of Exodus or something which was proved to be the case by Saint Thomas Aquinas. He says:

> As for Usury, the least that can be, is the Rent of so much Land as the money lent will buy, where the security is undoubted; but where the security is casual,

then a kinde of ensurance must be enterwoven with the simple natural Interest, which may advance the Usury very conscionably unto any height below
the Principal it self. [Petty, 1662, p. 48]

And then, finally, in this wonderful analytical chapter, he actually refers
back to the price of land near towns:

Parallel unto this, is something which we omit concerning the price of Land;
for as great need of money heightens Exchange

—he knew about the demand for money—

so doth great need of Corn raise the price of that likewise, and consequently
of the Rent of the Land that bears Corn, and lastly of the Land it self; as for
example, if the Corn which feedeth *London*, or an Army, be brought forty
miles thither, then the Corn growing within a mile of *London*, or the quarters
of such Army, shall have added unto its natural price, so much as the charge
of bringing it thirty nine miles doth amount unto [ibid.]

—and so on and so forth.

Well, I hope I've said enough to persuade you that Petty was an extremely remarkable man. He goes on, in the remainder of the book, to deal
with various kinds of taxes. On the whole he's against import taxes save if
the local trouble that's caused by imports is very adverse [chap. 6]. Then he
conceives poll money [chap. 7]—direct taxation per head:

I shall speak of Poll-money more distinctly, and first of the simple Poll-money
upon every head of all mankinde alike; the Parish paying for those that receive
alms, Parents for their Children under age, and Masters for their Apprentices,
and others who receive no wages. [ibid., p. 62]

And he says—he goes out of his way without involving the pseudo-princi-
ple of diminishing marginal utility compounded on the incomes of different people—he just says

The evil of this way is, that it is very unequal; men of unequal abilities, all
paying alike, and those who have greatest charges of Children paying most;
that is, that by how much the poorer they are, by so much the harder are they
taxed. [ibid.]

And he goes on [chap. 15] to recommend a fancy which has been the fancy
of a good many economists since—notably John Stuart Mill to some extent, Alfred Marshall to some extent, and no less a person than Lord Kaldor [1955], who has written what, in my opinion, is quite a good book on
the subject. He recommends a tax on consumption, levied in his case by
way of excise, and in the case of Kaldor and Professor Meade, in more complicated ways.

Well, I hope I've said enough to persuade you to have a look at *A Treatise of Taxes and Contributions.* It's all very penetrating—now, don't gather

your papers together just for a moment; I shall be finished before one o'clock—it's all very penetrating, but there is still no system. That's why I class Petty among the anticipators, rather than among those who contributed to the *emergence* of system in the eighteenth century. And I confined myself to the *Treatise of Taxes and Contributions,* although scattered about in his *Political Arithmetick* [1676] and in his *Verbum Sapienti* [1664], and in his quaintly called *Quantulumcunque* [1682], he investigates further— and here is the combination of monetary theory and political arithmetic— he estimates the amount of money which is necessary to keep trade going. And he lived before the age of index numbers, but presumably one can read into his estimates of the amount of money that is necessary to keep trade going, the amount which is necessary to keep trade going with fairly full employment at constant prices.

You will find in the *Quantulumcunque,* which is in volume 2 of the works of Petty, a series of short questions, questions such as you might have in final examinations, together with short answers by Petty. The whole thing is less than ten pages, but it throws a very, very vivid light on what I have been trying to convey to you this morning—that Petty really had very superior economic insight.

NOTES

1. See Marx, "Sir William Petty," in Marx (1952, pp. 15–23).
2. See Cassel (1903, p. 94; chap. 4, pp. 149–51, 156).

Child and Locke (Interest)

TODAY I conclude this section of the lectures which has been dealing with anticipations of the emergence of systematic economics, first in the works of the moral philosophers and then in ad hoc treatises and pamphleteering—of which Petty's treatise on taxation is, of course, an extremely superior example. The hundreds and hundreds of ad hoc pamphlets and treatises which come under this heading will not bear comparison with Petty's more or less systematic discussions of public finance.

But now I must go back to something which is not, I think, on quite the same intellectual plane as Petty, and in regard to which in certain respects, which I will draw your attention to, interpretation is perhaps more difficult. I want mainly to speak about the work of the philosopher Locke, but before I do that, let me connect up one of the two main subjects that Locke dealt with, namely, interest on loans, with what I had to say when I was talking about it in Aristotle and the medieval theologians.

In that connection I pointed out the extreme disapprobation of Aristotle in regard to trade in money, of all kinds of trade "the most unnatural" [Aristotle, 1948, p. 20], and the persistence of that among the early medieval theologians. I analysed, in particular, Saint Thomas Aquinas on this subject, his citations of Scripture and his attempt at an analytical justification of his contention that interest on loans was unnatural. Then I went on to show how, as time went on, and commercial institutions developed—particularly in Italy—various concessions were made to the commercial practice of the time, regarding some practices in regard to loans as not sinful. So by the time of the Reformation there was at any rate one tradition of thought—a Catholic tradition—which was certainly prepared to countenance the loss incurred by lending money at zero interest when using the money onself might have secured profit. And I then at the end of the lecture pointed out that while it was a Catholic theologian, Molinaeus, who really made the most systematic representation of this change of view, among the Protestants there was division: Calvin could see no harm in honest charging for loans; Luther was as emphatically against it as the early medieval theologians. And so the controversy drifted on. In this country the chief opponent, root and branch, was Thomas Wilson [1572], whose treatise on usury has been very well edited, and with a lengthy introduction, by R. H. Tawney. Well, as I said at the end of that lecture, by the seventeenth century there were very few people who remained of that total frame of mind, and the controversy regarding interest related to what the legal rate of interest permitted should be, and whether it should be reduced.

Now, let us confine ourselves to a brief view of the controversy in this country. By the teens of the seventeenth century, the legal rate of interest in this country was 6 percent, and the controversy of the seventeenth century was whether it should be reduced from that. And the most influential and famous early plea that interest should be reduced was by a Sir Thomas Culpepper, who in 1621 wrote a small treatise against usury which is fantastically difficult to get hold of, but it is reprinted as an appendix to the more famous work about which I am just about to talk about. The controversy ebbed and flowed, and it became significantly acute in the late 1660s, when the leader of the plea that the legal rate of interest should be reduced was one Sir Josiah Child, who published a pamphlet entitled *Brief Observations concerning Trade and Interest of Money* in 1668. And he includes a reprint of Culpepper's forceful pamphlet.

A great many people thought that, having regard to the politics of the day, the proposal would be defeated. And in fact it was turned down, for reasons which we need not go into, by the House of Lords, and the controversy died away. But it was renewed with much greater intensity in the early 1690s when Josiah Child—who incidentally was an official and became head of the East India Company—republished his old discourse of trade and the appendices under the heading *A New Discourse of Trade* [1693], which includes new arguments and new material.

Well, this was reprinted several times, and it became much read. And it is a work which the graduates among you should have a look at. It is from my point of view important because the main argument for the improvement of economic conditions was a plea that the legal rate of interest should be brought down. But the *New Discourse of Trade* becomes a compendium of recommendations and observations. Child expatiates on poor relief, on the law relating to companies; he discusses the Navigation Act, and he discusses commercial debt, and he—since I don't think that his book is very good from our point of view—he discusses in a very enlightened frame of mind—a value judgement on my part—the problem of naturalisation and recommends that it should be made freer. Those of you who are interested in that sociological problem would do well to look at his observations, which, for his day, were extremely enlightened. And I am willing to forgive his bad economic theory for his liberal attitude to the Jews—a very rare attitude among writers in this country at that time. He also talks about balance of trade, and about the trade in wool. And the thing which has made his book so rare is that he talks about the plantations—namely, the colonies which were growing up in the eastern seaboard of North America. And so it has become a rare book not only in economic areas, so to speak, but in the history of the United States.

But now there is no doubt that while he made all these incidental observations—some of them at great length—his main object in publishing the book, and republishing his *Observations* and Culpepper's and so on, was that he wanted to see the legal rate of interest reduced. Well, the arguments were poor. He pointed to the prosperity of the Netherlands where the rate of interest was actually lower, and he thought that if we imitated the Netherlands and forced the rate of interest down, we should achieve the prosperity of the Netherlands. He goes back into history, and he argues that whenever the legal rate of interest has been reduced in the past in this country, the country has prospered thereafter.

Well, Child's book is important for the reasons I have mentioned. It is important also because it provoked a reply by the philosopher Locke. Now, I am not going to insult an advanced class like this by dwelling on the importance of Locke as a philosopher, who made important contributions both to epistemology and to political philosophy. The first essay on Government is an argument with an obscure chap called Filmer, which you need not read, but you should be ashamed of not reading the second essay on Government, which was probably more influential in this country fifty years after it was written, or even more than that, than any other work. And if you want to know the details of his life there is the admirable work by Professor Cranston [1957], a professor in this institution.

I think myself that Locke has been to some extent underrated as an economist. This is not because I happen to go all the way with him, insofar as I understand him, on various questions, but because I think that his exposition is of a quality superior to that of all but two of his contemporaries, one of whom was Petty, that he does discuss at greater length certain matters which had not been discussed at such length, and altogether I think that he deserves a rather greater place in the textbooks. Now, his contributions relate to the coinage, to the rate of interest and to property. I'm not going to deal with his contributions to the theory of property because I find it convenient to deal with it when I come to deal with David Hume—needless to say, by way of contrast with the much more excellent theory put forward by Hume. But I do want to devote this lecture to saying a few words drawing your attention to his contributions to the other subjects.

Now, on coinage, Locke is tremendously historically important, whether you agree with him or not. By the 1680s and the 1690s, the coinage of this country, which chiefly consisted of silver, was in a pretty disgraceful condition. It was worn; it didn't represent the value that it weighed in the scales; it didn't represent the value of silver which was proclaimed, so to speak, by the stamp on the coin. It was worn, and it had been clipped. The device of minting was not general in the early history of coinage, and minting of course enables anyone of reasonably good sense to detect in a moment whether a coin has been clipped. Well, a controversy arose of what to do about it. And there were two schools of thought: the school of thought which argued that there should be a recoinage of the silver currency so as to make it worth the silver which it claimed to be, and another school of thought which argued that, although the alloy in the silver should not be changed, there was something to be said for what they called "raising the value of money," which is a confusing title for us because it means something quite different for us. They meant debasement—that is to say, saying that a thing which called itself a shilling was equal, so to speak, to fifteen pence. I simply use that illustratively, because Locke refers to it in his writing [Locke, 1695, p. 177].

Now, Locke was the extremely influential leader of the school which argued that there must be a recoinage at the old rate. His views on the subject are contained partly in his main work on the subject, which I shall be quoting later, *Some Considerations of the Consequences of the Lowering of Interest, and Raising the Value of Money*, which was published in 1691. And the main part of that extensive pamphlet is devoted to interest, which I shall be coming to in a moment, but he deals at large with the question of raising the value of money—that is to say, debasement, or, if you like, devaluation.

The controversy is an extremely interesting one, and it had some bearing on modern problems. Locke's chief opponent in this controversy was a man called Lowndes, who was the First Secretary of the Treasury and played a great part in founding the Bank of England and in the very prudent conduct of the finances of the day. And he wrote *An Essay for the Amendment of the Silver Coins* [1695], which was published in the middle of the 1690s, to which Locke wrote a *lengthy* reply called *Further Considerations Concerning Raising the Value of Money* [1695]. And this was, unlike most of the historic controversies of the times that we've been taking a brief survey of, a thoroughly good-tempered controversy. Locke's *Further Considerations* has a preface in which he acknowledges the excellence of Lowndes' exposition, his great public spirit, his friendliness in showing to Locke some of his thoughts before he published them, and altogether the controversy was a model to all who aspire in the twentieth century to be economists, in the way of good manners.

Now, Locke's position is very simple, and I can describe it very shortly. Locke was a pure metallist. He believed that the value of money should be the value of the metal which it contained—that is to say that, in the end, money must be judged by the weight of the metal and not the stamp or certificate that it contained that weight. And hence, he said, there is no point in changing the label as Lowndes had suggested. Lowndes had suggested a devaluation of considerable proportions—some 20 percent or so—but Locke said it was a proposal comparable to a proposal to "lengthen a foot, by dividing it into fifteen parts, instead of twelve, and calling them inches" [Locke, 1695, p. 145].

Well, there is something in that. But there was also something in Lowndes' point of view, because Lowndes' point of view was that, roughly speaking, the damage had been done, that the wearing and the clipping of the coins had in fact contributed to a diminution of the things that they would buy—that is to say, a raising of prices in the market. And it is very clear, judging with modern insight, that what Lowndes feared was that recoinage would involve a deflation, with all the difficulties and social frictions that that would imply. So, as one reads the controversy nowadays, one has a sneaking sympathy for Lowndes on the very cogent arguments which he presented.

Now, Hawtrey discussed this controversy in his *Currency and Credit* [1919], which all of you should read because it ranks with some of Robertson's writings, together with Keynes, as initiating the progress which has been made in our understanding of monetary phenomena in the twentieth century. I won't say that you won't find traces of it before, but Hawtrey's *Currency and Credit* is an absolutely seminal book. Sir John Hicks has recently written eulogies in various places of Hawtrey, drawing attention to the shameful nature of the neglect of this famous book of his. And the book does deal with various historical episodes, including the silver recoinages. And he there shows considerable sympathy with Lowndes, but points out that Locke was perhaps *right* in that there was an experiment going on in Government-authorised convertible paper money—the foundation of the Bank of England. And, says Hawtrey [1950, pp. 238–44], people would have said at the time if there had been Lowndes' devaluation: "Well, where will it stop? After all, we only have a guarantee of convertibility of this paper which is beginning to circulate as a result of the foundation of the Bank of England," and distrust would have been engendered by Lowndes' otherwise rather persuasive proposal.

Now, this is a frightfully superficial account, but even so the interest of it has let me run five minutes over my time. You should read a splendid book by Horsefield [1960], which I think is in my bibliography, on monetary experiments. And the chapters on the British monetary controversy, 1650–1710, give you all the detail, not only of Locke and Lowndes, but of all the other pamphlets which are worth thinking of. And he provides a splendid bibliography of pamphlets which are not worth thinking about.

Well now, I come to interest. Locke's writing on interest was also successful. When Child first published his book at the end of the 1660s, Locke, who was already friendly with various political figures of the reign of Charles II, was asked by one of them to write an essay on Child's advocacy of lowering the legal rate of interest. And Professor Letwin actually reprints the essay—it was a very crude essay—as an appendix to his splendid book on *The Origins of Scientific Economics*.[1] Well, when the controversy was rekindled in the 1690s, in 1691 Locke published this famous book, or long pamphlet, called *Some Considerations of the Consequences of the Lowering of Interest, and Raising the Value of Money*. Now, this is anti-Child. It is against a false lowering of the rate of interest by lowering the legal rate, but it deals with other matters, and I think I can direct your attention to six important matters which appear in the course of his reflections on interest.

First of all, he is definitely against lowering the legal rate of interest. And right at the beginning of his book—pages 5 and 6 of my collected edition of Locke's works, which was published in 1794 (ninth edition)—pages 5 and 6 enumerate his objections to lowering the legal rate:

1. It will make the difficulty of borrowing and lending much greater, whereby trade . . . will be obstructed. . . .

2. It will be a prejudice to none, but those who most need assistance and help; I mean widows and orphans, and others uninstructed in the arts and management of more skilful men, whose estates lying in money, they will be sure, especially orphans, to have no more profit of their money, than what interest the law barely allows. [Locke, 1691, p. 5]

On the other hand, thirdly, he thinks that it would "increase the advantage of bankers and scriveners" who knew how to get round all that sort of thing [ibid.]. And he, fourthly, reckons it "as one of the probable consequences of such a law" that it will increase crime, and he expatiates on the evils of administrative acts which are an incentive in some way or other to crime [ibid., p. 6]. By crime, in this case, he meant swearing false oaths concerning the rate at which you had made loans and so on and so forth.

Well then, he proceeds to argue—I am speaking very roughly here—that there is no particular reason to suppose that the legal rate of interest is not in harmony with what he calls the natural rate of interest. He derides on a later page—page 68 of the ninth edition—all Child's arguments about the greater prosperity of Holland. He doesn't deny that Holland is prosperous, but he inverts the causal connection. Interest is low in Holland *because* of the abundance of stock and because Holland is prosperous; Holland is *not* prosperous because interest rates had been forced down. And he then turns to this proposition: that if you try to force the rate of interest down by law, and the underlying conditions of supply and demand are such as not to justify that forcing down by law, then all sorts of things will go wrong. Trade will be impeded in various ways, and prosperity, far from being increased, will be less.

But now what was this natural rate? Now here I am compelled to make a confession to you that I am not sure, and the authorities are not sure. He actually says that natural interest is raised in two ways—when money is little in relation to debt and, secondly, when money is little in relation to trade. And in such conditions, he argues, it's vain to go about trying effectively to reduce interest rates.

But now the question arises: What did he mean by "money"? There are two modern authorities whom I would quote on this matter. The first is Professor Tucker of Australia, who wrote a book called *Progress and Profits in British Economic Thought, 1650–1850* [1960]—one of the best books on the history of this aspect of thought that I know. Tucker [1960, pp. 27, 35] thinks that by "money," in this connection, Locke meant "available and loanable funds," which rings a Robertsonian bell, and certainly fits the interpretation of a good many of the things that Locke says. But now, Professor Vickers, who I think is still at the University of Pennsylvania, has written a work called *Studies in the Theory of Money* [1960], a careful, historical work trying to trace Keynesian elements in various predecessors of Keynes. Vickers [1960, chap. 4, pp. 43–73] claims that Locke was an anticipator of Keynes, who, as you know, in a crude version, said that interest depended on liquidity preference and the quantity of money.

And the question is how to make up one's mind. I confess I find Tucker rather more persuasive than Vickers, but I can easily imagine that if Vickers were here—as he was here at one time writing his Ph.D. thesis, of which this book is an enlargement—he could quote sentences which seem to indicate that Locke was thinking of the total quantity of money rather than the loanable funds forthcoming. My own feeling is that Locke himself may have been a little bit muddled here. You may think that the burden of his argument favours the loanable fund interpretation, but my own feeling (and I think that this year, 1979; I give notice I may change that views again next year) is that he felt in a vague way that plenty of money, in the total quantity sense, made more loanable funds forthcoming.

Now certainly, until Hume wrote on interest, which I shall be coming to in a couple of weeks' time, the monetary interpretation of Locke, whether Locke intended this or not, the monetary theory of interest, was right. And it was not only Hume—who didn't mention Locke by name, but who argues against a pure monetary theory of interest—it was not only Hume, it was also a man called Massie [1750], who wrote a pamphlet in this splendid series of *Reprints of Economic Tracts* by John Hopkins. I shall say a word or two about Massie when I come to Hume.

Then here we are, in the most important part of Locke's reflections on interest, in some doubt. And I think it would be dishonest of me if I were to come down heavily on either side of the authorities here.

He then thirdly—and I think I should say this before I stop—on page 36 he provides a justification of interest, harking back to earlier controversies on the justification of interest as a whole. And he says: "Money therefore, in buying and selling, being perfectly in the same condition with other commodities, and subject to all the same laws of value, let us next see how it comes to be of the same nature with land, by yielding a certain yearly income, which we call use, or interest" [Locke, 1691, p. 36]. Well then, he goes on to argue, as many people had argued before him, that if you regarded the rent of land as justifiable, then why are you regarding as sinful or unjustifiable the loan which makes possible the purchase of rents? And so on and so forth.

Well, I am a little bit behind, and I must mention in the first five minutes of the next lecture the other points in which Locke cloaked his argument.

NOTE

1. See Letwin (1963, app. 5, pp. 273–300).

B. Emergence of Systems

Cantillon

I TIMED my lecture badly yesterday, and in regard to Locke I left undiscussed three points to which I feel that I must draw your attention. I'll be as brief as I can, because I, as well as the rest of you, am anxious to get on to the really interesting part of this course, and it's only ten minutes off.

I said that Locke's remarks on interest were valuable and deserve to be taken note of in regard to six matters: firstly, his animadversions about Child's thesis, the direct proposal to lower the rate of interest; secondly, his ambiguous discussion of the determination of the natural rate of interest, on which I declared myself rather unable to make up my mind concerning the interpretation thereof; thirdly, his justification of interest by comparing it with rent of land. The three points remaining, and one general observation, are as follows. Fourthly, that in the course of his development of these rather rambling remarks about the interest problem in general, he develops a quantity theory of money and a determination of the price level—I am using modern terminology here—which in some respects is ampler than anything else that you will find in the earlier literature, except in the terse remarks of Petty in his *Quantulumcunque* [1682]. And certainly on page 22 of the appropriate volume [vol. 4] in the ninth edition of Locke's works, there is an analysis of velocity of circulation, which certainly goes beyond anything which had been written before—at any rate, anything which to my knowledge had been written before.

Then, fifthly, on page 40 of the *Considerations* [1691], in the ninth edition, you have a discussion of the influences determining value—a general discussion of the influence of supply and demand on price and general reflections on the difficulty of conceiving stationary conditions as regards price. He is concerned, as the man I'm about to talk about later on says, exclusively with market price, and he makes some very shrewd remarks there. And then finally, and sixthly, on page 55 of the *Considerations*, he discusses at some length the incidence of taxation, and places himself among those who argue that, in the *end*, most taxation of his time, and presumably earlier times, eventually settled on the landowners.

Now, with that very superficial account of this aspect of Locke, I leave him, save for a mention of the quality which is praised by Professor Letwin in the book which I have already recommended to you, *The Origins of Scientific Economics*. Letwin [1963, pp. 160–62, 167–71] praises Locke's general approach to these matters because in the end he has some perception of the broad underlying forces in his discussion of *natural* rates of interest and *natural* influences on prices and the value of money and so on and so forth. So he edges a little nearer to the subject which I wish to discuss in three minutes' time.

Now, on the question of lowering the rates of interest by legal means, and raising the value of money in the special sense of devaluation, Locke is easily surpassed by Sir Dudley North in his *Discourses Upon Trade* [1691]. In very short papers he animadverts on these subjects and succinctly succeeds in undermining the arguments which have been advanced respectively with regard to interest and with regard to debasement. Letwin [1963, pp. 189–204], in his book, goes so far as to say that one must regard highly North's *Discourses Upon Trade*, which you can all find in the republication of the Economic History Society of *Early Tracts on Commerce*. I pass over it lightly because it's such good reading, and even the slowest of you could read it quite easily in fifty minutes. It is very brightly written and contains a preface, probably by his brother, Roger North, the author of the celebrated biography of the North family. And you can find it not only in the Johns Hopkins series of reprints but also in the Economic History Society reprints of the *Early Tracts on Commerce*, which were edited originally by McCulloch.

Now, much as I should like to give a whole lecture on North, I don't wish to delay any longer my discussion on the next part of these lectures, namely, the emergence of systematic economics in the eighteenth century. Neither Petty nor Locke, nor North, although arguing in terms which are more or less familiar to us—speaking our language so to speak—treated the economic system as a whole. There are hints of this in North's pamphlet, as Professor Letwin [1963, pp. 189–204] points out, but the explicit and systematic treatment of general economic relationships has to wait until the eighteenth century. And the emergence is to be detected principally in the works of the French economists who later on were called "the physiocrats," and in the work of the Scottish philosophers—chiefly, the greatest of all our philosophers, David Hume and Adam Smith.

But there is a third personality, a personality about whom we know comparatively little, who wrote a work which as a scientific treatise is superior to anything that the physiocrats produced and really, in many respects, bears a comparison with *The Wealth of Nations* itself, namely the *Essay on the Nature of Commerce* by Richard Cantillon [1755]. You all ought to know something about Cantillon, and the sources are not all easily accessible, so I propose to devote a little time to his history and his publication before I expound to you the system unfolded in this book.

Richard Cantillon—whom the French, of course, would call "Canteon"—was of Irish descent, and settled in Paris at an early age as a banker. He seems to have been an extremely shrewd and sharp-witted banker, and when John Law, about whom I will talk to you in connection with the physiocrats, launched his ill-fated Mississippi scheme, which was the French parallel of our South Sea Bubble in the early '20s of the century, Cantillon saw through it, probably in indiscrete conversation ventilated his doubts, and was sent for by John Law, who had established himself in royal esteem and high prestige in Paris. Law said to him: "Do you know that I could have you turned out of this capital city in twenty-four hours?" And Cantillon seems to have said, "But you won't. I can make a success of your scheme."[1] And for the time being he, so to speak, acted as a bull for the Mississippi bonds, but he got out in time and made a huge fortune. And then in 1734, having a house just round the corner in Covent Garden, he was murdered in his bed by his valet and his house set on fire and a great many valuable papers destroyed.

We know a certain amount of detail concerning his dealings with clients and the numerous lawsuits that he was involved in. We know something of his habits as an economist. He used to travel round in a carriage with an accountant to keep his observations on the economic phenomena that he witnessed. From time to time he would get out of the carriage, and, according to Mirabeau, he would taste the soil to see what sort of fertility, what chemical composition, it was of, and he would then presumably tell his accountant to take a note of this. And in the course of time he accumulated, apparently—because no one has seen it in this or presumably the nineteenth century—he accumulated a great deal of valuable economic information and statistics, which he refers to in the *Essay on the Nature of Commerce* as "the Supplement." And no trace of "the Supplement" has emerged. Very peculiar discoveries are still made in our subject. The truth about the origin of Quesnay's famous economic table—the thing on which the physiocratic system was based—has only been cleared up within the last twenty years, so there is hope still as regards Cantillon's "Supplement."

We don't really get to know the man except through this book. There is no photograph of him, and the learned Higgs, who publishes the original publication in French and with what he thinks was mostly the English original on opposite sides—so the book is not as formidable as you might think, as I hold it in my hand—well, the learned Higgs, wishing to provide all the information that he could, has published in this book—he persuaded the Royal Economic Society, which was flush of funds at the time, to publish—a photograph of a painting of Mrs Richard Cantillon and another photograph of his daughter who married into the aristocracy, on the principle, presumably, that in the process of subtraction of the daughter from the wife some idea of the father will emerge!

However, as regards the perplexities of publication, this was published twenty-one years after Cantillon's assassination—published by a bookseller called Gyles of Holborn in 1755. And it was published in French, and it was labelled "Translated from the English." And Mirabeau, about whom you will hear quite a lot later on—the father of the celebrated revolutionary statesman—who had had access to Cantillon's manuscript and had it copied out, incorporated long passages in an unpublished memoir on population of his own. Mirabeau said that he translated it into French at the suggestion of a friend. Other French contemporaries, when it was published as

"Translated from the English," protested that it wasn't so. But the extraordinary thing is that Cannan and Higgs between them discovered long passages in English in works of a general writer on industry and the author of a two-volume folio dictionary of commerce, called Postlethwayt. And Postlethwayt [1757a,b], particularly in the *Dictionary* [1757b], quotes a substantial part of the *Essay on Commerce*, and Higgs weaves that into the translation from the French which is on the opposite page of this book. Well, I could go on a great deal about that. Professor Yamey sent me only last week a new edition of Cantillon's *Essay* [1979], with further bibliographical detection by a learned Japanese professor, Professor Tsuda, of which I can only say that it kept me from more relevant work to these lectures for two nights last week. But I must go on.

When it was published, and through the work of Mirabeau, it had a very considerable réclame. I will dwell further on its influence on the physiocrats when I come to deal with the physiocrats next week. It is mentioned in all sorts of works of the period. And then its reputation entirely ceased, and, save for an obscure reference in Karl Marx,[2] it wasn't quoted or discussed for 100 years. And then Stanley Jevons hit upon a copy, realised that it was the work of a most remarkable man, and in 1881 he published an article—which is reproduced in Higgs' book (which was republished at a very low price by the Royal Economic Society, and I should imagine that you can still get some)—he published an article called "Richard Cantillon and the Nationality of Political Economy." And then Higgs, who was an admirer of Jevons' discovery, himself set to work on discovering more facts with regard to the *Essay* and with regard to its author, and he published articles in the first number of the *Economic Journal*, and again in 1892 in the *Quarterly Journal of Economics*.

Nowadays there is a splendid French edition edited by Sauvy [Cantillon, 1952], and it is easily accessible in our time. And it is now recognised generally as one of the most extraordinary documents in our subject. I am choosing my words carefully. You may think that I exaggerate, but I do not retract the words—one of the most extraordinary documents of our subject. The look of it is something which has not appeared before. It is a treatise on the working of the economic system—a systematic, abstract treatise, informed, however, by close acquaintance with the details of the commerce, finance and trade of the period in which it was written. A thousand pities we haven't "the Supplement" on which he based many of the propositions in his book.

And this treatise is unlike the treatises of the physiocrats, which went on to recommend policy, and unlike *The Wealth of Nations* which is at once a treatise and a polemic. Adam Smith wrote *The Wealth of Nations* partly in order to add to knowledge, partly in order to attack the principles of the mercantile system as he understood the mercantile system, as I explained it to you the other day. But Cantillon hasn't any axe to grind except in the last paragraph, where there is an indirect reference to the dangerous operations of John Law and the manufacture of credit. But for the rest of it, it is as detached as you can possibly conceive. In the course of part 1, he deals at some length with the population question. He completely anticipates Malthus on the tendency of population to multiply until the limits of subsistence. He utters the memorable phrase "Men multiply like Mice in a barn," provided that there is subsistence [Cantillon, 1755, p. 83]. And then he closes the chapter by saying whether it's a good thing to have an economy with a comparatively small population living at a good standard of life, or a good thing to have a larger population living more or less at subsistence level, is not my business to inquire [ibid., p. 85]—which is rather piquant in that connection, even if you are rather tired of twentieth-century economists who point out that various things involve value judgements when it's quite obvious that they do.

Now, the *Essay* is divided into three parts. The first part is a general analysis of the working of the economy. The second part is a more detailed discussion of monetary theory and interest theory, and the third part is an *incredibly* well-informed discussion of commerce and banking. And so I make no apology for leading you through it. I take it that you will all have access in some way or other to the Higgs edition, which is by far the easiest for you to read since what is probably the original is in English on the right-hand side of every page.

He begins with a short chapter, "Of Wealth," and the first few sentences run: "The Land is the Source or Matter from whence all Wealth is produced. The Labour of man is the Form which produces it: and Wealth in itself is nothing but the Maintenance, Conveniences, and Superfluities of Life" [ibid., p. 3]. And then chapters 2 to 6 are, so to speak, devoted to economic sociology. Chapter 2 discusses "Human Societies" in general, and in the course of this he discusses the function of property as he conceives it in any complicated human society. He then goes on in chapter 3 to deal with "Villages," and he argues that "To whatever cultivation Land is put" [ibid., p. 9], it's convenient for some people, at any rate, to live together near the source of their agricultural labour. He then goes on in chapter 4 to discuss "Market Towns," pointing out that a village is insufficiently large to provide a market for all sorts of things which, even in a comparatively primitive agricultural society, people may want, and hence it becomes convenient that shopping centres should be established in market towns.

And this leads him to chapter 5, "Of Cities." And there he distinguishes cities from market towns by reason of the fact that in cities some of the landowners will have taken up their habitation, and consequently, being richer than the peasants or agriculturalists, their wants will be more complicated, and therefore the commerce of the city will be itself of a more complex certain nature. And then in chapter 6 he goes on to "Capital Cities" and distinguishes capital cities by being the seat of Government—the residence of the Prince or the Monarch—and he is led to make very interesting remarks on the geographical features which lead to the location of a capital city. Now, there is none of this in the earlier literature at all. Cantillon must be attributed with terrific originality in planning a book of this sort.

Well, in chapter 7 he plunges into economic relationships, and the title of the chapter is "The Labour of the Husbandman is of less Value than that of the Handicrafts-man." And he explains why an agricultural "Labourer's Son at seven or twelve years of age begins to help his Father either in keeping the Flocks, digging the ground, or in other sorts of Country Labour which require no Art or Skill" [ibid., p. 19]. But now: "If his Father puts him to a Trade,"—I'm quoting Cantillon—"he loses his Assistance during the Time of his Apprenticeship and is necessitated to cloath him and to pay the expenses of his Apprenticeship for some years" [ibid.]. Therefore, economic forces bring it about that, in order to get a flow of apprentices, the financial reward of handicraftsmen—the people who have completed their apprenticeships—must tend to be greater than the financial reward of the agricultural labour.

And in chapter 8 he goes on with the theme. Incidentally, his book is very easy reading, because most of the chapters are pretty short. The title of the chapter again conveys to you the meaning: "Some Handicrafts-men earn more, others less, according to the different Cases and Circumstances." And he dwells upon the different lengths of training for different handicrafts, and the different risks which are involved: "By these examples and a hundred others drawn from ordinary experience it is easily seen that the difference of price paid for daily work is based upon natural and obvious reasons [ibid., pp. 21–23]. And then he warms up to the analysis, and in chapter 9 he argues that "The Number of Labourers, Handicrafts-men and others, who work in a State is naturally proportioned to the Demand for them." And if in a village the demand falls off, then there will be wastage by migration and diminution of population. If, on the other hand, the demand is greater, then there will be migration into the centre. And so you have the idea thrown out of an equilibrium relationship of the number of the different kinds of labourers to the demand.

And having got to that point, of course, he is confronted with the question of price, and in chapter 10 he plunges straightaway into what he calls the "Intrinsic Value of a Thing"—the price around which the market price will tend to oscillate: "the Price or intrinsic value of a thing [in general] is the measure of the quantity of Land and of Labour entering into its production" [ibid., p. 29]. And, well, that is the substance of that chapter.

Now, this extraordinary man had read Petty—or at any rate Petty's *Treatise of Taxes and Contributions* [1662]. And in chapter 11 he tackles the question of the par between land and labour: How do you assimilate quantities of land and quantities of labour in deciding what is the intrinsic value or price of this thing or that? And he alludes to Petty, and he advances in a quite complicated argument that you can solve this problem if you decide upon the area of land: not that which is necessary to produce the commodity in question—that goes without saying—but in addition to that if you can decide on the area of land which produces the subsistence of the labourers which are necessary to produce the particular commodity in question. He recognises that, of course, the subsistence will vary in different circumstances, and that this isn't an entirely exact method. But it is the best he can do, and it is the best attempt that has ever been made to solve Petty's question of the par between labour and land. It won't help you much in deciding the normal value of prices in advanced communities, but at any rate it is a very valiant attempt to solve the problem which Petty had attempted to discuss both in the *Treatise of Taxes and Contributions* and in his *Political Anatomy of Ireland* [1672], to which Cantillon also refers.

Well then, in chapter 12 he says that "All Classes and Individuals in a State subsist or are enriched at the Expense of the Proprietors of Land" [Cantillon, 1755, p. 43]. He's becoming a little physiocratic there, but this is advanced with reference to contemporary circumstances. It is not doctrinaire in the sense which made the physiocrats regard agricultural labour and extractive labour as the only productive labour, and all the rest as being unproductive. There are many anticipations of physiocratic doctrine in this part of Cantillon, but it is to my way of thinking at any rate not nearly so doctrinaire as the physiocrats.

And then in the marvelous chapter 13 he says, Well then, how are the goods circulated, and how is production organised? And the answer is—the chapter heading again gives you the substance of the chapter, although the chapter is very well worth reading—"The circulation and exchange of goods and merchandise as well as their production are carried on in Europe by Undertakers"—*entrepreneurs* in French—"and at risk." That's in the original French and is the first use that I know of the term *entrepreneur* in this technical sense. And he then enlarges on the role of the entrepreneur in agriculture and in manufacture and in commerce, in ways which have realistic reference to the circumstances of the time. And he then divides society into two groups: those who are hired at prices fixed beforehand—contractural remuneration—and those who are unhired and who are, in one sense or other, speculating on the future of markets for which they produce. No more useful demarcation of the various groups in society in this particular respect has ever been made, and it has taken the twentieth century to rediscover what is set forth with such vividness and such piquancy by Cantillon. And then, going on [chap. 14], he returns to the demand side, and he says, "The Fancies, the Fashions and Modes of Living of the Prince, and especially of the Landowners, determine the use to which Land is put in a State and cause the variations in the Market-prices of all things."

And in chapter 15, he then goes into the population question, to which I have already alluded, and the chapter is headed "The Increase and Decrease of the Number of People in a State chiefly depend on the Taste, the

Fashions, and Modes of Living of the Proprietors of Land." And he refers
to "the Supplement," in which

> will be found estimates of the amount of Land required for the support of a
> Man according to the different assumptions of his Manner of Living. It will be
> seen that a Man who lives on Bread, Garlic and Roots, wears only hempen
> garments, coarse Linen, Wooden Shoes, and drinks only water, like many
> Peasants in the South of France, can live on the produce of an Acre and a half
> of Land of medium goodness, yielding a sixfold harvest and resting once in 3
> years. [ibid., p. 71]

Now, that's the tone in which he discusses this matter. And according to
the whims of proprietors and of the ladies of quality,

> If the Ladies of Paris are pleased to wear Brussels Lace, and if France pays for
> this Lace with Champagne wine, the product of a single Acre of Flax must be
> paid for with the product of 16,000 acres of land under vines, if my calcula-
> tions are correct. This will be more fully explained elsewhere and the figures
> are shewn in the Supplement. [ibid., p. 77]

Then he goes on to quote the observations of Halley at Breslau in Silesia,
the famous scientist:

> it is found that of all Females capable of childbearing, from 16 to 45 years of
> age, not one in six actually bears a child every year, while, says M. Halley, there
> ought to be at least 4 or 6 who should have children every year, without in-
> cluding those who are barren or have still-births. [ibid., p. 79]

And he goes into the reason for that, and eventually he says:

> Sir Wm Petty, and after him Mr Davenant, Inspector of the Customs in En-
> gland, seem to depart from nature when they try to estimate the propagation
> of the race by progressive generations from Adam, the first Father. Their cal-
> culations seem to be purely imaginary and drawn up at hazard. On the basis of
> what they have seen of the actual birth rate in certain districts, how could they
> explain the Decrease of those innumerable People formerly found in Asia,
> Egypt, etc. and even in Europe? [ibid., p. 83]

And then comes the famous statement:

> Men multiply like Mice in a barn if they have unlimited Means of Subsistence;
> and the English in the Colonies will become more numerous in proportion in
> three generations than they would be in thirty in England, because in the Col-
> onies they find for cultivation new tracts of land from which they drive the
> [inhabitants]. [ibid.][3]

And so on. But he ends the chapter:

> It is also a question outside of my subject whether it is better to have a great
> multitude of Inhabitants, poor and badly provided, than a smaller number,
> much more at their ease. [ibid., p. 85]

And in chapter 16 he takes the common view that "The more Labour there is in a State, the more naturally rich the State is esteemed," and in the final chapter of part 1, "Of Metal and Money, and especially of Gold and Silver," he more or less reproduces, in much more vivid terms, the standard explanation, derived from Aristotle through the Fathers and the modern lawyers and so on and so forth, of the origin and uses of money, and especially of gold and silver. End of part 1.

But at the cost of encroaching on the next lecture, I'm going to stop there, because part 2 is even more surprising as regards economic analysis than the book that I have been outlining to you. Part 2 contains not only a theory of market price, it contains a minute elaboration of the quantity theory of money, and then he discusses why the quantity theory of money is insufficient to explain the changes in the value of money under dynamic conditions. And he provides what you have to wait for a very many years for, before you have any comparable analysis of that problem at all, in the sort of detail that he goes into. But more of that next time. I shan't linger so long on that because part 3, on banking and trade, is so crammed with details of what, after all, was his own trade and is so valuable a document. I would say that, on banking and money and trade, it's easily the best book before the twentieth century, save Thornton's *Paper Credit* [1802] at the beginning of the nineteenth century. And I shan't go into that in detail, expecting that those of you whose appetite has been whetted will read it for yourselves.

NOTES

1. This statement, translated from the French, appears on p. 336 of the *Essai*, in the reprint of Jevons' essay on Cantillon: W. S. Jevons (1881), "Richard Cantillon and the Nationality of Political Economy.'

2. See Marx, "Adam Smith and the Theory of Productive Labor," in Marx (1952, pp. 105–97, at 111), where Marx quotes Smith quoting Cantillon.

3. The word used by Cantillon here is *Savages*. Robbins' use of the word '*inhabitants*' was reflective of his desire to avoid giving offense in this more enlightened era. See also lecture 13, n.2 and accompanying text.

Cantillon (cont.)—Physiocracy

SO LET ME, without undue recapitulation, plunge into the remainder of what I have to say about Cantillon [1755]. I hope that the extracts that I read to you from part 1 were sufficient to make you feel that Cantillon was rather an important chap. Part 1, as you will have gathered, is devoted to a general description of economic organisation—the controlling power of demand, the nature of what he calls intrinsic value and its relation to market prices and incomes, and winding up with a description of the ordinary stuff about money, which I didn't trouble to recapitulate for you because I had reached the end of the lecture hour and I don't think that, although the style is characteristic, and it bears the same sense of authoritative contact with the subject he is talking about, I don't think that Cantillon's last chapter on money brings to light anything that is frightfully important.

But now part 2, which deals with prices, money and interest, although I think it would be easy for me to recapitulate it comparatively briefly, is far more important—not perhaps as regards form and scope in part 2, but as regards originality of analysis and proposition. It starts with a chapter on barter, and I don't think that there is very much to say about that. He sets out grounds for barter; he makes some allusion to Locke on market prices and the introduction of money.

Chapter 2, however, is extremely important. It deals with the formation of market prices. Having rebuked Locke in the first chapter for looking only to market prices, in chapter 2 he himself proceeds to make a most original contribution to the theory of market prices. I say it's original; of course it will all be absolutely old hat so far as you are concerned. But the chapter is, so far as I know, the first place in the economic literature which actually discusses the *mechanism* whereby the varying disposition to demand and the varying disposition to supply eventually produce market prices. He talks about bartering, and says some people

> are more clever in puffing up their wares, others in running them down. Though this method of fixing Market prices has no exact or geometrical foundation, since it often depends upon the eagerness or easy temperament of a few Buyers or Sellers, it does not seem that it could be done in any more convenient way. [Cantillon, 1755, p. 119]

And he then gives what is the equivalent of an early Austrian model of the market process. Let me read it to you:

> Several maîtres d'hôtels [at Paris] have been told to buy green Peas when they first come in. One Master has ordered the purchase of 10 quarts for 60 livres,

another 10 quarts for 50 livres, a third 10 for 40 livres and a fourth 10 for 30 livres. If these orders are to be carried out there must be 40 quarts of green Peas in the Market. Suppose there are only 20. The Vendors, seeing many Buyers, will keep up their Prices, and the Buyers will come up to the Prices prescribed to them: so that those who offer 60 livres for 10 quarts will be the first served. The Sellers, seeing later that no one will go above 50, will let the other 10 quarts go at that price. Those who had orders not to exceed 40 and 30 livres will go away empty.

If instead of 40 quarts there were 400, not only would the maîtres d'hôtels get the new Peas much below the sums laid down for them, but the Sellers in order to be preferred one to the other by the few Buyers will lower their new Peas almost to their intrinsic value, and in that case many maîtres d'hôtels who had no orders will buy some. [ibid., pp. 119–21, brackets in original]

And then he winds up the chapter by saying that of course distant markets will always have some effect on the price in the market that you are considering, varying with the distance, and, if the price in a particular market is particularly low, then some seller will think of going elsewhere [ibid., p. 121]. And so on and so forth.

Well then, in chapter 3 he turns to the circulation of money, and the opening sentence says:

It is the general opinion in England that a Farmer must make three Rents. (1) The principal and true Rent which he pays to the proprietor, supposed equal in value to the produce of one third of his Farm, a second Rent for his maintenance and that of the Men and Horses he employs to cultivate the Farm, and a third which ought to remain with him to make his undertaking profitable. [ibid.]

Well, he goes into this at some length, and I think he proceeds very cautiously and says that this is only a first approximation, roughly speaking, but this part of it is not unintelligible and it leads on to a further discussion, in chapter 4, on the circulation of money.

And he goes into the various classes and the frequency of their respective uses of money. He considers the demand for money for purposes of guarding against unforeseen risks. He considers the varying habits of the landowners and the people from whom they buy in the country, and how the people who manufacture products in the town spend their money. And so on and so forth. He takes note of the existence of banks and goldsmiths, who were turning themselves into banks at that time, and he argues that the existence of banks so to speak economises the demand for money and makes it circulate more rapidly.

And he then [chap. 5] discusses the geographical location of centres of hard money, and this leads him to a digression on location theory. He thinks that prices in general are likely to be lower in areas which are far distant from the market towns and the capital cities, and for that reason he thinks that it would be especially profitable for certain kinds of manufactures, not involving heavy costs of transport, to be set up in these distant places, rather than in places adjacent to towns where rents will be higher and all sorts of other costs will beset them.

And then, in chapter 6, he deals with "the increase and decrease in the quantity of hard money in a State." And he refers to Locke in this connection. Locke, who you remember had expounded some sort of quantity theory of money, had expounded, not in the same vivid detail as Cantillon, the causes of variations in demand for money. But now, in chapter 6, he refers to Locke again, and I am quoting:

> M. Locke lays it down as a fundamental maxim that the quantity of produce and merchandise in proportion to the quantity of money serves as the regulator of Market price. I have tried to elucidate his idea in the preceding Chapters: he has clearly seen that the abundance of money makes everything dear, but he has not considered how it does so. The great difficulty of this question consists in knowing in what way and in what proportion the increase of money raises prices. [ibid., p. 161]

And there follow for the next nearly twenty pages a more or less minute examination of various ways in which the quantity of money in circulation in a community may be increased: the flow of precious metals from the mines, favourable balance of payments, and so on and so forth.

And he then goes on to examine in regard to these various possibilities the way in which the money spreads itself through the community. And, having regard to his earlier dissertation on variations of the demand for money, the way in which prices tend to be affected depends, according to him, into whose hands the money gets first. If it gets into the hands of people whose demand for money is small, then they pass it on quickly and prices begin to rise. If it gets into the hands of people who tend to hoard money, then for that reason the price level is not so immediately affected, although sooner or later the hoards will get spent and sooner or later there will be some effect. And after all this analysis, which is thrillingly original—there is nothing like it in the literature, and there is nothing like it, I would venture to say, in Hume or Adam Smith; you would have to get to Thornton's *Paper Credit* [1802] before you find analysis on this dynamic level—he concludes on page 177: "From all this I conclude that by doubling the quantity of money in a State the prices of products and merchandise are not always doubled. A River which runs and winds about in its bed will not flow with double the speed when the amount of its water is doubled" [ibid., p. 177]. And so he goes on.

And then, towards the end of the book [chaps. 9 and 10], he deals with the interest question, and on that there is no need for me to linger so long. He quite definitely *attacks* the view that it is the quantity of money, just like that [Robbins snaps his fingers here], which affects the rate of interest. He says people may think that the increase in the quantity of money will bring the rate of interest down, but he quotes examples where the rate of interest has risen when the quantity of money has been increased. And he then goes forward to give a more or less loanable funds account of the money market, taking account of its *frightful* complexity—the different rates of interest which are normal to different buyers and sellers. He mentions consumption loans, but goes out of his way to say that these do not constitute the main demand for loans in this connection. The main demand for loans comes from the profit which is made by undertakers in manufacturing and cognate kinds of industry. Well, that's all very clear and vividly described, but there is no need, I think, for me to recapitulate.

Then you come to part 3, which is on trade, foreign exchange and banking. And there I won't attempt a recapitulation. It is written with a greater intimacy with trade and the foreign exchanges—remember he made his fortune by banking and dealing in foreign exchange and so on—than you will find in any of the subsequent literature. Anyone who wishes to broach this subject anew would be well-advised, at an early stage, to read Cantillon's account of these matters.

So far as banking is concerned, he *emphasises* that the existence of banking and bank credit and all that sort of thing economises the demand for hard money. And then he winds up with the one tendentious paragraph in his *Essay*. He argues that

> It is then undoubted that a Bank with the complicity of a Minister is able to raise and support the price of public stock and to lower the rate of interest in the State at the pleasure of this Minister when the steps are taken discreetly, and thus pay off the State debt. But these refinements which open the door to making large fortunes are rarely carried out for the sole advantage of the State, and those who take part in them are generally corrupted. The excess banknotes, made and issued on these occasions, do not upset the circulation, because being used for the buying and selling of stock they do not serve for household expenses and are not changed into silver. But

—final sentence—

> if some panic or unforeseen crisis drove the holders to demand silver from the Bank, the bomb would burst and it would be seen that these are dangerous operations. [ibid., p. 323]

So much for John Law and the Mississippi scheme.

Well, not so much for Cantillon, who I think is as thoroughly worth reading as the central parts of *The Wealth of Nations* and Hume's essay, to which I shall be coming some time next week.

Now, in the second half of this lecture, I want to begin to talk to you about the systematic emergence of economic analysis at the hands of the French economists who, later on, after the title of one of Quesnay's books [1888], came to be called the physiocrats.

Now, we want to have a little background to this. You'll want to know something—a nodding acquaintance—with conditions in France in the late seventeenth and early eighteenth centuries. And in particular you first of all must realise the tremendous and agonizing poverty of the majority of the inhabitants, the subjects of *Le Roi Soleil*, the great King Louis XIV. Have any of you ever read *The Characters* of La Bruyère [1698]? One of the most beautiful examples of French prose in literature. And in one of these essays there is a striking passage dealing with the countryside. And he describes that in the countryside you can see feeble, weatherbeaten animals, apparently unconcerned with what is growing in the countryside, and one of the creatures looks up—and behold, it is a man! I certainly don't know any description of poverty in those days which is equal to this short paragraph of La Bruyère's. War had impoverished them, iniquitous taxation, the exemption from taxation of all sorts of privileged people. *Le Roi Soleil* fostered in various ways what from the cultural point of view was one of the high points in human history: painting, literature, poetry, drama, these all flourished—but not the people.

And the second point that you ought to have some knowledge of is the commercial policy of those days, which was under the direction of a man called Colbert. Now, looking around, I am sure that there are people in this audience who have had that very delicious way of doing sole—sole Colbert. Well, that mode of cooking is named after the great commercial Minister of Louis XIV. And in Adam Smith's *Wealth of Nations*, Cannan's edition, page 161, there is a short description of Colbert, which I think is better read then summarised:

> a man of probity, of great industry and knowledge of detail; of great experience and acuteness in the examination of public accounts, and of abilities, in short, every way fitted for introducing method and good order into the collection and expenditure of the public revenue. That Minister had unfortunately embraced all the prejudices of the mercantile system, in its nature and essence a system of restraint and regulation, and such as could scarce fail to be agreeable to a laborious and plodding man of business, who had been accustomed to regulate the different departments of public offices, and to establish the necessary checks and controuls for confining each to its proper sphere. The industry and commerce of a great country he endeavoured to regulate upon the same model as the departments of a public office; and instead of allowing every man to pursue his own interest his own way, upon the liberal plan of equality, liberty and justice, he bestowed upon certain branches of industry extraordinary privileges, while he laid others under as extraordinary restraints. [Smith, 1776, 2:161]

Now, you will not fail to observe the bias in that utterance of Adam Smith, but it explains something which the physiocrats were up against and which was the chief subject of the polemical part of Adam Smith's *Wealth of Nations*.

Now, in this background—the reign of Louis XIV—economic discussion of the state of society was not favoured. The celebrated Marshal Vauban, who lived from 1633 to 1707, seems to have been a humane and a generous man, as well as being a very great soldier. And he was distressed, his heart was wrung, by the spectacle of the poverty, and he wrote a book called *d'une Royal* [1710]—the royal tithe—in which he proposed a total reorganisation of the system of taxation, and submitted it to the King. This was not greeted with any satisfaction at all. Vauban fell into disfavour and shortly afterwards died, it is said, of a broken heart.

Much more important than Vauban, who is only important for master's degree specialists among you, is a man called Boisguilbert, who lived from 1646 to 1714. He wrote several books which are collected in the most easily accessible book—or at any rate I've got a copy of it which I bought a long time ago—called *Détail de la France* [1707]. If any of you see a copy of that, for goodness sake do not dispose of it without consulting someone expert in these matters; it is worth quite a lot of money nowadays. He was a judge, and he too, together with Vauban, thought that the country of France was in a bad state. And his various writings substantiate this, which make them very valuable for the economic history of France. But he also attacks Colbertism—the favouring of manufacturers to the neglect of agriculture, which was the occupation of the majority of the people. And it can be argued—Boisguilbert is not a man who figures very large in the literature—that there is some anticipation of Cantillon's position as regards the very important position in the economy of the demand of the landowners—some anticipation, therefore, of the physiocrats.

Well then, we come then to John Law and the Mississippi scheme. John Law was a Scotsman. He was born in 1671, and he had to leave Scotland because he was involved in a duel. And before he left he had published in English a very bright book called *Money and Trade Considered*, 1705. It contains very many acute remarks on value and scarcity, almost anticipating Marshall's revolution in some respects. He was essentially an inflationist. He wanted money to be issued on the value of land, which was almost bound to lead to inflation. And while he failed utterly to persuade his Scottish colleagues, he managed to insinuate himself into the confidence of the Regent of France, and together they launched the Mississippi company. And they engineered the finance associated with the launching thereof, whose collapse eclipsed in magnitude and repercussions the collapse of the South Sea Bubble launched at about the same time in this country. So although Louis XIV was dead, the collapse of this scheme tended to prolong the discredit of public discussion of economic matters.

There are minor writers—Melon [1739], Dutot [1738]—whose books are not, I think, very worth your attention unless you are going to write a thesis on them. Montesquieu, in his *L'esprit des lois* [1748], had, in one of the books, incidental remarks on economic questions, but on the whole you can say that until the middle of the 1750s and 1760s there was very, very little economics written in France which is worth your attention except Cantillon, and his reflections were only published in 1755.

But in the second half of the 1750s and the 1760s there was a terrific outburst of economic speculation, due to the activities of the physiocrats— Dr Quesnay and his friends. Now, I promised to warn you when you should watch out for a certain bias. I do not find the physiocrats as impressive as the Scottish philosophers who were writing at the same time. Indeed, I am tempted to go with David Hume who, writing to a friend, described them as "of all men the most chimerical."[1] But of course that was an exaggeration. There are important contributions by the physiocrats, but I just warn you that I do not enter into this disquisition with the same enthusiasm as I entered the description of Cantillon or with which I shall discuss the contributions of Hume and Adam Smith.

Well now, who were these chaps? I'll read you an extract of a funeral oration. This took place on the 20th of December 1774, and it took place in a room which was full of people dressed in mourning. At the end of the room was a large pedestal surmounted by a marble bust, and the whole assembly was turned towards this bust in an attitude of great sorrow and respect. And the master of the house then uttered his oration as follows:

> Gentlemen, we have lost our master, the veritable benefactor of humanity belongs to this earth only by the memory of his good deeds and the imperishable record of his achievements. Socrates has been said to have brought down morality from the skies. Our master has made it germinate upon earth. Celestial morality was a guide only for a few chosen souls. The doctrine of the net product procures subsistence for the children of men, secures them in its enjoyment from violence and fraud, lays down the principles of its distribution and assures its reproduction. O bust! O venerable bust that represents to us the features of our common master. It is before you, it is to the vow of universal fraternity which our conscience, enlightened by the teaching of the excellent man whom you portrayed for us bids us observe. O Master, look down from your heavenly heights. Smile still on our words and works and our tears, while my trembling hand offers on your tomb laurels which will never perish.

The bust was the bust of Quesnay, the leader of the physiocrats; the speaker was the Marquis Mirabeau, the father of the famous Mirabeau, his first convert and follower; and the audience were the numerous members of the school which they had succeeded in forming.

Well now, a word or two about Quesney, who is clearly the leading intellect—save if you include Turgot, whom I shall treat separately—the leading intellect of the physiocrats. He was born of humble, agricultural parents in 1694. He was a surgeon by profession who became later on a physician because of eye trouble. He attained very considerable eminence in his profession by writing *On the Circulation of Blood*[2]—note the title there. And he achieved the utmost eminence in his profession, however, by an exhibition of social rather than medical skill. By this time his eminence as a doctor had secured him entrance to fashionable circles at Versailles, which was the centre of the French monarchy as you all know. And Quesnay was at a party when one of the high ladies of the court was seized with an epileptic fit. Well, Quesnay was called in and he realised—which shows that he was a man of general intelligence—that the lady would wish to conceal the nature of her trouble from her companions, and he therefore banished everybody from the room until the fit was over. And this tact, and the treatment that he gave her, so commended him to this lady that she recommended him as personal assistant to no less a person than Madame de Pompadour, the mistress of the King himself.

Well, Quesnay was then fifty-give, and from then until his death he remained at Versailles, moving in the highest circle and directly under the powerful protection of Madame de Pompadour. Those of you who are interested in personalities and in pictures will perhaps have noticed that in the last two years the National Gallery has secured the most *splendid* portrait of Madame de Pompadour in middle age. So, if you want to look at the highest person to patronise the physiocrats, you can go to the appropriate room in the National Gallery.

Well now, the feature of Colbertism was that it fostered manufacture at the expense of agriculture. Quesnay, because of his origin and because of his fortune, had himself acquired a certain amount of land and had become extremely interested in agriculture and agricultural politics, and he was very interested in technical improvements. So it was not unnatural that sooner or later he should turn to wider problems of agricultural reforms. He wrote two articles on farmers and grains for Diderot's *Encyclopedia*.[3] And this led him on to economic analysis in general, and his famous economic table—which you all ought to know something about, and which I will explain next time—his famous economic table [Quesnay, 1758] which dealt, not with the circulation of blood this time, but with the circulation of wealth. No accident.

But for all his excellence, Quesnay might have been an isolated figure like Cantillon if it had not been for his followers. And I must just tell you— and with this I will conclude—the story of the way in which he got his followers. Mirabeau had been interested in economic problems and had got hold of a copy of Cantillon. And he made copies of Cantillon before he handed it back to the rightful owner, and he then wrote the book for which he was always called in public discussion, a book entitled *L'ami des hommes* [1883]—"the friend of man," and, some wag added, since he was always quarrelling, "and the enemy of his wife and children."

Well, Mirabeau got access to Quesnay and sent Quesnay his manuscript. And Quesney read it and wrote in the margin, "The child has drunk bad milk. The strength of his temperament is indeed promising but he does not understand how to think."[4] So the first time Mirabeau went to see Quesnay, it wasn't frightfully successful. Quesnay opened by saying that he, Mirabeau, had put the plough before the ox, and that Cantillon was an ass.[5] And Mirabeau was rather upset about this, for he admired Cantillon very much, and he didn't feel that he had completely put the plough before the ox. And so he went away. But then, fascinated by what he had seen of Quesnay, he returned. They had a second conversation in which Quesnay succeeded in making a convert of Mirabeau, and Mirabeau was exactly the sort of person whom Quesnay needed to popularise his ideas. Mirabeau was essentially a social person. He gathered round him a set of people whom he indoctrinated with Quesnay's ideas—Mercier de la Rivière, Vauban and so on and so forth. They formed a veritable school. They had their journal—the *Ephémérides du Citoyen*, they published books, they held periodical meetings at Mirabeau's house and they became immensely fashionable. Royalty took an interest in them. The King of Sweden came to visit them at Paris. Catherine the Great sent for Mercier de la Rivière—not a frightfully successful visit. The Margrave of Baden actually wrote a book on physiocratic doctrine, and, so it is said—I am really not sure that I believe this—the Emperor of Austria himself did a day's ploughing in Moravia to indicate his sympathy with their system. I don't expect that the Emperor of Austria did anything but just to put his hand to the plough while it was dragged along for, so to speak, halfway in a furrow. But all sorts of people became as enthusiastic as the founders. They suddenly felt that here was a new branch of knowledge and a branch which would make everybody happy and just.

Well now, I could expatiate a good deal more on the biographical details, but I shall begin my lecture tomorrow by discussing the doctrines of the physiocrats and, particularly, Quesnay.

NOTES

1. Letter from Hume to Morellet, 10 July 1769, reprinted in Hume (1955, pp. 214–16).

2. See the collection of Quesnay's works in Quesnay (1958).

3. See Quesnay (1958) and the excerpts from Quesnay's writings translated in Meek (1962).

4. Robbins is paraphrasing here the following statement by Quesnay, which was written down by Mirabeau in a letter to Rosseau: "The child has been suckled on bad milk; the force of his temperament often puts him right so far as results are concerned, but he understands nothing as to principles" (quoted in Meek, 1962, p. 17, italics deleted).

5. Mirabeau actually uses the word "fool"; see Meek (1962, p. 17).

Physiocrats—Turgot

YESTERDAY'S lecture was in two parts: first of all, some detailed examination of part 2 of Cantillon's *Essay* and a brief indication of the content of part 3. And that was the first half. And the second half was devoted to providing some sort of background to the rise of physiocracy in France, the poverty of the people under Louis XIV, the characteristics of Colbertism and Adam Smith's opinion on that policy, and then a word or two about Vauban and Boisguilbert, and thenceforward to John Law, his part in the Mississippi catastrophe and the influence it had in restraining sensible economic discussion, and then, finally, the outburst of discussion, whether sensible or not, under the physiocrats in the second half of the '50s and the '60s. And I gave you Mirabeau's funeral oration on Quesnay to evoke something of the atmosphere of enthusiasm and excitement prevailing among these people, and I concluded with a discussion of Quesnay's followers mustered by Mirabeau, who was the orator at the funeral ceremony which I described.

Now all that was, so to speak, background material. I want to devote most of this lecture to a very, very broad analysis of what the physiocrats were up to. I warned you yesterday that my enthusiasm for the physiocrats is not as great as some other people have managed to evoke, and if you want to read an *extremely* scholarly and well-informed work by someone who finds their work extremely exciting, you should read Professor Meek's *Economics of Physiocracy* [1962]. It is quite first-class. Professor Meek's death within the last twelve months or so is a great loss to the history of our subject.

But now to get on to the substance. First of all, what were the general attitudes of the physiocrats? First of all—not foremost, but first, I think, in origin, as witness the account I gave you of Quesnay—they were pro-agriculture and anti the fostering of manufacture and so on, à la Colbert.

Secondly, you can say that their attitude to Government in general can truly, in most respects, if not all, be described as laissez faire. In that respect I think that you should make a fairly sharp distinction between the attitude of the physiocrats and the attitude of the Scottish philosophers—Hume and Adam Smith—whose point of view was much more complicated. I just throw that out at this moment; I will deal with the point of view of Hume and Adam Smith next week and the week after.

And thirdly, you can say—and this I think distinguishes them from Hume at any rate, and in my judgement, although not in the judgement of some authorities, Adam Smith—that whereas the background of Hume and I think Adam Smith can, roughly speaking, be described as utilitarian—although not in the same quantitative sense as you find utilitarianism as preached by Bentham and James Mill, and to some extent by John Stuart Mill (only to some extent there)—the attitude of the physiocrats was not utilitarian in that broad sense. It definitely relied upon what I should regard—and, again, guard against my bias—a rather *simpliste* conception of natural law. A conversation is reported as having taken place between Mercier de la Rivière and Catherine the Great, who inquired of this distinguished physiocrat what she should do to make the State prosperous and happy. And he replied to her, "You simply obey the laws of nature." And when she pressed him to further elaboration, the conversation became extremely vague. That may be unfair, but reading the physiocratic literature, my feeling is that nearly all of them, and indeed Quesnay himself, felt that natural law was something which could be written on two tablets of stone. Well now, whatever your conception, whether you regard natural law as being incumbent or whether you regard it as being an *ignis fatuous*, it is not as simple as that. Indeed, the sophisticated interpretation of natural law is a very complicated matter indeed.

Now, what economic analysis did they invoke to support these general attitudes? Well, the first thing that you have to notice is the classification of members of society. This was based upon the idea that only agriculture, and later on there was added extractive industry, were productive. All other kinds of labour were sterile. They didn't deny that other kinds of labour were useful in various ways, but they attached tremendous importance—analytical importance—to their division between productive and unproductive, or sterile, labour. And the productive classes consisted of labourers on the one hand and the landowners on the other. The landowners were entitled to this effectively termed adjective *productive* in virtue of their original advances which made the land fertile. And consequently, while the labourers received wages which tended at any rate to subsistence level, the landowners were, in virtue of their original advances, the recipients of the net product. But before you run away with the idea that this is a simple case of the interest of Quesnay and some of his friends favouring the landowners, you should take note of the fact that the result of their analysis was that the landowners should bear *all* the taxation, whatever the size of their holding, and that all other taxation should be abolished, which was scarcely pro-landlord.

Well, on the basis of this classification, they erected a theory of distribution. The labours of the productive classes were conceived to be an annual flow, and according as this annual flow was divided between further advances to the productive classes and purchases from the unproductive classes, so society was held to be in a healthy or unhealthy condition. It was fundamentally important, according to the physiocrats, that the payments made to the sterile classes, who were provided for out of the net product of the productive classes—so defined—did not encroach on the advances

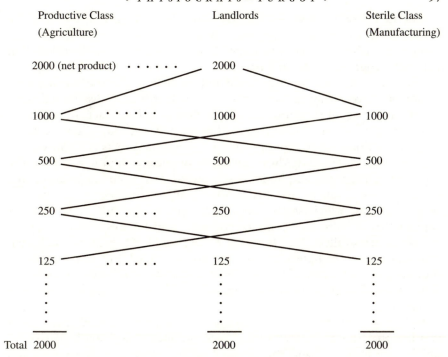

| Productive Class (Agriculture) | Landlords | Sterile Class (Manufacturing) |

Figure 1. Quesnay's Tableau.

made to the cultivators. If they did, the net product would be less, and society would be in decline.

Well now, this idea, this general concept of an annual flow of production and its distribution, whether healthy or unhealthy, was developed in the famous economic table, of which Mirabeau, prone to exaggeration as usual, said that the invention of the economic table could be compared to the invention of writing and money. Now, the economic table is a most mysterious business. If you want to study the economic table, the authentic version is reproduced in a quarto edition edited by Professor Meek and Dr. Kuczynski [Quesnay, 1972], various discoveries having been made with regard to the history of the economic table. And in Meek's *Economics of Physiocracy* [1962] you will find a very complicated and diligent analysis of what assumptions the economic table, all these various manifestations, depended upon.

But the general picture was as I have depicted on the board. You had three columns: the productive classes of labourers, the proprietors who received the net product, and the sterile class. And the proprietors spent so much on advances in the first process of the circulation: a thousand of the net product to the productive classes and a thousand to the unproductive classes, and then the unproductive classes spent 500 on the products of the productive classes, and they spent some of the proceeds on the products of the sterile classes, and so on and so forth. This is simply symbolic of the whole thing and is not to be taken as in any sense doing justice to the complications of Quesnay's thought. I simply put it on the board so that you can recognise the general nature.

Now, the original economic table and its main manifestations depicted a static state of affairs in which the net product was so distributed as to maintain, period after period, the annual flow of net product. In the *Philosophie rurale*, which Quesney and Mirebeau [Mirabeau, 1764] collaborated in producing, the economic table is developed so as to show declining states of society and advancing states of society. And it was from the economic table that the physiocrats deduced their recommendation that *all* taxes should fall on the net product. All intermediate taxes were to be swept away, which surely was a very, very over-simple idea, or so it appeared to Voltaire. Have any of you ever read Voltaire's little satire on the physiocrats called *The Man with Forty Écus* [1768]?[1] Here was a man who had a very small piece of land, but still it yielded him a very small net product. He was taxed, and he looked round and saw the sterile producers, at work producing other things, untaxed. And he thought that this was rather odd.

Well now, what does all this amount to? Well, first of all, you can say if you like that the division of society into productive and sterile classes, or unproductive classes, and the division of the product of agriculture and extraction on the one hand and manufactures on the other—being divided according to the economic table—is just semantic. And supposing you regard "productive" as being productive of food and minerals—well, only people with nothing better to do quarrel about words. And if you were to keep that in mind all the time, well, you would go on talking in that sense. But the fact is that the physiocrats meant more than this. Only the product of agriculture and extraction produced a surplus. All other kinds of labour, in equilibrium, only covered its cost of production. Only agricultural and extractive efforts produced, so to speak, new stuff. The rest, useful though it might be, simply worked up the new stuff without adding, in equilibrium, any new value.

But that, of course, according to our way of thinking, would be misleading. When I come to talk to you about Adam Smith, you will find that Adam Smith rejected the use of the term *productive* as applying only to agricultural labour, and he even had admitted that some of the physiocrats included extractive industry as well. He still retained the division between productive labour and unproductive labour, but his division was different, and although I'll dwell on this, let me mention it at the moment. The Smithian division, which persists in Marxian economics to this day, was between labour which left something behind it in the way of accumulation (capital producing) and that which did not. Unproductive labour—the labour of the King at the top and of ballet dancers at the bottom, to use

Adam Smith's very, very picturesque description of unproductive labour—in fact was very useful, but it didn't add to wealth in the sense of capital wealth. Now that, I think, has meaning. I don't myself prefer to use it in that way, but it certainly will bear much more analysis than the idea of the physiocrats that only agriculture and extraction added to the value of the annual product. So much for the terminology.

Now, a good mark for them. They did study the system as a whole. This is why they are to be classified among those who originated economics as a study of the economy taken as a system of relationships. Up to the end of the seventeenth century, even sophisticated analysis, like that of Petty and Locke, had been in bits. The physiocrats did conceive the economic table, misleading although its terminology may be, did conceive the whole of the system. Of course, they had been anticipated by Cantillon, but Cantillon's work had a limited circulation. And Cantillon's work of course was infinitely superior, but he can't figure large as an influence in the development of economics, whereas the physiocrats do figure large until they were superseded to a very large extent by the classical system. They did perceive that, staring at the system as a whole, you could try out hypotheses which would explain variations in the relationships of the system as a whole. They even attempted—Quesnay, occasionally—to give some sort of quantitative dimension to their speculations.

And thirdly, also a good mark, they conceived the system as a whole, as you can perceive from the economic table, as being not only connected at one point of time, but being connected through time. The emphasis of economic analysis was shifted by the physiocrats from the consideration of wealth as such. Whether it consisted in gold and silver, as some of the simple people might have thought, or whether it consisted in capital wealth, from their point of view the focus was the flow of wealth. And that, although it was not entirely new, was a contribution to economic analysis.

And now, what have we to say about the economic table? Now, this is a frightfully controversial subject. Mirabeau, as I have said, compared it to the invention of writing and money. Adam Smith, who was very friendly with Quesnay, and who at one time thought of dedicating the *Wealth of Nations* to Quesnay, thought that the economic table was founded on a mistake—this *factual* division, not merely a verbal division, of society into classes and the function of the classes. And in our own time there are still rival interpretations of the economic table, which has received far more attention in the last forty years than it received in the, oh, let's say, quarter of a century, or perhaps thirty or forty years after its initial promulgation.

Well, let me just try to sum up my own ideas on the subject, bearing in mind that these are controversial, and if you read the literature of the subject you will find views which are different. I don't really think that you can give Quesnay credit for having in that anticipated Walras and his system of interconnected economic relations. The economic table was certainly not a stable system. There was no general presumption in the analysis of the economic table that there were forces at work which would bring it into stability necessarily. It was certainly thought that if the payments to the sterile classes exceeded a certain figure, then the economy would get into difficulties, but there is no Walrasian connection between the relative prices and the disposition of resources and the relative prices of services and capital.

Secondly, what relation does it bear to the Keynesian system? Well, you can say if you like that it does consider a macroeconomic problem—the problem of expenditure and revenue. And occasionally there are thrown out hints of the inimical effects of hoarding, but there is no multiplier in the system, and I think it's very, very fanciful to regard it as an anticipation of Keynes.

Well then, coming to post-Keynesian speculation, what about dynamic analysis, in the sense in which you are taught by the great experts here? You can say that the physiocrats did have a conception of change, in the sense that, in the *Philosophie rurale*, the tables which show a declining society and the tables which show a more prosperous society have a dynamic aspect. But they are not dynamics proper. They are really, as it were, comparative statics, and again there is no intimate connection between prices either of ultimate goods or of factor services.

I think the best construction that can be put on the economic table is the construction which has been put by some American writers: that you can rewrite the economic table as a Leontief system. And, indeed, if you neglect the titles, so to speak, in the first row and you just look at the relationship of the figures, you can make it out to be a sort of primitive Leontief system. This has been worked at great length by various American writers. But of course the Leontief system of the twentieth century has no use for the physiocratic distinction between productive and unproductive labour, and therefore the Leontief up-to-date tables are talking about the distribution of a net product which is quite different from the distribution which is talked about by Quesnay and his friends.

As for the suggestion which has been made by some writers that they were anticipators of underconsumption theories—whatever that means— they certainly weren't against the maintenance of the net product, and they certainly weren't against the increase of the net product. They certainly weren't against investment in agriculture which would increase the net product. They attached enormous importance to agricultural improvement, but occasionally they threw out hints that they would be against financial hoarding, and they were against—and this distinguishes them from Malthus and his followers—they were against luxurious expenditure if it encroached on the net product. So I don't really think that one can take them frightfully seriously as anticipators of either the Malthusian version of underconsumption, which really meant overinvestment, or more modern versions which involve in some way or other some process which in a very wide sense can be regarded as Robertsonian hoarding.

Now, I want for the next quarter of an hour to talk to you about a man connected with the physiocrats, but who in my judgement—and this is a judgement of value—produced speculations which are far more congenial to the modern outlook than the physiocratic speculations. All honour to Quesnay and his enthusiastic followers, but if you read Turgot's *Reflections on the Formation and the Distribution of Wealth* [1770]—which is certainly available, translated by Professor Meek with a very scholarly introduction— you feel, save where he lapses into physiocratic distinctions, that he is talking much more our language than the physiocrats did, and he is, to my way of thinking, much easier to read. I find Quesnay almost intolerably difficult. You need a towel round your head to read Quesnay, and the watered-down editions of Quesnay, well, they don't give you the real stuff. You've got to tackle the economic table at some time or other.

Well, Turgot was friendly with them, and his *Reflections on the Formation and the Distribution of Wealth* was first published by Dupont de Nemours in the journal of the physiocrats, the *Ephemerides du Citoyen*, in '69 to '70 of the eighteenth century. And it purports to be notes for conversations on the economic system with two learned young Chinese who were purported to have visited France in those years.

Well, let me run very rapidly through the various parts of this book, which I recommend the serious-minded among you to read. You can read it, I would imagine, in about an hour and a quarter. Well, the first part of it is tinged with physiocracy in various aspects. It talks about land and the inequality of its distribution, the importance of the husbandman, and on page 123 of Meek's translation you get in chapter 8 of this alleged exposition to Ko and Yang a "Primary division of society into two classes: first, the *productive* class, or the Cultivators; and, second, the *stipendiary* class, or the Artisans." And he then goes on to discuss the inequalities, the relations between the two classes, and he distinguishes the cultivator and the proprietor and the division of product between the cultivator and the proprietor. He talks about the net product in physiocratic terms at this stage. And then on page 127 he begins to see similarities between the cultivators and the artisans, and then he dwells on their differences.

But the importance of his book comes a little later on, when he has delivered himself of these physiocratic sentiments, and it comes on page 134 of the Meek translation, in which he deals with "capitals in general, and the revenue of money." "There is another way of being wealthy," he says, "without working and without possessing land of which I have not yet spoken. It is necessary to explain its origin and its relation with the rest of the system of the distribution of wealth in society, of which I have just sketched the outlines" [Turgot, 1770, pp. 134–35]. And then he diverges, because he wants to do full justice to the capital question, into monetary theory, and he discusses "the use of gold and silver in commerce" [ibid., p. 135]. He discusses the "Birth of Commerce" and the "Principle of the valuation of . . . things" [ibid.]. And then on page 137, having dealt with value, there is an amazingly up-to-date paragraph in which he says: "Each commodity can serve as a scale or common measure with which to compare the value of all others."

And he goes on to discuss what would be an ideal currency and then points out on page 138 that "Every commodity does not present an equally convenient scale of values. Preference was bound to be given in practice to those which are not susceptible to any great difference in quality and thus have a value which is in the main relative to their number or quantity." He expatiates on this at length. And he then comes back to gold and silver and their variations, all of which is reasonably well known. But on page 145, having got his reflections on money, which are truly originally stated, out of his system, he comes back to money in the economic system and its functions, and it "facilitate[s] the separation of different labours as between the different Members of Society."

And he then goes on to talk about "the reserve of annual produce, accumulated to form capitals" [ibid., p. 145], and he then proceeds to discuss "Movable wealth [as] an indispensable prerequisite for all kinds of remunerative work." This is on page 146, in answer to question number 51. And question number 52 discusses the "Necessity of advances in cultivation" before the net product can be achieved. And he discusses the various kinds of agricultural capital—livestock, slavery—and then proceeds to the "Evaluation of land in accordance with the proportion which the revenue bears to the amount of movable wealth"—the proportion which is "called the number of years purchase of the land [ibid., p. 149]. But then he goes on to say—this is on page 150—that "Every capital in the form of money, or every sum of values of whatever kind, is the equivalent of a piece of land producing a revenue equal to a particular fraction of this sum."

And so the first employment of capital may be the purchase of a landed estate. But another employment of capital, on page 151, is the advances necessary in manufacturing and industrial enterprises. And he then expatiates on the nature of these advances: "he who set men to work, provided the materials himself and paid from day to day the wages of the Workman." And he subdivides at this stage, which is a queer business, having regard to what he had said under physiocratic influence at the beginning. On page 153, he subdivides "the industrial stipendiary Class"—he doesn't call them the sterile class, but he calls them the stipendary class as distinct from cultivators—he subdivides them into "capitalist entrepreneurs and ordinary Workmen." And so he proceeds with the "Subdivision of the Class of Cultivators" [ibid., p. 155]. All these have in common "that they buy in order to resell; and that their traffic depends upon advances which have to be returned with a profit, in order to be newly invested in the enterprise" [ibid., p. 157].

And he then returns at the end to objections to the Scholastic contribution—the condemnation of usury—and he attacks the interpretation of interest which makes it depend upon the quantity of money in circulation.

The quarter of an hour that I have devoted to talking about Turgot is odious in its superficiality and in the injustice that it does to a truly great man. But you can read the *Reflections* for yourself, and you can read what is written about Turgot. To keep up with the programme, I intend next week to start the lecture on David Hume, about whom I shan't give you biographical details because, whatever intellectual biographies you are ignorant of, *none* of you have any excuse for being ignorant of the biography of David Hume, the greatest philosophical mind in the English language.

Note

1. The original French title is *L'homme aux quarante écus*.

Locke and Hume on Property—Hume on Money

I WANT now to begin a series of lectures which go at greater length than I have been able to go so far into the development, from the point which I reached last week, of what can be called classical economics. I have said inadequate words about the development of systematic economics in France at the hands of the physiocrats, and even less satisfactorily I have drawn your attention to the work of Turgot, who, in my judgement, was in all sorts of ways a very superior type. I should like to go on, and I should even like to go on expatiating at considerable length, on the physiocrats, but I now come to the Scottish philosophers.

I said last time that I would not give you any biographical details of David Hume, who is the man I'm going to talk about today, because I should expect you all, being highly educated people, to know, roughly speaking, the facts of his life. I was challenged as I came out from the lecture room by a very intensive question: Where should we find out these facts? And I said I was a little surprised about this very good-natured question, and I said, "Well, of course the best biography is by Mossner" [1954]. And I then reflected that, after all, Mossner's is a rather long book, and for those of you who are under the shadow of examinations and so on, Mossner is rather a tall order to take on. Then I thought, well, *why on earth* didn't I say before and recommend to all of them the very short autobiography—which occupies nine pages, I think, in the Green and Grose edition of Hume's papers—the very short autobiography which Hume wrote on the eve if his death, "My own Life" [1776]. His first sentence is: "It is difficult for a man to speak long of himself without vanity; therefore, I shall be short" [ibid., p. 1]. And he is short; it does occupy, actually, eight of these pages. So there is no excuse for you at all to remain ignorant of Hume.

Now, to deal with Hume I think the appropriate order—since Hume himself didn't elaborate a system, although there was a system in his mind—the appropriate order is to deal first with his reflections on property and then to proceed to the more analytical parts of those essays which deal with economics. And here, with his thoughts on property, we have to go back to Locke, whose remarks on that subject I drew your attention to but said I would postpone until I came to deal with Hume. Well, again I'm using the fourth volume of the 1794 edition of the *Works* of Locke, but it is a different part of the volume. The part to which I want to draw your attention is his second essay on Civil Government [1690],[1] which those of you who have paid any attention to political science should be acquainted with—one of the great seminal works of political philsophy and political science, the great apologia for the principles of the great and glorious and bloodless revolution of 1688.

The first essay deals with a bore called Filmer, who quoted all sorts of Scripture against the Whiggish outlook which Locke represented, and is not worth your attention unless you are a political science specialist. But the second essay on Government is an important essay, but I'm not urging you to read it all. I'm simply going to give you a summary—a very short summary—of his views on property. It is chapter 5 of the second essay on Government. And how can I compress it? If I keep my book open I shall give you too many quotations. Following my unswerving rule of refreshing my memory on things that I am going to talk about, I read it myself in half an hour—in less than half an hour, because I was interrupted for family reasons halfway through.

The substance of his essay at first appears to be a justification of the institution of property in terms of labour. God gave the earth to all mankind, he says in the first paragraph [ibid., p. 353]. How then shall we justify people owning little bits of it? And he then develops what you feel nearly towards the end is a labour theory of property. The Red Indian who kills a deer is surely entitled to the deer, which in the America of his day was nobody's property; it was just roaming about common land. The man who gathers the fruits of the earth—acorns, for instance (why he should gather acorns, I am not quite sure, but that is Locke's example)—he's entitled to keep them. But neither in the case of the deer, nor in the case of the acorns, should he keep it just to be spoilt. The deterioration of the acorns, if there was an excessive supply—and so far as I was concerned the number of acorns that I would want to eat would be very small—the deterioration of the acorns would be socially undesirable; the spoiling of the flesh of the venison would be undesirable. And then what about land? In the beginning there's so much land that you need only take account of the labour element in commodities, but he who clears land—you must remember that this is all against the background of the late seventeenth century when there was land for the asking throughout the North American continent—he who clears the land of its trees and all that sort of thing is surely entitled to keep it [ibid., p. 356].

So up to this point you have a labour theory of property. And he goes out of his way to say that, even in more advanced societies, nine-tenths of the majority of commodities is due to the labour which has been expended on raw materials [ibid., p. 361]. But then, as you would think, if you don't know it already, and as I think every time I read it, he perversely draws attention to the fact that gold and silver do not deteriorate by keeping [ibid., p. 365]. And he then goes on to argue that since by common agreement—he was a social contract theorist, the greatest writer in the English language on the social contract—he says by common agreement and contract people have agreed to the use of money [ibid., pp. 365–67]. There is therefore no objection to the accumulation of money and using money to buy land. Well, that doesn't make particularly convincing sense to me, but it's certainly an apologia which was bandied about in the political discussion of the eighteenth century, and you ought to know about it.

Now Hume. Hume develops his ideas on property in his essay *Concerning the Principles of Morals* [1751], which he himself thought was his best-written book. Of course, his most famous book is the *Treatise on Human Nature* [1739–40]; it is *that* which justified my rather daring remark last time that he was the best philosophical mind contributing to the English language. He himself was very disappointed with the reception of the *Treatise*. He wrote more popular essays: the essay *Concerning Human Understanding* [1748], and then another essay—a long essay—which occupies most of this book, *Concerning the Principles of Morals*.

And in the essay on the *Principles of Morals*, in section 3, he deals with justice. Now, his use of the term *justice* mustn't confuse you here. When he talks about justice, he is not talking about criminal justice. You mustn't believe that because he talks about justice in relating to property and contract and all that, that he is forgetting that part of justice which, let us say, applies to persecution and murder and to offences against the person. But he deals with justice and his beginning is "That justice is useful to society, and consequently that *part* of its merit . . . must arise from that consideration" [Hume, 1751, p. 179]. And he then says that he's going to argue

> That public utility is the *sole* origin of justice [in this sense], and that reflections on the beneficial consequences of this virtue are the *sole* foundation of its merit; this proposition, being more curious and important, will better deserve our examination and enquiry. [ibid.]

Have any of you read the *Enquiry Concerning the Principles of Morals?* Well then, I won't say that you are going to have a treat from me, but insofar as I read you passages you *will* have an intellectual treat.

He develops his argument by a series of models. He doesn't call them models in the pretentious way in which we envelope, very often, pure banalities in this jargon, but his first model is a model which excludes scarcity:

> Let us suppose, that nature has bestowed on the human race such profuse *abundance* of all *external* conveniences, that, without any uncertainty in the event, without any care or industry on our part, every individual finds himself fully provided with whatever his most voracious appetites can want, or luxurious imagination wish or desire. His natural beauty, we shall suppose, surpasses all acquired ornaments:

—male and female—

> The perpetual clemency of the seasons renders useless all cloaths or covering: The raw herbage affords him the most delicious fare; the clear fountain, the richest beverage. No laborious occupation required: No tillage: No naviga-

tion. Music, poetry, and contemplation form his sole business: Conversation, mirth, and friendship his sole amusement. [ibid., 179–80]

Well, he goes on to say,

> It seems evident, that, in such a happy state, every other social virtue would flourish, and receive tenfold encrease; but the cautious, jealous virtue of justice [relating to property] would never once have been dreamed of. For what purpose make a partition of goods, where every one has already more than enough? Why give rise to property, where there cannot possibly be any injury? Why call this object *mine*, when, upon the seizing of it by another, I need but stretch out my hand to possess myself of what is equally valuable? Justice, in that case, being totally USELESS, would be an idle ceremonial. [ibid., p. 180]

And he goes on to argue that, of course, there *are* among the amenities with which human life is lived on this planet, cases where there is no scarcity of things which are very useful: air, for instance, he quotes, and water—not in the Sahara Desert but in many places—"are not challenged as the property of individuals; nor can any man commit injustice by the most lavish use and enjoyment of these blessings" [ibid.]. He goes on to mention that water is subject to exceptions. Model number 1.

Model number 2. Again, forgive me for reading. Adam Smith said of the professors at Oxford, who had long ago abandoned "the pretence of teaching" [Smith, 1776, 2:251], that they sometimes saved their self-respect by reading aloud boring books [ibid., 2:253]. Well now, I hope I don't read aloud to you boring books. I only read aloud to you, rather than depend on my own improvisation, because I think that the passages are more vivid than anything I can make them. Now,

> suppose, that, though the necessities of the human race continue the same as at present,

—that is to say, we need food and clothing and housing and all that sort of thing—

> yet the mind is so enlarged, and so replete with friendship and generosity, that every man has the uttermost tenderness for every man, and feels no more concern for his own interest than for that of his fellows: It seems evident, that the USE of justice [in relation to property] would, in this case, be suspended by such an extensive benevolence, nor would the divisions and barriers of property and obligation have ever been thought of. Why should I bind another, by a deed or promise, to do me any good office, when I know that he is already prompted, by the strongest inclination, to seek my happiness, and would, of himself, perform the desired service; except the hurt, he thereby receives, be greater than the benefit accruing to me? in which case, he knows, that, from my innate humanity and friendship, I should be the first to oppose myself to his imprudent generosity. [Hume, 1751, pp. 180–81]

Beautifully subtle, isn't it?

> Why raise land-marks between my neighbour's field and mine, when my heart
> has made no division between our interests; but shares all his joys and sorrows
> with the same force and vivacity as if originally my own? [ibid., p. 181]

Well, he goes on to make observations about this.

> In the present disposition of the human heart, it would, perhaps, be difficult
> to find compleat instances of such enlarged affections. [ibid.]

Then he goes on to say—and I am paraphrasing here—that the case of families approaches it. He obviously had a happy family life himself. And he says:

> the stronger the mutual benevolence is among the individuals, the nearer it
> approaches; till all distinction of property be, in a great measure, lost and con-
> founded among them. [ibid.]

And again, although he hadn't married himself, he says, with a benevolent outlook on the very varied frontier of human life in that connection:

> Between married persons, the cement of friendship is by the laws

—you see, he interposes a little qualification—

> supposed so strong as to abolish all division of possession: and has often, in
> reality, the force ascribed to it. [ibid.]

He doesn't give either the family or marriage completely full marks, but he said what, after all, is certainly common observation, that in families, except in extremely eccentric cases, there are large stretches of life where things are enjoyed in common. And in happy marriages at any rate there are no fundamental disputes about possessions, although it needed—lest you think that I am not up to date in history—it needed not Hume's humanity, but the Married Women's Property Act, which was also the product of the meditations of an economist, John Stuart Mill, to bring that state of affairs more readily prevalent. Model number 2 ended.

Model number 3 is the reverse of these: "Carrying every thing," he says [ibid., pp. 181–82], "to the opposite extreme, . . . what would be the effect of these new situations"?

> Suppose a society to fall into such want of all common necessaries, that the
> utmost frugality and industry cannot preserve the greater number from perish-
> ing, and the whole from extreme misery: It will readily, I believe, be admitted,
> that the strict laws of justice are suspended, in such a pressing emergence, and
> give place to the stronger motives of necessity and self-preservation. . . . [I]f a
> city besieged were perishing with hunger, can we imagine, that men will see
> any means of preservation before them, and lose their lives, from a scrupulous
> regard to what, in other situations, would be the rules of equity and justice?
> [ibid., p. 182]

And I am skipping a bit.

> The public, even in less urgent necessities, opens granaries, without the consent of proprietors; as justly supposing, that authority of magistracy may, consistent with equity, extend so far: But were any number of men to assemble, without the tye of laws or civil jurisdiction; would an equal partition of bread in a famine, though effected by power and even violence, be regarded as criminal or injurious? [ibid.]

End of model number 3.

He then goes on to say—I'll just read a few paragraphs:

> Thus, the rules of equity or justice depend entirely on the particular state and condition, in which men are placed, and owe their origin and existence to that UTILITY, which results to the public from their strict and regular observance. Reverse, in any considerable circumstance, the condition of men: Produce extreme abundance or extreme necessity: Implant in the human breast perfect moderation and humanity, or perfect rapaciousness and malice: By rendering justice totally *useless*, you thereby totally destroy its essence. [ibid., p. 183]

But, and here is the case he's arguing,

> The common situation of society is a medium amidst all these extremes. We are naturally partial to ourselves, and to our friends; but are capable of learning the advantage resulting from a more equitable conduct. Few enjoyments are given us from the open and liberal hand of nature; but by art, labour, and industry, we can extract them in great abundance. Hence the ideas of property become necessary in all civil society: Hence justice derives its usefulness to the public: And hence alone arises its merit and moral obligation. [ibid.]

And then he goes on [Hume, 1751, pp. 188–89] to argue at great length that property will be, in the majority of cases, more carefully looked after if the owners of property and the persons or small groups have a direct interest in its preservation, and that if there is no direct interest in its preservation, then, even though there may be no violation of law, there may tend to be a more wasteful use of it.

Then he goes on [Hume, 1751, pp. 189ff.] to say—and I recommend all this to your further perusal; I mustn't linger on this—he goes on to argue, as against those who suggest that there is, so to speak, a natural instinct of property and the laws relating to property (he is against the idea of natural laws in that sense), "Look round at society. Look at the ways in which the law of property differs in different societies." You would need a hundred—I do not know that he uses this particular phrase—different instincts to explain the hundred different variations in the law relating to property, if you rely, as many philosophers of that day did, upon some original natural instinct in that respect. And he dwells upon the fact that the law relating to property is subject to change by evolution, by consideration of changes in the conception of public utility, all of which he argues in beautiful prose and at much greater length than it would take me if I were to appropriate the remaining twenty minutes devoted to this lecture.

Now, you'll find Hume's contribution, not to the background of political economy, which is what I have been talking about now, but to analytical economics, in the *Essays*, which he wrote in middle age. The *Treatise*, as you know, was written at a preternaturally early age. If ever there was a bright young man, it was Hume. And I quote again from this edition, which I am sorry to say is out of print—the *Essays Moral, Political and Literary*, edited by Green and Grose [1907], and if I refer to pages it will be the pages in volume 1. There is, however, I think, in print a collection of Hume's economic essays, not the things from the considerations on *The Principles of Morals* that I've been talking about so far, but the three essays on money, interest and the balance of payments, and other essays on the populousness of ancient nations and public credit and all that sort of thing—an American edition edited by a man called Rotwein [Hume, 1955].[2] One must be grateful to him for making these things readily available. And he has a long essay on Hume's psychological approach and so on and so forth, which only those of you who have a great deal of time to spare need read. What you *must* read are the essays on money, on interest and on the balance of payments, because these set the tone, and in some ways are superior to most propositions of Adam Smith and most of the transitory comments of nineteenth-century classical economists, with the exception always of the never-to-be-forgotten Thornton, whose *Paper Credit* [1802] was born out of due season, so to speak.

Now, plunging in straightaway, I must give you brief notes on these things, introducing you to his main propositions. He starts the essay on money by saying that: "Money is not, properly speaking, one of the subjects of commerce; but only the instrument which men have agreed upon to facilitate the exchange of one commodity for another. It is none of the wheels of trade: It is the *oil* which renders the motion of the wheels more smooth and easy." [Hume, 1907, 1:309, emphasis added by Robbins]. And he then advances the proposition, which is a static proposition, I warn you, "If we consider any one kingdom by itself, it is evident, that the greater or less plenty of money is of no consequence; since the prices of commodities are always proportioned to the plenty of money" [ibid.].

Now, don't think that he was a crude monetarist because he opens the argument in that way. And I pass over the fact that in a paragraph quite near the beginning of the essay on money he expresses an awareness of the complications introduced by banking credit into one's conception of the functions of the different kinds of money. That comes in the essay on the balance of payments.

And so I skip his general and historical observations there, and following up his statical observation that the quantity of money is in equilibrium (I am using twentieth-century terminology—a matter of indifference), he says:

It was a shrewd observation of ANCHARSIS, the SCYTHIAN, who had never seen money in his own country, that gold and silver seemed to him of no use to the GREEKS, but to assist them in numeration and arithmetic. It is indeed evident,

—says Hume—

that money is nothing but the representation of labour and commodities, and serves only as a method of rating or estimating them. Where coin is in greater plenty; as a greater quantity of it is required to represent the same quantity of goods; it can have no effect, either good or bad, taking a nation within itself; any more

—and write this down if you take notes—

than it would make an alteration of a merchant's books, if, instead of the ARA-BIAN method of notation, which requires few characters, he should make use of the ROMAN, which requires a great many. Nay, the greater quantity of money, like the ROMAN characters, is rather inconvenient, and requires greater trouble both to keep and transport it. [ibid., 1:312–13]

Those of you who feel inclined to use monetarism as a dirty word, a term of reproach and so on and so forth, should go on to the next sentence, page 313 of the Green and Grose edition [1907], volume 1:

notwithstanding this conclusion, which must be allowed just, it is certain, that, since the discovery of the mines in AMERICA, industry has encreased in all the nations of EUROPE, except in the possessors of those mines; and this may be justly ascribed, amongst other reasons, to the encrease of gold and silver. Accordingly we find, that, in every kingdom, into which money begins to flow in greater abundance than formerly, every thing takes a new face: labour and industry gain life; the merchant becomes more enterprising, the manufacturer more diligent and skilful, and even the farmer follows his plough with greater alacrity and attention. This is not easily to be accounted for. [ibid., 1:313]

So you see, poor Hume was not a simple-minded monetarist, if such a person exists.

And then comes this very illuminating paragraph:

To account, then, for this phenomenon, we must consider, that though the high price of commodities be a necessary consequence of the encrease of gold and silver, yet it follows not immediately upon that encrease;

—whether Hume had read Cantillon in manuscript is very, very doubtful, but he had hit on the same point that Cantillon had hit on—"but some time"—I'm going on reading Hume—

is required before the money circulates through the whole state, and makes its effect be felt on all ranks of people. At first, no alteration is perceived; by degrees the price rises, first of one commodity, then of another; till the whole at last reaches a just proportion with the new quantity of specie. [ibid.]

Remember, he's not talking about paper at all. He reserved that for another essay.

In my opinion, it is only in this interval or intermediate situation, between the acquisition of money and rise of prices, that the encreasing quantity of gold and silver is favourable to industry. When any quantity of money is imported into a nation, it is not at first dispersed into many hands; but is confined to the coffers of a few persons, who immediately seek to employ it to advantage. Here are a set of manufacturers or merchants . . . who have received returns of gold and silver for goods which they sent to CADIZ. They are thereby enabled to employ more workmen than formerly,

—he wasn't even assuming, as is sometimes said of the classical economists, perpetual ultra-full employment—

who never dream of demanding higher wages, but are glad of employment from such good paymasters. If workmen become scarce, the manufacturer gives higher wages, but at first requires an encrease of labour; and this is willingly submitted to by the artisan,

—remember, he was writing for the eighteenth century—

who can now eat and drink better, to compensate his additional toil and fatigue. He carries his money to market, where he finds everything at the same price as formerly, but returns with greater quantity and of better kinds, for the use of his family. The farmer and gardener, finding, that all their commodities are taken off, apply themselves with alacrity to the raising more; and at the same time can afford to take better and more cloths from their tradesmen, whose price is the same as formerly, and their industry is only whetted by so much new gain. [ibid., 1:313–14]

From the whole of this reasoning

—I've been skipping a good deal—

we may conclude, that it is of no manner of consequence, with regard to the domestic happiness of a state, whether money be in a greater or less quantity. The good policy of the magistrate consists only in keeping it, if possible, still encreasing . . .

—he is only meaning gold and silver, and Adam Smith thought that he was a little bit on the side of the mercantile system in this respect—

by that means he keeps alive a spirit of industry. [ibid., 1:315]

Then he goes on to say that

A nation, whose money decreases, is actually, at that time, weaker and more miserable than another nation. [ibid.]

And he explains the process.

And then the rest of the essay goes on to discuss the introduction of money into primitive societies, and the increase of the demand for money as the utility of the use of money is recognised by wide stretches of the population who at first had not realised these benefits. And so he thinks that in fact prices have not risen commensurately with the spread of the money economy, which accompanied the discoveries of the West Indies and North America by Christopher Columbus and which caused no inconsiderable inflation of prices in different western countries. But he thinks that prices have not risen—he may or may not be correct here—in proportion to the increase of money because the demand for money has increased also, and money-raising habits have spread to wider and wider sections of the population.

Now, I won't start to try to teach you what he says about interest, although it's much shorter. The balance of payments will take rather longer, but I'll stop here. I hope reading these copious extracts aloud will not deter you, harassed undergraduates under the shadow of the final examinations, equally with advanced people who are taking an M.Sc. or any of you who are taking doctorates, from reading these three essays of Hume. If you have grasped the substance of those three essays, you have grasped the substance of a great deal of even nineteenth-century classical economics.

NOTES

1. Locke, *Two Treatises of Government*, in *The Works of John Locke* (9th ed., 1794), pp. 207–485. First essay, "Of Government," pp. 212–337; second essay, "Of Civil Government," pp. 338–485.

2. "Of Money" (pp. 33–46), "Of Interest" (pp. 47–59), and "Of the Balance of Trade" (pp. 60–77), in Hume (1955).

Hume on Interest and Trade—Precursors of Adam Smith

LET US get on with Hume. Such is the interest of Hume's arguments that I lost a little time yesterday. I won't recapitulate what he said about money, but I will proceed straightaway to what he said about interest, and that can be, as a matter of fact, summarised much more quickly.

Although he doesn't mention the monetary interpretation of John Locke's theory of interest, he does attack, root and branch, the view which some people have attributed to John Locke: that the rate of interest is affected by the quantity of money—a purely monetary theory of interest. Now, all of you who have studied the modern controversy on the subject know that some people have been betrayed into very false indignation with Keynes' *General Theory* because they interpreted him as propounding an entirely monetary theory of interest. He has himself to thank for it a little bit because again and again he talks about liquidity preference on the one side and the quantity of money on the other. The catch is, in Keynes, that he translates the quantity of money always into wage units, so eliminating all influences on prices and so on. And whether the view as thus qualified is right or wrong is for another set of lectures. It's an intricate matter.

But coming back to Hume, he attacks the crude view that the quantity of money, not reduced to wage units, affects the rate of interest. He said:

> Were all the gold in England annihilated at once, and one and twenty shillings substituted in the place of every guinea, would money be more plentiful or interest lower? No surely: We should only use silver instead of gold. Were gold rendered as common as silver, and silver as common as copper; would money be more plentiful or interest lower? We may assuredly give the same answer. Our shillings would then be yellow, and our halfpence white; and we should have no guineas. No other difference would ever be observed; no alteration on commerce, manufactures, navigation or interest. . . .
>
> Now, what is so visible in these greater variations of scarcity or abundance in the precious metals, must hold in all inferior changes. If the multiplying of gold and silver fifteen times makes no difference, much less can the doubling or tripling them. All augmentation has no other effect than to heighten the price of labour and commodities. [Hume, 1907, 1:321]

What he is actually saying is what one would say nowadays to a crude monetary theory of interest: that an upward change in the quantity of money affects both the prices of income and capital goods, and interest is essentially a ratio between income and capital goods, and in statical conditions would presumably be unaffected. Note I say "in statical conditions"—there is much more complication as soon as we come to changing conditions.

And then he goes on—he dwells a little on the fictitious value of money, and so on and so forth—but he goes on to propound his own theory of interest, which is that "High interest arises from *three* circumstances" [ibid., 1:322, emphasis in original], and low interest from the reverse. The three circumstances are: "A great demand for borrowing [consumption loans]; little riches to supply that demand; and great profits arising from commerce: And these circumstances are a clear proof of the small advance of commerce and industry, not of the scarcity of gold and silver" [ibid.]. And he goes on to develop the argument: "suppose, that, by miracle, every man in GREAT BRITAIN should have five pounds slipt into his pocket in one night; this would much more than double the whole money that is at present in the kingdom; yet there would not next day, nor for some time, be any more lenders, nor any variation in the interest" [ibid., 1:323–24]. And so on.

Well, I think that's all that I need say about Hume's theory of interest, although it is "must" reading for all of you. I would only say that, in my judgement, much as I admire Hume, I am disappointed in this essay—that, in contradistinction to the essay on money and to the essay on the balance of payments which I am just going forward to, he didn't discuss the effect of the impact of change, which quite clearly is one of the factors that you have to take into account in interpreting the structure of interest rates in contemporary conditions. And in a way, the beautiful argument of Hume's essay on interest deflected the attention of the nineteenth-century classical economists in such a way as to concentrate their attention on the *real* factors affecting the rate of interest—as we should put it, the marginal efficiency of investment and the schedule of time preference (this is all in Fisher's splendid book on the theory of interest)—and led many of the classical economists—not quite all—to ignore too much the monetary complications. And in a way, even with the qualification which I have introduced into crude versions of Keynes, I think you can regard the emphasis that Keynes lays on these factors, thus interpreted, as being, in a way, a reaction from some of the nineteenth-century crude statements which hoped to show that the rate of interest was determined, in changing conditions, only by real factors. But that's by the way.

Essay 3,[1] *Of the Balance of Trade*, is in a way the most entertaining and the most ingenious of the essays. He starts by referring to the state of mind of people who "prohibit the exportation of commodities" and

> preserve among themselves whatever they think valuable and useful. They do not consider, that, in this prohibition, they act directly contrary to their intention; and that the more [that] is exported of any commodity, the more will be raised at home, of which they themselves will always have the first offer. [ibid., 1:330–31]

And he goes on to "the same jealous fear with regard to [the export of] money," which has "prevailed among several nations" [ibid., 1:331]—the mercantile system, as Adam Smith called it, and as I lectured on it three weeks ago.

Then he passes on—and I can pass over this very quickly: "all calculations concerning the balance of trade are founded on very uncertain facts and suppositions" [ibid.]. And he makes fun of a man called Joshua Gee, who wrote a book on the state of the nation in which—Hume is satirical here—he

> plainly demonstrated, by a detail of particulars, that the balance was against them for so considerable a sum as must leave them without a single shilling in five or six years. But luckily, twenty years have since elapsed, with an expensive foreign war; yet is it commonly supposed, that money is still more plentiful among us than in any former period. [ibid., 1:332]

"In short," he says,

> this apprehension of the wrong balance of trade, appears of such a nature, that it discovers itself, wherever one is out of humour with the ministry, or is in low spirits; and as it can never be refuted by a particular detail of all the exports, which counterbalance the imports, it may here be proper to form a general argument, that they may prove the impossibility of this event. [ibid.]

Well now, he goes on to prove the impossibility of this effect—a worrying state of the balance of payments—for conditions under which all payments inside and out are payments in gold and silver. He is leaving paper credit out and takes account of it later on.

But his specie flow theory of the self-righting nature of the balance of payments is highly ingenious and is worthwhile bearing in one's mind when one is thinking about these things. And he says, "Suppose four-fifths of all the money in GREAT BRITAIN to be annihilated in one night, and the nation reduced to the same condition, with regard to specie, as in the reigns of the HARRYS and the EDWARDS" [ibid., 1:333]. What nation could possibly dispute with us on the assumption that, if the prices of goods and services have been reduced by that subtraction, our exports would flourish, our imports would diminish and there would be a flow back of money until we were in, roughly speaking, the same relation with other parts of the world as we were before.

Or "Again,"—he is very pleased with this argument and he repeats it in inverse terms—

> suppose that all the money of GREAT BRITAIN were multiplied fivefold in a night, must not the contrary effect follow? Must not all labour and commodities rise to such an exorbitant height, that no neighbouring nations could afford to buy from us; while their commodities, on the other hand, became

comparatively so cheap, that, in spite of all the laws which could be formed, they would be run in upon us, and our money flow out; till we fall to a level with foreigners. [ibid.]

And then he goes on, warming to the subject, with this famous passage:

> How is the balance kept in the provinces of every kingdom among themselves [within Great Britain], but by the force of this principle, which makes it impossible for money to lose its level, and either to rise or sink beyond the proportion of the labour and commodities which are in each province? [ibid., 1:334–35]

And then he lapses into his irony:

> Did not long experience make people easy on this head, what a fund of gloomy reflections might calculations afford to a melancholy YORKSHIREMAN, while he computed and magnified the sums drawn to London by taxes, absentees, commodities, and found on comparison the opposite articles so much inferior? [ibid., 1:335]

"And, no doubt," he says, warming to the argument, "had the Heptarchy subsisted in ENGLAND"—the heptarchy, for those of you who come from abroad, took place over a thousand years ago when Great Britain, let alone Scotland, was divided into sections, each with a monarch—

> had the Heptarchy subsisted in ENGLAND, the legislature of each state had been continually alarmed by the fear of a wrong balance; and as it is probable that the mutual hatred of these states would have been extremely violent on account of their close neighbourhood, they would have loaded and oppressed all commerce, by a jealous and superfluous caution. [ibid.]

So there you are. And provided that paper substitutes for metallic money are *freely* convertible and the banks are obliged to preserve some return so that convertibility can be preserved, and supposing all sorts of other complications as regards the reserve ratios of other countries and so on, what Viner calls Hume's specie flow analysis still holds, roughly speaking, good. And it explains the comparative state of equilibrium prevailing between many countries of the world during the various parts of the nineteenth century.

But, before you say that Hume was not a pure monetarist as regards internal conditions—witness the essay on Money—and is now a pure monetarist as regards international monetary relations, read on:

> I scarcely know any method of sinking money below its level,

—that is in the foreign exchanges—

> but those institutions of banks, funds, and paper credit, which are so much practised in this kingdom. These render paper equivalent to money, circulate it throughout the whole state, make it supply the place of gold and silver, raise

proportionably the price of labour and commodities, and by that means either banish a great part of those precious metals, or prevent their farther encrease. What can be more short-sighted than our reasonings on this head? We fancy, because an individual would be much richer, were his stock of money doubled, that the same good effect would follow were the money of every one encreased; not considering, that this would raise as much the price of every commodity. [ibid., 1:337]

And so he goes on, expatiating on the effects of the unwise use of paper currency, than which he says there is no more effective measure of diverting from a country all its reserves of precious metals. And so he goes on. But I have lectured you too much on my favourite eighteenth-century philosopher, and we must proceed.

And what I want to do in the remaining half hour is to begin—rather more detailed lectures than you have had in the past—a survey which will take me certainly the whole of next week, and perhaps part of the lecture afterwards, of the relevant parts of Adam Smith's *Wealth of Nations* [1776].

Now, let me say a word about reading, because I know how pressed some of you are. You must read all of part 1 of the *Wealth of Nations*. You must read part 2. As regards part 1, you can omit the digression on silver, and you can skip some of the sections on rent. Part 2 is comparatively short and should be read, save where he gives you detailed banking history towards the end of the book. Part 3 gives you his historical perspective and is worth reading. Part 4 deals with systems of political economy, most of which is devoted to the mercantile system, and when I come to it I will tell you which parts you ought to read there. And book 5 is devoted to the functions of government, and again there you will need some guidance if you are pressed for time. But some reading of the *Wealth of Nations* is quite essential if you are to be a serious student of this subject, and, of course, graduates should go further.

Well now, having said all that by way of dissipating terror, I want to devote most of this lecture to certain predecessors, apart from Hume, of the *Wealth of Nations*. And I want to talk in particular about three: Mandeville, Steuart and Hutcheson. I need not say too much about any of these.

Bernard Mandeville is very important. He was a doctor of Dutch extraction, who came to this country—the date is perhaps disputable—but towards the end of the seventeenth century. And he set up in medical practice in London, and in 1705 he created for himself a scandalous reputation, a reputation only as scandalous in moral philosophy as the reputation of Machiavelli was in the Renaissance time in regard to the conduct of the state—how to keep order and how to defeat one's enemies and so on.

Now, Mandeville's publication in 1705 was called *The Grumbling Hive, or, Knaves Turn'd Honest,* and it was just published as a sixpenny pamphlet in doggerel. His argument was that society was kept in order, some sort of division of labour practised, employment maintained, by the vices of mankind rather than their virtues. He used the word "vices" in a very peculiar sense. He used it as equivalent to the normal wants of average sensual man and woman. Everything which was not—and this was ironical on his part, clearly—completely ascetic and austere was designated as a vice. It is necessary for me to enter on that terminological explanation in order that you may understand what I am going to say.

I am going to read to you part of his doggerel poetry. *The Grumbling Hive* was an allegory of a human society, and the grumbling hive prospered so long as it was full of vice. This is reprinted—for those of you who like to take notes—in the first volume of Cannan's *Wealth of Nations* [1776], which, although it's not the most up-to-date—the most up-to-date is a very expensive edition issued by Glasgow two years ago [1976] in commemoration of the two-hundredth anniversary of the *Wealth of Nations*—is still comparatively cheaply obtainable. And I shall give you all the page references from there. Well, in Cannan's introduction, on page 44, he quotes the significant passage:

> The worst of all the multitude
> Did something for the common good.
>   This was the state's craft, that maintain'd
> The whole, of which each part complained:
> This, as in musick harmony,
> Made jarrings in the main agree;
> Parties directly opposite,
> Assist each oth'r, as 'twere for spight;
> And temp'rance with sobriety
> Serve drunkenness and gluttony.
>   The root of evil, avarice,
> That damned ill-natur'd baneful vice,
> Was slave to prodigality,
> That noble sin; whilst, luxury
> Employ'd a million of the poor,
> And odious pride a million more:
> Envy itself and vanity
> Were ministers of industry;
> Their darling folly, fickleness
> In diet, furniture, and dress,
> That strange ridic'lous vice, was made
> The very wheel that turn'd the trade.
> Their laws and cloaths were equally
> Objects of mutability;

—he had female fashion in mind—

> For what was well done for a time,
> In half a year became a crime;
> Yet whilst they altered thus their laws,
> Still finding and correcting flaws,
> They mended by inconstancy
> Faults which no prudence could foresee.
>> Thus vice

—in his particular sense of the word—

>> nursed ingenuity,
> Which join'd with time and industry,
> Had carry'd life's conveniences,
> It's real pleasures, comforts, ease,
> To such a height, the very poor
> Lived better than the rich before;
> And nothing could be added more.

>>> [Smith, 1776, 1:xliv–xlv]

And then the bees grumbled and grumbled and grumbled and grumbled about all sorts of things until Jove, in anger, said that he would rid the hive of fraud, and the hive became virtuous in Mandeville's sense. They foreswore mutability in fashion, diet and dress, they lived austerely, and at once the economic system dropped to pieces—widespread unemployment took place, and so on.

Well, in 1714 he repeated this doggerel poem and added to it, in non-doggerel, beautiful English prose. No eighteenth-century writer, not even the most famous names, wrote more beautiful and persuasive English than Mandeville. He republished it under the title *The Fable of the Bees, or Private Vices, Public Benefits*. And he went on expanding this until—the final edition was 1729—it eventually expanded to two thick volumes, the second of which contains a very long and very amusing dialogue in the Platonic manner. Very interesting and good bedside reading, I am bound to tell you.

Well, it was obviously designed to shock. There is no doubt about that. He was writing with his tongue in his cheek. Now, what were his intentions? If you read the introduction to the wonderful American edition of *The Fable of the Bees* by a man called Kaye [Mandeville, 1924], which is published by the Oxford University Press, you would think that Mandeville was really an idealist who wanted to shock people out of their grumbling habits about the behaviour of the average man, and he invented this terminology to make them think again. And, well, to some extent I would say that my great friend von Hayek thinks that Mandeville's intentions may be regarded as being in a sense to promote knowledge by thinking, by the means of these shocks. I personally don't agree. I think if you read the essay on charity schools, in which Mandeville argues against the education of very poor boys and girls who have been, by the death of parents or something of that sort, consigned to charity schools, you will find that he actually does argue *against* the education of these unfortunates. I think there was a sinister streak in Mandeville. But this is a subject not for serious academic discussion; it is rather for after-dinner conversation.

The great importance of Mandeville was that he produced a shock among moral philosophers—as was his intention, whether for good reasons or bad—comparable, as I have said, to the moral shock that was produced and is produced even to this day by the reading of Machiavelli's *The Prince* [1950]. How many of you have read *The Prince?* Well, you have felt a little shocked, and then perhaps you reflected that Machiavelli had also written other writings and was probably not such a bad chap. But he was being severely scientific. But nearly all the moral philosophers for the next two centuries, including that not altogether moral character, Frederick the Great of Prussia, wrote refutations of Machiavelli. And eighteenth-century moral philosophers, once *The Fable of the Bees* was widely read, all wrote refutations of Mandeville.

And Adam Smith refers to him in his *Theory of Moral Sentiments* [1792], and refutes the point of view that it is vice that makes the wheels of the world turn round. But Adam Smith, who was a cunning fellow, was *tremendously* impressed by Mandeville's argument that the average wants of mankind—which Mandeville called obsessional and sometimes erring mankind—that demand in fact, played an important part in sustaining the division of labour. There can be no doubt at all that the effect of Mandeville on Adam Smith's way of thinking is part of the background of the first chapters of Adam Smith, which I shall be describing to you next time.

Well now, Mandeville is the most interesting of the three people I am going to talk about. Sir James Steuart was a Scottish baronet who, to his great misfortune, became involved in the Jacobite rebellion of 1745. For those of you who come from other parts of the world, after the great and glorious revolution which dethroned James II, his nearest relatives— the son, who was called the Old Pretender, and the grandson, who was called the Young Pretender—staged attempts to come back to the throne of Great Britain and Scotland. First, in 1715, was the Old Pretender's attempt. Then, in 1745, the Young Pretender, who was rather a romantic character much beloved by various virtuous women, staged a more successful attempt, and because of the inefficiency of the British Army they did succeed in penetrating as far south as Derbyshire before an army could be scratched together, which then had no very great difficulty in defeating them.

Now, poor Sir James Steuart became involved in the Young Pretender's entourage when the Young Pretender had managed to capture Edinburgh. And after the defeat of the 1745, Sir James Steuart spent years in exile, travelling from continental resort to continental resort. Eventually he was given a free pardon, largely as a result of that extraordinary woman, Lady Mary Wortley Montagu, and other people who took compassion on him and realised that he hadn't played a very great part in the rebellion and that in other respects he was a worthy citizen. He spent his years in exile making careful and interesting studies of other people's economic systems, and in 1767 he published a two-volume *Principles of Political Economy*—the first time that title appears in the English literature. It had appeared in the French literature in the seventeenth century in a comparatively worthless book which I won't expatiate on.

And what can one say of this? It is in many respects an intelligent and careful and well-argued book, synthesising, in a way, many of the principles of the mercantile system—not in the narrow sense in which Adam Smith used it and popularised the name, but rather in the wider sense in which you get it in Heckscher and in Schmoller and in people who write about the mercantile system as though it meant just any old piece of *national* economic policy. In a way, it's the best exposition of the wider mercantile system in the literature, but it had hardly any influence. Poor Sir James. It was completely eclipsed by Smith's *Wealth of Nations*, which was published, as you all know, in—need I mention the date?—1776. And Smith very carefully, as he explained in a letter to a friend, didn't mention Sir James Steuart's book, but he went out of his way to refute the various arguments, as he thought, in Sir James's exposition.

Professor Terence Hutchison [1967], who is a great friend of mine, and for whom I have the greatest respect as an historian of economic thought, did write a review of a modern work—a publication of Steuart and modern publications reviving his reputation—and Professor Hutchison thinks that was rather shabby of Adam Smith. I don't quite share my friend Professor Hutchison's view on that. I think it was perfectly legitimate for Smith, writing in those days, having on an intellectual plane disposed of the arguments, refraining from giving his opponent, who was by that time returned to Scotland and was mixing in much the same circles as Adam Smith, a free advertisement. But those specialists among you—the master's degree people—may find it worthwhile having a look at the modern reprint which, as I was told by a member of the audience, is now at a reduced price in the antiquarian bookshop. There is a very, very good introduction by the editor, Andrew Skinner, and it contains most of what is worthwhile in Steuart's writings.

There is just time for me to mention the third influence, now positive. Mandeville's influence was positive, but Smith shied away from the morals that he drew from his peculiar terminology. Steuart's influence was negative, in that Adam Smith went out of his way to deal with various arguments advanced by Steuart, but he was influenced—and he confessed the influence, not so much on the *Wealth of Nations*, but on his general thinking—by Francis Hutcheson, who was his predecessor in the Chair which he occupied during part of his life at Glasgow, and during which he, Adam Smith, gave the lectures which became first the basis of *The Theory of Moral Sentiments* and then the basis of the *Wealth of Nations*.

Hutcheson must have been an extremely nice chap. He was born in 1694 in Ireland, and he was educated in Glasgow, and then he migrated again to Ireland in 1730. His early works on moral philosophy were produced while he was there. For those of you who are interested in aesthetics or the history of moral philosophy, his inquiry into the origin of our ideas of beauty and virtue [1729] is a thing which is thoroughly worth reading. Now, I don't say that this is obligatory on even Ph.D. specialists, but if you like reading about aesthetic theory, Francis Hutcheson is rather good on that.

He was appointed professor at Glasgow in 1730, and he had a tremendous influence in the intellectual renaissance of the Scottish universities, who, while Oxford and Cambridge—with the exception of the Newton tradition at Cambridge—were wallowing in sloth and idleness, were second only to the intellectuals of France. And he abandoned the habit of lecturing in Latin, and he was, apparently, extraordinarily friendly and *eloquent* as a lecturer. Adam Smith calls him the "never-to-be-forgotten" Francis Hutcheson [Rae, 1895, p. 411]. And after his death, a disciple of his published his lectures on moral philosophy [1755] in two volumes—a quarto edition—which, if you see it in secondhand bookshops, you shouldn't surrender without consulting knowledgeable people.

Now, Hutcheson's importance, insofar as Adam Smith is concerned, is that he taught Adam Smith that part of moral philosophy which included remarks on ethics. And Francis Hutcheson was the transmitter to Adam Smith of much of the Aristotelian philosophy which had survived the medieval theologians and modern lawyers, like, *especially*, a German called Pufendorf. Francis Hutcheson's own treatment of economics in his *System of Moral Philosophy* [1755]—this book published after his death— very closely follows the treatment of this part of moral philosophy— the part originating in Aristotle's stray remarks on economics: it follows Pufendorf.

The rest of his writings are not without interest. Francis Hutcheson was definitely a radical for his time. If you read his remarks on colonies, he expresses considerable sympathy for those who, even in his day, were beginning to be restive as being under the domination of the British Government. And Hutcheson is certainly worth reading as the bridge between Aristotle and Adam Smith's analytical economics, on all of which, if you want to read more, there is a book by a man, William Taylor, who is a professor (or was a professor—I don't know what's happened in the last two or three years) at the University of Salisbury, Rhodesia, on *Francis Hutcheson and David Hume as Predecessors of Adam Smith* [1965]. And

he has most of the stuff there. It is quite a good and a studious book.
He doesn't make Hume quite as exciting as I think Hume ought to be
made, but his remarks are sagacious and helpful, usually very helpful, to any
of you to whom I have been too superficial or too brief or too given to
asides.

NOTE

1. Robbins presumably calls this "essay 3" because it is the third of Hume's
economics essays which he is discussing in his lecture. However, this essay is in fact
essay 5 in Green and Grose, vol. 1.

General Survey of Smith's Intentions—
The Wealth of Nations: Analytical (I)

IT IS TIME to catch up, just at the point at which these lectures become, I won't say respectable, but less negatively respectable than they were. That is to say that I am going to lecture to you for two or three lectures on Adam Smith and the beginnings of classical economics.

I won't assume, as I did with Hume, that all self-respecting people will know the details of the life of Adam Smith, and I can rehearse the leading events very quickly. Let me get the dates right. He was born at a place north of the Firth of Forth called Kirkcaldy, which must have been a much more agreeable spot than it is nowadays. I once went up to try to buy a printing works there, and the shade of Adam Smith wasn't particularly evident. He was born in Kirkcaldy in 1723. His father was a civil servant of kinds. Adam Smith studied at Glasgow University under the "never-to-be-forgotten" Francis Hutcheson, of whom I was talking to you last time. He studied from 1737 to 1740, and then he had the good fortune, or the misfortune, to get a Snell Exhibition to Balliol College, Oxford, where he lived from 1740 to 1747. What he did there is to some extent veiled in mystery; his correspondence isn't very revealing. We know that he thought extremely poorly of the educational arrangements at Oxford: At the University of Oxford the professors have long ago abandoned "even the pretence of teaching," he says in the *Wealth of Nations* [Smith, 1776, vol. 2:251].

He must have made pretty good use of his time in the libraries there because he emerged an extremely well-read man, and from 1748 to 1750 he was a sort of extension lecturer at Edinburgh, which then, as now, was, so to speak, the capital city of Scotland and the home of perhaps 40 percent of the intellectual life—the other 40 percent being at Glasgow and leaving 20 percent scattered about the country. In 1751, he was made Professor of Logic at Glasgow, but in 1752, the Chair of Moral Philosophy having become vacant, he transferred from logic to moral philosophy, and the lectures that he gave there, of which we now have two sets of student notes, covered political economy incidentally.

When Adam Smith was dying he summoned his executors and exhorted them to burn all his papers except sundry philosophical papers. But student notes were discovered by Cannan in 1896, and a second set of student notes was discovered in Aberdeen in the fifties and are now published in the very expensive but very scholarly book issued in celebration of the bicentenary of the *Wealth of Nations* by the University of Glasgow [Smith,

1978]. In 1759—this is an important date—he worked up that part of his lectures which dealt with moral philosophy, a work which would have made him famous even if he had not written the *Wealth of Nations*— namely, the celebrated *Theory of Moral Sentiments*.

In 1764 he gave up his Chair halfway through the session. Townshend, the famous politician who was responsible in many ways for the quarrel with the American colonies, persuaded Adam Smith to accompany the young Duke of Buccleuch on a journey in France. The better-to-do people, more right-thinking people, among the aristocrats who ruled the country in those days for the most part, despairing of getting their sons a good education at the English universities, used to send their sons on continental trips which lasted two or three years, and for the most part they came back, if they had aesthetic tastes, loaded with works of art. Much of the richness of the artistic heritage of this country comes from the trips of the young British aristocrats in Italy and elsewhere. Townshend thought that the young Duke of Buccleuch, who seems to have been a nice chap and a virtuous man, might acquire bad habits if he were abroad unaccompanied, and he conceived the—from the Duke of Buccleuch's point of view—marvellous idea of getting this famous professor to be his companion.

And they stayed in France for some time, and it was there that Adam Smith made the acquaintance of the physiocrats. And he got on quite well with them. He thought well of Quesnay, and it is rumoured that if Quesnay had not been dead—I think I said this before—Adam Smith intended to dedicate the *Wealth of Nations* to him. Not that he agreed with him, but he had a respect for his character and for his intellect.

In 1766 the Buccleuch family pensioned Adam Smith off, and for ten years he spent his time between Kirkcaldy, London and Edinburgh, writing the *Wealth of Nations*, which was published in 1776—a date which is famous for other reasons to those of you who come from abroad, and which also saw the publication of the first of Jeremy Bentham's works. It was an *annus mirabilis* in many ways. In 1778 Adam Smith was made a Commissioner of Customs, and in 1790 he died.

As you can see, it was a comparatively uneventful life. He seems to have got lost when he was a child, and he was recovered without any damage done, but academically it was about as favourable as can be conceived. He was a great friend of David Hume. Some of Hume's best letters are written to Adam Smith, and Hume's best letters are among the best letters in the language.[1] Adam Smith was a great influence in the University of Glasgow. He was apparently quite a good administrator, and highly respected by his colleagues and by his students.

Have I told you the story of his retirement? Well, he retired halfway through a session in order to accompany the Duke of Buccleuch, and this weighed on his conscience very much. He made arrangements for a substitute—a good substitute, in his judgement—but he thought that the students, who in those days paid fees to the lecturers, were not getting a fair deal, and so at his last lecture he lugged along a bag of silver. And he announced to the students that compelling reasons necessitated his retirement and that his place would be taken—and worthily taken, I daresay he said—by his successor. But he felt that they had not got value for money out of him, and he proposed therefore to give them back a proportionate amount of their fees. And apparently they said, "Oh dear Mr Smith, we love you so. We really don't want the fees back," and he was so distressed at this that eventually they agreed, and they filed up to the rostrum, and he dropped in the hands of each of the students a proportionate repayment of the fees.

He was in many respects an absent-minded man. He was a bad correspondent. He was a companionable, a clubbable man. He belonged to clubs in Glasgow where he had very worthy intellectual companionship. He belonged also to clubs in Edinburgh, and he was sometimes apt to interrupt the conversation by saying out loud that he thought that some person was talking nonsense.

I must correct an impression that you may get from reading Schumpeter. You know how much I admire Schumpeter's book, but Schumpeter wasn't so careful about facts as he ought to have been. And Schumpeter had a down on Adam Smith, not that he didn't realise the importance of the *Wealth of Nations*, but, Schumpeter-wise, he wanted slightly to denigrate it, to say that it contained no original thoughts [Schumpeter, 1954, pp. 184–86], and that his handling of the world of reality was a bit—what shall I say?—stepmotherly. And Schumpeter [ibid., p. 182] actually says that it is noticeable that there was no woman in his life except his mother. Now, if Schumpeter had taken the trouble to read Dugald Stewart's [1811] biographical sketch, published after Adam Smith's death, he would have known that there was a lady to whom Adam Smith was very attached for many years, and his friends always were surprised that in the end it didn't end in marriage. He also, when he was a young man, went about with girl called Jeanie, and that didn't come to anything either. Perhaps Jeanie was not a particularly fascinating person, or at any rate drifted off. Adam Smith and his mother went to a ball and Jeanie was there, and Adam Smith didn't recognise her. And his mother said to him, "Adam, don't you realise that this is your ain Jeanie?" So there he was—a rather lovable character, and he put political economy on the world map as a serious subject.

If you read French works of the nineteenth century, you will find that the authors are inclined to think that Adam Smith got his system from the physiocrats, but that was before Cannan's discovery of the student's notes, and the later discovery at Aberdeen of other student's notes. These are very good students' notes; the Cannan discovery is extremely well written. God grant that notes taken in this institution are half as good as the students' notes of Adam Smith's lectures on jurisprudence and political economy. These lectures, which were delivered before he went to France and mixed with the physiocrats, and other evidence which is produced in Scott's quite important book on *Adam Smith as Student and Professor* [1937], make it quite clear that the main parts of his system were discovered before he knew the physiocrats. But it may very well be that from the physiocrats or from Turgot he was inspired to write parts of book 2, particularly those parts which depict capital as advances. And it may well be that he derived more, I think, from the physiocrats, whom he liked but whom he thought were wrong, and that he derived more from Turgot, although again Turgot's dialogue, which I explained to you, was not published until the late 1760s, and the students' notes show that the system was elaborated before then.

Well now, let's begin to tackle the *Wealth of Nations.* And first of all, I want you to realise the mixed nature of the *Wealth of Nations.* And I can best convey that to you by reading to you the titles of the five books. The first book is called—you needn't take notes about this because you will all be reading book 1—"Of the Causes of Improvement in the productive Powers of Labour, and of the Order according to which its Produce is naturally distributed among the different Ranks of the People." Book 2 is called "Of the Nature, Accumulation, and Employment of Stock." Book 3, "Of the different Progress of Opulence in different Nations." Book 4, which occupies a tremendous space, "Of Systems of political Œconomy"— the mercantile system and the agricultural system, as he called it, of the physiocrats. And book 5 is called "Of the Revenue of the Sovereign or Commonwealth."

Well, you can see from that list of contents that Adam Smith's *Wealth of Nations* is *not* wholly or nearly scientific, in the sense that Cantillon's *Essay on Commerce* was almost 99 percent detached and scientific. Book 3, *Of the different Progress of Opulence in different Nations,* contains a normity of overtone. It is clear what he thinks that the progress ought to have been, and how it had been stopped at different stages. And book 4, *Of Systems of political Œconomy,* is overtly polemical. Adam Smith was out to kill the mercantile system and all the regulations which went with it. And you can see that the scientific part of his book, although, once he comes airborne, is pretty candid and scientific, had an overtone of controversy, in it in that, since he was anxious to kill the mercantile system and abolish all sorts of regulations, he was anxious to set out in a systematic way how the economic system worked in the absence of the mercantile system, or how it would work in the abscence of the agricultural system. But the agricultural system, in his judgement, was never likely to come into being.

But now, I put this first lest you should say that, in the lengthy discussion that I'm going to give to the scientific foundations of classical political economy, I have concealed from you the background of the controversy and controversial sections. But you will go completely wrong if you write off the *Wealth of Nations* simply as a polemic, simply as an apologia for a bourgeois society which was coming into being, and so on and so forth. It was the work of a profound thinker anxious to discover the nature of things. And once he was embarked on the discovery, then an impulse to tell the truth as he saw it, whether it was favourable or not, inspired his writing. And lastly I would say, on this mixture of polemic and scientific work, that it is not without significance that Smith is appealed to not only by the classical economists, but by Marxian economists, by nationalist economists—by almost all schools of thought which have succeeded the writing of the *Wealth of Nations.*

Well now, let us now get down to the scientific side of it. The main content of the scientific side of it—and here I am being a spot controversial; not all historians of economic thought would put it this way, but I am saying to you that in my opinion the main content of the *Wealth of Nations* is a theory of productive organisation and a theory of the causes of economic growth. Some people will fasten attention on the theory of value and distribution. And it is true that the theory of value and distribution in book 1, and some parts of the theory of money and capital in book 2, have attracted most attention among theoretical economists. But my own belief, which has grown through years of reading and thinking about the *Wealth of Nations*, is that you get the perspective wrong if you focus too much— even I may have done this in earlier lectures or earlier footnotes—on the value and distribution side, although I'm going to give you quite a strong dose of value and distribution in a moment.

The scientific content can be more broadly summarised by saying that the first book lays it down that growth depends on the division of labour, and the division of labour is organised by the market and the force of what he called self-interest. And the scientific part of the second book is devoted to explaining how the possession of stock facilitates the division of labour—promotes it—and the accumulation of stock promotes the increase. It also contains Adam Smith's analysis of money, which he covers under the heading of capital. Now, you must put up with this, and I'll try to make it as interesting as I can, but we must go through books 1 and 2 in greater detail.

The book starts with an introduction and plan, which I think you should all read, and which I won't read to you. But book 1, which, as I have said, deals with the improvement of the productive powers of labour and the order according to which it is distributed, begins with the most famous chapter in political economy, possibly: chapter 1, "Of the Division of Labour." And the first sentence runs: "The greatest improvement in the productive powers of labour, and the greater part of the skill, dexterity, and judgment with which it is any where directed, or applied, seem to have been the effects of the division of labour" [Smith, 1776, 1:5].

And then comes an example which has become very famous, and which he probably got from the French encyclopedia—not this application of it, but the technology involved. He takes the example of pin-making and shows how if labour is appropriately divided between casting the pins and casting the head and then fitting the two together and so on and so forth, many times as much pins can be produced per man in an institution practising the division of labour than could be produced if each man applied himself to all the operations necessary for doing the division of labour. Well, you should all read that.

On page 9 of Cannan, however, he sums up the causes of the increase of the quantity of work which, in consequence of the division of labour, the same number of people are capable of performing. It

> is owing to three different circumstances: first, the increase of dexterity in every particular workman; secondly, to the saving of time which is commonly lost in passing from one species of work to another; and lastly, to the invention of a great number of machines which facilitate and abridge labour, and enable one man to do the work of many. [ibid., 1:9]

Now, there are two comments to be made on this ennumeration. First of all, contrast it with Plato, who emphasises the genetic factors—the inborn differences between people. I dwelt upon that sufficiently. Adam Smith, following the tradition of the eighteenth-century enlightenment, and following Locke in this particular respect, thought that we all come into the world with, roughly speaking, equal potentiality, and what happens afterwards is a matter of education and experience—a thought which did him credit, but which was not, I think, exactly right. Don't think I underestimate the importance of experience and education. Don't think that I want to thrust down your throats the genetic differences, about which we know very, very little indeed, and most people who talk about them are frauds. But there it is.

The second comment I have to make is that he omits what a minor classical economist called Torrens [1833] called the territorial division of labour—the differences in the division of labour which derive from the fact that different parts of the earth's surface are differently suited for different kinds of activity—agricultural and industrial and commercial and so on and so forth. But he deals with that splendidly later on when he is dealing with the mercantile system.

And then he broadens out, and he gives you an extensive view of what the division of labour really means for society in general. The pin factory is often quoted as being his proof of the advantages of the division of labour, but the last paragraph of chapter 1 is much, much more important than that, and I propose to read you extracts from it:

> Observe the accommodation of the most common artificer or day-labourer in a civilised and thriving country, and you will perceive that the number of people of whose industry a part, though but a small part, has been employed in procuring him this accommodation, exceeds all computation. The woollen coat, for example, which covers the day-labourer, as coarse and rough as it may appear, is the produce of the joint labour of a great multitude of work-

men. The shepherd, the sorter of the wool, the wool comber or carder, the dyer, the scribbler, the spinner, the weaver, the fuller, the dresser, with many others, must all join their different arts in order to complete even this homely production. How many merchants and carriers, besides, must have been employed in transporting the materials from some of those workmen to others who often live in a very distant part of the country! how much commerce and navigation in particular, how many shipbuilders, sailors, sail-makers, rope-makers, must have been employed in order to bring together the different drugs made use of by the dyer, which often come from the remotest corners of the world! [Smith, 1776, 1:13]

And then—I am missing out a lot in order to save time—

if we examine, I say, all these things, and consider what a variety of labour is employed about each of them, we shall be sensible that without the assistance and co-operation of many thousands, the very meanest person in a civilized country could not be provided, even according to, what we very falsely imagine, the easy and simple manner in which he is commonly accommodated. Compared, indeed, with the more extravagant luxury of the great, his accommodation must no doubt appear extremely simple and easy; and yet it may be true, perhaps, that the accommodation of an European prince does not always so much exceed that of an industrious and frugal peasant, as the accommodation of the latter exceeds that of [kings in other parts]

—I am paraphrasing, lest this terminology should give offence to any of you—

the absolute master of the lives and liberties of ten thousand [of his subjects]. [ibid., 1:14]

The last sentence is a little watered down, since this is an international institution and he was writing about the eighteenth century.[2]

Now, chapter 2 is just as important. And he thinks that the division of labour—from which we get so many advantages which really, as he depicts it, given an apparatus of justice and law and order and so on and so forth, is the thing which binds a society together, whether justly or unjustly—is the basis of the economic aspect of the civilisation. And he thinks that this arises from a propensity in human nature—a "propensity to truck, barter, and exchange one thing for another" [ibid., 1:15]. And then he goes on with a rather dubious remark that "Nobody ever saw a dog make a fair and deliberate exchange of one bone for another with another dog" [ibid.], to which Cannan, who was something of a wit, says in a footnote: "It is by no means clear what object there could be in exchanging one bone for another" [ibid., at note 2].

But he then goes on to say that

A puppy fawns up on its dam, and a spaniel endeavours by a thousand attractions to engage the attention of its master who is at dinner, when it wants to be fed by him. Man sometimes uses the same arts with his brethren, and when he has no other means of engaging them to act according to his inclinations, endeavours by every servile and fawning attention to obtain their good will. He has not time, however, to do this upon every occasion. In civilized society he stands at all times in need of the co-operation and assistance of great multitudes. . . . In almost every other race of animals each individual, when it is grown up to maturity, is entirely independent, and in its natural state has occasion for the assistance of no other living creature. But man has almost constant occasion for the help of his brethren, and it is in vain for him to expect it from their benevolence only. He will be more likely to prevail if he can interest their self-love in his favour. [ibid., 1:15–16]

And notice that the self-love is on the side of the chap or lady from whom he wants to get something. "His favour" clearly means his immediate circle, his family.

As Wicksteed says in his *Commonsense of Political Economy* [1910], which probably most of you haven't read nowadays, the important aspect of Adam Smith's emphasis on self-love, as he calls it, is the non-tuism of the person with whom he bargains. He doesn't interest himself—he may, but he doesn't necessarily, interest himself—in what the person with whom he's bargaining is doing with his family. He may be interested in all sorts of things with which he favours his family and wider circles in society. We'll talk more about self-love later on.

Whoever offers to another a bargain of any kind, proposes to do this. Give me that which I want, and you shall have this which you want, is the meaning of every such offer; and it is in this manner that we obtain from one another the far greater part of those good offices which we stand in need of. It not from the benevolence of the butcher, the brewer, or the baker, that we expect our dinner, but from their regard to their own interest. We address ourselves, not to their humanity but to their self-love, and never talk to them of our own necessities but of their advantages. [Smith, 1776, 1:16]

Well, I see that the time is up and perhaps that is a piquant way in which to end this particular proposition, but I shall be going on to talk about self-interest and the market and the width of the market tomorrow, and then I shall get on to value and distribution.

NOTES

1. See Hume (1932; 1954).
2. The actual phrase used by Smith is "exceeds that of many an African King, the absolute master of the lives and liberties of ten thousand naked savages."

The Wealth of Nations: Analytical (II)

THE LECTURE yesterday was interrupted by the fire alarm, and consequently I had to break off just at the point at which the most interesting
developments of the *Wealth of Nations* were becoming obvious. Let me
recapitulate that chapter 2 of book 1 is headed "Of the Principle which
gives Occasion to the Division of Labour," and the famous passage dwells
upon the fact that, although if one is closely allied in friendship within
one's family or in one's circle, one can obtain scarce commodities by way
of gift or common use, that in a civilised society most of us are in need of
scarce commodities, goods and services which are the produce, as had been
explained in chapter 1 of the *Wealth of Nations*, of thousands and thousands of people, and it is the impersonal relationship of exchange which
provides the incentive to division of labour: "Whoever offers to another a
bargain of any kind, proposes to do this. Give me that which I want, and
you shall have this which you want. . . . We address ourselves, not to their
humanity but to their self-love, and never talk to them of our own necessities but of their advantages" [Smith, 1776, 1:16]. Now, let me dwell on
this just a little bit.

I was explaining this to you in the last lecture by reference to Wicksteed's extensive discussion of the meaning of self-love in this part of the
classical analysis, dwelling upon the fact that the person negotiating a purchase may be interested in his own welfare—self-love—in his family welfare—family love—in his circle of intimate friends—friendship—or he may
be interested on behalf of people with whom he hasn't the same friendly
interest. It's notorious, if you are at all worldly wise, that the people who
make the hardest bargains in contemporary life are people who are executors of other peoples' wills, or who are trustees of charitable foundations.
And why? Because in that case you are not free to indulge yourself in relatively disinterested action; you are under instructions by the trust or by the
will. Well, that relationship—the relationship in exchange described by
Adam Smith—was described by Wicksteed as "non-tuism," and that, I
think, is all that needs to be said about that.

But I was asked a question as I came out whether Adam Smith did actually think that all actions in society were conducted on the basis of this
enlarged conception of self or family or trust interest. And the answer is
"No." The answer is that if you look—which most of you won't do—at his
other famous book, *The Theory of Moral Sentiments* [1759/1792], you will
find that Adam Smith's chief conception of the criteria of moral action vis-
à-vis one's fellows and so on and so forth is sympathy, and he judges, he
sets out as a criterion of, right moral actions the estimate which would be

made of the motives and the effects of actions by an impersonal spectator. He creates the fiction of an impersonal spectator who is not interested on one side or the other, and that impersonal spectator is, in the last analysis, subject, if you like, to the rules of high heaven—in which Adam Smith was, in contradistinction to David Hume, a believer. Subject to the rules of high heaven, the impartial spectator was, so to speak, the criterion of moral action in general.

This is not to say that there is a contradiction between *The Theory of Moral Sentiments* and the *Wealth of Nations*. If challenged, I have absolutely no doubt at all that Adam Smith would have said, in regard to the organisation of production and the division of labour, that the impartial spectator would judge that social utility was best served by the exchange relationship, and the exchange relationship is as I have described it. However, this is a matter on which controversy has prevailed, and my point of view may not be right, although it's not one of the points of view about which I have any very great queasiness of conscience, I am bound to say.

The chapter goes on enlarging on the way in which the possibility of exchange gives rise to the division of labour, and then he divagates and talks about the differences of natural talent, which he had mentioned in chapter 1 as giving rise to the division of labour. And it's here that he says: "The difference between the most dissimilar characters, between a philosopher and a common street porter, for example, seems to arise not so much from nature, as from habit, custom, and education" [Smith, 1776, 1:17]. I am skipping an awful lot. "By nature a philosopher is not in genius and disposition half so different from a street porter, as a mastiff is from a greyhound, or a greyhound from a spaniel, or this last from a shepherd's dog" [ibid., 1:18].

Well, when I think of the difference between me and Einstein, I'm not at all sure that he's right, and I don't think that Einstein's genius, or the genius of Newton and many other people, arose simply from circumstances and education, although no doubt it played a part. I wouldn't have been an academic for so long if I didn't think that education was sometimes some good to some of you.

Well, now, chapter 3. This chapter is, I think, one of the most important chapters in the history of political economy, but I can summarise it very quickly. Indeed, the summary is given to you by the chapter heading: "That the Division of Labour is limited by the Extent of the Market." If you conceive a very small village community, for instance, isolated from the rest of the world, it is not worth anybody's while concentrating on a minute division of labour or inventing very expensive machines to serve a wide market. You have to have an extensive market in order to take account of, as it were, to use a modern phrase, the indivisibilities of character or machinery. Now, I say that's important because I have no doubt at all that the nineteenth-century classical economists would have acknowledged that it was obvious and, of course, that it was in the background of their thoughts. But certainly in the twentieth century, in my young days in the 1920s and early 1930s, there arose discussions with regard to the nature of the firm, initiated by a very important article by Mr Sraffa in the *Economic Journal* [1926]. And there were infinite discussions concerning the conception of increasing returns—a downward-sloping supply curve within the firm. And tremendous ingenuity was displayed, as had been displayed by Marshall, criticising a proposition of Cournot's which I will explain to you next term. But all this was quite out of perspective until the contribution of the great American professor who presided over the Economics Department at the School of Economics from 1927 to 1929 and then died suddenly. He had been a Harvard professor—Allyn Young.

How many of you know the name of Allyn Young? Very few. But his influence on American economics during his lifetime was enormous. You only have to read the preface to Chamberlin's *Economics of Monopolistic Competition* [1933] to realise that. He was a man who on the whole published comparatively little, and he wasn't a popular lecturer. He used to hesitate a long time, and students at the School of Economics used to compile books on the intervals which would elapse between important sentences. But he was a truly great man, and he wrote what, in my opinion, is one of the most important articles to be published in the *Economic Journal*—namely, his presidential address to the British Association, delivered shortly before he died, on "Increasing Returns and Economic Progress" [Young, 1928]. He drew attention to this chapter of Adam Smith's, and drew attention to the fact that the important examples of increasing returns in modern manufacturing industry are constituted by the disintegration of firms. Just think, for instance, of the history of the automobile industry, the pioneers of this mode of travel, which takes us about quickly on Sundays but which hampers progress nowadays on weekdays. The pioneers assembled all their parts and put them together. The motor industry now covers a variety of different firms, each making one, two or three components of the complicated machines which now carry us about under that title. And of course a narrow theory of the firm—a geometrical theory of what happens within the firm—really gives you no idea of increasing returns as it takes place through society in general via the division of labour. And Young, in modern terms—I have been talking colloquially to you— drew attention to this and thus restored the perspective which economists should have preserved absolutely prominently in their minds after reading Adam Smith.

Chapter 3 goes on giving illustrations of the limitations of the division of labour by the extent of the market. And that I won't expatiate upon. Chapter 4 deals with "the Origin and Use of Money," and although it's quite a lively chapter and is, I think, quite important if you are concentrating on Adam Smith's theory of money, I will do nothing but mention it.

Chapter 5 is more important. It distinguishes between the real and the nominal price of commodities, the nominal price being their price in money. Now, the fact of the variation in the value of money had been realised for centuries. The way that we use—an imperfect way—of distinguishing between money prices and real prices is by way of the device of index numbers, which as you know, at its most refined, has in it the element of the arbitrary and the approximation. It's essentially a sample and subject to all the reservations which beset a conscientious use of sampling theory. But in Adam Smith's day, index numbers had not been invented. They were first hinted at just shortly after Adam Smith's death, and only came into operation, really, halfway through the nineteenth century. So that Adam Smith, in this chapter, takes as his measure of real price, as distinct from nominal price, the price in labour terms, with all the qualifications that that involves and all the controversies to which his treatment gave rise when you came to Ricardian classical economics. Ricardo wanted to measure the real price by the quantity of labour expended. Adam Smith wanted to measure the real price by the quantity of labour which the commodity would command. And as Ricardo pointed out, there is all the difference in the world between those two measures. But this is an esoteric subject; I don't want to expatiate on this at this juncture—it would take a whole lecture. I will allude to it when I come to Ricardo. I draw your attention to its sequence in the development of Adam Smith's argument.

Much more important from my point of view in giving you an idea of Adam Smith's value and distribution theory and book 2 of the *Wealth of Nations* is chapter 6. With his emphasis on the importance of the market, its connection with the division of labour, behind him—his great achievement in Book 1—he then goes on to talk of "the component Parts of the Price of Commodities." And here you have got to watch your step very carefully, because at the opening of the chapter he talks about primitive conditions:

> In that early and rude state of society which precedes both the accumulation of stock and the appropriation of land, the proportion between the quantities of labour necessary for acquiring different objects seems to be the only circumstance which can afford any rule for exchanging them for one another. If

—and now this is a famous couple of sentences; it's often referred to as the parable of the beaver and the deer—

> If among a nation of hunters, for example, it usually costs twice the labour to kill a beaver which it does to kill a deer, one beaver should naturally exchange for or be worth two deer. [Smith, 1776, 1:49]

Well, I hope that that's obvious to all of you. When you have an economy in which the only scarce factor service is unskilled labour, then the ratio of the quantities of labour expended provides a key to what Adam Smith calls the natural, and what we should call the normal, price. Those of you who like monkeying about with geometrical economics can easily draw it on the blackboard. I won't take time by doing it. If you do quantity of labour necessary to kill a beaver on one axis and the quantity of labour necessary to kill a deer on the other axis, then if you draw a straight line connecting different points on the two axes, you have the production function, and wherever it is touched by an indifference curve you have the same price.

Then Adam Smith goes on to discuss differences of skill. And he doesn't really solve the problem, but he thinks that in the advanced state of society *allowances* must be made for superior hardship and superior skill. Those allowances, of course, are in value terms, and Adam Smith has begged the question by just casually treating it that way. But let us go on:

> In this state of things, the whole produce of labour belongs to the labourer; and the quantity of labour commonly employed in acquiring or producing any commodity, is the only circumstance which can regulate the quantity of labour which it ought commonly to purchase, command, or exchange for. [ibid., 1:49–50]

Then he switches to an advanced society, a society in which real capital has been accumulated in one form or another—wage goods or machines or anything you like—and land has been appropriated. And then he switches to a value cost of production—a value cost of production—theory of natural price: "As soon as stock has accumulated in the hands of particular persons, some of them will . . . [wish] to make a profit by the sale of their work, or by what their labour adds to the value of the materials" [ibid., 1:50]. And the stockholder would "have no interest to employ [people], unless he expected from the sale of their work something more than what was sufficient to replace his stock to him" [ibid.,] so that you have profits emerging.

> As soon as the land of any country has all become private property,

—and, inferentially, scarce—

> the landlords, like all other men, love to reap where they never sowed, and demand a rent even for its natural produce. . . . This portion, or, what comes to the same thing, the price of this portion, constitutes the rent of land, and in the price of the greater part of commodities makes a third component part. [ibid., 1:51]

You will notice that I said that once Adam Smith became airborne, he was not arguing a particular case for a particular class of people. The passage in question, I think, shows that. Well, he expatiates on this. He distinguishes between the excess of outlay and receipts of common farmers, where he detects an element of remuneration for their labour as well as an element of remuneration for the stock that they employ and so on. Again, each of these chapters needs your earnest attention.

Chapter 7 deals not with the real or nominal prices of commodities—that was dealt with, his problem not having the index number partial solution to help him, and that I've left behind—but chapter 7 deals with "the

natural and market Price of Commodities." And he says that he has explained the natural price of commodities—he'd begun to explain it in the
last chapter—and he sums up:

> When the price of any commodity is neither more nor less than what is suffi-
> cient to pay the rent of the land, the wages of the labour, and the profits of the
> stock employed in raising, preparing, and bringing it to market, according to
> their natural rates,

—a hint of the distribution theory to come—

> the commodity is then sold for what may be called its natural price.
>   The commodity is then sold precisely for what it is worth, or for what it
> really costs the person who brings it to market. [ibid., 1:57]

But prices are not always at their natural level, and the rest of the chapter
is devoted to explaining the variations and the effect of the variations of
actual market prices from natural or normal prices.

> The market price of every particular commodity is regulated by the propor-
> tion between the quantity . . . brought to market, and the demand of those
> . . . willing to pay. [ibid., 1:58]

And he distinguishes the demand in the market, which is given by the incomes of the people who are in the market, and what he calls absolute
demand:

> A very poor man may be said in some sense to have a demand for a coach and
> six; he might like to have it; but his demand is not an effectual demand, as the
> commodity can never be brought to market in order to satisfy it. [ibid.]

And he then goes on to explain what happens when the market demand
results in a price which is above the natural price, given, roughly speaking, competitive conditions. People will see an unusually high rate of profit
and surge in until the increase of supply in relation to the demand brings
the price down to something like the normal price. Conversely, if the state
of demand is such that the market price is below the natural price, then
some people will leave that particular kind of supply and new recruitment
will cease, and consequently supply will eventually diminish, and so the
market price will rise to the competitive normal price. Well, so much for
chapter 7.

   Chapter 8 deals with "the Wages of Labour" and is extremely perplexing
until you reach halfway through. He says that the wages of labour tend
towards subsistence level. And then he proceeds to explain it in terms of
the weakness of the labourers, uncombined, vis-à-vis the strength of the
employers who perhaps have not got an official combination but, according to Adam Smith, always tend to be in a tacit agreement to keep wages
low. And he actually says:

We rarely hear ... of the combination of masters, though frequently of those of workmen. But whoever imagines, upon this account, that masters rarely combine, is as ignorant of the world as of the subject. Masters are always and every where in a sort of tacit, but constant and uniform combination, not to raise the wages of labour above their actual rate. To violate this combination is every where a most unpopular action, and a sort of reproach to a master among his neighbours and equals. We seldom, indeed, hear of this combination, because it is the usual, and one may say, the natural state of affairs which nobody ever hears of. [ibid., 1:68–69]

And he then goes on to expatiate on this state of affairs.

But then he reverts to the supply side for a moment, and he says that of course masters can't force wages down below what is the subsistence level in the climate, and given the habits of the people in question: "A man must always live by his work, and his wages must ... at least be sufficient to maintain him. They must even upon most occasions be somewhat more; otherwise it would be impossible for him to bring up a family" [ibid., 1:69]. And he expatiates on the fact that half the children born, it is computed, die before the age of manhood, so that the subsistence wage must make allowance for that.

But then he suddenly switches over—after all, the *Wealth of Nations* is essentially an empirical book as well as a speculative book—and he observed that wages were not at subsistence level in his own country, that they differed in different parts—in some parts they were very low, in other parts they were higher—and that in other countries they were sometimes far above subsistence level, and in other countries at subsistence level, and in other countries still, below subsistence level—giving rise to the most horrible state of affairs. And he then enunciates the reason why:

When in any country the demand for those who live by wages ... is continually increasing; when every year furnishes employment for a greater number than had been employed the year before, the workmen have no occasion to combine in order to raise their wages. The scarcity of hands occasions competition among masters, who bid against one another, in order to get workmen, and thus voluntarily break through the natural combination of masters not to raise wages. [ibid., 1:70]

And so he unfolds.

In countries where accumulation is taking place, Smith sees a fairly cheerful prospect for mankind, as distinct from the very uncheerful prospect of the countries in which net accumulation is not taking place. And he says:

It is not the actual greatness of national wealth,

—by which he means national capital, not wages per head in this case—

but its continual increase, which occasions a rise in the wages of labour. [ibid., 1:71]

And then he gives the example of America, where wages were far in excess of subsistence level even in those days. And he also discusses other parts. He then gives the most terrible description of a stationary State, which he thought had existed in China,

> long one of the richest, that is, one of the most fertile, best cultivated, most industrious, and most populous countries in the world. It seems, however, to have been long stationary. [ibid., 1:73]

And he then gives a description of the absolutely lamentable condition of the working population, and particularly in the neighbourhood of Canton, which he hadn't visited—he took his knowledge from various books that he had read. And then he goes on to take the case of Bengal, which had been in a state of more or less civil chaos for some time, with people living on past accumulation. Capital wealth was actually declining. The description of the state of Bengal, well, it's such that I won't read it aloud to you. But that is the declining State.

And having, so to speak, contrasted the United States of America and the neighbourhood of Canton and Bengal as progressive, stationary and declining States, he then says—and this is a famous paragraph—

> It deserves to be remarked, perhaps, that it is in the progressive state, while the society is advancing to the further acquisition, rather than when it has acquired its full complement of riches,

—whatever he meant by that—

> that the condition of the labouring poor, of the great body of the people, seems to be the happiest and the most comfortable. It is hard in the stationary, and miserable in the declining state. The progressive state is in reality the cheerful and the hearty state to all the different orders of the society. The stationary is dull; the declining melancholy [ibid., 1:83]

—which is putting it mildly. He goes on . . . —"Of the Wages of Labour" is a long chapter.

I can deal quickly with the remaining chapters of book 1. Chapter 9 is entitled "Of the Profits of Stock." I will only point out to you at this stage that he thinks that "The rise and fall in the profits of stock depend upon the same causes with the rise and fall in the wages of labour, the increasing or declining state of the wealth of the society" [ibid., 1:89]. But as wealth increases, so Adam Smith explains the declining rate of profits in progressive society. He thought—and he thought rightly—that the rate of profit had declined since the Middle Ages. And that was that. I mention it thus briefly because I shall be coming back to Ricardo's very difficult theory of profit, which was directed against this version of the theory of profits which you find in Adam Smith's chapter "Of the Profits of Stock."

And in spite of what is said by the writers of cheap textbooks on the history of economic theory, he was not in favour of the merchants and manufacturers. The last section, page 100 of Cannan's edition, says:

> Our merchants and master-manufacturers complain much of the bad effects of high wages in raising the price, and thereby lessening the sale of their goods both at home and abroad. They say nothing concerning the bad effects of high profits. They are silent with regard to the pernicious effects of their own gains. They complain only of those of other people. [ibid., 1:100]

That was not the utterance of the paid emissary of the rising bourgeoisie. You have to go back to the original texts, you know, to get the truth.

Chapter 10 is "Of Wages and Profit in the different Employments of Labour and Stock." And this is a chapter which in a way has stood up to criticism much better than any of his other chapters. You all know how, in elementary lectures on economics, you were told to contemplate first of all a state of affairs in which labour and capital are completely mobile and consequently rates of wages are the same in all different industries and rates of profit are the same in all different industries, and then you are shown that there are differences of skill, differences of risk, differences of other elements in the environment than the earnings of wages or profits, and then you are given the picture of a tendency in a competitive society for an equality of net advantages, provided that there is sufficient equality. And then, following Adam Smith in part 2 of his chapter, you are told of the effects of various kinds of monopolistic restriction, both as regards the movement of labour and as regards the movement of capital. I won't insult an advanced class by expatiating on that, delicious though many of the side remarks are. He explains the comparatively low remuneration of the average lawyer by the inordinate conceit which people have of their own abilities. So that because the prizes of Queen's Counsel are very high, even at this day all sorts of people who never earned £100 arguing a case in a police court crowd into the industry, and then do occasional journalism and so on and so forth, and eke out their not very opulent existence because they have overestimated their own abilities in that particular line. Well, Adam Smith expatiates on that and on many other things.

Well then, at last we come to "the Rent of Land" [chap. 11], and again I will come back to this when I'm dealing with Ricardo. Adam Smith deals with the rent of land very thoroughly, and the descriptive method and historical material there is very good. He regards rent, however, as a component part of price. And when David Hume received the first edition of the *Wealth of Nations*, although he was dying, he took up his pen and said, "Bravo, Mr. Smith. You have done marvellously. Were we able to meet there are various little points I should like to take up with you. I rather think that rent is a consequence of price rather than a cause of price."[1] Well now, Adam Smith had said occasionally in the long chapter on rent that rent differed slightly from wages and profits in some respects, not having a variable supply function. But that again I can deal with when I come to deal with classical economics in general.

Well, so much for book 1. I'm nearly caught up now. I shall be briefly dealing with book 2 in the first lecture next week, and I shall get on to Adam Smith on "Policy" halfway through that lecture.

NOTE

1. Paraphrase of parts of a letter from Hume to Smith, 1 April 1776, reprinted in Hume (1955, pp. 216–17).

The *Wealth of Nations*: Analytical (III)—Policy I

I RECOMMEND to you Professor Samuel Hollander's [1973] book on Adam Smith. He's one of our most distinguished academic alumni, and I am now reading his recently published book on Ricardo, and it makes me feel sorry for you that you have to listen to me rather than to Professor Hollander, who is so good. He really surpasses all previous historians of economic thought, especially on Ricardo [1979], but his book on Adam Smith is quite first rate. All of you who are specialising in this subject are recommended to read the relevant chapters of his books, at any rate. He gives you a good deal of background history so far as Adam Smith is concerned, and when you get on to Ricardo, although it's pretty stiff reading and it's 679 pages, I think, there are chapters in it which really throw a new light on Ricardo.

Now, last time I finished an extremely inadequate account of book 1 of the *Wealth of Nations*. I now want to go on to book 2, and that ought not to take so long. Book 2 is called "Of the Nature, Accumulation, and Employment of Stock," and it is quite as important in the history of economic thought as book 1. It starts with an introduction which lays it down that division of labour depends upon the accumulation and employment of stock, which is his name for what we should call real capital. And he explains that the "stock of goods of different kinds . . . must be stored up . . . sufficient to maintain [those who participate in a division of labour which is at all advanced, supplying] with the materials and tools of his work, till such time, at least, as both these events can be brought about" [Smith, 1776, 1:258].

Well, he then sets out what he's going to do in the different chapters, which I needn't elaborate. Then chapter 1 discusses the kinds of stock, and it is important because it contains a distinction between circulating capital and fixed capital, which is perfectly all right if you are thinking of the point of view of an individual firm, but is *wrong*, or unhelpful, if you are thinking of the economy as a whole. According to this distinction, circulating capital is capital which reaps a profit by being sold, whereas fixed capital is something like a machine or a factory building which simply facilitates production, but which is not necessarily sold.

Well, that, of course, corresponds to a conversational usage among the directors of firms, and it is quite useful to keep one's head clear about the division of capital in any firm that one is in control of, based on this distinction. But as you can all see at once, it won't do for society as a whole because it depends entirely on the accidental degree to which production is integrated. In a vertical integration, all sorts of things are of course passed forward from stage to stage which do not make a profit unless they are priced inside the firm, which is a very sophisticated method of modern management. But an integrated industry makes the profit that Adam Smith regards as being made on circulating capital only when you get to the end of the integration, and the product, which has undergone various vicissitudes as it is passed from the earlier part of the integration to a later part, is, on this definition, "fixed."

So, subsequent economists have not used Adam Smith's definition very much. They have rather made any distinction that they want to make between fixed and circulating capital depend upon the durability of the capital involved. This is a semantic matter; it's not a fundamental one, but it's quite important to bear it in mind to preserve yourselves from confusion when you are reading the different historic authors.

Well then, chapter 2 deals with "Money." He regards money as part of national capital and deals with the expense of maintaining it. But I don't myself think that what he says about money is particularly relevant to this part of my lectures. I shall refer back to Adam Smith on money when I come to certain controversies of nineteenth-century classicism.

Chapter 3, however, I must dwell on. Chapter 3 is entitled "Of the Accumulation of Capital, or of productive and unproductive Labour." And here he uses the same terms as the physiocrats, but whereas the physiocrats effectively applied the term *productive* only to agriculture, and some of them to extractive industry, Adam Smith uses it in an entirely different way, and let me read the opening sentences: "There is one sort of labour which adds to the value of the subject upon which it is bestowed: there is another which has no such effect. The former, as it produces a value, may be called productive; the latter, unproductive labour" [ibid., 1:313].

Well now, that has some analytical sense: the distinction between a consumption service, which perishes in the moment of its production, although it may be remunerated, and investment, whether in material objects or—well, the classical economists called it education—investment in human capital. And presumably they thought that lectures didn't perish in the moment of their production. Having been a lecturer for nearly sixty years of my life, I am not quite so sure.

And then there comes a comic paragraph which I must read to you, because it is one of the most famous paragraphs in Adam Smith's book 2:

> The labour of some of the most respectable orders in the society is, like that of menial servants, unproductive of any value, and does not fix or realize itself in any permanent subject, or vendible commodity, which endures after that labour is past, and for which an equal quantity of labour could afterwards be procured. The sovereign, for example, with all the officers both of justice and war who serve under him, the whole army and navy, are unproductive labourers. They are the servants of the public, and are maintained by a part of the

annual produce of the industry of other people. Their service, how honourable, how useful, or how necessary soever, produces nothing for which an
equal quantity of service can afterwards be procured. [ibid., 1:314]

I am not quite sure about that.

> In the same class must be ranked, some both of the gravest and most impor-
> tant and some of the most frivolous professions: churchmen, lawyers, physi-
> cians, men of letters of all kinds; players, buffoons, musicians, opera-singers,
> opera-dancers, &c. The labour of the meanest of these has a certain value,
> regulated by the very same principles which regulate that of every other sort of
> labour; and that of the noblest and most useful, produces nothing which
> could afterwards purchase or procure an equal quantity of labour. Like the
> declamation of the actor, the harangue of the orator, or the tune of the musi-
> cian, the work of all of them perishes in the very instant of its production.
> [ibid.]

Well, there you are. And Marx adopted that division, and I understand that
it still figures in some Russian statistics.

But then he goes on to discuss the proportion between productive and
unproductive labour as so defined. And this leads on to the proposition
that productive labour is productive of capital, in some sense or other, and
unproductive labour, while it may produce a revenue of consumption to
those who enjoy it, is not productive of capital. And this leads him to expatiate at some length on the formation of capital: "Capitals are increased by
parsimony"—saving—"and diminished by prodigality and misconduct."

> Whatever a person saves from his revenue he adds to his capital, and either
> employs it himself in maintaining an additional number of productive hands,
> or enables some other person to do so, by lending it to him for an interest,
> that is, for a share of the profits. As the capital of an individual can be increased
> only by what he saves from his annual revenue . . . so the capital of a society,
> which is the same with that of all the individuals who compose it, can be in-
> creased only in the same manner. [ibid., 1:320]

Well, that's OK. It leaves out of account forced saving, for instance, which
takes place in the early days of inflation, and it leaves out of account monetary complications of a like character.

But he then goes on to reassure people that saving does not mean a diminution of employment, and he says, in a very well-known sentence:

> What is annually saved is as regularly consumed as what is annually spent,
> and nearly in the same time too; but it is consumed by a different set of people.
> That portion of his revenue which a rich man annually spends, is in most cases
> consumed by idle guests, and menial servants, who leave nothing behind them
> in return for their consumption. That portion which he annually saves, as for
> the sake of the profit it is immediately employed as a capital, is consumed in
> the same manner, and nearly in the same time too, but by a different set of

people, by labourers, manufacturers, and artificers, who re-produce with a
profit the value of their annual consumption. [ibid.]

Now that fateful sentence leaves out entirely the possibility of variations in
the velocity of circulation, which are the same as attempts to hoard. Now
it is quite true, as Keynes pointed out (and many other people have pointed
out too), that, provided that the quantity of money, either metallic or
paper, in a community is constant, attempts to hoard will influence simply
the volume of production and employment, but they won't diminish the
amount of hoarded money in the community. The effect is on the velocity
of circulation. But that is a very important effect: It is one of the ways in
which we can partially explain fluctuations in trade and employment.

And this remark of Adam Smith's was emulated by the majority of the
classical economists and found further development in the celebrated, but
possibly misnamed, Say's Law. J. B. Say was a French economist of great
distinction, who popularised Adam Smith and rearranged his exposition in
a very French logical way, and who is an economist of stature. And the idea
that aggregate supply must always be equal to aggregate demand has in
modern jargon been described as Say's Law. And all sorts of people, great
and small, have made some reputations for themselves by explanations why
Say's Law doesn't always hold.

Well, if you read Professor Baumol [1977] in quite a recent number of
Economica—I think it is 68—on the eight different meanings of J. B. Say,
you will realise that J. B. Say did realise the possibility of hoarding, and he
did realise all sorts of other possibilities, so that it's really rather a mistake
to blame Say for mistakes into which James Mill fell—or at least I think that
he fell—and which Ricardo certainly maintained from time to time, and
indeed employed with tremendous effect in his arguments with Malthus
about depressions and things of that sort. But there it is: Give a dog a bad
name and it will stay with him. And I suppose this will go on being called
Say's Law even though the history of economic thought shows that Say was
not so guilty as other people.

Well, the rest of the book dwells on the benefits to society of accumulation, and it makes a distinction between private individuals and Governments. Adam Smith, being slightly Marxian at this moment—I may remind
you, he was a Scotsman—Adam Smith thinks that private individuals
on the whole tend to save, to make safeguard against the future, whereas
he finds it extremely hard to believe that Governments save. On the contrary, Governments are always exceeding their revenue, and if only they
would stop messing private individuals about, one need not worry about
the accumulation of capital. But both Adam Smith and Hume, with
the very, very small National Debt hanging about in those days, were very,
very much worried by the prodigality of Governments, and both Adam
Smith and Hume denounced the prodigality of Governments in no uncertain terms.

Then you go on to a chapter [chap. 4] on "Stock lent at Interest," which is interesting, but which employs no new concepts.

He then goes on in book 3 to suggest that the policies of States have distorted "the Natural Progress of Opulence," and he expatiates on "the Discouragement of Agriculture in the ancient State of Europe after the Fall of the Roman Empire." Then in chapter 3 he discusses "the Rise and Progress of Cities and Towns." In chapter 4 he discusses the mutual relationship of towns and country given in the policies of the State. That is all that I need to say about book 3.

In book 4 he talks about "Systems of political Œconomy." The introduction gives a new slant to political economy. Books 1, 2 and 3—although there is a spot of polemic in book 3—may be regarded as analytical, but book 4, "Of Systems of Political Œconomy," is polemical. He says:

> Political œconomy, considered as a branch of the science of a statesman or legislator, proposes two distinct objects: first, to provide a plentiful revenue or subsistence for the people, or more properly to enable them to provide such a revenue or subsistence for themselves; and secondly, to supply the state or commonwealth with a revenue sufficient for the public services. It proposes to enrich both the people and the sovereign. [Smith, 1776, 1:395]

He adds:

> The different progress of opulence in different ages and nations, has given occasion to two different systems of political œconomy, with regard to enriching the people. The one may be called the system of commerce,

—later on he calls it the mercantile system—

> the other that of agriculture. I shall endeavour to explain both as fully and distinctly as I can, and shall begin with the system of commerce. [ibid.]

The system of commerce occupies the rest of chapter 1 and a good part of chapter 2, and I do not propose to go into it at great length, because, while it is of *immense* value to historians, as indicating the appraisal which Adam Smith made of various historical interventions and regulations, I do not think that it falls much within the compass of these lectures.

Chapter 1, which deals with "the Principle of the commercial, or mercantile System," inveighs against the idea that wealth consists in money, or gold and silver—a popular notion which naturally arises from the double function of money as the instrument of commerce. He then goes on to indicate that he disagrees with the mercantile or commercial system, which holds that it should be the object of commercial policy to secure a constant inflow of the precious metals. He thinks that the country which has no mines of its own must undoubtedly draw its gold and silver from foreign countries in the same manner as one that has no vineyards of its own must draw its wine. He thinks that that is all that there is to it. He is here relying on what I have already referred to in discussing Hume—the specie flow hypothesis, which Hume expounded in a notable way. Adam Smith must have been acquainted with Hume's refutation, although he does not refer to it in the *Wealth of Nations*, which is felt to be something of a mystery. At any rate, he is not as good as Hume in that particular connection.

Chapter 2 discusses restraints on particular imports, and he thinks that the interests of various kinds of producers will guide them, and he uses some rather rocky arguments here about the amount that goes into foreign trade and our domestic trade. That leads up to his famous remarks about the invisible hand, which I must read to you, because you must all know about it:

> the annual revenue of every society is always precisely equal to the exchange-able value of the whole annual produce of its industry, or rather is precisely the same thing with that exchangeable value. As every individual, therefore, endeavours as much as he can both to employ his capital in the support of domestic industry, and so to direct that industry that its produce may be of the greatest value; every individual necessarily labours to render the annual revenue of the society as great as he can. He generally, indeed, neither intends to promote the public interest, nor knows how much he is promoting it. By preferring the support of domestic to that of foreign industry, he intends

—he said earlier in the chapter that domestic industry tends to be more productive than foreign industry, which is very, very questionable if you apply it to particular historical instances—

> only his own security; and by directing that industry in such a manner as its produce may be of the greatest value, he intends only his own gain, and he is in this, as in many other cases, led by an invisible hand to promote an end which was no part of his intention. Nor is it always the worse for the society that it was no part of it. By pursuing his own interest he frequently promotes that of the society more effectually than when he really intends to promote it. I have never known

—this is the so-called apologist for the bourgeoisie—

> much good done by those who affected to trade for the public good. It is an affectation, indeed, not very common among merchants, and very few words need be employed in dissuading them from it. [ibid., 1:421]

Then he goes on to say that

> The statesman, who should attempt to direct private people in what manner they ought to employ their capitals, would not only load himself with a most unnecessary attention, but assume an authority which could safely be trusted, not only to no single person, but to no council or senate whatever, and which would no-where be so dangerous as in the hands of a man who had folly and presumption enough to fancy himself fit to exercise it. [ibid.]

This passage is always quoted by those who describe Adam Smith as a laissez-faire extremist. Of course if you take it by itself, it sounds that way, but if you read on in the book you will find that he assigns all sorts of functions to the State which really distinguish him from those who regard laissez-faire as a dogma. I intend to go on to discuss that sort of thing in the next lecture. I will say on that passage only what I have said already: that, analytically, the part about the invisible hand directing people to domestic investment until domestic investment is less profitable than foreign investment is not frightfully convincing, although it seems clear that Adam Smith set some store by it. His praise of the invisible hand guiding self-interest when not supported by monopolistic restriction of one kind or another would have been very much better if he had not used that particular example. But perhaps this is esoteric stuff.

Let me go on to what he says about the physiocrats. There is only one chapter devoted to physiocracy, as distinct from many chapters devoted to details of the mercantile system. But his reaction to physiocracy is quite interesting and deserves just a little attention.

I have already introduced you to the chapter on physiocracy when I read to you Adam Smith's rather contemptuous appraisal of Colbert, a plodding man who was very efficient at looking after accounts, but who was not, in Adam Smith's opinion, efficient in managing the affairs of a great country because he devoted all his attention to fostering industry, and consequently left agriculture at a disadvantage. He goes on to say: "If the rod be bent too much one way, says the proverb, in order to make it straight you must bend it as much the other" [ibid., 2:162].

The French philosophers had been rather offputting so far as Hume was concerned—I think that I quoted to you the saying that they were of all men the most chimerical—but they rather attracted Adam Smith. And he says:

> The French philosophers, who have proposed the system which represents agriculture as the sole source of the revenue and wealth of every country, seem to have adopted this proverbial maxim; and as in the plan of Mr. Colbert the industry of the towns was certainly over-valued in comparison with that of the country; so in their system it seems to be as certainly under-valued. [ibid.]

Then he goes on to explain the physiocratic system, which I have already tried to explain to you. He mentions the physiocratic table, which he obviously regarded with a certain amount of respect. He calls Quesnay's system "this liberal and generous system" [ibid., 2:170], but he thinks that "The capital error of this system . . . seems to lie in its representing the class of artificers, manufacturers and merchants, as altogether barren and unproductive" [ibid., 2:172]. He says that the following observations may serve to show the impropriety of this representation:

First, this class, it is acknowledged, reproduces annually the value of its own annual consumption, and continues, at least, the existence of the stock or capital which maintains and employs it. But upon this account alone the denomination of barren or unproductive should seem to be very improperly applied to it. We should not call a marriage barren or unproductive, though it produced only a son and a daughter, to replace the father and mother, and though it did not increase the number of the human species, but only continued it as it was before. . . .

Secondly, it seems, upon this account, altogether improper to consider artificers, manufacturers and merchants, in the same light as menial servants. The labour of menial servants

—and the Sovereign, I interpolate that—

does not continue the existence of the fund which maintains and employs them. Their maintenance and employment is altogether at the expence of their masters, and the work which they perform is not of a nature to repay that expence. That work consists in services which perish generally in the very instant of their performance, and does not fix or realise itself in any vendable commodity which can replace the value of their wages and maintenance. [ibid., 2:173]

And so on and so forth.

On the page before there is a slight dig at Quesnay, which I think is worth reading to you because it shows Adam Smith's much more eclectic attitude to the constitution of society and the possible control of society. He says:

Some speculative physicians seem to have imagined that the health of the human body could be preserved only by a certain precise regimen of diet and exercise, of which every, the smallest, violation necessarily occasioned some degree of disease or disorder proportioned to the degree of the violation. Experience, however, would seem to show, that the human body frequently preserves, to all appearance at least, the most perfect state of health under a vast variety of different regimens; even under some which are generally believed to be very far from being perfectly wholesome. . . . Mr. Quesnai, who was himself a physician, and a very speculative physician, seems to have entertained a notion of the same kind concerning the political body, and to have imagined that it would thrive and prosper only under a certain precise regimen, the exact regimen of perfect liberty and perfect justice. [ibid., 2:172]

Then after a few sentences he says:

If a nation could not prosper without the enjoyment of perfect liberty and perfect justice, there is not in the world a nation which could ever have prospered. In the political body, however, the wisdom of nature has fortunately made ample provision for remedying many of the bad effects of the folly and injustice of man; in the same manner as it has done in the natural body, for remedying those of his sloth and intemperance. [ibid.]

Then he bestows a little praise on the system. He says of the agricultural system:

> This system, however, with all its imperfections, is, perhaps, the nearest approximation to the truth that has yet been published upon the subject of political œconomy, and is upon that account well worth the consideration of every man who wishes to examine with attention the principles of that very important science. [ibid., 2:176]

Now, why did Adam Smith praise the physiocrats and Hume denigrate them, with the exception of Turgot? It was clearly because Adam Smith felt that the physiocrats, in the course of their analysis of the system as a whole, denounced all sorts of regulations—regulations which prevented the passage of corn from one district where it was plentiful to another district where there was famine, and so on and so forth. He felt that they were on to a good thing in emphasising the benefits of greater freedom of markets and greater freedom of individual enterprise. He did not agree with their definition of "productive" and "unproductive" labour; he felt that the economic table—not to use his words—was not as important as the invention of writing, or the wheel, or something of that sort. He thought that the physiocrats exaggerated its importance, but he thought that it was a liberal and generous system and deserved attention.

But he winds up book 4 with a very important passage, in which he says that the mercantile system, having proved its rottenness in various ways, and the agricultural system being shown to be defective in various ways, with "All [these] systems either of preference or restraint, therefore, being thus completely taken away, the obvious and simple system of natural liberty establishes itself of its own accord" [ibid., 2:184].

He then defines the system of natural liberty and that is very important, lest you should have got wrong ideas from superficial reading of the passage on the invisible hand:

> According to the system of natural liberty, the sovereign has only three duties to attend to; three duties of great importance, indeed, but plain and intelligible to common understandings: first, the duty of protecting the society from the violence and invasion of other independent societies. [ibid., 2: 184–85]

He said earlier, in praising the navigation laws which confined various kinds of trade to British ships, that they had built up a powerful navigable force which was capable of being used for military purposes, and defence was more than opulence. He said that in the chapters on the mercantile system.

> [S]econdly, the duty of protecting, as far as possible, every member of the society from the injustice or oppression of every other member of it, or the duty of establishing an exact administration of justice. [ibid., 2:185]

I think that Adam Smith was a bit wrong there in saying that justice was plain and intelligible to common understanding. Hume was more right when he drew attention to the fact that systems of justice—systems relating to property (in Hume's terminology) and contract—are extremely complicated, not capable of being written on two tablets of stone or anything of that sort, but demanding from very superior intellects the minute attention of a lifetime. But *thirdly*—and this is the one that I want you to keep in your heads—

> and, thirdly, the duty of erecting and maintaining certain public works and certain public institutions, which it can never be for the interest of any individual, or small number of individuals, to erect and maintain; because the profit could never repay the expence to any individual or small number of individuals, though it may frequently do much more than repay it to a great society. [ibid.]

That third duty of the State is not the utterance of a dogmatic supporter of the police State or (was it Marx or Lassalle who called it) the "nightwatchman theory of the State."[1]

What he thought about the duties of the State, and what he thought about public finance, I shall endeavour to compress within my lecture tomorrow, so as to be able to go on next week with the much more difficult nineteenth-century classicists.

NOTE

1. It was Lassalle.

The Wealth of Nations: Policy II

WE HAVE more or less caught up, and at the conclusion of my last lecture I read you Adam Smith's discussion of the functions of the State under the system of natural liberty, dwelling especially on the third function, which was for the State to carry out branches of enterprise or undertakings which it could never be to the profit of any individual or small collection of individuals to undertake, although it might be to the benefit of a large country.

The only thing I want to say about that is that I forgot as I was walking out of the room to exhort you to compare that definition of the functions of the State with that in Keynes' famous pamphlet *The End of Laissez-Faire* [1926]. I don't think at that stage Keynes, who was a marvellous man, but had an extremely bad memory—an *extremely* bad memory; it explains all sorts of things which have been ascribed to him for unrighteousness, and quite unfairly so—but he obviously hadn't read this last chapter of Adam Smith's fourth book, because his own definition of the functions of the State runs in almost the same words and it has exactly the same formal purport, although of course all sorts of things have happened since 1776, and I am inclined to say that any reasonable person would regard the specific functions of the State falling under this heading as meaning more in the twentieth century than they did in the eighteenth. Well, that's all that I want to say about the general enunciation.

But now I want this morning to talk to you about Adam Smith's elaboration in book 5 of the expenditure and regulations of the State and the various heads that they fall under, and to take a brief glance at public finance. So I had better get on with it.

Well, the beginning of book 5 deals with the first of the duties of the State in liberal circumstances, namely, defence. I am not going to dwell on that. He gives an interesting account of the evolution of defence from the time of the lowest and rudest state of society in which every man is a warrior as well as a hunter, and possibly a shepherd, to times which were modern at the time when he wrote the *Wealth of Nations*. And he dwells, not unnaturally, on the increased costs of defence since the invention of gunpowder and the greater specialisation of defence. And that doesn't involve economic analysis, and I pass on.

He then deals with the question of justice, and although he does not use the word *justice* in the rather narrow sense in which Hume uses it when dealing with law relating to property and contract, he does go out of his way to say that where there is no property and where therefore there can be no theft and violence concerning property, the execution of justice is a comparatively narrow matter. And he then proceeds to expatiate on the execution of justice in more advanced society, particularly as regards property, which he thinks owes its origin either to good fortune or to birth. And he concludes that section by tracing the evolution of institutions of justice, showing how in the past the institutions were such as to permit those who administered justice to accept gifts and in various other ways to be corrupted, and he dwells upon the extreme importance of the independence of the judiciary.

Well, what we're concerned with, mostly, is the third duty of the State— that of fostering or actually carrying out undertakings which it can be to the interest of no private individual or group of individuals to foster. And first of all, on page 215 of Cannan's edition [vol. 2], he dwells upon the importance of institutions of this sort, and he recommends that in many cases, as for instance a road system or a bridge system—that sort of thing— these works could be financed by means other than taxation, and he comes down pretty heavily in favour of tolls—tolls both for roads and for canals, which were beginning to come into fashion in a large way in his day. And to show his empiricism in this respect, he says that if canals are not looked after continually, the banks tend to fall in, and consequently it will be to the self-interest of the people who maintain canals to keep them navigable. The same is not true of roads, where a road can be usable although it has been allowed to fall into grave deterioration. And he consequently thinks that the ownership of roads must reside in some public authority.

And he then goes on—the final point in his general treatment of this matter, before he comes to particular institutions—he says that public works of a local nature should be locally administered because the local authorities are more affected in one way or another, however they may be constituted, than the central authority. And he contrasts the good lighting of cities where local authorities control them with cities where that is not the case.

Then he proceeds to particular branches of commerce, and there is a long disquisition on the authorisation by the State of regulated or joint stock companies. Now, on the whole, as I shall be revealing in a moment, Adam Smith had a strong suspicion both of the administration of such companies and of their efficiency if they were to reach out beyond certain very specified functions. He thinks that there is some justification for the regulated companies where the trade was concerned with comparatively primitive communities enjoying different systems of law, and where there was very great risk for individual traders. But he goes on to say that there is a great risk in affording particular status even to the regulated companies, and he has, in this part of his book and other parts of his book, pretty harsh things to say about the East India Company, which had such tremendous powers as regards the subcontinent of India and elsewhere.

And then when he gets to joint stock companies he says again that the joint stock principle is all right, provided that it is extinguished in a comparatively short time. And he follows up what he said about the regulated companies by very grave reflections on the more limited purposes of the joint stock companies:

> Without a monopoly, however, a joint stock company, it would appear from experience, cannot long carry on any branch of foreign trade. To buy in one market, in order to sell, with profit, in another, when there are many competitors in both; to watch over, not only the occasional variations in the demand, but the much greater and more frequent variations in the competition, or in the supply which that demand is likely to get from other people, and to suit with dexterity and judgment both the quantity and quality of each assortment of goods to all these circumstances, is a species of warfare of which the operations are continually changing, and which can scarce ever be conducted successfully, without such an unremitting exertion of vigilance and attention, as cannot long be expected from the directors of a joint stock company. [Smith, 1776, 2:245]

Well, if you were a critic of Adam Smith, you could have a perfect field day as regards his further observations elaborating this particular generalisation. He actually goes on to say:

> The only trades which it seems possible for a joint stock company to carry on successfully, without an exclusive privilege, are those, of which all the operations are capable of being reduced to what is called a routine, or to such a uniformity of method as admits of little or no variation. Of this kind is, first, the banking trade; secondly, the trade of insurance from fire, and from sea risk and capture in time of war; thirdly, the trade of making and maintaining a navigable cut or canal; and, fourthly, the similar trade of bringing water for the supply of a great city. [ibid., 2:246]

Well now, whatever one thinks of the present law relating to joint stock companies and the present efficiency of joint stock companies, it must historically be admitted that Adam Smith was very wide of the mark in saying that. Successful joint stock companies which haven't been granted a State-conferred monopoly have been conspicuously successful—some of them being conspicuously unsuccessful—at subsequent times in history. You should read that part and reflect on it, and try to think out the various generalisations applicable to joint stock companies which didn't occur to Adam Smith. There are some generalisations appropriate to joint stock companies as *we* know them which are by no means entirely favourable, but that is another question.

I pass to the much more fascinating—and, since you have given me this splendid birthday card, much more relevant to today—chapter, "Of the Expence of the Institutions for the Education of Youth." And he talks first of all about universities. "Have those public endowments," he asked, contributed in general to promote the end of their institution? Have they contributed to encourage the diligence, and to improve the abilities of the teachers? Have they directed the course of education towards objects more useful, both to the individual and to the public, than those to which it would naturally have gone of its own accord? It should not seem very difficult to give at least a probable answer to each of these questions. [ibid., 2:249]

Then he goes on to make a generalisation which some of you may think to be true and which I think is partially true, but not wholly:

In every profession, the exertion of the greater part of those who exercise it, is always in proportion to the necessity they are under of making that exertion. This necessity is the greatest with those to whom the emoluments of their profession are the only source from which they expect their fortune. [ibid.]

That is to say that, as regards university professors, he thought that the ideal state of affairs was that they should derive their incomes from the pay which their students contributed. And so if they gave good lectures they would get a good many students, and if they gave bad lectures they would get few students.

Now, you mustn't think that that is an entirely unreal supposition. Do any of you come from Germany? Does the *Kollegiumgeld* still function in different universities in Germany? [A student seems to respond in the negative.] It has only been abolished, then, since the Second World War. Indeed, I know professors of business administration, who may be dead now, who used to make an enormous fortune from the very successful lectures which they gave by the *Kollegiumgeld*.

And he says that

The greatness of the objects which are to be acquired by success in some particular professions may, no doubt, sometimes animate the exertion of a few men of extraordinary spirit and ambition. Great objects, however, are evidently not necessary in order to occasion the greatest exertions. [ibid., 2: 249–50]

And he then says that

The endowments of schools and colleges have necessarily diminished more or less the necessity of application in the teachers. . . .

In some universities the salary makes but a part, and frequently but a small part of the emoluments of the teacher, of which the greater part arises from the honoraries or fees of his pupils. [ibid., 2:250]

He was thinking of his own university of Glasgow, which he obviously thought was pretty efficient.

The necessity of application, though always more or less diminished, is not in this case entirely taken away. Reputation in his profession is still of some importance to him, and he still has some dependency upon the affection, gratitude, and favourable report of those who have attended upon his instructions. . . .

In other universities the teacher is prohibited from receiving any honorary or fee from his pupils, and his salary constitutes the whole of the revenue which he derives from his office. His interest is, in this case, set as directly in opposition to his duty as it is possible to set it. It is the interest of every man to live as much at his ease as he can; and if his emoluments are to be precisely the same, whether he does, or does not perform some very laborious duty, it is certainly his interest, at least as interest is vulgarly understood, either to neglect it altogether, or, if he is subject to some authority which will not suffer him to do this, to perform it in as careless and slovenly a manner as that authority will permit. . . .

If the authority to which he is subject resides in the body corporate, the college, or university, of which he himself is a member, and in which the greater part of the other members are, like himself, persons who either are, or ought to be teachers; they are likely to make a common cause, to be all very indulgent to one another, and every man to consent that his neighbour may neglect his duty, provided he himself is allowed to neglect his own. In the university of Oxford, the greater part of the public professors have, for these many years, given up altogether even the pretence of teaching. [ibid., 2: 250–51]

And Adam Smith had been a Snell scholar at Balliol for seven years!

He then goes on to discuss French universities, and he thinks pretty badly of the French universities. I must read this, which perhaps you may interpret against me!

If the teacher happens to be a man of sense, it must be an unpleasant thing for him to be conscious, while he is lecturing his students, that he is either speaking or reading nonsense, or what is very little better than nonsense. It must too be unpleasant to him to observe that the greater part of his students desert his lectures; or perhaps attend upon them with plain enough marks of neglect, contempt, and derision. . . . Several different expedients . . . may . . . blunt the edge of all those incitements to diligence. The teacher, instead of explaining to his pupils himself the science in which he proposes to instruct them, may read some book upon it;

—which is what I am doing now—

and if this book is written in a foreign and dead language, by interpreting it to them into their own. [ibid., 2:252–53]

And he then goes on in the immortal paragraph which makes you love Adam Smith, even if, as I shall be saying in a moment, you don't totally agree with him:

The discipline of colleges and universities is in general contrived, not for the benefit of the students, but for the interest, or more properly speaking, for the ease of the masters. Its object is, in all cases, to maintain the authority of the master, and whether he neglects or performs his duty, to oblige the students in all cases to behave to him as if he performed it with the greatest diligence and ability. It seems to presume perfect wisdom and virtue in the one order, and the greatest weakness and folly in the other. Where the masters, however, really perform their duty, there are no examples, I believe, that the greater part of the students ever neglect theirs. No discipline is ever requisite to force attendance upon lectures which are really worth the attending, as is well known wherever any such lectures are given. Force and restraint may, no doubt, be in some degree requisite in order to oblige children, or very young boys, to attend to those parts of education which it is thought necessary for them to acquire during that early period of life; but after twelve or thirteen years of age, provided the master does his duty, force or restraint can scarce ever be necessary to carry on any part of education. Such is the generosity of the greater part of young men,

—and women, I would add—

that, so far from being disposed to neglect or despise the instructions of their master, provided he shows some serious intention of being of use to them, they are generally inclined to pardon a great deal of incorrectness in the performance of his duty, and sometimes even to conceal from the public a good deal of gross negligence. [ibid., 2:253]

So then he goes on to expatiate on the history of education in medieval times—how it was the instrument of the Church—and he expatiates on the contrast between contemporary universities, Oxford and Cambridge, and the conditions among the Greeks, where there were no universities, but where the great philosophers—Plato and Aristotle and their followers— each took pupils and, according to Adam Smith, succeeded in giving them a pretty good education. And he then goes on to say that where subjects are not taught in universities, such as dancing or fencing, and where the instructors are paid for by fees, then the instruction is pretty good; otherwise the demand falls off. And he expatiates too on the fact "that there are no public institutions for the education of women, and there is accordingly nothing useless, absurd, or fantastical in the common course of their education" [ibid., 2:266].

Now, it is historically the case that, whatever you can say about Oxford and Cambridge—and there is quite a lot to be said against them in some ways in the twentieth century—you cannot really say that they are idle. The so-called tutorial system, which is dying out in many faculties (the small-group system of tuition is coming into vogue), was, of course, a rich man's privilege. A one-to-one relationship is all right and is indeed absolutely necessary in the graduate school, but you can arrange reasonable intimacy with a small group, I think, at the undergraduate level.

Well, in my day at Oxford—I was there for a few years in the 1920s, and I was at first on a part-time engagement—I used to go up on Wednesdays very early and come away on Saturdays at midday, and every hour of the day was devoted to the old-fashioned tutorial system—1:1. When a man brought you along an essay taking so much of a foolscap page, you were supposed to go on talking to him for the rest of the hour, instead of saying, "Well, Mr X, next time perhaps your essay might be more interesting. You might take some regard to this authority and that, if you haven't already studied them." And I must say that in those days, by the time I came to have lunch on Saturday, I was so exhausted—I went on until 10 o'clock at night—that I didn't want any lunch.

And it was my impression in those days that very distinguished people actually overworked. Note I am talking about people who are dead now, but the very distinguished historian of mediaeval economic thought A. J. Carlisle told me that he used to give 1:1 tutorials thirty hours a week. Now, that was very different from the state of affairs described by Adam Smith. I think that lecturing at Oxford in my day was taken very lightly indeed by most of the tutors. It was a statutory obligation, and they did not take much trouble about it; anybody who did take trouble with lectures had no difficulty in having an enormous crowd of students. But somehow or other, and I say this not in vindication of the universities, which are in all sorts of ways sometimes no better than they should be, but as a matter of historical fact, Oxford and Cambridge reformed themselves in the nineteenth century so that, if you may say, *excessive* devotion to the 1:1 tutorial system replaced this state of absolute neglect in the eighteenth century. And this was due, not to an alteration of the market system at all; it was due to the influence of a few powerful personalities—I know Oxford much better than Cambridge: In Oxford such as Mark Pattison at Lincoln, Jowett at Balliol, Newman and his friends at Oriel, and so on. So that although I would be far from saying that there are no people at those ancient universities who neglect their tutorial duties, on the whole, in my time at any rate, it was thought to be something that was not done—not to conform to those rather arduous regulations.

I would also say, as regards universities, that I think that there is more of a problem—if you are not completely laissez-faire as regards education—as regards the emoluments of the people who teach very esoteric subjects. Now, for instance, a professor, however diligent he may be, who lectures on, shall we say, Egyptology, is not likely to get so extensive an audience as the man who lectures on, let us say, accounting or engineering. I myself think—this is a value judgement, if you like—that Egyptology is a very respectable subject and that it should be incumbent on a university of sufficient size, such as London University, to have professors in those narrow fields which don't attract a large number of undergraduates. And therefore the fee system which Adam Smith recommended, which served its purpose perfectly well in the very distinguished state of the Scottish universities, was not, I think, universally applicable for that reason.

However, Adam Smith then goes on to talk—what is really much more important than university education—to the education of people who don't have the benefit of university or college education. And he thinks that the division of labour, which he has so praised in book 1 of the *Wealth of Nations*, has a bad effect on those who are involved in the division of labour at a lower level, insofar as they receive no education. And there is a memorable paragraph that I'll read, again despite what Adam Smith says about those who read things:

> In the progress of the division of labour, the employment of the far greater part of those who live by labour . . . comes to be confined to a few very simple operations. . . . But the understandings of the greater part of men are necessarily formed by their ordinary employments. The man whose whole life is spent in performing a few simple operations, of which the effects too are, perhaps, always the same, or very nearly the same, has no occasion to exert his understanding, or to exercise his invention in finding out expedients for removing difficulties which never occur. He naturally loses, therefore, the habit of such exertion, and generally becomes as stupid and ignorant as it is possible for a human creature to become. The torpor of his mind renders him, not only incapable of relishing or bearing a part in any rational conversation, but of conceiving any generous, noble, or tender sentiment, and consequently of forming any just judgment concerning many even of the ordinary duties of private life. [ibid., 2:267]

And he goes on to say that it even corrupts the activity of his body and renders him incapable of exerting his strengths of adventure and perseverence and so on.

> And so, in order to avoid these deplorable results, he thinks that though the common people cannot, in any civilized society, be so well instructed as people of some rank and fortune, the most essential parts of education, however to read, write, and account, can be acquired at so early a period of life, that the greater part even of those who are bred to the lowest occupations, have time to acquire them. . . . For a very small expence the public can facilitate, can encourage, and can even impose upon almost the whole body of the people, the necessity of acquiring those most essential parts of education. [ibid., 2:270]

And he goes on to recommend the establishment

> in every parish or district [of] a little school, where children may be taught for a reward so moderate, that even a common labourer may afford it; the master being partly, but not wholly paid by the public. . . . In Scotland the establishment of such parish schools has taught almost the whole common people to read, and a very great proportion of them to write and account. [ibid.]

And so he goes on, and he suggests that certain professions should be free only to those who have passed certain examinations. He doesn't believe altogether in university examinations, but he does believe that certain degrees of competence can be imposed. And so on.

He goes on to discuss the expense of religious instruction [ibid., 2:273–99] and indulges in a very amusing controversy with Hume, whom he describes as "the most illustrious philosopher . . . of . . . the age" [ibid., 2:275]. Hume had said that it's a very good thing to have a State religion, with the people in it maintained by the State, because, Hume says, this discourages fanaticism and fanaticism is a very disturbing thing. Indeed, diligence is a very disturbing thing in the promulgation of everything—and here surely Hume is being ironical—everything except the "true" religion, which he inserted obviously to keep at arm's length those who criticised him for being an agnostic. Adam Smith enters into controversy with him not so much on religious grounds, but on the ground that if there is a multiplicity of sects in competition with one another, none of them will become sufficiently predominant, and they won't be sufficiently wealthy to attract very distinguished people, and the universities will be able to attract from—in such a state of affairs in the organisation of a multiplicity of sects of religion—the more distinguished people, because the universities can afford by way of fees and salaries to offer superior advantages. All that is very amusing, but I don't think it is analytically very important.

The important thing which I just want to draw your attention to is the section in the rest of the book which deals with questions of taxation and debt.[1] Now, as regards taxation, you will receive very superior lectures on taxation elsewhere in your specialisation here, and it would therefore be totally superfluous for me to go through Adam Smith's arguments about taxation in detail. It is necessary, however, just to mention the famous canons of taxation which he laid down at the beginning of this discussion of a good tax system.

The first canon is that a tax system should conform to equality of burden. Now, the interpretation of that is ambiguous. In parts of his treatment he seems to mean proportionality to income, and there are other parts which can be picked out by those who favour progressiveness of income taxation. The second canon of taxation is certainty. People ought to know what taxation they are charged, either direct or indirect. The third canon is convenience. Taxation should be collected in a way which causes least inconvenience. And the fourth canon is economy in collection [ibid., 2:310–12].

Well, he then goes on to discuss various taxes, direct and indirect, and sometimes you agree with him and sometimes you don't. It is all very interesting, but I think it is below the horizon for a course of 35 lectures on the history of economic thought.

The last part of the book deals with public debt [book 5, chap. 3]. And since there are sufficient of you here, how many of you come from America? Hands up, please. Well now, here is something which is rather piquant so far as you're concerned. Way back in the second volume of Cannan's edition, on page 124, he has revealed his extreme concern about the public financial arrangements as between the American colonies, as they were, and Great Britain. And he doesn't think that these are at all fair, and he thinks of it in some respects from the British point of view. He points out the great expense of maintaining an army and a navy to guard the colonies from the depredations of the French and the Red Indians and so on and so forth. And so he suggests a federation, and he thinks that that would be almost ideal. And he says—and this I read to you to show his open-mindedness:

> The people on the other side of the water are afraid lest their distance from the seat of government might expose them to many oppressions. But their representatives in parliament, of which the number ought from the first to be considerable, would easily be able to protect them from all oppression. The distance could not much weaken the dependancy of the representative upon the constituent, and the former would still feel that he owed his seat in parliament, and all the consequence which he derived from it, to the good-will of the latter. [ibid., 2:124]

Well, I am a little bit in disagreement with Adam Smith considering that it took two months to communicate with the eastern seaboard of the United States; I think that that might be regarded as a disadvantage. But he says that this distance would not be of very long continuance:

> Such has hitherto been the rapid progress of that country in wealth, population and improvement, that in the course of little more than a century, perhaps, the produce of American might exceed that of British taxation. [ibid.]

And then—listen carefully, see that he was not a good internationalist, at any rate as regards the English-speaking world—

> The seat of the empire would then naturally remove itself to that part of the empire which contributed most to the general defence and support of the whole. [ibid.]

And then he returns to this at the very end of the book, and he says that—I mean, people preen themselves on possessing an empire—

> The rulers of Great Britain have, for more than a century past, amused the people with the imagination that they possessed a great empire on the west side of the Atlantic. This empire, however, has hitherto existed in imagination only. It has been, not an empire, but the project of an empire; not a gold mine, but the project of a gold mine; a project which has cost, which continues to cost, and which, if pursued in the same way as it has been hitherto, is likely to cost, immense expence, without being likely to bring any profit. . . . It is surely now time that our rulers should either realize this golden dream, in

which they have been indulging themselves . . . ; or, that they should awake from it themselves, and endeavour to awaken the people. If the project cannot be completed, it ought to be given up. If any of the provinces of the British empire cannot be made to contribute towards the support of the whole empire, it is surely time that Great Britain should free herself from the expence of defending those provinces in time of war and of supporting any part of their civil or military establishments in time of peace, and endeavour to accommodate her future views and designs to the real mediocrity of her circumstances. [ibid., 2:432–33]

Well, you may agree with that or you may disagree with it, but no one can say that Adam Smith was not candid.

Well, I apologise for dealing with Adam Smith in three short lectures. It would be a pleasure for me to deal with him in twenty lectures. But time presses, and I shall go on next week to the beginnings of nineteenth-century classical economics.

NOTE

1. See Smith (1776, vol. 2, book 5, chaps. 2 and 3, respectively).

C. Nineteenth-Century Classicism

General Review—Malthus on Population

Now, we have finished with Smith, or at any rate with an attempt to have a systematic glance at the various doctrines and attitudes, particularly in the *Wealth of Nations*, and I now therefore enter on a series of lectures, which will slop over into next term, on the nineteenth-century classical period.

Now, just a word or two about the personalities and derivations. For me, at any rate, it is very difficult to draw a sharp line between Adam Smith and Hume and the position of the early (or the first half of the) nineteenth-century classical writers. For me at any rate—this is a controversial judgement, if you like—the classical economist *accepted* the *main* perspective of the *Wealth of Nations*, which was, as I have said, an analysis of the machinery of productive organisation and a discussion of the nature of growth and the causes or objectives of growth.

The typical characteristic of the nineteenth-century classical economics was that it crossed the t's and dotted the i's, and in some respects differed considerably from the value and distribution part of the *Wealth of Nations*. But that doesn't, I think, exclude a continuity of fundamental conceptions in the way in which I am formulating them. In some respects, the nineteenth-century classical economists developed parts of Smith; in other respects, they corrected it and amplified it, especially as regards value and distribution, money, and international trade. And in the end, you get a resynthesis, which is avowedly an attempt to bring Adam Smith up-to-date, in John Stuart Mill's *Principles* [1848].

Now, if you want a general period, I would say 1798, which is the date of the publication of the first edition of Malthus' *Essay on Population*, to 1874, which is the date of Cairnes' *Leading Principles*.

The personalities involved fall into two groups—two generations. The leaders of the first generation were Ricardo, 1772 to 1823, who wrote pamphlets on money and trade [1810; 1815] and eventually wrote his stupendously important *Principles* [1817], which developed the analytical method to a degree hitherto not attempted. Malthus, whom I shall be talking to you about later on today, is chiefly important for his *Essay on Population*, but it must be remembered that he wrote a principles of economics and engaged in argument and analysis and criticism with his fellow economists. His friendship with Ricardo, with whom he usually disagreed, is one of the famous friendships in the history of our subject. And then, still in the first generation, you must mention James Mill, a rather austere figure whose habits you may find described in his son John Stuart Mill's *Autobiography* [1873]—a friend of both Bentham and Ricardo, who made his name as an economist by a pamphlet called *Commerce Defended* [1808], and who eventually turned Ricardo into simple English, which he at first dictated on walks to his little son, John Stuart Mill, who had a rather horrific childhood (you must read about it).

And then there is Colonel Robert Torrens, who lived a long time. He was born in 1780 and he died in 1864, so that he really straddles the first generation and the second generation of classical economists. In the first generation he was famous for his *Essay on the External Corn Trade* [1815], which was a plea against the reimposition of the regulation of trade in corn. His monetary works in this first period were, from the point of view of the classical economists, heterodox. He lived on into the second generation, where his main works were a book on the colonisation of Australia—an extremely distinguished work—and his collection of pamphlets called *The Budget* [1844]. If any of you pick up a copy of the collected pamphlets known as *The Budget*, you know you've got a very valuable thing. And he wrote at length on Peel's Act of 1844 and the controversies surrounding it [Torrens, 1848].

These people were all founders of the famous London Political Economy Club, which still meets roughly once a month in the main seasons of the year at the Reform Club. It was founded by Ricardo, Malthus, Torrens and Mill, and, in a way, one rough definition of a British classical economist would be to say that he was usually a member of the London Political Economy Club.

Standing apart from the first generation, but belonging to the same period, is the famous Henry Thornton, whose work I think that I have already described to you: his *Paper Credit* [1802], and then his two speeches in the House of Commons on the Report of the Bullion Committee [1811] in the early years of this century—in my judgement by far the best things written on money before the twentieth century.

Then in the second generation you have Nassau Senior, who was a solicitor, but who held the Drummond Chair of Political Economy at the University of Oxford on two occasions. You were elected to the Drummond Chair to give a few lectures, which had to be published, for a short period, and then you gave way to someone else. He was twice Drummond Professor, and he wrote important pamphlets, which have been reproduced by the London School of Economics, on *Transmission of Precious Metals* [1827], *The Cost of Obtaining Money* [1829a] and *The Value of Money* [1829b]. He also wrote an extremely important letter to a man called Lord Howick on principles of social reform [Senior, 1831]. He took part in the famous report on the Poor Law and the equally famous report on the position of the handloom weavers. Senior's dates are 1790 to 1864.

Then there was McCulloch, 1789 to 1864. He and Torrens and Senior all died in the same year. McCulloch was the disciple of Adam Smith and Ricardo, and in a sense a populariser of both. He wrote many works, and he has been the subject of an extremely distinguished study by Professor O'Brien [1970] of Durham University in our own generation. And then, of course, transcending all these but Ricardo as an economist was John Stuart Mill, 1806 to 1873, important not only as an economist, but as a logician and a general writer on philosophy and politics. You all ought to know quite a lot about John Stuart Mill outside the subject of these lectures. And then finally, there is J. E. Cairnes, who lived from 1823 to 1875, who was to some extent a disciple of John Stuart Mill, and whose works are his *Some Leading Principles of Political Economy* [1874], his *Essays in Political Economy* [1873], which are among the best essays on applied economics in the nineteenth century, and an extraordinary book which he wrote during the War between the States on the economics of slavery [1863]. But perhaps more about Cairnes later.

Now, I want to talk to you for the remainder of this lecture about Malthus and population. It provided a somewhat sensational background to nineteenth-century classical economics. But you mustn't think that Malthus was the first person to write about population. There was a learned American, now dead, called Stangeland, who wrote a book on pre-Malthusian theories of population [1904] which occupied three or four hundred pages dealing with relatively obscure figures of one kind or another. I have already drawn your attention to the anticipation of Malthus in Cantillon, with his famous remark that "Men multiply like Mice in a barn" when they have access to subsistence. And Adam Smith's eventual theory of wages invoked a tendency, which might be averted for many, many years, for wages to fall to subsistence level if the accumulation of capital diminished so as not to keep pace with the population.

Well, it was Malthus who really succeeded in putting the subject of population on the popular map. And you should all have a look at the *first* edition of his *Essay on Population* [1798], which was published anonymously, but which has been republished by the Royal Economic Society. I'm not sure whether it's in print, but they republished a sufficient number of them for you to be able to pick it up pretty easily.

His theory was a direct result of a hostile reaction to the uprush of Utopian speculation, utopian optimism, which accompanied the first years of the French Revolution. Have any of you ever read Wordsworth's *Prelude* [1805]? The famous Wordsworth, who became rather stuffy in his old age, was thrilled by the early idealistic phase of the French Revolution, and he wrote:

> Bliss was it in that dawn to be alive,
> But to be young was very heaven!
> [Wordsworth, 1809/1982, p. 340]

Well, you can see Malthus' attitude by the title of his essay: *An Essay on the Principle of Population as It Affects the Future Improvements of Society with Remarks on the Speculations of Mr Godwin, Mr Condorcet and Other Writers.* You all know who Godwin was I hope. Anybody who doesn't? Candour is always a virtue. He was Shelley's father-in-law, and he was the writer of a great two-volume quarto *Principles of Political Justice* [1793], which is the locus classicus of philosophical anarchism. His view was that if law and property were abolished, then crime would disappear from the face of the earth, human relations would be perfectly harmonious, human health would be perfect and man might even become immortal. I would live for that!

Malthus explains in his preface his motives. He says:

> The following Essay owes its origin to a conversation with a friend, on the subject of Mr. Godwin's Essay, on avarice and profusion. . . . The discussion, started the general question of the future improvement of society; and the Author at first sat down with an intention of merely stating his thoughts to his friend, upon paper, in a clearer manner than he thought he could do, in conversation. But as the subject opened upon him, some ideas occurred, which he did not recollect to have met with before; and as he conceived, that every, the least light, on a topic so generally interesting, might be received with candour, he determined to put his thoughts in a form for publication. [Malthus, 1798, p. i]

Well, in fact the "friend" was his father, a very generous, lovable old crank who was a disciple of that scoundrel Rousseau. I say scoundrel, not because I disagree with his political views, which I do, but because of his quarrel with Hume, in which he was 100 percent wrong and Hume was 100 percent right.

Well, Malthus' father was a friend of Rousseau, and, when Rousseau thought he was being persecuted in France, with the encouragement of Hume he fled to England, and Malthus' father found him a cottage for the time being. Malthus himself, whose relations with his father were of the most admirable and pleasant type, was just down from Cambridge, where he had taken mathematics and been a Wrangler, and presumably the rather facile optimism which informed his father's views as they talked about things over nuts and wine after dinner rather jarred, and so he set himself to refute the theory of Godwin and other such optimists in a systematic way.

Well now, the argument of the *first* essay—underline "first" all the times here—isn't difficult to summarise, and those of you who don't like reading books as a whole can get the argument from the first chapter. (This is rather base of me to say, but I have compassion on the sort of things that you're supposed to learn outside of this subject nowadays.) The chapter starts by posing the question which had been raised by Godwin and Condorcet, who, as you know, was one of the great French intellectuals of the latter part of the eighteenth century and was eventually done to death by the Revolution, but that is neither here nor there. The question posed by Godwin and Condorcet—who was much more moderate than Godwin—was: Can man improve its position by changes in social arrangements? Malthus says: "the great question is now at issue, whether man shall henceforth start forwards with accelerated velocity towards illimitable, and hitherto unconceived improvement; or be condemned to a perpetual oscillation between happiness and misery, and after every effort remain still at an immeasurable distance from the wished-for goal" [ibid., pp. 2–3]. He then says that he has read some of the speculations on the perfectibility of man with *great pleasure*, but he says—I quote—"I see great, and, to my understanding, unconquerable difficulties in the way" [ibid., p. 7].

He begins by laying down two postulates. One is very banal, and the other is rather piquant. The first is: "That food is necessary to the existence of man" [ibid., p. 11]. I'm quoting. Well, that's banal; we don't need to argue about that. The second is: "That the passion between the sexes is necessary, and will remain nearly in its present state" [ibid.] Well now, why should he have thought this last quaint generalisation necessary? Well, quite simply, Godwin, in his book—his very optimistic book—had predicted the gradual decay of sexual passion. But of course if that were likely, then of course the whole Malthusian thesis in the first edition would fall to the ground. Hence, Malthus felt it necessary to lay down his second principle.

And later in the book—later in the first chapter—he says:

I put out of the question, at present, all mere conjectures. . . . A writer may tell me that he thinks man will ultimately become an ostrich. I cannot properly contradict him. But before he can expect to bring any reasonable person over to his opinion, he ought to shew, that the necks of mankind have been gradually elongating; . . . that the legs and feet are daily altering their shape; and that the hair is beginning to change into stubs of feathers. And till the probability of so wonderful a conversion can be shewn, it is surely lost time and lost eloquence to expatiate on the happiness of man in such a state; to describe his powers, both of running and flying. [ibid., p. 10]

And so on and so forth. Well now, assuming that these postulates are granted, he proceeds to argue first that "the power of population"—I'm quoting; take this down—"the power of population [to increase] is indefinitely greater than the power in the earth to produce subsistence for man" [ibid., p. 13]. Why? And here, after having stated what is pretty obvious, if you imagine mankind multiplying without deliberate limitation of families at a reasonable speed, it is very clear that within a few thousand years the weight of mankind would outweigh the weight of the planet.

But he at this moment tries to make his argument more exact, and he says: "Population, when unchecked, increases in a geometrical ratio [and] [s]ubsistence [for man] in an arithmetical ratio" [ibid., p. 14]. And then he puts up in his book [ibid., p. 25] the arithmetical and the geometrical ratios: "1, 2, 3, 4, . . ." and so on like that—constant additive factors—"1, 2, 4, 8, 16, 32, . . ." and so on.

Well now, if one may criticise Malthus a little bit, that's all right, but that is simply one arithmetical illustration of the contrast between arithmetical ratios and geometrical ratios. Obviously, if the figures are supposed to represent the possibility of multiplication of food—arithmetical ratio—and the possibility of the multiplication of the population—geometrical ratio—of course the argument is very compelling. But this is not the only geometrical ratio conceivable. You can imagine that the characteristic of a geometrical ratio is simply that it increases by some common multiplying factor, and you can imagine the multiplying factor being very, very small indeed, and consequently the growth in population would be able to keep up with the multiplication of food for quite a long time.

But of course what Malthus was really getting at, although this has sometimes been questioned—Cannan [1953, pp. 113–14] questioned it—was the simple law of diminishing returns. And if the law of diminishing returns on a constant factor—on earth—is stated sufficiently cautiously, Malthus can do without his spurious arithmetical illustration, which has given all sorts of superficial people golden opportunities to think that they have refuted the fundamental Malthusian population theory, and he could have got away with it.

Well, I am prepared to give Malthus credit for having the idea of diminishing returns at the back of his head. He actually uses language in the second edition [1803] which gets nearer the law of diminishing returns, and he was one of the people who invented the law of diminishing returns later on. And in his article on "Population" [1823] in the *Encyclopaedia*, round about 1830, he actually invokes the law of diminishing returns, so that I think that you must give him the credit for having something more fundamental in his mind than this rather spurious arithmetical illustration.

Therefore, he says, since population can't increase without food, it must somehow or other be kept in check. And then comes a passage which I will read you, and it's a moving passage, and it's a famous passage:

> Through the animal and vegetable kingdoms, nature has scattered the seeds of life abroad with the most profuse and liberal hand. She has been comparatively sparing in the room, and the nourishment necessary to rear them. The germs of existence contained in this spot of earth, with ample food, and ample room to expand in, would fill millions of worlds in the course of a few thousand years. Necessity, that imperious all-pervading law of nature, restrains them within the prescribed bounds. The race of plants, and the race of animals shrink under this great restrictive law. And the race of man cannot, by any efforts of reason, escape from it. Among plants and animals its effects are waste of seed, sickness, and premature death. Among mankind, misery and vice. [Malthus, 1798, pp. 14–15]

Later on, in the body of the essay, he develops this concept of the checks on human multiplication. This is in the first essay still. They fall into two classes: the "preventive check"—that's anything which actually prevents people from multiplying—and secondly, the "positive check"—anything which reduces their numbers when they are actually here. But whatever the technical nature of the check—the positive or the preventive—he thinks that the checks are accompanied either by misery or vice. And consequently, he goes on to argue that Godwin's "beautiful system," as he [ibid., p. 181] called it, was hopeless. Put men in the most opulent surroundings, remove all the imperfections of institutions, which Godwin had insisted on, and remove the governments, and in a short time population will catch up with the greatest conceivable rate of increase of subsistence and be kept from outrunning them only by vice or misery.

Godwin had actually urged in his book that, as a matter of fact, population didn't outrun subsistence. And here I'm quoting from Malthus; Malthus quotes Godwin: "There is a principle"—he said (he, Godwin)—"in human society, by which population is perpetually kept down to the level of the means of subsistence" [ibid., pp. 175–76]. Malthus comments: "This principle, which Mr. Godwin thus mentions as some mysterious and occult cause, and which he does not attempt to investigate, will be found to be the grinding law of necessity; misery, and the fear of misery" [ibid., p. 176].

Well, there you have the argument as he elaborated it in this essay. It is a comparatively short book. The majority of the human race were doomed to live on the margin of subsistence, and only those who were privileged to own property were, in the long run, above that margin.

Well, this was very discouraging to all sorts of hopeful people, not merely Godwin. But now, Malthus was not content with having made a sensation. His book was published anonymously, but his name speedily got out. He was anxious to extend knowledge, and so he set himself to collect information. He travelled extensively. His diary of his travels in Scandinavia [Malthus, 1966] to investigate the population problem has recently been published and is edited by Mrs James. And the second edition which appeared in 1803—the first edition was in 1798—was virtually a new book. The first essay was a brilliant tract from a man just down from Cambridge. The second edition is a rather dull treatise with all sorts of statistics and empirical facts. It is safe to say that if the theory of population had been brought to public attention in the second edition, the first not having existed, it would not have made the stir it did.

But it's very important to understand the change that had taken place. Malthus had changed his mind a little bit—not as much as you would expect, but a little bit. Cannan always used to say that it was because between 1798 and 1803 he had become engaged to be married and discovered that this involved states of mind which were neither miserable nor vicious. And so, in this edition, he admits the existence of a *third* check, which he calls moral restraint, or the prudential check, and this doesn't involve either vice or misery. He says:

> Throughout the whole of the present work, I have so far differed in principle from the former, as to suppose another check to population possible, which does not strictly come under the head either of vice or misery; and, in the latter part, I have endeavoured to soften some of the harshest conclusions of the first essay. [Malthus, 1803, p. vii]

Now, you must realise that, by the prudential check, Malthus did *not* mean contraception. He went out of his way in the fourth edition of his work to *repudiate* the suggestion that he should have supported anything which he regarded as being so vicious. All that he meant was delayed marriage. He had somehow got it into his head that perhaps when a young couple came along to the clergyman to ask him to proclaim the banns of marriage, the clergyman would give them a short lecture on the Malthusian principle of population, and then that the boy would look at the girl and say: "I am sorry, it is all off, my dear."

But people who read Malthus—the other classical economists, or some of them at any rate—were not thus inhibited. Bentham had already suggested deliberate family planning by a primitive form of contraception. James Mill [1826] suggests, rather more delicately, that means exist for limiting the geometrical increase of population, such that the wage level might be raised to any height deemed desirable[1]—which is an exaggeration on the other side. Francis Place, whom you may have heard of—those of you who study economic history or political history (Francis Place was one of the great radical reformers behind the Reform Act of the 1830s and behind the repeal of the Combination Acts in the 1820s)—Francis Place [1822] wrote a book defending Malthus. Godwin had turned on Malthus and had written another essay on population, and had attacked Malthus in ways which Francis Place thought were unfair. But Francis Place went out of his way to say that Malthus really did not understand what happens in the ordinary life of this world, and he then went on definitely to recommend deliberate family planning, and he gave rise to other literature concerning that habit.

Young John Stuart Mill, interpreting Malthus as his father had interpreted him and as Francis Place interpreted him, says in his *Autobiography* [1873, p. 105] that the principle of population enunciated by Malthus became not a cause of pessimism, but, I quote, "a banner" of hope. And I would say that you simply don't understand the nineteenth-century classical economists' attitude to social reform and all that unless you realise what their attitude was to the population problem.

Well, be that as it may, that's the history of political economy rather than the history of economics. But in economics, the admission that mankind need not live at the margin of subsistence—which, of course, had been suggested by Adam Smith when he suggested that capital, if multiplying faster than population, could sustain population at wages far above the limits of subsistence, so long as capital continued to accumulate—meant that, in the analytical theory, the very long run limit of wages was not, as it were, physiological subsistence, it was psychological subsistence—a much more complicated and difficult matter to formulate exactly.

Well, you should observe, however, that while the attack on perfectability was dropped by Malthus, provided that his kind of moral restraint were exercised—family planning, contraception, he regarded as vice, but not so James Mill and the circle around him—the idea of the abolition of law and property was not dropped. On the contrary, it was thought that the framework of law, including the framework of law relating to property, provided the incentive to restraint of population of one kind or another, and it's that which I had in mind when I said that you simply don't understand the classical theory of economic policy unless you read it with this interpretation of Malthus in mind.

Now, I think I've said enough to convince you that Schumpeter here, as so often in interpreting the English economists of that period, was wrong when he said that the theory of population was something alien to the central analysis of nineteenth-century classical economics. It provided, together with Adam Smith, the essential background. But you mustn't think that the importance of Malthus and his *Essay* is confined only to economic theory or the theory of economic policy. You must remember that, among other things, it was the reading of Malthus which convinced Darwin of his fundamental principle of evolution. And since Darwin's theory has done more to alter our conception of mankind and its destiny than anyone except perhaps Copernicus, you can't regard that as a minor influence.

Well now, that is not all about Malthus. We shall come up against him in the lecture tomorrow when we discuss the evolution of the theory of rent and his controversy with Ricardo. He will come up again in the next term when we discuss the theory of overall equilibrium. The pity of it all is that Malthus' more scientific books are rather dull to read, not only the second edition of the *Essay on Population*, but also his *Principles of Political Economy* [1820]. You will have to put a towel around your head and brace yourself to keeping at it for quite a long time before you get at Malthus' point. Not that Malthus lacked common sense, as we can see when we come to the monetary controversies. While Ricardo was able to refute his logic, Malthus' appraisal of the current situation had considerably more in it than can perhaps be attributed to the other classical economists. But more of that later on.

Tomorrow I shall try to give you a very rough account of the evolution of the classical theory of value and distribution, before going on to a more detailed account of the various items in the theory of value and distribution, which will have to be taken up the week after next.

NOTE

1. See James Mill (1826, chap. 2, section 2), reprinted in Mill (1966, pp. 228–44, esp. pp. 242–43).

Value and Distribution:
Historical Origin—Analytical (I)

IN THIS lecture I shall give you a superficial view of the emergence of the nineteenth-century classical view, or views, on value and distribution. I warn you that I shan't be finished with the subject this time. What I shall do is to is to give you a brief account of how it emerged in the pamphlet literature and in a definite political controversy. And I hope, if I get through, that I shall then have prepared the way for a systematic survey of each of the main theories, which takes some time and will require rather more intricate analysis than anything I have dealt with so far.

Now, I am going to give you this historical account in terms of the controversy relating to the reimposition of control of the import of corn, which emerged, as we shall see, toward the end of the Napoleonic Wars. Let me warn you that this account is slightly superficial in the light of Professor Hollander's [1979] researches, only recently given to the world. Professor Hollander thinks that Ricardo had in mind his theory of distribution before he became interested in its application to the Corn Law controversy, and he produces very interesting examples of correspondence between Ricardo and Malthus, which we now owe to the labours of Mr Sraffa, to refine that view. I am not going to go into these arcana; I propose to give you a pretty straightforward account of something which was connected with this controversy.

Now, the historic background that you ought to know is, what you probably do know, that the Napoleonic Wars cut off the supplies of corn from abroad. Well, this meant two things. Firstly, high prices. Thus, at an earlier time in the eighteenth century, from 1711 to 1794, the price of wheat was never above just over 60 shillings per quarter; by Michaelmas 1795 it was 92 shillings; on Lady Day 1801 it was 177 shillings, and from 1808 to 1813 the price did not fall below 90 shillings. If you are interested in these statistics, look up Cannan, *Theories of Production and Distribution* [1924], page 148.[1] He takes his statistics from Tooke, who is not always completely reliable.

Now, you mustn't think that all this rise in price of wheat was due to the particular circumstance of the import of corn being cut off from abroad. As we shall see next term, there was an inflation going on, and, needless to say, agricultural products were subject to inflation equally with other goods. But the shutting off of imports of corn by the war played its part, and as a result of the high prices of corn—I use the word "corn" in its generic sense to cover wheat and rye and oats and so on—as a result of this change of prices there was an extension of cultivation. And again, if you look up Cannan's early book on *Theories of Production and Distribution* [1953, p. 118] you will see a table showing the correlation—a rough correlation—between the average price of wheat and the number of Enclosure Acts. Those of you who come from abroad should know that there were common lands which were used by the common people for tethering their cattle and so on and so forth, and gradually they were, from the reign of Elizabeth onwards, subject to enclosure, and enclosure was quickened up very much by the high prices of the Napoleonic Wars.

Well, the agricultural community viewed the prospective end of the war with apprehension. They were in a panic lest the cessation of the mutual blockade should mean that the high prices were brought down by imports from, let us say, Poland, and elsewhere. Poland was a great source of wheat in those days. It was argued by the agricultural interests—the agriculturalists, the landowners and farmers, and possibly anyone who was articulate on behalf of the agricultural labourers—that it was in the interests of the nation to keep prices high. If it was not done, then corn land would go out of cultivation, and there would be in the end a greater shortage of corn than ever before. And so committees of both Houses of Parliament were appointed, and they collected evidence which went to show that the lands recently taken into cultivation were more expensive to cultivate, and therefore that if prices fell they would go over to grass again.

Well now, these facts—and they were facts—were very significant for the opponents of the reimposition of duties. If they could show, firstly, that increased investment of capital in agriculture was diminishingly efficient, and, secondly, that the price of corn was to some extent determined by the quantity of labour employed in production, then they could argue that the recent rise in the price of this essential food was due to the extension of cultivation and the consequent increase of labour necessary to produce what we should call the "marginal" bushel. And so, they argued, it was obviously fruitless to divert investment to encouraging domestic agriculture and to abstain from importing cheaper corn from abroad.

Four theories sprang out of this discussion—theories which, in some respects, followed Adam Smith, but in other respects called Adam Smith in question, and in other respects introduced elements which Adam Smith had not thought of. The so-called Law of Diminishing Returns in agriculture was almost formulated by some of the witnesses before the House of Lords Committee, which on balance I think is—for graduates amongst you who are interested in this subject—the more interesting of the two committees. And reading the evidence of these witnesses, Ricardo and a man I've not mentioned to you hitherto, Edward West—who became a high official in the service of the East India Company and wrote a very interesting tract in the 1820s on money and all that sort of thing—Ricardo and West were struck by the implication of the evidence given to the committees in Parliament, and they rushed into print with their theories almost simultaneously. Sraffa, in his edition of Ricardo, reproduces an inscription in Ricardo's hand saying that his pamphlet was written before West's pamphlet appeared, and since Ricardo was one of the most truthful and candid persons that God ever made, we must accept his evidence.

But I'm going to quote to you Edward West's essay. It's entitled *An Essay on the Application of Capital to Land, with Observations Shewing the Impolicy of Any Great Restriction of the Importation of Corn* [1815]. You notice the moderation of the title. And Ricardo was moderate in a sense that shocked some of his followers, because he thought that, insofar as there were special burdens on agriculture, a slight duty counterbalancing those burdens could be retained on the importation of corn. But that is quite incidental to his system, and henceforward I shan't mention that exception to the strong argument which Ricardo brought against the limitation of imports.

But let me read you a bit from West's pamphlet. West's pamphlet is much the more readable of the two. You will remember that Ricardo was always protesting that he was a stockbroker and had not had systematic education, although his writing is, while occasionally obscure, very vivid and lingers in one's mind. But West obviously had the quality of clear exposition although, as you will see in the next second or so, he failed to make an analytical distinction which is quite important, or failed to realise all that could be made of it. He says:

> each equal additional quantity of work bestowed on agriculture, yields an actually diminished return, and of course if each equal additional quantity of work yields an actually diminished return, the whole of the work bestowed on agriculture in the progress of improvement, yields an actually diminished proportionate return. [West, 1815, pp. 6–7]

Now, you see, he has hit on the distinction between average and marginal returns in that sentence. What he doesn't realise is that the average and the marginal are not coincidental, save in exceptional circumstances. Do I need to put a Knightean curve on the blackboard to show you the difference? Well, West has enunciated a law of diminishing returns, although he failed to distinguish the point at which marginal and average returns diminish.

Well then, the second theory which arose out of the discussion was of course the labour theory of value. Now, as I need hardly remind you, Adam Smith had coquetted with a labour theory of value in his so-called parable of the beaver and the deer. In the rude state of society preceeding the appropriation of land and the accumulation of stock, the quantity of labour, said Adam Smith, was the circumstance which determined the normal rate at which commodities exchanged for one another. The market rate might fluctuate, but the market rate would tend to come to the normal rate indicated by the ratio of the quantity of unskilled labour. Then he went on to refine it, and when he came to deal with the accumulation of stock—useful machines and wage goods accumulated and so on—and the appropriation of land by the landowners who loved to reap where others had sown, his theory of value undergoes a transformation in kind. It's no longer concerned with quantity of labour; it's concerned with value of labour, value of the use of stock—profit—and value of the use of land—rent.

Now, to Ricardo and his friends, surveying the rise of price in the light of their new-found law of diminishing returns, this substitution by Adam Smith of a cost of production theory of normal value for his quantity of labour theory of value must have seemed a change for the worse, which is absolutely clear nowadays, although you won't find it in the comparatively recent literature always. For instance, Jacob Hollander [1910], who is no relation of Sam Hollander, in his rather excellent survey of Ricardo's life and contribution, thinks that Ricardo only gradually perceived the modifications that had to be made to the labour theory of value to get it right. But we now know that he did perceive them at an early stage, but he did say that they were rather unimportant, which has led George Stigler [1958], in his excellent article on the Ricardian theory in general, to call it—What is it? Does anyone remember it?—the 92½ percent labour theory of value, or ninety-three.

At any rate, Ricardo and his friends were therefore apt to revert to the theory implied by the parable of the beaver and the deer. And you can see the application thereof if you look at Ricardo's *Essay on the Influence of a Low Price of Corn on the Profits of Stock*. I am not quite sure whether Sam Hollander would agree with me in the light of his discoveries in correspondence between the lines, but I am still inclined to regard Ricardo's *Essay on the Influence of a Low Price of Corn on the Profits of Stock*, which together with West's book was published in 1815, as the great seminal tract of this part of classical economics. And the critical passage is here, and I'll read it to you. This is in the *Essay on the Influence of a Low Price of Corn on the Profits of Stock*; it is not an extract from the *Principles*:

> The exchangeable value of all commodities, rises as the difficulties of their production increase. If then new difficulties occur in the production of corn, from more labour being necessary, whilst no more labour is required to produce gold, silver, cloth, linen, etc. the exchangeable value of corn will necessarily rise, as compared with those things. On the contrary, facilities in the production of corn, or of any other commodity of whatever kind, which shall afford the same produce with less labour, will lower its exchangeable value. [Ricardo, 1815, p. 16]

Clear enough, although if you read Ricardo in the *Principles* [1817] you will find more difficulty in disentangling, because Ricardo's theory in the

Principles is concerned not only with the *causes* of changes in value, but also with the *measure* of value, for which, to the end of his life, he was, in a way, vainly searching. In the *Principles*, he *assumes* the measure to be an invariable gold, after qualifying that in various ways, but in the *Essay*, these arcana, although quite important, do not obtrude themselves.

And so, after the passage that I have read you, he goes on to argue [Ricardo, 1815, pp. 17–18] that improvements in modes of cultivation will lower value, and then—and now we come to the controversial point—since importing the product of superior lands abroad is like having recourse to an improvement at home, to prohibit importation is similar to prohibiting improvements [ibid., pp. 20–25]. Perhaps I have used the word "superior" in a sense which is a little misleading in this respect. I think that you should substitute the word "cheaper," although when I come to deal with Ricardo's theory of international trade I will tell you why I have done it. So to prohibit importation is similar to prohibiting domestic improvements. Now, there you have the raison d'être of the law of diminishing returns and the labour theory of value.

A theory of rent and a theory of profits were also the outcome of these discussions, and, indirectly, a theory of wages too. Let us look a little more closely at the way in which they developed.

Take rent first. In the earlier days before the eighteenth century, high rents were looked upon as a sign of prosperity. And quite clearly this was due to the fact that, in those days, the governing class, the oligarchy, was on the whole composed of landowners, and they felt, and their apologists felt, that when rents were high that was a sign that the nation was doing pretty well, whereas low rents were thought to be a sign that the country was going to the dogs. And these views were not contradicted by earlier theoretical discussions. The physiocrats thought that a high net product, composed mainly of agricultural and—in brackets—extractive production, was to be the aim of economic policy. They then added, which you must never forget, that they thought that all taxation must fall on the net product. And Adam Smith did not think that the interests of the landowners were particularly opposed to the interests of society. His reasons for that are not absolutely clear, considering that he had said that the landowners, like all other men, loved to reap where they hadn't sown [Smith, 1776, 1:51]. But certainly, if you read through the very long chapter on rent in Adam Smith's book, you don't find rent held up as the villain of the piece—far more high profits and the interests of merchants and manufacturers, for whom he is supposed by ignorant people to be the apologist.

But with the Corn Law controversy this thing came into prominence, and while Ricardo and West were reflecting on the law of diminishing returns and all that, Malthus published a pamphlet entitled *Inquiry into the Nature and Progress of Rent* [1815]. And this is an interesting and illuminating book, and Malthus' other pamphlet, actually apologising for the

Corn Laws [1814], is by far the most intelligent apology of the multitudinous literature apologising for the Corn Laws. Quite worth reading, and worth reading his arguments with Ricardo. But in the *Inquiry into the Nature and Progress of Rent*, which is more theoretical, he argues that rent is due to three causes:

1. Land produces a surplus over the expenses of cultivation;
2. That this surplus always creates in the long run new demand—the argument of his theory of population; and
3. That the most fertile land is scarce. [Malthus, 1815, p. 8]

And therefore, for these three reasons, rent is to be regarded as a beneficial feature—a beneficial social institution.

Now, this didn't appeal at all to Ricardo. And if you read the superficial books, you will find that Ricardo is represented as being an apologist for stockbrokers, but by the time that Ricardo took part in this controversy, he was at least as much a landowner as he was a holder of stock. Indeed, in one of his letters to Malthus he said he simply would not know how to value his estate in those terms. And he was a rich man. Starting from zero, roughly speaking, and never indulging in risky speculation, he accumulated a fortune of something like three-quarters of a million pounds, which in those days was big money—much more than Keynes accumulated in our own day. Keynes left, roughly speaking, a million pounds, and some pictures which, of course, would be very much more valuable now.

But Ricardo was against high rents for intellectual reasons, and he realised that Malthus' number 3—the scarcity of the most fertile land—was the means of turning the tables on Malthus. And so he argues in this pamphlet that I am discussing, the *Influence of Low Price of Corn on Profits of Stock*, that only Malthus's third reason is responsible for rent. The fact that land produces a surplus over expenses of cultivation doesn't mean that rent should exist if it produced an indefinite surplus and the surplus was always creating new demand. That would be too dogmatic for Ricardo, who realised that the surplus need not create a new demand always. Rent was only paid because—famous phrase—of the niggardliness of nature in providing fertile land, and rent only consists of profits transferred from the investors to the landlords. He says:

> If all land had the same properties, if it were unlimited in quantity, and uniform in quality, no charge could be made for its use, unless where it possessed peculiar advantages of situation. . . . It is only, then, because land is not unlimited in quantity and uniform in quality, . . . that rent is ever paid for the use of it. [Ricardo, 1821, p. 70]

There you have the Ricardian theory of the origin and cause of rent.

But that wasn't all. Having shown rent to be an indication of poverty rather than riches, Ricardo went on to try to show by a complicated argument that the interests of the landlord were always opposed to the interests of society, at any rate in the short run, in that, he argued, the progressive improvement or the admission of cheap corn always diminished rent. You've seen already from what I have read to you how he compared improvement with cheap corn, and he dwells on this with unusual rhetoric. He says:

> If the interests of the landlord be of sufficient consequence, to determine us not to avail ourselves of all the benefits which would follow from importing corn at a cheap price, they should also influence us in rejecting all improvements in agriculture, and in the implements of husbandry; for it is as certain that corn is rendered cheap, rents are lowered, and the ability of the landlord to pay taxes, is for a time, at least, as much impaired by such improvements, as by the importation of corn. To be consistent then,

—he says, rising to his rhetoric—

> let us by the same act arrest improvement, and prohibit importation. [Ricardo, 1815, pp. 49–50]

So that landlords were to be watched. But what about the interests of the capitalists?

Well, this brings us to the theory of profit. And what I am about to say, I warn you is extremely superficial; I shall be devoting half a lecture to the theory of profits next week, but I want to give you the controversial side of the Corn Law debate before I get down to analytical detail. Ricardo thought that, in the end, wages would tend to subsistence level, although he was aware by that time that subsistence level would be a psychological subsistence level and not a physiological subsistence level. I shall come back to that next time. Profits, according to Ricardo were a residue—something left after wages and rents had been paid. So that if corn was made more expensive by extension of cultivation at the margin— and by the margin he clearly had in mind the less fertile land, or the marginal return to the more fertile land when additional investment was put on it—if corn was made more expensive—the labour theory of value and the Law of Diminishing Returns—then wages must rise, and the amount left for the profit maker must fall in consequence, so that the influence of the profit maker was opposed to the interests of the landlords. For the landlords, the prohibition of importation was desirable because it made corn dear and rents high. For the capitalist it was undesirable because it made corn dear, wages had to rise in consequence, and consequently less was left for profit.

But you must not leave it there. Ricardo, with Smith, thought that the interests of the wage earners were to be fostered by accumulation, and accumulation was chiefly out of profits. He hoped that the stationary state was not near. Professor Hollander proves that he thought that it might be far distant. He hoped that accumulation, mainly out of profit, would go on outstripping subsistence wages and therefore raising wages, and he hoped that would go on long enough for the labourers to learn expensive habits, and, consequently—and this is a modern phrase but I just use it to make vivid my point—the psychological subsistence level would be raised.

Well, there is the controversial part of the emergence of the classical theory of value and distribution. I want now to go on to discuss the analytical development by Ricardo in the *Principles*, in Torrens' *Essay on the External Corn Trade*, and so on.

Well, I think that I have time to deal with the Law of Diminishing Returns, which you hear so much about in modern theory that I can, I think, assume that I can go very quickly.

The classical economists on the whole were inclined to confine the Law of Diminishing Returns to agriculture, and to it they opposed the Law of Increasing Returns in manufacture—rather ill-defined, not always appealing to the extent of the market as Adam Smith had done. But in modern times West's distinction between marginal and average returns has been emphasised, and with the Knightean production function, which, you know, shows aggregate returns rising to a maximum aggregate, and then the inflexion of the curve shows marginal returns beginning to diminish, and the tangent to the aggregate curve shows average returns beginning to diminish.

Well, in modern times again—and this started before modern times; you find it in Senior to some extent, but it must be regarded as figuring large in modern analysis—the Law of Variation of Returns has been generalised in the shape of the production function, and you can draw a simple production function in three dimensions and get most out of it that way, if you like. The production function derives from what Edgeworth [1911], with his rather amiable way of inserting a comic jest in order to drive home his analysis, which was not always as clear, as is comic jest, talked about, first of all, dosing—which is a very common word—dosing land with increasing amounts of capital and labour. And Edgeworth suggested: Well, why not reverse the relationship between patient and dose, and dose a constant of labour with varying amounts of land? And you will get a production function of roughly speaking the same sort of curvilinear order.

And thirdly, in modern times, the original Law of Diminishing Returns has been supplemented. The nineteenth-century classical economists did not succeed in supplementing it as well as Adam Smith had supplemented his treatment of the division of labour by his emphasis on the extent of the market. The classical economists and the neoclassical economists under the leadership of Marshall got all muddled up by trying to apply the conception of increasing returns to two-dimensional diagrams showing the increasing returns curve as a function two variables, whereas, as Allyn Young [1928] points out—and I talked to you about this when I was talking about Adam Smith's chapter—increasing returns through a society as a whole is a function of the disintegration of industry with the increasing division of labour.

So much for the diminishing returns side of the controversy. Next time I will plunge into the arcana—and there will be more of Keynes than hitherto—of the classical theory of value and distribution and its modifications.

NOTE

1. See also Cannan (1953, p. 117).

Value and Distribution: Analytical (II)

Now, in my last lecture last week I tried to explain how broad principles relating to value and distribution were invoked in the course of a specifically political controversy—the controversy relating to the reimposition of limitations on the import of corn. I drew your attention to West's very precise formulation of the laws of return, but I concentrated chiefly on Ricardo's *Essay on the Influence of a Low Price of Corn on the Profits of Stock*, leading up to his triumphant conclusion that the effects of cheap imports were strictly analogous in this connection to the effects of improvement and urging therefore, to be consistent, that we should both prohibit improvements and importations, if one was of that way of thinking. But of course, it was his direct intention to denounce and to satirise. Then in the last five minutes of the lecture I went on to indicate various ways in which the so-called laws of return, the Law of Diminishing Returns in agriculture, as some classical economists called it, had been extended and reformulated and revised in more modern development. And I won't say anything more about that.

I want to talk today, and possibly tomorrow—This is not the last lecture, is it? It is the last lecture but one—about value and distribution. And I shall be concentrating principally on Ricardo here, not merely because Ricardo is so much more difficult than the other writers on the subject, but because, whether he reached the right conclusions or not, which is a controversial matter, he was so much more profound, so much more worthwhile puzzling your heads about—difficult though he may be.

I say this to warn you that Ricardo must not be regarded as being typical in this respect. There has been controversy in recent years about the extent to which the classical system, broadly defined, as I defined it last week, did retain Ricardian influence. There are some people who deserve to be taken seriously who think that the Ricardian influence, such as it was, had dwindled away by the beginning of the 1830s, and you had Senior and McCulloch edging away from it to some extent, and John Stuart Mill, whose exposition has certainly a different look from the exposition of Ricardo. That's a point of view which on the whole, I think, is overdone. I think that the Ricardian habit of thought and the questions raised by Ricardo continued to influence men's minds. Torrens, for instance. I don't expect you to know very much about Torrens, but he is one of those quoted by people who insist on the minimal influence of Ricardo after 1830. At a meeting of the Political Economy Club he said, "Well, how much is left of the Ricardian system?" This was in about 1830. But in the 1840s, in that rare book, the collection of his pamphlets on money and on other matters, Torrens [1844] recanted and said that his criticisms of Ricardo had been wrong, and he made what, for anybody else, would have been an unusually humble apology. But Torrens was slightly rhetorical in his exposition, and he certainly bites the dust as regards his earlier criticisms of Ricardo.

I think Ricardo's influence stayed on, and, after all, as you will see next term when we come to early modern stuff, Ricardo was enormously influential on Marshall. People search about for the various influences which played on Marshall and they are right to do so, and occasionally they will find obscure writers whom Marshall had read. But Shove, who wrote the really authoritative work on the Marshall centenary, which has been reprinted in all sorts of collections of essays, Shove [1942] was surely right when he argued that Marshall started by trying to translate John Stuart Mill and Ricardo into geometry or into mathematics.

So, what I shall be saying in this lecture and part of the next at any rate will chiefly be about Ricardo. And there will be a good deal of stuff that you won't find, specifically, in the [inaudible].

What was the classical theory of value as developed by Ricardo? Well, it was something more than a simple labour theory of value. I said that the labour theory of value was employed in Ricardo's arguments about the Corn Laws, but contrary to certain authorities, Jacob Hollander and Cannan for instance, at a quite early stage Ricardo realised that the simple theory of value, which he would very much have liked to preserve, was not so easy as all that. And that's why we have to go into it. It's no use leaving the labour theory of value as the resuscitation of the parable of the beaver and the deer of Adam Smith.

Well, let us notice first certain *essential* characteristics and assumptions which are common to Ricardo and to anyone who follows Ricardo in this respect. First of all, notice that it did definitely rule out utility, as commonly understood, as a determining factor. It didn't deny that the possession of utility was essential to value; what it denied was any quantitative connection between utility and value. And in that Ricardo followed Adam Smith's celebrated paradox of value, which was formulated in terms of his comparison between the utility of water and its value and the utility of diamonds and their value. Now whether Adam Smith thought that was the last word to be said on the subject is perhaps a controversial question. In recent years, the complexities of Adam Smith's thought have been dwelt upon in a notable essay by Professor Marian Bowley [1973], but Ricardo certainly didn't really very often give a thought to utility beyond the fact that utility was essential to value.

Secondly, and here I needn't expatiate, it was essentially what, using Marshallian terms, would be called a long period theory of value. It did not contend, any more than Adam Smith contended, that market prices always conformed to long period values. It only urged that under certain conditions market prices *tended* to conform to normal or long period values.

Now, at this point I must dwell upon the fact that Ricardo did not deny the influence of supply and demand. Schumpeter and others have accused him of denying the influence of supply and demand. And I am bound to say that while I think that these people who make this accusation show that they have not read Ricardo at all carefully, I am bound to say that Ricardo himself is to blame to some extent, because he took the influence of demand and supply for granted and actually had a chapter in his book in which he more or less went out of his way to say that anybody who says that value is determined, given other conditions, by demand and supply is frightfully superficial. But the fact is that when Ricardo was challenged on this matter—Malthus challenged him, for instance—Ricardo was rather grieved: How could people think that he didn't attach importance to supply conditions? How could people think that, in his view, cost of production, however interpreted, did not work on the market through its influence on supply? He says that more than once. There is a celebrated passage in his *Notes on Malthus*, and Professor Samuel Hollander gives you several passages.

But now, what were the conditions under which Ricardo thought that there was something to be said—notice my words: something to be said—for a labour theory of value? Well, these conditions are worth stating explicitly. It did not apply to articles, the supply of which was rigid or at any rate not capable of increase. If you think, for instance, of the supply of things which are rigid upwards, save in the event of forgery, you think of pictures of Old Masters. Old Masters may be destroyed, but the supply of Raphaels in someone's hand or other cannot, in the twentieth century, be increased. And of course Ricardo realised that there were many articles of that kind. Secondly, it didn't apply to paper money. How could it? Nor, thirdly, did it apply to monopolised products. And, finally, and most important of all in the Ricardian system, it did not apply to goods entering into international trade. Why? Because goods entering into international trade came from areas between which factor services, labour and capital, were not mobile. Consequently, the market price of such a good might be such as to involve considerable profitability in one area, but, because of the immobility of labour in other areas, it couldn't be multiplied indefinitely. But more of that later on. Ricardo was one of the originators of the theory of comparative costs in international trade, whereas the labour theory of value, such as Ricardo developed it and qualified it, was essentially a theory of absolute costs in some sense or other. That is to say, putting things in a nutshell, the labour theory of value that Ricardo tried to elaborate assumed substantial and effective mobility of capital and labour.

Now, granted those conditions, Ricardo thought that a labour theory of value was a good enough approximation for certain purposes. But now let us examine the difficulties, and let us examine these difficulties as they present themselves to us nowadays. Supposing all labour is of one quality and the disposition to work is quantitatively the same among different labourers, then, as in Adam Smith's parable of the beaver and the deer, a labour theory of value is perfectly all right. If the production function is a straight line, and you measure on the base the quantity of labour involved to produce one article and on the *y* axis the quantity of labour to produce another article, and if there is no variation of returns, then the production function is a straight line and, whatever your indifference curve, it will be tangent to that straight line, giving the same price ratio. But that, after all, is a very, very limited range indeed. On the theoretical plane, Ricardo might argue— I don't think he would argue very successfully in the modern world, but he might argue at his time—that, well, this was a good enough approximation for the conditions in which I want to apply it.

But it is a very, very limited theoretical example. First of all, let us take into account the factors which Adam Smith took into account when elaborating the parable of the beaver and the deer. As soon as there are different psychological experiences, differing in the sense that they are not in some sense or other equivalent and equal, then the normal ratio of exchange will not necessarily be equal to the pure quantity of labour ratio. If, for instance, hunting deer is a very, very pleasurable occupation, as it is for a great many males even at the present day, and if catching beaver means standing up to your neck in icy water, then you would expect that something more would have to be given for a beaver than would be the case if there were no such pleasurable or unpleasurable experience associated with the production of beaver and deer. Well, Adam Smith realised that, and that would have been realised by all the classical economists, but they wave it aside, you see—too obvious for words.

But in advanced societies there are three difficulties to contend with. First of all, there are differences of quality of labour, quite apart from the psychology associated between labour in different occupations—differences of skill. Now, supposing you believed the splendid eighteenth-century belief that, at first, alone among animals, the humankind is exactly equal in all potentialities, and all differences of skill or assiduity and so on come from the influence of the home and education and so on and so forth. Well then, of course, you could regard the problem as being partly solved—not wholly, but partly solved—by regarding the differences in reward of different kinds of labour as being due to differences of investment of various kinds. And up to a point, you could satisfy yourself with that, but I don't think that we can satisfy ourselves with that. People do differ in latent potentiality. We do not know much about it, and, as I have said before, people who pretend that they know much about it are usually using it for what I would regard—and this is a judgement of value—as rather despicable ends.

Well, there are, first of all, differences of quality of labour which have got to be explained unless you hold the optimistic eighteenth-century view. Secondly, there are differences in the quantity of land involved. And thirdly, there are differences in quantities of capital.

Well now, how were these difficulties met by Ricardo and, dare I say it, to some extent by Marx and others? Well, so far as differences of quality of labour were concerned, they were for the most part ignored. It was said that labour is determined by the higgling of the market, but that, of course, is circular reasoning. If you are trying to explain value by something other than value, by quantity of something, it's no use invoking value to explain value. Ricardo shows a little awareness of this when he says, well, the wage differentials change very slowly, they persist over long periods more or less the same. That's not really very satisfactory; it shows some uneasiness. Marx said that these differences were determined by a social process which goes on behind the backs of the labourers, but he meant much the same as Ricardo there, I think.

The difficulties concerning land were evaded by a mistake—I am being rather dogmatic here—by a mistake which persisted for a very long time and which still from time to time shows itself in various forms. It was thought possible to leave out the influence of different quantities of land by going to the rentless margin, by going to the use of capital and labour on the margin—either the internal or external margin—which yielded no rent. In classical times, this was regarded as a sort of *pons asinorum*. Any poor businessman who turned up and said, "Well I have to take rent costs into my consideration when I am totting up my profit and loss account" would be dismissed as an unutterable philistine; he doesn't understand that rent doesn't enter into cost of production—contemptible.

It is extraordinary that so many clever people were taken in by this. Of course, supposing you can think of land which is *completely* specific in the technical sense of the term—that is to say, which only has one use and one use only, no alternatives—then there is no opportunity cost for the land. You can regard the rent that it uses as a surplus and not as a cost in any sense. But specificity in that sense has to be looked for, because it means also specificity in time as well as in place, as well as in occupation. It's just a theoretical plaything. Theoretically speaking, and in certain purposes, you can perhaps regard all land as being specific to the production of corn. You are still very much remote from reality, but that is the way in which Ricardo and the Ricardians tended to think of it. And even Marshall perhaps went out of his way to think out excuses for them in that way.

But coming back to reality for a moment, just think of some alternative agricultural products. Think, for instance, of a fruit tree which demands exactly the same quantity of labour to plant and to look after and to pick as another fruit tree of a different kind. But its roots go down in a comparatively narrow stretch of land, and the other fruit tree occupies, if it is to flourish, three or four times the square yards of land as are necessary for the first. You cannot think that the exchange ratios of the different kinds of fruit would be as 1:1. You would have to count the use of the land with the latter kind of tree, the tree whose roots spread out, as costing something which it did not cost to produce the former kind of fruit. And so there has emerged in modern times the realisation that, for all sorts of purposes, it is no use going to the rentless margin. It would be just as sensible, to use the phrase which I used last time—Edgeworth's phrase—as reversing the relation between patient and dose.

You can eliminate rent from costs if you go to the rentless margin. Here [referring to figure 2] we are with the application of labour to a constant quantity of land, and the wage is represented by that straight line parallel with the x axis, and aggregate wages therefore represented by this rectilinear area, and rent, which is much too large, as the differential surplus. But you are now considering the variation of labour on a constant quantity of land. Exactly the same thing, you can imagine a fixed labour force and varying its application to quantities of land. And then, the quantities of land being regarded as homogeneous, you get something, not of the same value but of the same geometrical form, with wages as the differential surplus and rent as the rectilinear area. The thing is a trick—the elimination of rent from cost. You can just as easily eliminate wages. And on the theoretical plane—perhaps not empirically, but just theoretically—you are just as wrong-headed, because in invoking rent as the way out from considering quantities of land, you are passing from quantities—you are operating with quantity of labour, that is the essence of the labour theory of value—you are passing into the category of value of land. No one would have said that the quantity of land used in most kinds of production did not influence relative value. It was only because Ricardo hit on this business of eliminating rent from the quantity of labour and capital that he wanted to focus attention on that this thing arose.

Well now, descending just a little from the realm of pure theory—geometry and algebra and so on and so forth—for some of the things that Ricardo discussed it was perhaps an approximation to regard *most* of the land—not all (there was a different problem with site value), but *most* of the land—as devoted to the production of general agricultural commodities. You see, it's a frightfully crude simplification, but in that case, well, then he could perhaps regard the land as specifically agricultural and contrast agriculture with manufacturing industries in this respect. And you can see how he and his followers got into this habit of mind.

Now, Marshall, of course—who said once in a letter to Edgeworth that it was "*wisest not* to say that 'Rent does not enter into cost of production,'" but "*wicked*" to say that it does[1]—Marshall, of course, knew all about the alternative uses, and Marshall's margin of building is an indirect way of recognising that fact.[2] But Marshall fastened on something which was suggested in the Ricardian literature: the contrast, as he thought, in an old country at any rate, between the comparative rigidity of supply of land and the comparative elasticity of supplies of labour and capital. And, well, that contrast is there. It is not necessarily so in new countries, not necessarily so as regards the planet as a whole at this stage of history, although it is rapidly becoming so. But of course, if you conceive such a situation with the land

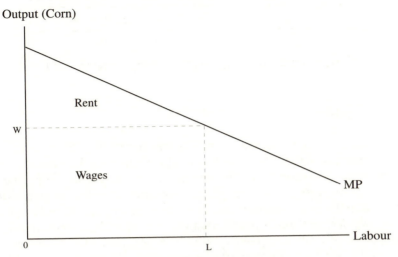

Figure 2. Ricardo's Rentless Margin.

supply rigid and the labour and capital supplies elastic, then this has a bearing on the theory of taxation.

And it was obviously for that reason that Marshall was so queasy about any attempt to throw overboard the doctrine that rent does not enter into cost of production. But moving on the plane on which Ricardo elected to move, the doctrine that rent didn't enter into cost of production was something which just evaded him, preventing him from considering the problem of alternative costs—opportunity costs, as we call it nowadays.

I think for once I will stop there. The capital business is so much more complicated that, if I start, I shall leave off at an inconvenient moment. I will do the capital complications, which are the really interesting ones. Some of this must be very familiar to those of you who are advanced students, but capital complications are in a way interesting and figure very largely in Ricardo's thought. I think it's better to leave off now rather than to start and then have to leave off at an inconvenient moment.

NOTES

1. Letter from Marshall to Edgeworth, 28 August 1902, reprinted in Pigou (1925, pp. 435–38, at 436).
2. See Marshall (1920, book 4, chap. 3, §7; book 5, chap. 11, §4).

Value and Distribution: Analytical (III)

I AM continuing the treatment which I began yesterday of the classical theory of value and distribution, with special reference to Ricardo. You may remember that I began by some general observations concerning the assumptions, the essentially long period relevance of most generalisations, and the mistake of Schumpeter and Malthus in saying that Ricardo ignored supply and demand, and I then stated the area of exchange where the approximation to a labour theory of value was not deemed to be in any way valid, and I went on to discuss the conditions under which a pure labour theory of value, as exemplified in Adam Smith's parable of the beaver and the deer, would be valid, and then I addressed myself during the greater part of the lecture to the complications arising in advanced societies—the complications being headed differences of quality of labour, differences of quantity of land, and differences of quantity of capital. And I went on to deal with the first two of those differences. I dealt rather summarily with the labour differences, as was only inevitable since these were, so to speak, assumed out of the way by both Ricardo and Adam Smith, and others. And I went on in the last part of the lecture with the attitude of classical economists to the problem of varying proportions of land combined with labour and explained how they kidded themselves into thinking that, by going to the rentless margin, they could get rid of that complication. I dwelt on that for some time; I even put a little diagram on the board, and I think I concluded by explaining the extraordinary reluctance of Marshall to abandon some of the classical theories of rent. I shall come back to Marshall's attitude towards the end of this course of lectures when I deal with Marshall's contribution to the neo-classical economics in the early modern age.

I want to address myself this morning partly to the complications involved by the fact that the productive process involves quantities of capital in one form or another. And then I want to run rapidly through the theory of distribution as it was treated by Ricardo and many of his followers.

Well now, what is the problem here? Very clearly, any labour theory of value which deserves any respect at all will take into account not merely the *direct* labour involved in the production of any commodity in its exchange relationships with other commodities, but also the *indirect* labour involved in manufacturing the instruments and the raw materials that were involved. That was common ground, and that, of course, was in line with a pure labour theory of value. And James Mill and McCulloch—at any rate at the beginning (I do not intend to follow up all the vicissitudes of McCulloch; you can find them all in Professor O'Brien's [1970] splendid book)—James Mill and McCulloch thought that they could deal with the capital complications by reducing all capital to indirect labour.

But that, of course, won't wash. It is perfectly true that the indirect as well as the direct labour counts as part of the cost of production. But it is not true that that accounts for the normal value in which, at a constant value of money, commodities may be conceived to exchange for one another. In some way or other, the quantity of capital, in whatever form you conceive of it—and the quantity of capital is a very, very ambiguous term; it may mean what Sir John Hicks [1932] has called the "materialist" conception, raw materials and machinery and so on and so forth; it may mean a fund of some sort, a nonmaterialist conception which itself involves valuation—but whichever way you think of it, it should be surely intuitively clear that in exchange economies, in long-period normal equilibrium, some payment, not payment to labour, is included in the cost of production and consequently influences supply.

Now, whatever may have been the delusions of John Stuart Mill and McCulloch that you can simplify all this out of the world by reducing it all to indirect labour, Ricardo had no such illusion. But his first approximation was to assume that the proportionate combination of labour and capital was the same in all industries. Now, if that were empirically true, of course, the variation in the quantity of labour which the different commodities employ would provide an indication of the ratios in which the commodities would exchange. And this, you should notice, would be true whatever conception you have of capital or the nonlabour material instruments of production. If the proportion of land was exactly the same in all branches of production, then you could rely upon the differences in the quantity of labour to give you the ratio in which the commodities would exchange for one another.

But Ricardo realised that that wasn't so. From time to time in his *Principles*, when he is arguing about broader questions, he elides the further question and does talk as if the quantity of capital employed were proportionately the same in the different industries. But you mustn't read too much into that elision because Ricardo spent an awful lot of time—headaches—in trying to take account in some way or other of nonproportionate combinations of labour and capital, however conceived. First of all, proceeding from models which you can depict as involving only circulating capital, and circulating capital involving chiefly wages, where the proportionate combination idea would not seem too silly, proceeding from that he—what shall I say?—messed about with various combinations of circulating and fixed capital, giving appallingly complicated illustrations of the combination of circulating capital and fixed and the way in which value would be affected in these connections. And then he took more and more account of the relative durability of fixed capital, which obviously affects costs of production of particular units, however you conceive it. And he gave the complicated examples of that.

And eventually, in a famous letter to McCulloch, he said he found the theory of value intolerably difficult—why, I will tell you why in a moment—but if he were to write his book again—this was at the end of his life, roughly speaking—if he were to write his book again, he would say that value was determined by relative quantities of labour and relative *times* in which the product appeared on the market—which formula, of course, included circulating and fixed capital of different degrees of durability.[1] And that really was very clever of Ricardo. But he threw out this hint, and you can see that it's in the back of his mind, progressively, in various editions of the *Principles*. But he didn't follow it up. And that was as far as he got. When he came to deal with larger problems, his plea was that, after all, in many lines of production the use of capital in its various forms was comparatively small, as compared with the quantity of labour. And therefore, as a first approximation, you might proceed as if the quantity of labour was the important thing. And hence Stigler's description of the Ricardian theory of value as a 93 percent labour theory.

Now, why was Ricardo so bothered about this? To discover that, you have to go back to Adam Smith's theory of value, where you realise he had thrown overboard the parable of the beaver and the deer as regards advanced societies and had produced what you may call a circular argument explaining the value of the product by the addition of the component parts of price—wages, profits and rent. And this led him to believe that, for instance, state intervention, such as bounties and taxes, would affect the price of corn and affect the price level in general.

Now, this stuck in Ricardo's gizzard. Ricardo felt that under a metallic system, at any rate, in the long period—he didn't neglect the velocity of circulation, as we shall see next term, although he probably underestimated it—but Ricardo felt that any theory of value, to be comprehensive, must take into account the labour cost of obtaining money. And so, so long as the cost of obtaining money remained constant, changes in relative wages, or more complicated changes such as subsidies or bounties, would simply affect the relationship between wages and profits and not affect the general value of money, as expressed by the vague idea of prices in general. (Ricardo didn't use the primitive index numbers which had been thought of but were not generally used in those days.) And this led him to what obviously intrigued him very much: that if there were some general rise in wages, for instance, but no rise in the cost of obtaining money, the rise in wages would lead to a fall in relative profits, and therefore the more capital-intensive commodities would actually fall in price with a rise in wages. And in reply to a question by Malthus, he admitted that the contrary would be the case, which presented him, you see, with a horizon which, minutely considered—rises in wages, falls in wages due to changes in the rate of profit—was almost intolerably complicated for some of the things he wanted to handle.

So he continued to worry, and his search for a measure of value—not a cause of value but a measure of value—continued to the end of his life. Even his unpublished paper on absolute and relative value doesn't solve this, and he knew it. But he felt that, so far as gold was concerned, the changes in the real cost of production, even though capital was involved, were very, very small. This was a purely empirical assumption, which may have justified the use of metallic currencies in the past, but affords no justification for confidence that the changes will be smaller or larger in the future. But he, when he wasn't just talking, broadly speaking, as though the labour costs of production would be the same, was rather apt to fall back on the assumption that, so far as the various instruments assisting the production of a metallic currency—other than labour—were concerned, that cost of production represented a sort of mean which could be contrasted with the variations between capital intensive and labour intensive (I am using the modern terms here in order to simplify) in the other commodities. And so, for various purposes, you could go on assuming that the metallic money was the measure of value.

Well, so much for the capital complications, which are, as you will see, pretty considerable. But at the same time, while they are pretty considerable and while in the end you must judge Ricardo had failed in providing a fully fledged long-period, real-cost theory of value, they do show the much greater profundity of insight of Ricardo as compared to the other classical economists. Senior [1836, p. 58], for instance, provided an easy get-out for himself and for other people by saying that so far as the use of capital was concerned—rent being convincingly banished by the fact that it didn't enter into the cost of production—there must be something corresponding to the real cost which wages represented, and he called that "abstinence"—the psychological effort which lay behind saving and/or (these matters were not very profoundly investigated) the psychological attitude which prevented you from consuming capital when capital became free. Well, there is something in that, but the word "abstinence" was frightfully unfortunate from the general sociological and propagandist point of view and gave wonderful opportunity—I think it was Lassalle who, I think, started it off, but it has been a wonderful opportunity ever since—for anybody making fun of the classical economists at that stage to discuss the *abstinence* of the Rothschilds of that time. This was what frightened Marshall into using the term *waiting* rather than abstinence, as it didn't involve such an immense moral effort, so to speak, as abstinence would.

Well, nowadays of course, we have got away from all that: We talk about variations of time preference. And that will cover any community you can think of, any community which pretends to any degree of rationality. Of course, interest rates and profit rates are regarded as evil things in certain highly populated parts of the world. I can remember putting a question to the very distinguished academy which was responsible for all sorts of publications in one of those parts of the world: How did they chose their works to publish? And I said—my question was partly silly—supposing you are (perhaps I've told you this story) called upon to choose between a complete edition of the works of Tolstoy and some obscure scientific work. Well, they said that choice is quite easy because Tolstoy pays for itself; the first edition of the works of Tolstoy was 100,000, and they had reason to be proud of the extent to which Tolstoy was read. But as for the scientific works and academic works, of course there are some, they said—being very human—which you just must publish, however small the circulation. But on the whole, they said, to my inward delight, "We try to publish books whose circulation is limited to under seven years." Well, if that's not the rate of interest crawling back by the number of years' purchase, I don't know what is.

Well now, let us pass on to a brief glance at distribution theory. I don't think that I need deal at length with the distribution theory of rent. I shall be coming back to that when I deal with Marshall. If you want just a brief summary of the various aspects of the classical distribution of rent, there is first of all the origin and cause of rent—scarcity, the niggardliness of nature and the impossibility of annihilating distance. Secondly, there is a static theory of relative rents—the excess of the yield of capital employed on that particular piece of land over the yield of capital on the marginal land. And then there was this dynamic theory which is invoked by Ricardo again and again and in his *Essay on the Influence of a Low Price of Corn on the Profits of Stock*, to the effect that in the beginning, at any rate, the impact effect of improvements in agriculture is to diminish rent. Now Ricardo was sticking his neck out there. If you will read Marshall's [1920] Appendix L on the effect of taxation and improvements on rent, you will find that Marshall shows that it all depends upon the way in which improvements affect the productivity of different kinds of land whether they diminish rent or whether they increase it. And then, finally, there is the doctrine about rent not entering into cost of production.

Well, the theory of general wages I have more or less indicated in the treatment of Adam Smith's theory of wages and what I've already said about Ricardo and Malthus. The long-run theory of wages—wages in the stationary state, which, don't think that either Adam Smith or Ricardo thought was necessarily very near in western countries—was a sort of psychological subsistence theory. And since it has ceased to be a physiological subsistence theory, the psychological subsistence theory, the long-run equilibrium theory of wages, allowed that wages could be rather high. Ricardo said, in a well-known passage that I copied out this morning:

The friends of humanity cannot but wish that in all countries the labouring classes should have a taste for comforts and enjoyments, and that they should be stimulated by all legal means in their exertions to procure them. There cannot be a better security against a superabundant population. In those countries, where the labouring classes have the fewest wants, and are contented with the cheapest food, the people are exposed to the greatest vicissitudes and miseries. [Ricardo, 1821, pp. 100–101]

—page 100 of Sraffa's edition of Ricardo's *Principles*.

Now, by missing out the adjective "psychological" subsistence, the critics of nineteenth-century classical economics have had great fun for themselves saying that the classical economists always expected wages to be, in the long run, at subsistence level. But as you will see, from Ricardo's point of view the hope was that, being persuaded to limit population in one way or another, the psychological subsistence level might be made very high. Indeed, I think that I quoted to you James Mill on population, who said that if judicious methods were employed to limit the size of the labour force then wages might be raised to any height desirable.[2] But remember that both for Ricardo and Adam Smith, so long as capital was being accumulated, and being accumulated faster than the rate of increase of population, the stationary state was a long way off.

In the short run, the general level of wages, given mobility and all that sort of thing, was determined by the size of the funds destined for the maintenance of labour in relation to the labourers offering themselves for contract services. This is another complicated way of saying the wage fund theory, but the actual term *wage fund* was only invented, was only used, by John Stuart Mill.[3] But the conception dates from Adam Smith. And you should realise that it was used in this connection as regards the possible raising of wages. It was not used by the classical economists, whatever may have been its use by popular writers, against the labouring classes. It was not used to any extent against the unions. If any of you doubt that, there is an excellent work on the classical theory of wages and capital by the one-time Professor at Harvard, the famous Taussig [1897]. And while I dare say it's out of print now, it was reprinted by the London School of Economics, and many copies of it should be about in the Library.

Well, I think that that is enough on wages, but in this connection you might revert to Ricardo who, in his first meditations on the subject, thought that all improvements were favourable to wages. And he preached this with some emphasis. Under various influences which there is no time to go into now, including the reading of the famous pamphlet by an obscure man called Barton [1817], Ricardo changed his mind. And greatly to the discomfiture of McCulloch, who had followed Ricardo in his first meditations on this subject, Ricardo published a chapter on machinery and wages in the third edition of his *Principles* [1821, chap. 31] in which he said that in the short run, if there were a great conversion of circulating capital—the wage element in circulating capital into fixed—then, for the time being, this might be inimical to the interests of the labouring classes. I emphasise "for the time being" because he thought that if the improvements raised the rate of profit, since, in his opinion, a good deal, although not always all, accumulation was out of profit, indirectly, in the long run, the labouring classes would profit too. But his recantation of the over-simple, optimistic view that improvements always in the short run were to the benefit of the working classes is, I think, one more proof of the fact that Ricardo, once he was airborne, was pretty detached.

Well, finally, the theory of profits, which is obscure and intricate. The best short chapter on the classical theory of profits is in Tucker's book on *Progress and Profits* [1960, chap. 5, pp. 74–89], which I have already recommended to you. By far the best treatment—but it extends over something like 100 pages—is in Sam Hollander's [1979, chaps. 3 and 4, pp. 101–90] new book, which I won't attempt to reproduce in ten minutes. The Ricardian theory of profits arose probably from his questioning of the Smithian theory. Adam Smith thought that profits were determined by demand and supply, and in the long run he thought that the accumulation of capital would lead to a fall of profits due to this competitive process. Ricardo questioned this. Ricardo's objections really added up to this: If there is proportionate expansion of capital and labour, why should there be any fall in the rate of profits, having regard to the fact that the demand for scarce commodities is almost insatiable? It must be something to do, said Ricardo, with diminishing returns.

Now, that is a short summary of the Ricardian theory of profit. Now we go into it rather more deeply. Profits, in his opinion, were a residue after paying wages; rent then derives at the margin on production. And he tended to assume that movements in this residue were the same as the rate of profit on all capital. But in this he tended to neglect the complications of fixed capital. As Tucker [1960, pp. 119–22] says, since his theory of profits on the whole abstracts from technical change, this is fatal. But—and this is very important for you to bear in mind—when he is talking about the rate of profits and the rate of wages, he is always talking about a *share* of the national income, in real terms. And while shares may move in one direction, the absolute amounts may move in another. And so when he talks of a fall in wages, he may, Ricardo-wise, be contemplating a situation in which absolute wages have risen but not have risen enough to offset the proportionate increase in the real rate of profit. All of which makes Ricardo very hard reading at this juncture.

[A student says: "Could you repeat what you just said, please?"] I am emphasising that Ricardo was always talking about shares in real income, measured somehow or other. And while it's a tautology—that if the share of one set of factors increases, the share of the other factors must fall, relatively—it is quite possible that the absolute amounts in both cases have risen. I hope that makes it clear.

So, in Ricardo's theory of wages there are really two influences which may affect profits. In the short run, which may last quite a long time, wages may be bid up by accumulation. Perhaps you should omit "in the short run" and say simply from moment to moment wages may be bid up by accumulation. But you must remember, both from Adam Smith onwards, and from Malthus, certainly, this would be followed by an increase of population, save unless it kept ahead of the increase of population or if the increase of population was restrained by some method or other. But in the very long run—and I think you're justified in using "the long run"—the extension of production to meet a growing population would lead to diminishing returns in agriculture, and this would lead to a rise in the price of wage goods, and this would be bound to lead to increased wages, and thus there would be a diminished rate of profit in the long run.

Well, the mechanics of this are set out in the *Essay on the Influence of a Low Price of Corn on the Profits of Stock*, in terms of what Sraffa calls a corn model. Here there is no problem of value, and capital is represented by the corn, the seed or the wage goods, and the *return* on corn is represented by corn. And so it's simply just a question of considering quantities. Now, Hollander, I think, has proved pretty conclusively that the corn model was not the only model in Ricardo's mind when he wrote the *Essay on the Influence of a Low Price of Corn on the Profits of Stock*. Certainly, when he proceeded to the *Principles* he couldn't fall back on a corn price because he was preoccupied with *value*, and value involved more than one commodity involved in distribution. Hence, all his wrestlings in the first chapter of the *Principles* with the problem of value. But in the long run, diminishing returns leads to an extension of cultivation, greater labour costs per bushel, and hence price rises to compensate for the cost increases. But wages must rise in order to continue to purchase subsistence. And prices, measured in gold at constant value, *cannot* rise to compensate the farmers, and consequently there must be a fall in profit. And here the important point to realise is the point that I spent some time in driving home earlier in the lecture: that Ricardo was insisting on the fact that, under a metallic currency at any rate, a rise in wages cannot lead to a general rise in prices if the labour price of gold and the other things are unaltered. Indeed, some prices would rise and some prices would fall, but overall the value of money would remain unchanged. On this hypothesis—tremendously remote from the world of reality—his argument had a good deal in it.

I don't think that Ricardo was a pessimist, as sometimes has been assumed. In the *Quarterly Journal of Economics* for 1977, there is this splendid joint article by Hollander and Hicks which arose from a conversation between Hollander and Hicks in which Hollander reproached Hicks for assuming that Ricardo thought that subsistence wages were near at hand.

And he quoted all sorts of passages which persuaded Hicks, and they then combined in an article which I think all of you—and you can read it in half an hour; it involves only elementary geometry for the most part—I think all of you will find extremely illuminating on the classical theory of distribution in general.

Well, that's all for this term, and I wish you all a very happy holiday.

Notes

1. See Ricardo's letters to McCulloch, 8 August and 21 August 1823, in Ricardo (1951–73, vol. 9, pp. 330–31, 358–62).

2. See James Mill (1826, chap. 2, section 2), reprinted in Mill (1966, pp. 228–44, esp. pp. 242–43).

3. See J. S. Mill (1965, pp. 337ff.).

Overall Equilibrium

I HAVE given you a rough ordered summary of the main views of nine-teenth-century classical economics on money and banking.[1] I had previously given you a rough history of the controversies of the Napoleonic Wars and what followed, and the last lecture was an attempt to present the results of the controversy in a more or less orderly form. I wound up with a discussion of the famous banking and currency controversy, which centered upon the question of whether a convertible note issue could be left to look after itself, so to speak, guided by the prudence of the Bank, or whether some control was necessary. The currency school which represented the control business was victorious in the Act of 1844. I don't want to recapitulate further; I just wanted to hitch on to what I am going to say.

What I want to talk about this morning is the classical conceptions of the broader conditions of overall equilibrium, leaving out until next time international complications.

Now, the classical conceptions of overall equilibrium are best approached, I think, by asking what was their attitude to saving. And saving, in the context of the classical system, was regarded as being, roughly speaking, equivalent to investment—not only ex post, but ex ante, so to speak. Now, the general attitude as regards the effects of saving is to be found in Adam Smith's *Wealth of Nations* where, in the chapter in book 2 concerning productive and unproductive labour and accumulation, he lays it down that what is annually saved is annually consumed, and in more or less the same period, but by a different set of people. I have drawn your attention to that passage before, and I think I said at the time that it was equivalent to a deliberate denial that there might be gaps between saving ex ante and investment. It was equivalent to the ignoring of the possible hoarding of saving, rather than putting saving into some form of real investment.

Now, this point of view was transmitted directly to the classical economists who, of course, all read Adam Smith, but it was reinforced by some observations originating in the *Traité d'Économie Politique*, published in 1804 by the French economist Jean Baptiste Say. Now, you ought to be warned that, in modern discussions—the sort of discussions that you read, or I hope you read, in regard to overall equilibrium—Say's Law of Markets is referred to in a way which suggests that the users have not read J. B. Say. It is extraordinary the number of people who have made reputations for themselves by denouncing Say's Law simpliciter. Say's Law, simpliciter, was that supply creates its own demand, and therefore there can be no general glut.

Now, the fact is that Say's pronunciation in the 1804 edition of his remarks on this subject was much looser than that. And there is an extremely useful article in *Economica* for 1977 by Professor Baumol, referring to Say's possibly eight laws and their signification. And although I don't want to go into the eight possible significations of Say's Law, I draw your attention to that by way of warning. Say actually, as Professor Baumol shows, did recognise the possibility of hoarding, and it can be argued, as Baumol argues in this article, that Say was simply enunciating his law of markets with regard to the developments of an economy over the long period, where history up to date surely showed—and *up to our own date* showed—that there could be a very considerable increase of production per head without any permanent congestion of the economy—production per head giving rise at the same time to income and, in the long run, possibly but not certainly, the probability that that income would be spent. It can be argued in defense of Say that he was considering the long-run possibilities of growth, and that he was not considering the short-run possibilities of congestion in the capital market due to failure to spend savings.

Well, so much by way of Say. The matter was taken up in this country by James Mill, the father of John Stuart Mill. James Mill had read the first edition of Say's *Traité* when he issued a pamphlet called *Commerce Defended* [1808], which was a counterblast to an obscure pamphlet, which only doctorate specialists among you need read, by a man called William Spence, who was rather influenced by physiocratic views. And Spence, in the middle of the Napoleonic blockade, which was supposed to paralyse our external trade, published a pamphlet called *Britain Independent of Commerce* [1808], in which he said: Why worry about Napoleon and his paralysis of international trade? Britain can be independent of commerce and still be reasonably prosperous because the increased money going to the landowners, owing to the probable rise in the price of corn and so on and so forth, *will almost certainly be spent* by the landowners, and not "not spent," as it might be if it fell into the hands of the monied classes. This is a very, very crude idea of Spence's pretty crude pamphleteering.

Well, James Mill, and Torrens [1808] also, replied to Spence. I'm not going to deal with Torrens' reply, in this context at any rate; the important reply is by James Mill. And James Mill deals with Spence's contentions on Adam Smithian lines. He says (I quote): "Let not Mr. Spence, however, be alarmed. Let him rest in perfect assurance, that the whole annual produce of the country will be always very completely consumed, whether his landholders choose to spend or to accumulate" [James Mill, 1808, p. 71].[2] Well, that's Smithian lines, but later on he goes on to develop the argument, which does not appear so strongly in the first edition of Say, although it peeps out in the second edition, as Baumol shows, and he goes on to say, warming up to the controversy:

No proposition . . . in political œconomy seems to be more certain than this which I am going to announce, how paradoxical soever it may at first sight appear; and if it be true, none undoubtedly can be deemed of more importance. The production of commodities creates, and is the one and universal cause which creates a market for the commodities produced. . . . When goods are carried to market what is wanted is somebody to buy. But to buy, one must have wherewithal to pay. It is obviously therefore the collective means of payment which exist in the whole nation that constitute the entire market of the nation. But wherein consist the collective means of payment of the whole nation? Do they not consist in its annual produce, in the annual revenue of the general mass of its inhabitants? But if a nation's power of purchasing is exactly measured by its annual produce, as it undoubtedly is; the more you increase the annual produce, the more by that very act you extend the national market, the power of purchasing and the actual purchases of the nation. . . . [T]he demand of a nation is always equal to the produce of a nation. [ibid., pp. 81–83][3]

Now, in this *extremely* illuminating article of Baumol's in this recent number of *Economica*, he goes a little further than I would in giving credit to Mill for taking into consideration the long-period considerations which Baumol shows certainly influenced Say to some extent. I think this is possible, and it may explain John Stuart Mill's attitude, which I will be coming to in a moment. But I think the general impression you get from reading Mill's pamphlet *and*—and this is more important—the general impression which *Ricardo* derived from Mill's pamphlet (and he afterwards read Say) was much more to insist on the universal applicability of this law of markets, in contradistinction to Malthus, who had his own interpretation of the possible causes of non–full employment, of economic depression, and so on and so forth.

Now, you can find passages in Ricardo which perhaps can be quoted against the rigid interpretation which I have put on James Mill and Ricardo's habit in controversy with Malthus of referring to the law of markets in the short term, but let us look at Malthus. In contradistinction to his great friend Ricardo, who on the whole was concerned with long-period tendencies, and tended to ignore short-period tendencies, and was given to long chains of reasoning based, in a masterly way, on simplified models, Malthus was not so logical as Ricardo in developing these models, but Malthus had some sense of contemporary goings-on.

A letter to Ricardo from Malthus [7 July 1821] was discovered in our own day by Mr Sraffa and tremendously impressed Keynes. And Keynes actually said: "If only Malthus, instead of Ricardo, had been the parent stem from which nineteenth-century economics proceeded, what a much wiser and richer place the world would be to-day!" [Keynes, 1933/1972, pp. 100–101]. Well, the thing to do is to look at Malthus, and in this letter he does put up what seems to be a Keynesian explanation. He says, "We see in almost every part of the world vast powers of production which are not put into action." And he goes on to explain this by saying (I'm quoting again):

> from the want of a proper distribution of the actual produce adequate motives are not furnished to continue production. . . . I don't at all wish to deny that some persons or others are entitled to consume all that is produced; but the grand question is whether it is distributed in such a manner between the different parties concerned as to occasion the most effective demand for future produce: and I distinctly maintain that an attempt to accumulate very rapidly which necessarily implies a considerable diminution of unproductive consumption,

—the spending of the landowners and so on and so forth—

> by greatly impairing the usual motives to production must prematurely check the progress of wealth. [Malthus to Ricardo, 7 July 1821, quoted in ibid., p. 99]

Now, it was that passage that impressed Keynes. I have read it in a sympathetic way, and I do sympathise with Malthus for getting irritated with Ricardo's rather simplistic *simpliste* interpretation of the model.

But when you consider it closely, and what Malthus said in his books, you find that, far from being Keynesian, it's the antithesis of Keynes. For Keynes, depression arose, to use the terminology of the *Treatise on Money* [1930], or, if you like, to use Swedish terminology, from ex ante saving—planned saving—exceeding planned investment. Now, it was Malthus' contention, for the most part, that depression arose because *too much* was invested and too little consumed, and Malthus actually goes out of his way—I warn you, this is a controversial matter; there is a man called Lambert in Belgium who maintains, against me among other people, that Malthus was a true Keynesian—but Malthus actually says in his *Principles of Political Economy*, page 32:

> No political economist of the present day can by saving mean mere hoarding; and beyond this contracted and inefficient proceeding, no use of the term, in reference to national wealth, can well be imagined, but that which must arise from a different application of what is saved, founded upon a real distinction between the different kinds of labour which may be maintained by it. [Malthus, 1820, p. 32]

So that, in contradistinction to Keynes and modern denouncers of the so-called Say's Law, Malthus believed that *overinvestment* was the cause of depression. He didn't believe it as much as Lauderdale, who was a brilliant economist, not of classical views, who wrote at the same time—wrote an essay on the production of wealth [1804], which is very well worth reading. Lauderdale thought that capital accumulation with known techniques was very speedily exhausted and after that the savings would necessarily run to waste. Malthus didn't go as far as that. Malthus said that Lauderdale went a little too far, but that there *was* a proportion between saving, in the sense of investment (in his sense), and consumption which guaranteed maximum growth.

Well, Ricardo and Malthus exchanged endless letters on this subject, and Ricardo wrote *Notes on Malthus' "Principles of Political Economy"* [Ricardo, 1928], which are thoroughly worth reading for those of you who are taking graduate schools degrees (quite a lot of time to wade through the notes, but it's volume 2 of Sraffa's marvelous edition [Ricardo, 1951]). Malthus, I think, lost out, as the saying is, in his controversy with Ricardo. Malthus, holding this conception of real overinvestment, was particularly vulnerable to Ricardo's use of the simplified version of Say's Law presented by James Mill.

But now, where have we reached in the history of theory? I think we've reached this conclusion: that good sense was lacking as regards what was happening in the deflation phase of monetary history during the Napoleonic Wars. Malthus didn't give the monetary explanation, as Attwood did, but Malthus was right, surely, against Ricardo and against other classical economists who gave any reason for the depression other than the right one. *Malthus was right that something was wrong*—something was wrong—but he didn't give the right reason for it. And on the plane of argument on which the letters to Ricardo and the notes of Ricardo on his *Principles* operated, *on that plane* Ricardo's remote logic had it nearly every time over Malthus' attempts at logic.

But now, this state of affairs worried John Stuart Mill, and he actually wrote to a friend, warning the friend, who was going to write on subjects of this sort, that he mustn't say anything which contradicted the truth implied in his father's and Ricardo's point of view. But he went on to say of this point of view and that of the under-consumptionists, particularly a man called Wakefield—Gibbon Wakefield [1849]—and Chalmers [1832] (also obscure people—I don't think that John Stuart Mill had much regard for Malthus in this particular connection, although he admired him very much as regards population): "The two points of view can be reconciled." And he wrote an extraordinary essay in the late '20s or early '30s, which he didn't publish until the middle of the '40s, which is published in his *Essays on Unsettled Questions of Political Economy* [1844]. And the paper is called—and you must all read it, undergraduates as well as graduates—"On the Influence of Consumption on Production." And he breaks through the sterile logic of the simplified interpretation of Say's Law and shows how holding back expenditure may produce the appearance of a general glut. He recognises that business is liable to alterations of prosperity and depression, so that general eagerness to buy and general reluctance to buy succeed one another at brief intervals. He says, "In this last case [that is, depression], it is commonly said that there is a general superabundance" [Mill, 1844, p. 68].

Now, how is that to be reconciled with the position of his father and
J. B. Say? Well, first of all, he says, and I'm quoting—I am quoting so much
in this lecture because I want you to be sure that I am not just improvising
and paraphrasing, in a favourable or unfavourable sense, the people whose
opinions I am giving you the history of—he says that the proposition that
supply is at the same time demand is, and I quote, "evidently founded on
the supposition of a state of barter. . . . When two persons perform an act
of barter, each of them is at once a seller and a buyer. He cannot sell without buying" [ibid., p. 69]. Very simple, absolutely incontrovertible, but
analytically, by way of contrast, an extraordinarily deep insight. He goes on
to say:

> If, however, we suppose that money is used, these propositions cease to be
> exactly true. . . . [T]he effect of the employment of money . . . is, that it en-
> ables this one act of interchange to be divided into two separate acts or opera-
> tions. . . . Although he who sells, really sells only to buy, he needs not buy at
> the same moment when he sells; and he does not therefore necessarily add to
> the *immediate* demand for one commodity when he adds to the supply of
> another. . . . [T]here may be . . . a very general inclination to sell with as little
> delay as possible, accompanied with an equally general inclination to defer all
> purchases as long as possible. [ibid., pp. 69–70]

And so he goes on:

> to render the argument for the impossibility of an excess of all commodities
> applicable to the case in which a circulating medium is employed, money must
> itself be considered as a commodity [in demand and supply]. It must, un-
> doubtedly, be admitted that there cannot be an excess of all other commodi-
> ties, *and* an excess of money at the same time. [ibid., p. 71, emphasis added by
> Robbins]

I'm quoting. And he then goes on to say—and this is Baumol's charitable
interpretation of what Say might have meant, but inferentially perhaps
what his father might have meant—he concludes—he's very careful—by
emphasizing that "The argument against the possibility of general over-
production is [still] quite conclusive, so far as it applies to the doctrine that
a country may accumulate capital too fast" [ibid., p. 73]. One in the eye for
Malthus. And then he gives, what I shall not quote to you, a splendid account of a trade cycle which starts by people being eagerly optimistic, pre-
ferring goods to money and getting rid of money quickly, culminating,
under a metallic standard, when there are strains on the ratios of the banks
in a financial crisis, and then, the relative preference for money and goods
being changed, and money being in demand and not goods, there appears
to be a superabundance of goods other than money.

Baumol wrote another article with Professor Becker—I don't know how
much Professor Becker contributed to it; it reads to me very much like
Baumol—in 1952, and it's called "The Classical Monetary Theory: The

Outcome of the Discussion" [Becker and Baumol, 1952]. And Baumol and Becker say in that article that if you read Mill's essay "Of the Influence of Consumption on Production," you wonder what the fuss has all been about in the modern controversy, in which *dozens* of people have made their reputation by pointing out that the oversimple formulations of Say and the still more simple formulations of James Mill, Ricardo, and so on were certainly wrong in the short period. So there you are. And that article by Baumol and Becker is in *Economica* for November 1952.

Now, as regards overall equilibrium, there are other fragments of theory which anticipate modern thought on this subject, and I want to spend the last ten minutes drawing your attention to them. I remind you first of the fact that Hume, in his discussion of the effects of an increase of gold supply in a community, pointed out that the effects in enlarging the circulation only dribbled through gradually, and if this gold got into the hands of people who were spending and giving employment, the effects might be an increase of employment and prosperity.

Now, this Humian doctrine rather dropped out of view, but among classical economists, including Jeremy Bentham, there was developed a doctrine which is in modern days has been called the doctrine of forced saving. And you will find an extremely splendid discussion of the history of the doctrine of forced savings as an appendix to a later edition of Hayek's famous lectures delivered here in the '30s on *Prices and Production* [1931].

The first elaboration of the doctrine of forced saving was by Jeremy Bentham, who in part of his *Manual of Political Economy* [1843] deals at some length with what he calls forced frugality. And forced frugality can take two forms. It can be extracted from the citizens by taxation and used by the Government. Well, that's quite straightforward, and Adam Smith would have recognised that (but he would have said that the Government would have wasted the forced frugality). But then Bentham goes on (and I'm quoting): "The effect of forced frugality is also produced by the creating of paper money by government, or the suffering the creation of paper money on the part of individuals" [Bentham, 1843, p. 44]. If the additional money comes into the hands of those who use it as capital, then—I'm quoting—"All hands being [fully] employed," it is a tangible effect offset to the loss of real income on the part of the rest of the community [ibid., p. 45]. And he goes on to say: "as in the above case of forced frugality [through taxation], national wealth is increased at the expense of national comfort and national justice" [ibid.]. Well, you get the same in Thornton's marvelous book. He says: "provided we assume an excessive issue of paper to lift up, as it may for a time, the cost of goods though not the price of labour, some augmentation of stock"—he meant capital—"will be the consequence" [Thornton, 1802, p. 263].[4] And he then expatiates on the effect of this on the people with fixed incomes.

And you will find reference to this in Malthus, and you will find reference to this in Torrens and in the work of a man who is more obscure than he deserves to be, Joplin—*An Illustration of Mr. Joplin's Views on the Currency*, 1825. But you also find it in John Stuart Mill in his essay on profits,[5] and in the *Principles*. In the *Principles*, there's a clear explanation of the process which he calls forced accumulation:

> The circulating medium . . . is partly employed in purchases for productive, and partly for unproductive consumption. . . . If, then, an addition were made to the circulating medium [which is] in the hands of unproductive consumers exclusively, a larger portion of the existing stock of commodities would be bought for unproductive consumption . . . ; and on the contrary, if the addition be made to the portion of the circulating medium which is in the hands of the producers . . . , a greater proportion of the commodities . . . will for the present be employed as capital, . . . And there is a real increase of capital. [Mill, 1965, 2:528]

But he doesn't agree with this; he thinks that it's unjust. Well, that's the first fragment of dynamic elements in the treatment of various classical economists of overall questions.

The second part which I want to emphasise is the contrast between natural and money rates. This has its origin in Adam Smith's doctrine that if the banks increase their convertible issues on discounts on real transactions—real trade—then there's no danger of over-issue. The danger of over-issue on Adam Smith's conception arose if they increased their issues on artificial finance bills not corresponding to the needs of trade. And that argument was brought up by the anti-bullionists, as I explained last time.

But Thornton, in his *Paper Credit*, edited by Hayek [1802/1939], page 254, points out that the real bills doctrine is all nonsense as stated in that sense, because it pays no attention to the short-term rate of interest: The volume of bills coming up for discount will vary according to the short-term rate of discount. And consequently, Thornton makes a distinction between the money rate of interest—short and long—and the real rate of profitability, which reminds you of Wicksell and his contrast between money rates of interest and the natural rate of interest.

And finally, in the speeches of Thornton [1811] on the Bullion Committee's report,[6] he makes the third dynamic fragment that I want to draw your attention to in the discussion of overall equilibrium: He makes the distinction between money rates of interest and real rates of interest, which is not the same as the distinction between money rates of interest and the natural rate of interest, or profitability. It is the distinction between what you get in money terms and what the money rate of interest will purchase in real terms, which is a doctrine which I do not need to expatiate upon. With a minimum money rate of interest at 17 percent in this unfortunate country, the real return, with prices rising at 17 percent on investments of that sort, is zero. No more glaring contrast can be conceived.

But of course we didn't have to wait for our own day of reckless inflation on the part of governments that ought to have known better—value judgement—to discover this. The distinction which Thornton drew between money rates and real rates—the real return—is elaborated in that marvelous early work by Irving Fisher on *Appreciation and Interest* [1896a]. Those of you who are Americans here must never forget, what is sometimes forgotten, I think, in your country, that Irving Fisher was the most marvelous theoretical economist—analytical economist—produced in the last 100 years in the English-speaking world. His book on the theory of prices [1892], written as a doctor's thesis, and his book on *Appreciation and Interest*, and his book on the *Nature of Capital and Income* [1906] and his book on *The Rate of Interest* [1907] are *absolutely outstanding*, and all sorts of people in more modern times have got great credit for rediscovering what was writ large in the books which were recommended to me as a student—standard obligatory reading—by Fisher.

Jacob Viner, who was a great friend of mine, once said to me that if Irving Fisher and Frank Taussig—who was a senior professor at Harvard and who wrote a very good principles of economics for his day and who wrote many works on applied economics—Jacob Viner said that if Irving Fisher and Frank Taussig were rolled into one, then America would need no economists for a hundred years.

Tomorrow I shall be switching over to the classical theory of international trade.

NOTES

1. Again, lectures 23 and 24 (as per the numbering scheme given in Robbins' outline; see appendix A), to which Robbins is referring here, were not recorded.
2. This can also be found in James Mill (1966, p. 129).
3. This can also be found in James Mill (1966, pp. 135–36).
4. See also Thornton (1939, p. 329).
5. "On Profits, and Interest," in Mill (1844).
6. These speeches are reprinted in Thornton (1939).

International Trade

THE explosion in the west end has disorganised traffic and disorganised my morning program. I want to talk to you today about the classical theory of international trade. Now, you may remember that when I was dealing with Adam Smith's chapter on the division of labour, I specifically pointed out that among the advantages of the division of labour he did not enumerate the advantages of dividing labour spatially. But of course, whatever the reason for the omission, you mustn't think that Adam Smith did not give attention to this particular problem. The greater part of book 4 on the mercantile system rests upon his conception that there were great advantages in the division of labour between different parts of the world.

There's a celebrated passage which, because of the disorganisation of my morning, I have not marked before coming along—ah, here it is—in chapter 2 of book 4 in which he says: "The natural advantages which one country has over another in producing particular commodities are sometimes so great, that it is acknowledged by all the world to be in vain to struggle with them." And this is the famous passage:

> By means of glasses, hotbeds, and hotwalls, very good grapes can be raised in Scotland, and very good wine too can be made of them at about thirty times the expence for which at least equally good can be brought from foreign countries. Would it be a reasonable law to prohibit the importation of all foreign wines, merely to encourage the making of claret and burgundy in Scotland? But if there would be a manifest absurdity in turning towards any employment, thirty times more of the capital and industry of the country, than would be necessary to purchase from foreign countries an equal quantity of the commodities wanted, there must be an absurdity, though not altogether so glaring, yet exactly of the same kind, in turning towards any such employment a thirtieth, or even a three hundredth part more of either. Whether *the advantages* which one country has over another, be natural or acquired, is in this respect of no consequence. As long as the one country has those advantages, and the other wants them, it will always be more advantageous for the latter, rather to buy of the former than to make. It is an acquired advantage only, which one artificer has over his neighbour, who exercises another trade; and yet they both find it more advantageous to buy of one another than to make what does not belong to their particular trades. [Smith, 1776, 1:423–24]

Well, the grapes in Scotland illustration very vividly brings out the good sense of this matter, and I say that of the twentieth century as much as of the eighteenth century, making all allowances for exceptional cases covered by the famous infant industry argument.

But analytically, the nineteenth-century classical economists carried the matter considerably further than Adam Smith's homely illustration of the disadvantage of growing grapes in Scotland. You may remember that when I was giving you a schematic account of Ricardo's 93 percent labour theory of value and pointing out the various exceptions—which added up to a very large volume—I mentioned that it did not apply to the exchange between areas between which there was no mobility of labour and capital. Now, I put it in those very general terms because the analysis which emerges from Ricardo and the other classical economists is usually dealt with under the heading of "international trade." And all sorts of people have acquired some sort of ambiguous reputation by pointing out that there *is* mobility of capital and labour between the areas called *nations*. From time to time, in particular cases, the mobility of labour is impaired by quota regulations and so on, and the same applies to the mobility of capital. Well, all that, of course, is true enough, and it was true even of the time of Ricardo. Ricardo, for some reason or other—I do not pretend to explain this, because his forefathers had come from Portugal and his immediate ancestors had come from Holland—but on the whole, at any rate, as regards the movement of capital, he says that he would *regret* mobility of capital between different national areas. This is just an idiosyncrasy on his part and has nothing to do with the analysis that follows.

Now, on the 93 percent labour theory of value, or the real cost theory of value, not applying to international trade or trade between areas between which there is no mobility, Ricardo was compelled to think out further analysis. And his further analysis, which is called the theory of comparative costs, has, on the whole, stood up, with modification, to analytical developments since that day much better than his 93 percent labour theory of value. I say that it has stood up; it has undergone extensive modifications, but to anticipate, if you like, the famous theory of opportunity costs, which is still alluded to in lectures and in political discussions on economic policy, bears a family resemblance to the theory of comparative costs as it was developed by Ricardo and indeed by one of Ricardo's contemporaries, namely, the strange man Torrens.

Now, the theory of comparative costs is associated with the name of Ricardo. It appears in the first chapters of the *Principles of Economics.* It was, in fact, enunciated before Ricardo, although not under that name, by Robert Torrens in his *Essay on the External Corn Trade* [1815]. There is really no doubt about Torrens' priority in that respect. But having paid that tribute to my favourite minor economist, I shall now explain to you in Ricardian terms the theory of comparative costs.

Well now, let us take the simplest possible example. Let us take exchange between a hypothetical England and a hypothetical Germany. And let us not get muddled by going straightaway into comparative costs. Let us go back to the fundamentals of absolute productivity. And there are three possible cases here:

	1		2		3	
	Germany	England	Germany	England	Germany	England
Wool	2	1	4	1	2	1
Corn	1	2	3	2	2	1

Let us take two commodities, wool and corn. And the first case, which is the simplest I can devise, is two units of wool produced in Germany for one unit in England, and as regards corn the reverse relationship applies. In the second case, four units of wool are produced in Germany to one in England, and three units of corn to two in England. In the third case, two units of wool are produced in Germany for one in England, and similarly for corn.

Now, the first of these cases is called *absolute* cost differences, and you can see that, whether there is mobility of labour or not, there is advantage in exchange because in one case Germany is twice as good in the production of wool and half as good in the production of corn. I ought to say that these productivity figures are exactly the reciprocal of the cost figures, hence the eventual designation of these propositions as the theory of comparative costs. Well now, that's the case of absolute cost differences.

Here [pointing to the board], in the second case, there are *comparative* cost differences. Now, here you observe that Germany is superior to the hypothetical England in both wool and corn, but if you work out the cost differences you can see that the superiority is different in the cases of the two commodities. And so this case is called the *comparative* cost case.

Now we come to the third case, in which Germany is twice as good, both at the production of wool and the production of corn, as England, but the cost differences are the same in either case. Well now, if you think a little bit, it's very clear indeed, isn't it, that in the absolute cost difference case there is obvious advantage in concentration of one commodity in one area and the other commodity in the other area and exchange being effected. You don't need the theory of comparative cost to show that. But in the second case, where the comparative costs differ, there is still advantage in exchange. It might be—although it would be rather improbable—that some distinguished academic was superior to his gentleman's personal gentleman at cooking meals, but his superiority in his academic line was so much greater than his superiority in cooking meals that there would still be good sense in his concentrating on his academic stuff and leaving the cooking to be done by his gentleman's personal gentleman.

But supposing the superiority in *each* line was the same, as it is in my case 3, then there would be nothing in it. You can see that perfectly well. Let us suppose that you have one of these—I won't say tedious, I will say useful—

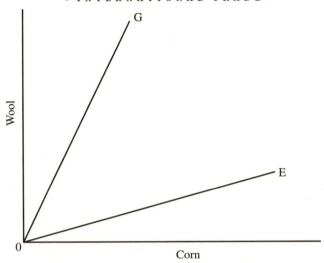

Figure 3. Comparative Costs and Gains from Trade.

apparatuses, and you measure wool along there and corn along there, you will find that; if you plot them out, the cost differences resolve themselves into straight-line vectors in the simple case where there is no variation of cost, whatever the operation undertaken. And you would find if you worked out some example that the division of labour which would arise, both in the absolute cost case *and* the different comparative cost case, would simply resolve themselves into angular magnitudes of the sort indicated by radius vectors from the origin. But supposing that you had the third case, then the radius vector would be the same for England and Germany, and there would be no opportunity for advantageous exchange between the two areas.

I have given you the simplest case possible—two commodities and two countries. Various complications arise when you have more than two commodities, even if you stick to the two areas "at home" and "abroad" to simplify things. But you mustn't regard the classical theory as stopping at this point which depends upon, here [pointing to the board], the revelation of the range of advantageous exchanges between England and Germany, even if there are comparative cost differences. You mustn't think that the classical analysis, which is really rather beautiful in this respect, stops there. It is not necessarily the case that, out of equilibrium, the real comparative cost differences create a situation in which there is, immediately, advantageous exchange between real commodities.

Let us think of a case—the simplest possible case. And if any of you are confused in this, the diagram that I'm going to reproduce is a diagram which I don't know of elsewhere, but is in an Italian book of which there is a German translation, *Principles of Theoretical Economics*, by Barone [1927].

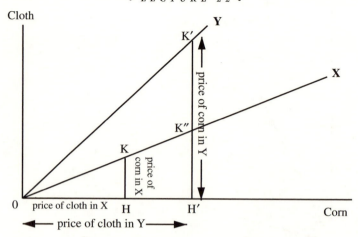

Figure 4. Barone's Trade Diagram. *Source:* Barone, 1929, p. 98.

And Barone's case starts by assuming that there is a gold currency in
both Germany and England, but for some reason or other the price of
wheat and the price of corn in Germany are both lower than in England, so
that here [in figure 4] you have the initial gold price of wheat in Germany
and here the gold price of corn—these being derived, obviously, from the
productivity slopes. And suppose that the same thing applies in England,
but at higher gold prices. Well now, what happens in that case? Clearly, if
there is free trade, no German buys anything from England, and England
buys *both* wheat and corn from Germany. On the very simple quantity theory assumptions which the classical economists used in this connection,
and simplifying just a little bit—assume that the purchases from England to
Germany are paid for in gold, but they are paid for out of hoards—all that
happens is that coming into Germany these payments are spent and affect
the price level. Well then in that case, you will get a movement of the gold
prices in Germany along here and along here, until the gold price of corn
is the same in Germany as it is in England. And at that point the exchange
of real goods will come into view. Germany will go on producing wool, but
England will now get an opportunity of selling some corn.[1]

Now, I give Barone very high marks indeed for thinking that one out.
But Barone's diagram is simply a simplified version of one of the most famous propositions of Ricardian and classical economics regarding the distribution of the precious metals. This in a sense is an elaboration of Hume's
specie flow analysis. Ricardo felt that under conditions of free trade, and
assuming a specie currency composed of gold, there would be movements
of gold which brought it about that the real exchanges in equilibrium between the different countries were the same as they would have been under
conditions of barter—the redistribution of gold bringing about the underlying real conditions of comparative costs.

Now, this is quite a complicated matter, and Ricardo does not make it frightfully intelligible unless you know it already. For those of you who have never heard of the theory of comparative costs before, I recommend Senior's pamphlet *On the Cost of Obtaining Money* [1829], or, in modern times, Taussig's book on international trade [1927], which, because he deals with arithmetical examples, is regarded with some disparagement by those who know advanced matrix analysis and so on and so forth, but still contains a great deal of matters which are relevant to international trade and are better explained there than anywhere else, up to this point. There is an article by Taussig around the turn of the century on "Wages and Prices in . . . International Trade" [1906], and that's in the *Quarterly Journal of Economics*, but the book on international trade was published when he was quite an old man, in the '20s.

But now, those of you who are very quick to follow this sort of exposition, even if you haven't known this before, will realise that the labour theory of comparative costs, while it did provide a theory of the division of labour under these simplified conditions, and while it did show a range of possible exchange rates which would be advantageous to both of the parties in between these radius vectors, says nothing about the equilibrium price between the cost vectors—that there's just an area within which bargaining may take place. That is to say that the theory of comparative costs, by itself, does not deal with demand conditions, and demand conditions prove, in the last analysis, when you have more than two commodities, to be extremely important. And they *are* important when you have two commodities.

Now, how did demand conditions come in? Well, you can find it in Ricardo where he's dealing with colonial trade [1821, chap. 25], but I think that you would have to use a microscope. The theory of demand in nineteenth-century classical economics arises from various sources.

First of all, it arises in connection with the argument regarding the effects of absenteeism on the part of the Irish landowners, around about the first quarter of the century—Ireland having been included in Great Britain by the Act of Union at the beginning of the century. There began to be complaints that the absentee landlordism, which had all sorts of bad effects apart from trade, meant that the Irish were poorer off than if the landlords had resided on their estates. And some of the classical economists—and McCulloch was a culprit in this respect—scouted this idea, said, after all, exports and imports paid for each other and the balance of payments eventually balances, so why bother? Well, that was very superficial, and a very clever man called Mountiford Longfield, whom I shall have to talk about when I talk about the anticipators of modern analysis as distinct from nineteenth-century classicism, Mountiford Longfield wrote a lecture, which was published, on absenteeism [1835]. And he pointed out with non-mathematical terms that if the absentee landlords spent a great deal of their rents, let us say on lace for their lady friends in Paris, that meant a switch of demand which might have been focussed on factors of production in Ireland to the lacemakers in the neighborhood of Paris, and thus the factorial terms of trade might be affected by absentee landlordism. That was the first case.

The second case was the frightful behaviour of Colonel Robert Torrens. Colonel Robert Torrens had been a *stalwart*, in his *Essay on the External Corn Trade* [1815], in resisting the imposition of protection for agriculture after the Napoleonic Wars. And he continued until the end of his life to be a stalwart for the general Smithian position that there are advantages in the territorial division of labour. Indeed, Torrens himself invented the term *territorial division of labour* which is so useful. But as time went on and the cry arose for Great Britain to go free trade whatever else was happening elsewhere, Torrens became convinced that there were disadvantages in unilateral free trade. And he wrote some *Letters on Commercial Policy* [1833], which are in the London School of Economics series, in the 1830s which caused no splash at all. It's an extremely rare book, and I coaxed the London School of Economics to reprint it, partly because I had never been able to find a copy of it myself except in museums. But in the 1840s, when the movement for unilateral trade was gathering strength, Torrens published a series of letters, partly on monetary policy and partly on trade policy, which he gathered together in a book called *The Budget* [1844]—a series of letters, *The Budget*, by Robert Torrens. And incidentally, that too is a rare book. I've got a copy, so if you find a copy, you don't run any risks in consulting me. But don't get rid of it. It's really one of the rarest books, and I am surprised that it's not been reprinted by photography, because it is so important in the history of thought.

Torrens devised a series of bartering examples and monetary examples in which he showed that there was a possibility, other things being equal, that if England went free trade unilaterally, the terms of trade might turn against her. He *fantastically* exaggerated this possibility, but analytically there was something in it. It caused *no end* of a row among the classical economists. Senior [1843] wrote a review of Torrens' book in the *Edinburgh Review*, in which he paid tribute to Torrens' eminence and all that sort of thing, but said that he was quite analytically wrong. And there were others who took exception to Torrens' attitude here.

But Torrens was quite defiant, and John Stuart Mill, reading Torrens' *Budget*, recollected that in the late '20s he had written an analysis, realizing the gap in the Ricardian theory, of the conditions of demand in international trade. And reading Torrens, he felt that he might publish this essay together with the essay that I was praising yesterday on the influence of consumption on production and a couple of other essays in a book—which is not so rare, the *Essays on Unsettled Questions of Political Economy* [1844]. We have reprinted it, but it's not such an extraordinary thing to come across a copy either of the original or of its reproduction in Bohn's Library in the nineteenth century [Mill, 1897].

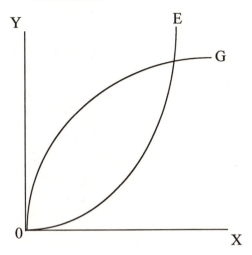

Figure 5. Marshallian Trade Diagram.
Source: Marshall, 1923, app. J.

And of course, analytically, Mill was far ahead of even Longfield in this respect, and *far* ahead of Torrens, who used the most extravagant arithmetical examples which prevented the analytical point that he was making from being taken sufficiently seriously. Mill worked out tables of international supply and demand and showed that, in certain circumstances, there could be a certain amount of finance to be extracted from the foreigner by a revenue tax on his goods. He didn't believe in protective tariffs, and he didn't believe in milking the foreigner, but he felt himself obliged to confess that analytically it was possible to conceive of that.

Well, I see my time is up. But it only remained for Marshall to translate Mill's essay on international exchange, which was illustrated by *arithmetical* illustrations, in order for Marshall [1879; 1923] to devise his aggregate demand and supply curves which exhibit conditions of equilibrium between the relevant cost situations at their intersection [see figure 5]. (You can call one of these G and the other E.) That's more modern theory. We can leave it at Mill having discovered and set forth the real cause of the gap in the Ricardian theory.

And so I'm getting to the end of the classical system. I'm not going to lecture on taxation, which you can read up in Ricardo or can read up in the book by Shoup [1960] which is recommended in my list. But I think that I will wind up my exposition on nineteenth-century classical economics by giving you a lecture next week on John Stuart Mill himself, who, so to speak, after all this exchange of pamphlets and books and so on and so forth, thought that it would be desirable to have a book on the same scale as Adam Smith's *Wealth of Nations* which introduced the various complications which had occurred since the writing of the *Wealth of Nations*.

NOTE

1. To further assist the reader in interpreting the Barone diagram, we provide the following explanation. The two radius vectors in the two goods (cloth and corn) space refer, respectively, to country X and country Y. Their slopes are different because of different *relative* prices in the two countries. This means that the quantity of corn OH′ is exchanged with a quantity H′K′ in Y and H′K″ in X.

Now, suppose that we measure the absolute prices in the same currency—or, as Robbins puts it, in terms of gold. If the same quantity of cloth can be bought with OH amount of currency in X and OH′ in Y, it follows that the price of corn in X (HK) is lower than in Y (H′K′). With both absolute prices in X lower that in Y, there will be export of both goods from X to Y. According to the quantity theory, the consequent monetary movement in the opposite direction makes absolute prices increase in X until, according to Barone, H coincides with H′.

We are indebted to Andrea Salanti for his assistance with this translation.

John Stuart Mill

I'LL SKIP the lecture in the program on the theories regarding taxation of the nineteenth-century classical economists, but before quitting that general field, I think that I ought to devote a lecture to talking to you about John Stuart Mill.

John Stuart Mill, whose *Principles of Political Economy* was published in 1848, is not the last of the classical economists. The last was J. E. Cairnes, who held a chair at University College, and whose various works are still worth looking at, despite the fact that he didn't appreciate Jevons' theory of value—which has earned him a bad name in the minds of certain somewhat superficial people. But John Stuart Mill occupies, so to speak, a terminal position as regards the general evolution of thought between himself and Adam Smith. And his *Principles of Political Economy* avowedly intends to do for the subject—widely conceived, as we shall see, as Adam Smith's conception was—definitely proposes, with due respect, to bring Adam Smith up to date. And therefore I think that although John Stuart Mill is much easier to understand than Ricardo and will not involve at any stage in this lecture the kind of analysis which I have been led into at various stages in this section of my lectures, he is, I think, worth paying a little attention to.

Now first of all, a few words about his life. He was born in 1806, and he died in 1873. His life is enormously important in the cultural history of this country in the middle of the nineteenth century. He was not only an economist, he was an outstanding logician. He was an authority on the metaphysical philosophy of his day, he wrote extensively on morals and political science, and dominated the intellectual life of his like-minded contemporaries—the radical wing of the Whig party—and eventually came perhaps to dominate rather too much the life of the universities.

When I was a young man there was a tradition in this school—clearly created by Cannan—of rather looking down one's nose at John Stuart Mill. And I have no doubt that this arose in Cannan's mind when he was a young man, and when John Stuart Mill was probably rammed down his neck at Oxford as having uttered more or less the last word on the subject. Nowadays I hope that that tradition has ceased to exist in this institution, and although I am pretty clear that John Stuart Mill will never come back as having said the last word on this, that, and the other thing, he does take his place as among the great writers in our subject.

Now you ought to read—this is not for economics—his *Autobiography* [1873]. It is a short document. You can read it in an evening, and I would say—sticking my neck out—that it's one of the outstanding autobiographies in the language, one of the three outstanding autobiographies of the nineteenth century—the other two being, and you won't suppose that I agree with this, Newman's *Apologia pro Vita Sua* [1864] and Mark Pattison's *Memoirs* [1885]. [Seemingly in response to a student's query:] Newman's *Apologia*—he had been accused by Charles Kingsley of being a hypocrite in his departure from the Church of England and joining the Church of Rome, but his *Apologia* is written in the most eloquent and aesthetic prose. Well, John Stuart Mill's *Autobiography* is, I think, incumbent on students of the history of the broad field which is taught in this school—political science, ethics, philosophy and so on and so forth, as well as economics.

He had a very peculiar life. James Mill, who was an intellectual of eminence, though not as great as his son, had very peculiar ideas with regard to the way in which children should be brought up, and, at a very early stage, John Stuart Mill was learning Greek and Latin. And by the time that he was seven or eight he was giving instructions to other members of the Mill family. John Stuart Mill never went to public school or anything of that sort. He was taught by his father, who would set him a very rigid set of exercises or take him for a walk. His father's *Elements of Political Economy* [1826][1] was compiled from the youthful John Stuart Mill's notes of the utterances which James Mill—who was an austere sort of chap—used to make during these expeditions. And such is the naïveté—there was a naive side of John Stuart Mill—that, when apologizing for writing his journal, he says that if he has been able to do anything in the world it is not due to any innate ability; it is entirely due to the way he was educated [Mill, 1873, p. 30]. Well, I just don't believe that. The way that he was educated led to complete emotional starvation, and, in his twenties, when he was the rising hope of James Mill and Jeremy Bentham and all that distinguished circle of philosophical radicals, he had a nervous breakdown.

He had already written, on Benthamite lines, on morals and political economy. He was a *strict* utilitarian in those days. By strict utilitarian I mean a strict follower of Bentham, who doubtless was a very great man, but who used the broad outlook of utilitarianism, which, of course, springs from the eighteenth century and Hume, to elaborate proposals for constitutional reform, legal reform, and so on and so forth, which were very precise and very dogmatic, and are open, if I had many more hours in which to lecture to you, to various criticisms.

Well, in his twenties, John Stuart Mill helped Bentham edit his *Rationale of Judicial Evidence* [1827] in five volumes. And after that, and perhaps because of that, and because of the emotional starvation of his life, he had a nervous breakdown. One evening he thought to himself, "If all that you have recommended as regards social reform and so on and so forth were realised, would you be any happier?" And the answer was: "No." And he went through a period of profound intellectual and emotional despair. He got himself into a terrible state by thinking that the almost infinite combination of notes on the musical scales would eventually be exhausted and that then there would be nothing further for the human race to do in that line. Well, it's an interesting thought—it sometimes occurs to one—but it's not a thing to have a nervous breakdown about.

Eventually Mill achieved salvation, partly through reading poetry. Wordsworth and Coleridge revealed to him a whole world of emotional experience which James Mill had not cultivated in his plan for John Stuart Mill's education. And partly he was redeemed by falling in love with a young woman—Harriet Taylor her name was—who was unhappily married to a man very considerably older than herself. The affair, I ought to say, for the inquiring minds among you, was strictly platonic, in the way in which the word *platonic* used to be used in this regard. Eventually Mr Taylor died, and Mill married Harriet. And in his *Autobiography*, you will find *unbelievable* eulogies of all that Harriet had meant to him and all that she had contributed intellectually to his work. [George] Grote, who was one of the Benthamites and the celebrated historian of Greece, and incidentally one of the founding fathers of London University, said that only a man of John Stuart Mill's excellence could survive the extravagance of the inscription which Mill placed on Harriet's tomb.

And the biographers of Mill have been quarrelling about her influence ever since. Laski seems to have told someone that Morley told him that Harriet ingratiated herself with John Stuart Mill by repeating to him every morning his conversation of the previous evening. I don't believe that in the least. I don't believe that Harriet was the overwhelming intellectual innovator which John Stuart Mill thought her to be, but I don't believe that John Stuart Mill was the sort of person who would have been flattered by his wife repeating to him his own opinions of the night before. Whether Morley repeated this to Laski or not, or whether Laski invented it or heard it from some other person, is open to question, but Alexander Bain [1882], who was a philosopher of some distinction—now, I think, not read, but who wrote an extremely good biographical sketch of John Stuart Mill—says quite the contrary. He doesn't go into such raptures about Harriet, but he does say that Harriet, by querying Mill's ideas and stimulating him to push them further, had an important influence on his life.

Well, she died after seven years of marriage, and Mill thought that he was shattered, and shattered no doubt he was, in the sense of this absolutely irreparable emotional loss. But far from being shattered, some of his most outstanding works were written after that date: the *Liberty* [1859], which all of you ought to read—it's very good and has very great bearing on contemporary controversy; the *Utilitarianism* [1877]; his work on

Representative Government [1861], which is still one of the most thought-provoking works on that subject; and, above all, the ladies among you should read his immortal work on *The Subjection of Women* [1870]. The emancipation of women, which is one of the good things in the last 100 years, owes itself partly to a few heroic women who agitated for status in the universities and so on and so forth, and to John Stuart Mill's remarkable essay, which brought about the change in the law which really, much, much more than the vote gave rise to the emancipation of women. Although the vote was very important, and it was very unjust to deny women—one-half the human race—equal voting rights with the male half, the turning point in the subjection of women is, of course, the Married Women's Property Act. Before that time, if a girl married, the management of her property passed to her husband—legally—and if he turned out to be a bad egg, well, that was too bad. And that humiliating position certainly slopped over into my boyhood; I rather fancy that it's dying away now. Now, I hope I've said enough, and quite deliberately, to interest you in this classic.

Now, his contribution to economics. Specialists in the MSc who are taking this subject certainly should read the *Principles of Political Economy*, which is highly readable. Indeed, Professor Bladen, who founded the famous Department of Economics at Toronto University, which is issuing Mill's *Works* in umpteen volumes—about twelve or fourteen of them are already ready and have appeared—Professor Bladen said that it should still be used as a textbook. I really cannot go all the way with Bladen on that matter. Economics and what I call political economy have taken different paths, and although the mixture of economics and political economy and politics in Mill's *Principles* makes it a much more interesting book than the sort of things that *you're* introduced to the subject by—very interesting books and excellent in their own way, but no one would say that Samuelson's book [1948], for instance, is as interesting as John Stuart Mill's *Principles of Political Economy*, or anything like as profound on the fringe questions of the two centuries involved.

Well, so much for the *Principles of Political Economy*. Then there's the work that I mentioned in the last lecture, which was provoked by Torrens' publication of *The Budget*: the *Unsettled Questions of Political Economy*, which was published in 1844—thoroughly worth reading and much shorter than the *Principles of Political Economy*. It contains five important essays. The first one being the "On the Laws of Interchange between Nations," which made contributions to the theory of international trade that I dealt with last time. The second one is "Of the Influence of Consumption upon Production," which, roughly speaking, as Baumol and Becker say, rendered unnecessary all the fuss as between the supporters of Say and the neo-Keynesians and so on. The third one is of less importance. It's "On the Words Productive and Unproductive" labour. It's the least important of the essays, but it does make out a case for the Smithian distinction, which, as you know, still persists in economics as taught according to the tradition of Karl Marx and influences statistics too. Then there is a very interesting essay "On Profits, and Interest," which, for those of you who have any difficulty in following Ricardo on profits, is *much* more intelligible. It is not as up-to-date as Hollander's [1979] marvelous book, but it is much shorter, and, incidentally, it contains the plainest statement of the theory of forced saving, which I was talking to you about three lectures ago.

Well now, there are people who belong to the category of those who manufacture pseudo-problems. They contrast the *Essays on Some Unsettled Questions of Political Economy* with the *Principles* and argue that there's an incompatibility between the *Unsettled Questions*, which are economics in the strict sense of the word—economic science—and do not branch out into questions of political philosophy and application and so on, and the *Principles*. That, with all respect to the people who have said it, is nonsense. Mill's *Principles* [1848] is headed on the title page, which these people should have read or have looked at before they got down to making false representations in this respect, "with Some of Their Applications to Social Philosophy." He makes it quite plain that he's not only going to talk about economics in the narrow sense of the word, but he's going to talk about applications as well. And while he may have changed his mind on particular subjects and brought some things up-to-date—he was continually changing his mind about applications and political philosophy, changing the text and, in some respects, changing the balance of the argument—there is no incompatibility. Mill is Mill throughout, and there is no sharp break of opinion in regard to economics.

It *can* be argued that there was a break of opinion in regard to political philosophy at the time in the 1830s, when, having read Wordsworth and Coleridge, and having heard their point of view, which was sharply opposed in some respects to the Benthamite point of view, he actually did write an essay on Bentham in which he drew attention to Bentham's shortcomings while acknowledging his greatness, and drew attention, which upset the strict Benthamites, to the insights, although interspersed with muddle, of Wordsworth and Coleridge [Mill 1950]. Later on I think he shifted his position a little bit back, and, if you read his *Utilitarianism*, there is far less about the shortcomings of Bentham and perhaps, even inferentially, of his father.

Now, the arrangement of the *Principles*. It is in two volumes in the Toronto edition [1965], and—did I mention this?—in the Toronto edition there is a volume called *Essays on Economics and Society* [1967] which contains reprints, so there's absolutely no excuse for you to say that you can't get hold of it in the library. I don't recommend you to buy it. It is very expensive. And I also don't recommend you to buy it because it contains a very long preface by me on Mill's economics, and I get a small roy-

alty on that preface—just a few dollars every year. So I don't recommend
you to buy it, but I do recommend having a peek at it and reading the
Essays on Unsettled Questions, which are there.

Well, coming back to the *Principles,* there are five books: One is on
"Production," the second is on "Distribution," the third on "Exchange"
and money, the fourth on the "Influence of the Progress of Society on Production and Distribution," and the fifth on "the Influence of Government" on the economic system. And there he sets forth a broad picture of
the universe of discourse unfolded in Adam Smith's *Wealth of Nations,* but
with the corrections of the theory of value and distribution, introduced by
Ricardo and lesser economists, which Mill thought worthwhile interweav-
ing with this broad picture of a society founded on the division of labour
and guided by the market.

I don't need to expatiate on the detailed contents, as I did on Adam
Smith. I should point out that Mill divided production and distribution in
his work as he does because he believed that the so-called laws of production which he wished to elaborate were of universal applicability, whereas
the laws of distribution, which he proposed to go into in the section
headed "Distribution," were to some extent guided by institutional arrangements. Well, you can see what he means. It is very, very difficult indeed to imagine a society in which some form or other of the so-called law
of returns, or substitution in production, would not prevail. Although Mill
was a near-Malthusian, he didn't believe in Malthus' third ground, which
involved neither vice nor misery—his moral restraint. Indeed, it is said—
although even Professor Pedro Schwartz [1972], who has written a very
up-to-date book on Mill, was not able to check it because city police archives are not accessible to research—that Mill did spend a night in prison
for distributing, as a young man, leaflets on contraception to redeem, as he
hoped, the people who, by reason of the multiplication of the population,
found themselves in unnecessary poverty. But he did believe in the broad
Malthusian outlook, which he thought was applicable to any society—that
if population were not restrained in some way or other, sooner or later that
society would get into a mess. And that, looking around the world of the
twentieth century, has not been altogether refuted, although a great many
people have written books pretending that it has.

That was the one distinction that he introduced which you don't find
in Adam Smith, and it is a distinction which is open, I think, to some question. I ran into my friend Friedrich Hayek in the summer, and he was
saying that he thought that Mill had done great harm by his distinction
between the laws of production and distribution. Well, I can see what
Hayek meant. Certainly some of the things that you want to say about production are influenced by institutions affecting distribution. The theory is
blurred, but, at the same time, I think you can see what Mill was getting
at, and I defended Mill a little bit to my friend Hayek in that particular
connection.

Another fundamental distinction which you won't find there, but which you will find in modern economics, is Mill's distinction between what he calls "statics" and "dynamics" of political economy. He got this from an allegedly great sociologist. I am prepared to believe that Comte still commands the affection and respect of a diminishing number of people who swallowed Comte's teaching hook, line and sinker. There is a Comte series of lectures, which is given at the London School of Economics, without strings, so that the lecturer of the day can criticise Comte as well as pointing out any excellence that may be found in him. But it was Comte who influenced Mill at the time, until Mill found out what Comte's views on women were. Comte was a very peculiar person in this respect. On the one hand he felt that women should be worshipped, and on the other hand he was a crank on phrenology, and because the dimension of their heads was smaller, he thought that they were intellectually inferior. And Comte had behaved rather disgracefully to Mill, who got a subsidy from Grote and Molesworth for Comte. Comte had been turned out from examining for the University of Paris and was living in some poverty, and when Grote and Molesworth stopped the subsidy, Comte read Mill *the most terrific lecture* of their conduct versus his case—the most extraordinary exhibition of egotism, I think, in the history of respectable philosophy. But Mill didn't twig the slightly bogus element in Comte until Comte started to talk about women.

Harriet, I must say, when she saw the letters which Mill exchanged with Comte—which are most fascinatingly edited by Lévy-Bruhl [Mill, 1899], and which might be read by any of you who have any spare time and really want to have amusement at the communication of thoughts between these two people, the humble Mill and the egocentric, almost paranoiac, Comte—when Harriet saw the letters she at once twigged the nature of Comte, and she said to Mill—and this bears out Bain's interpretation of their relationship—that she was ashamed of Mill for taking so much notice of this dry root of a man. But Comte's distinction between statics and dynamics in sociology struck Mill's attention, and he introduced it into economics. And for good or bad, it has persisted up to the modern day.

Now, the anti-Mill myth, which persisted in my young days, and which was not only held by Edwin Cannan, but all sorts of other people in my sphere of work, used to dwell upon the fact that Mill was not original—Mill was just, at best, a very good systematiser in political economy. (They couldn't really say that *On Liberty* was not an original book.) But this is not the case. And if you read Stigler's *Essays in the History of Economics* [1965], you will find that he has an essay on originality in economics,[2] and he picks out John Stuart Mill as having made extremely important original contributions to classical economics. And, since you ought to read Stigler on this subject, I can go through this very quickly.

Stigler picks out, so far as the treatment of wages is concerned, Mill's innovation of the theory of noncompeting groups and the effect that that has on relativities in the wage level. If you read Adam Smith's famous chapter, you might almost think that, if it were not for the policy of Europe—which he denounces—that there was complete mobility of labour between different industrial pursuits. And Mill deals with that much more satisfactorily. Secondly, Stigler points out that Mill is the originator of the treatment, in the theory of value, of joint products, which hadn't been dealt with at any length by Ricardo and Mill's predecessors. Thirdly, he points out that Mill actually saw through the slightly fallacious element in the Ricardian theory of rent, insofar as it emphasised rent not entering into cost of production. Mill realized that if land had more than one use, then there would be opportunity costs for the use of land, and rent, in that sense, might enter into cost of production. Fourthly, Stigler points out that the economics of the firm first makes its appearance in John Stuart Mill's *Principles of Political Economy*. You don't find much about the firm in Ricardo or any of the earlier generation, and he treats economies of scale at reasonable length. Fifthly, Stigler points out that, after all, Mill did, in his *Essays on Some Unsettled Questions of Political Economy*, treat supply and demand as functions of price and set out arithmetical illustrations of that relationship. And finally, Stigler doesn't omit to point out that his discussion of Say's Law, although you can find anticipations of this in Torrens, for instance, and in one or two other cases, is absolutely masterly and does succeed in illuminating all the buzz that prevailed in his time and has prevailed until quite recently since.

Now, as regards Mill's applications, I can't do more than elaborate them for you. But they stand out, I think, as standing for his main contributions—and here I'm casting my net rather wider than the *Principles of Political Economy* and discussing not all his contributions to political philosophy, but regarding those which have bearing on economics. He was very much in favour of peasant proprietorship. He believed, with the famous writer on agriculture—Young [1794]—in the eighteenth century, that the magic of peasant proprietorship turns sand into fertile soil, and he was especially urgent in his view that Governments should foster that proprietorship.

Secondly, his vision of the future was a vision in which the organisation of industry eventually resolved itself into cooperative enterprises. There is a great dispute about whether Mill was a socialist or an individualist. Fabian socialists have claimed him as a socialist, and individualists have claimed him as a chief individualist. And Mill himself added to the confusion by, in the first edition of his *Principles*, stating the case for certain forms of socialism in a rather mild way and stating the case for individualism in not a very strong way, but stronger way. And then he modified the second edition. He was rather disgusted at being taken up by extreme individualists and quoted as lending his authority to their rather dogmatic point of view. In the *Autobiography*, he explains that he and Harriet had been *influenced* in various ways by contemporary movements, in such a way that they were prepared to be called socialists. And this has provoked the controversy which I have referred to.

Now, if you go into Mill's socialism in detail, by comparison of the various editions of his *Principles* and his posthumously published essays on socialism [Mill, 1967, vol. 5], various things emerge. First of all, it is absolutely clear that Mill was not a total collectivist. I don't think that Mill was acquainted with Marx, but Mill was acquainted in the latter part of his life with the continental international socialism which tended towards totalitarian collectivism, and Mill denounced that.

Mill was not against the State ownership of certain public utilities: He wrote on water supply; he was not unfavourable to nationalisation of railways—he discusses it in a judicial manner. But in the end, the main part of his socialism, his aspirations for the future of the working classes, which he and Adam Smith recognised as constituting the main part of the population, his aspirations were based upon experiments in producers' cooperation—small groups of producers getting together and cooperating; not consumers' cooperation, but producers' cooperation. And even there, I would say that the case is stated more strongly in the third edition of his *Principles* than it is in the posthumous and unfinished essays on socialism. Certainly the thing is open to controversy, and reasonable people, provided that they define their terms, are entitled to claim him on one side or the other.

May I go on for two minutes longer? As regards corporations, he was in favour of limited joint stock companies, about which there was a tremendous debate among the classical economists. And as regards the ancient universities and all that, he was in favour of disregarding the original, many-hundred-years-old deeds of trust and using the funds of the corporations for what, in the given environment, was to be regarded as more socially suitable. The essay on corporations is in his collected essays [ibid., vol. 4].

As regards taxation, he was at once what some of you would regard as reactionary and in other respects very radical. As regards income tax, he was utterly against progressive income tax, save insofar as progression is involved by a small exemption limit at the beginning. As you know, a small exemption limit at the beginning implies a certain degree of progression, but it is not what we regard as progressive taxation, which he regarded as penalizing the enterprising against those who preferred not to be enterprising.

As regards inheritance, he was far more radical than any Government has ever been so far. He was in favour of an absolute limit being placed upon the amount of money which a man might inherit—a few hundred thousand, that was all. And he would certainly have been in favour of splitting up inheritance by way of legacy duties rather than duties on the estate as a whole. He was also in favour of special taxation on land on more or less Ricardian terms.

Well, I see my time is up, and I think I've said enough to you about his emphasis on the subjection of women. I haven't said enough on his essay *On Liberty* and his distinction between self-regarding and other regarding actions, which some people think is out of date, but which is still, I think, rather thought-provoking.

NOTES

1. The first edition of James Mill's *Elements* was published in 1821.
2. "The Nature and Role of Originality in Scientific Progress," in Stigler (1965, pp. 1–15).

D. Other Mid-Nineteenth-Century Thought

Mill (cont.)—Saint-Simon and Marx

I WANT to give you some sort of conspectus of the relevance of John Stuart Mill to the history of economic thought. I have nothing further to say on his contributions, particularly as regards the *Principles*, but there is something which remains to be said about his ascendancy and its decline.

The book was published in 1848, and I would think that it was no exaggeration to say that it was *the* influential work on political economy for the next forty years or so. Until Marshall published his *Principles of Economics* [1890], I would guess that Mill was the most read. But it was a declining influence, and the decline is, I think, relevant to the history of thought, dealt with as superficially as I am compelled to deal with it.

There occurred an apparently sensational change of mind on Mill's part as regards the theory of wages, not as regards the long-period theory of wages, but as regards the demand for labour in the short run—what Adam Smith called the funds destined for the maintenance of labour, and which were invoked in one shape or other by the nineteenth-century successors of Adam Smith. It was Mill who called it the wage fund, and in a way it could be argued that Mill gave it rather more precision than its popular repute in history would give it.

As I think I explained to you at an earlier stage, I think that Taussig's *Wages and Capital* [1897], which is a book that I've recommended you to read for the general history of economic thought, shows quite successfully that, contrary to popular mythology, the theory of the wage fund was not commonly used by classical economists against the trade unions. Nevertheless, there was the theory of the wage fund which, in Mill's formulation, seemed to indicate pretty tight upper limits on the share of the national production going to the wage-earning classes.

And then—it was 1869—there was a man called Thornton (not to be confused with the early-nineteenth-century monetary authority), who was a friend of John Stuart Mill, worked with John Stuart Mill in the India Office, and took an interest in social questions. And he published a book entitled *On Labour: Its Wrongful Claims and Rightful Dues* [1869]. And it's a book which is quite worth perusing. Part of the book consisted in strictures on the way in which the theory of the market was formulated, and this led him to discuss the theory of the labour market. Now—not to labour too long on this—Mill reviewed *On Labour: Its Wrongful Claims and Rightful Dues* in the *Fortnightly Review* [Mill, 1869] when it came out in 1869. And his review was cordial and friendly, as befitted a review written by one of one's friends (and should be of most of one's enemies). But Mill had little doubt in showing that some of Thornton's argument about the general theory of demand and supply was based on misapprehension—that the strictures of the central classical tradition in that respect, although interesting, were capable of being refuted.

But when Mill came to review the part on the labour market, he made a confession of error. He said, roughly speaking, that his exposition of the wage fund theory indicated too precise a limit to the share going to the wage-earning classes, and in other ways he thought that Thornton's mild strictures were justified. Now, this created something of a sensation. That Mill, who had been taken as the last word on this subject, should have admitted error, without providing an alternative theory, upset thoughtful people. And then the last edition of Mill's *Principles* [1871] came out, and he hadn't altered the text very much. He referred in the preface to a controversy at present going on with regard to the wage fund and all that, but said that it was not yet time for him to reformulate the argument of the *Principles*, at any rate on any very large scale.

Well, in Cairnes' *Leading Principles* [1874], there is a section which remonstrates with Mill for abandoning a wage fund theory. And he certainly puts the best face he can on the use of this conception in explaining the short-run demand for labour. But he wasn't successful. It was not rehabilitated, and it drops out of economic theory thenceforward. It appears in a very modified form in Böhm-Bawerk's *Positive Theory of Capital* [1891], about which I shall be talking to you later in the term, and in the positive part of Taussig's *Wages and Capital* [1897]. Taussig declares that he is a little put to it to understand why Mill made such an almost abject confession of error—partly because Taussig thinks that the thing could be reformulated so as to be reasonably elastic, and yet to play some part in the theory of capital. Well, I think it was necessary to draw your attention to that. You will find the matter thoroughly dealt with in Taussig's book.

Now, I've got forty minutes left, and I think that I ought to say forty minutes about Marx and his connection with nineteenth-century classical economics. It is not my plan to deal with Marx at greater length. You get other lectures on this subject, and the subject is an extremely, extremely difficult one. But it is perhaps worthwhile tracing the connection with nineteenth-century classical theory, or what Marx would have regarded as superior nineteenth-century classical theory—he was very sarcastic about what he regarded as the decline after Ricardo. But the comparison and the contrast are not insignificant. I hasten to say at the beginning that I certainly don't think that what I have to say, either positively or negative, is all that there is in Marx as a pure economist. There is a great deal which, perhaps until modern times, has passed unnoticed and has not perhaps been given sufficient justice to. But that's not my intention this morning.

Well, let me say just a word or two about the background of Marx's economics in the more popular sense of the term. To understand Marx at all you certainly have to realise the background of the French Revolution and the stimulus that this gave to all sorts of revolutionary or semi-revolutionary thought. You find fragments of what Marx contemptuously called

Utopian socialism in the works of Robert Owen, who you know about from the economic history of this country; in the works of Fourier, who was certainly a very, very peculiar person, but who possibly owes his fame partly to the fact that Mill paid a good deal of attention to Fourier;[1] and chiefly in the works of Saint-Simon and the Saint-Simonians. And if you are thinking of the history of socialism—not the influence of socialism, but the history of socialist theory—I have really no doubt at all that, Marx apart, Saint-Simon, and especially his disciples, were the most intellectually interesting and, I think, influentially the most important thinkers.

Saint-Simon himself was a very strange man. He was a French aristocrat. He fought in the American War of Independence on the American side. He came back to France loaded with approbation, and he renounced his nobility. And then, the Revolution proceeding, as revolutions sometimes do, further and further into the hands of extremists, Saint-Simon got into trouble with the Jacobins—Robespierre and Saint-Just and all that—and he suffered a brief term of imprisonment. And he was lucky, perhaps, to escape with his head; all sorts of people were executed on rather slight pretexts in those days.

And then afterwards he had a very miscellaneous career, sometimes being in funds and sometimes not being in funds, sometimes being supported by powerful people and sometimes not being supported. But he devoted the rest of his life (he died in 1825) to—what shall I say?—messianic writings, in which he pronounced on internationalism, the union of Europe, and rewrote Christianity. Those of you who are interested in his more eccentric works will find a very good translation of the typical Saint-Simon—translated by a man called Markham [Saint-Simon, 1952]—published by Blackwell in that very useful series of standard texts in political science. Saint-Simon gathered around him a body of enthusiastic followers who treated him as a sort of messiah, but who, in a way, as I shall be saying in a moment, were I think rather more considerable thinkers.

So far as economics was concerned, Saint-Simon's attitude can be designated as a sort of "apostle of industrialism." And I can illustrate his apostolic attitude by quoting one of his remarks. (I am paraphrasing.) He makes the sensational remark: If all the kings and all the apparatus of courts were to die, what difference would it make to the rest of society? Whereas, if the leading industrialists were to die, the society would collapse. Hence, he argued that all class distinctions based upon feudalism and all that were obsolete. Politics were a sham. He expatiated on that at length, and he thought that all political institutions in France ought to be replaced by a sort of economic parliament with a very complicated constitution of industrialists and scientists and so on and so forth, and they were to organise France on the scale of a large factory.

Well, so much for Saint-Simon—limitations of time. His disciples—the chief names are Enfantin, Bazard and Rodriques—formed themselves into a not wholly unisexual monastic sect. They produced a journal called *The Producer*, and they gave a series of lectures systematizing the thought of

Saint-Simon. And these lectures—which I don't think are translated into English, but are beautifully edited by Bougle and Halévy [Saint-Simon, 1829], two of the great French social historians and scholars of my young days—were published under the name of the *Doctrine de Saint-Simon: Exposition*. And they go considerably further than Saint-Simon towards something that we should recognise as part of the background of nineteenth-century socialism. The emphasis on the importance of industrialism, yes, but they go on to attack the arbitrary nature of the distribution of private property. They go on to pose the problem of the distribution, which they think in its present form is inequitable and also led to the inefficient organisation of production. And the remedy was some sort of collective organisation of industry run by a rather complicated hierarchy of clever people.

Well, so much for the Saint-Simonians, whose book *Saint-Simon* is in a way profound and in a way a joke. The *Doctrine Saint-Simon*, which was written by people about your average age, is really a very superior piece of work indeed, and thoroughly worth reading. They were, so to speak, alpha quadruple plus undergraduates. Their behaviour in the monastic community caused great scandal in Paris, and they were brought to court. The account of their trial, which has been written by one of the Pankhursts—one of the nephews of the Mrs Pankhurst of suffragette fame—is very entertaining reading. You feel that it has all been got up as an undergraduate joke in a way. Obviously the court gets very much the worst of it. But then they served a short term of imprisonment, which certainly reflected on the sense of humor of the court, and then, on the whole, their enthusiasm waned. Some of them departed to the Middle East in search of the ideal woman. I should not say nothing about the Middle East at all, and it may be that the ideal woman would be discovered there; but they did not discover her. And then some of them came back to be great mid-nineteenth-century industrial leaders—supreme capitalists.

Well, Marx regarded all this as Utopian socialism, and his own brand was specifically labelled "scientific socialism." Marx, in his young days, certainly passed a great many value judgements, and all the early writings of Marx regarding alienation and so on are absolutely teeming with value judgements. But by the time he came to write systematically on political economy—the preliminary to *Das Kapital* [1867], which in a way, if you want to get what he was in the main driving at in longer works, is thoroughly worth reading, *The Critique of Political Economy* [1859]—his work was described as scientific socialism. It was supposed to be composed all the time not of condemnation, but of historical record and economic analysis. And he certainly discouraged any speculation as to the form of the eventual communist society. If you did that, you were infected by bourgeois habits; the future would unfold itself according to implicit laws of history.

Well, so much for the background of Utopian socialism. I only draw attention to the background of Hegel, against whom Marx was in violent revolt. Hegel is certainly not one of my favourites, and I won't trust myself to evaluate his contribution to philosophy, which is still a matter of controversy. Suffice it to say that my reading of Hegel roughly speaking corresponds to an opposite estimate. But Marx, so to speak, derived from Hegel the concept of history as positive statement, antithesis and synthesis. History proceeded like that in the past. But Marx's filling in of those categories was very different from Hegel's. You get a very good idea of the philosophy of history in Popper's attack on historicism—*The Poverty of Historicism* [1960]. Popper always sets out the point of view that he proposes to attack more clearly than the point of view of those he attacks, and his account of the attitude of mind springing from Hegel is worth reading.

But chiefly—and I don't expect I shall get through this quite in this hour—you have to take account of Marx's background of classical economics. Now, there's a lot been said about Marx having cribbed from the so-called Ricardian socialists. There is a learned book by Anton—not Carl—Menger, which is called *The Right to the Whole Produce of Labour* [1899], which contains a good deal of interesting history and a famous preface by Foxwell, who used to be Professor of Money and Banking at the time of the early days of the London School of Economics. And Foxwell and Menger suggest that Marx got a great deal of his inspiration from the so-called Ricardian socialists here. Well, I think there is very good ground for saying that so-called Ricardian socialists were either not socialists or not Ricardian. But that's another story. There is no doubt at all of the inspiration which Marx got from Smith, and to some extent from Ricardo. And it's difficult, I think, certainly in any short statement, which is bound to be wrong about so complicated a person as Marx, to say which he owes most to.

Marx, I ought to say, whether you agree with him or disagree with him, was probably the best historian of economic thought of his time, although I personally think—and this is a value judgement—that Marx was *frightfully* unfair to some of the people he criticised, as, for instance, when he criticised poor Malthus for having broken his vows in getting married and begetting children. It was not true at all; it was absolutely not contrary to the rules of the Church of England, to which Malthus belonged. But you mustn't be put off in your respect for Marx by that sort of silly remark. Marx had an eye for what was important far better than, let us say, the classical historian of economic thought, McCulloch. And McCulloch is a very valuable person for looking up rare people and so on and so forth, but it was Marx who detected the excellence of Petty, and it was Marx who detected the inventiveness of Quesney in the economic table, and it was Marx who realised the importance—well, the classical economists recognised that—of Smith and Ricardo. I would say myself that in the end Marx got rather more from Smith than he got from Ricardo, although what he derived from Smith was either very simple or, in a complex way not revealed by anything in volume 1, a realisation that Smith's simple statements weren't absolutely correct.

But now we come to the central feature of Marxian economics in volume 1 and volume 3—value and distribution, and the theory of price. Volume 1 of *Das Kapital* [1867] opens with a pure labour theory of value, not frightfully unlike, as regards analysis, the Smithian parable of the beaver and the deer, whose exchange value in the long run was thought to reflect more or less exactly the ratios of labour time expended in their production. And even where there is recognition of complications, Ricardo and Smith, at this stage of the development of their theory, ignore differences of wages, differences of labour skill, and say that that's settled by the market, which is obviously circular reasoning, as I have said. And in Marx you find that this is rather more pretentiously attributed to a social process which goes on behind the backs of the producers, but what he meant was indeed the market.

In volume 1 the argument is developed in terms of value and surplus value, which we'll be coming to, and the simple part of Adam Smith, which, after the beginning paragraphs, suggests that when capital has been accumulated and land has been appropriated the whole produce of labour does not go to the labourers. And you can read that into Smith, although it is doubtful whether he meant by his analysis what Marx derived starting from a similar point. But up to this point, those of you who get the theory of value from volume 1 will not find anything very different from the citations from Smith which I have given you.

The difficulties begin, and differences begin, with the theory of wages. All values being determined by the labour cost of production, *the value of labour* was determined in the market by the labour cost of producing labour—you know, with all the complications of the family and all that thrown in. Now, if you like, you can say this is pure classical theory of conventional subsistence—a long-run theory of wages. But it isn't. The classical economists' long-run theory of wages would certainly involve conventional subsistence (in Ricardo, for instance) and appealed to the supply side. And they hoped that if the supply side were sufficiently limited, that the labouring classes would acquire expensive habits, so that in the long run conventional subsistence would be very much above what the term *subsistence wages* means.

But all that is in Adam Smith's final formulation of the general theory of wages. While, at any rate, the funds destined for the employment of labour are increasing, wages can be above subsistence level, as they were in America and in Great Britain and elsewhere. And then Malthus elaborated the tendency to subsistence, and the classical near-Malthusian economists elaborated a conventional subsistence level which was much higher than the Malthusian subsistence level.

But Marx did none of these things. Marx was anti-Malthus. He didn't realise, or he didn't emphasise, what there is of truth in Malthus—namely, that if there is no check to the supply side of labour, that the world will get into a mess, which at this time in history has certainly not yet been refuted. Marx goes back to Adam Smith's subsistence theory, which he shares with

Turgot, and referred to the superior bargaining power of the employer. Adam Smith goes out of his way to say we hear a great deal about the combinations of labourers, but we do not hear enough of the combinations of employers. And according to Smith, at that stage of the chapter, the employers are always in an implicit combination to lower wages to subsistence level, which combination only breaks up in the progressive society when employers compete with one another and drive wages up. Well, Marx wasn't talking about the progressive society. On his view, the tendency of society was eventually to deteriorate so much that it would explode. And Marx's theory of normal wages is a "cost of production theory of labourers"—the wage being forced down by superior bargaining power on the part of the owners of capital.

But from this Marx goes on to deal with surplus value. The value of goods is determined by their labour cost of production, but labour, although remunerated at cost of production levels, produces a surplus above its cost of production. And Marx was very interested in the surplus. His interest in Quesnay is obviously due to the fact that Quesnay's interest was really in *a* surplus, but it was a surplus produced by land. Marx was interested in the surplus produced by labour, and labour, whose value was determined, like the value of everything else, by the structure of society and by the labour cost of production, produced a surplus value.

If, for instance, general labour can produce, let us say, its cost of production—its subsistence level—in seven hours, and the capitalist can force labour to work longer than that—twelve hours if you like—then a surplus emerged, and that was what Marx argued actually happened. And he went on to argue that profit was only derived from exploitation—profit in the large sense, the residue after meeting expenses.

I see that it's three minutes to twelve. I will leave you suspended as Marx did in volume 1. In volume 1 Marx pointed out that there are some difficulties in reconciling the rate of profit and his conception of surplus value, and Engels, who wrote the preface to subsequent editions of Marx, challenges people to solve this problem. There is reason to suppose that Marx had solved the problem to his satisfaction when he wrote volume 1, but the solution only emerges in volume 3, and that I can deal with shortly at the beginning of my lecture next week.

NOTE

1. See, e.g., Owen (1949) and Fourier (1901).

Marx (cont.)—List and the Historical School

IN THE last part of my last lecture I tried to give you a very brief résumé of Marx's relation to the classical position. I underlined that description of what nature was intended to do. There are other lectures given in this institution which deal with Marxian philosophy in its wider implications, and I certainly was performing a much humbler task than that. So much for the limitations.

But the clock compelled me to leave off at the point at which Marx himself had left his readers in a state of uncertainty. He had focussed the attention in volume 1 on a theory of value which, combined with the theory of wages which depended on the superior bargaining power of the employers, gave rise to the appropriation by the employers of surplus value—at any rate, surplus value (and this is the question in point) on the employment of labour, the value of labour being determined by subsistence cost, and value of machines and inanimate factor services being determined by their labour cost of production. And so you have the emergence of surplus value, but surplus value deriving only from investment in the employment of labour. Now, since the proportion of labour to capital—the organic composition of capital—would vary in different industries, this presented a problem: namely, how under relatively competitive conditions could you account for the fact that the rate of profit in different industries tended to be the same—not at any moment, but it was always tending in that direction—while the extraction of surplus value depended upon the organic composition of capital.

Well, this problem was left unsolved in volume 1. In volume 3 Marx comes back to the determination of the exchange ratios and in volume 3 the norm to which exchange ratios tend depends upon their prices of production. So that, in the end, Marx, in this respect, reached much the same conclusion as Ricardo, whose theory of value was, after all, in the last analysis, a real cost theory of value, which admittedly mostly depended upon labour cost, but which took account of other factors as well.

Now, why did Marx do this? Because there is evidence in a letter, which Professor Baumol later discovered, from Marx to Engels that he did know that this conclusion was the conclusion that he would eventually arrive at. But the motive to me is a mark of interrogation. We don't know an awful lot about Marx's mental processes in the evolution of his stupendous work, and so far as I am concerned, the mark of interrogation remains. Did he conceive of the first volume being just, so to speak, a first approximation, like the first paragraph of Ricardo's chapter 1 of the *Principles*? Well if so, he made a lot depend upon it in volume 1. But, as I say, I don't know the answer. I draw your attention simply to the puzzle and its eventual solution on more complicated lines.

For the rest of Marx's theory—the theory of the declining rate of profit; the theory of the growing rate of concentration in manufacturing industry; the much disputed, as regards interpretation, theories of the trade cycle; not to mention the sociological generalisations which were coupled with that theory of the economic interpretation of history—the theory of the class war and its eventual determination in the expropriation of the expropriated, and then history would reveal what came next—all that is much more important than what I have said to you in relation to Marx's conception of the classical system. I ought to add that if you plug through the three volumes of *Das Kapital*, you will find interesting additions to capital theory which, so to speak, go in some ways beyond what other classical economists have achieved. But so much for Marx in this series, having made quite clear the very limited nature of my treatment of him.

I now come in this series to a brief account of the critics of the nineteenth-century classicists—brief because I should like to finish in this lecture. Whether I shall is an open question.

There are two groups of critics which, historically speaking, you should take account of. First of all, there's the critics which fasten on a particular aspect of the Smithian system and which are to be described as the economic nationalists. Secondly, there is the famous historical school, chiefly centred in Germany, but having anticipators and followers in this country. Now, all that I want to do is to pull aside the curtain. Reams of doctoral words might be written on both of these schools, and have been written. But that's not my intention. My intention is simply to place what I conceive to be the position of each of these groups in the perspective of economic thought—the history of economic analysis—in its proper place.

Well now, a few words about economic nationalism—much the easiest to deal with. Speaking very broadly—and all simple generalisations in this sphere are liable to be misleading—you can draw a contrast between the typical outlook of eighteenth-century intellectuals and some, at any rate, of the nineteenth-century intellectuals. The eighteenth century, in all sorts of ways, was cosmopolitan in outlook. It discussed man—man including woman in this particular instance—and not, except with regret, the groupings of men into places and nations and so on. The people whom I am going to talk to you about were, for the most part, nineteenth-century thinkers, whose views have permanently altered the structure of international relations in the twentieth, and their emphasis was precisely the opposite: on national entities—group entities.

In a way, the French Revolution, which started by having its roots in the eighteenth century, ended up by arousing nationalism as a response to the ambitions of Napoleon and his associates. Certainly the French Revolution may be regarded as being the dividing line as regards thought, although one of the most important thinkers is rather detached from that. If you want another crude contrast—and it's a value judgement on my part—you can make the contrast between the classical outlook and the romantic outlook. But all that belongs to the history of society and to history in general. Our concern in the history of economic thought is confined, I think, to the context of what may be described as the rise of the infant industry argument.

Now, of course you have to go far back in history before you don't find infant industry arguments. The literature of the so-called mercantilist period abounds in the exhortations to governments to foster infant industries within their own borders. Adam Smith was prepared to believe that, in extremely risky circumstances involving foreign trade, some government intervention might be called for, but on the whole he was against it. And the emphasis of the fourth book of the *Wealth of Nations* is in a sense a critique of government interventionism as regards the fostering of particular industries and commercial enterprises.

Now, this raised up in the minds of persons of Adam Smith's own age some reaction, and the reaction is given a splendid, and in many ways a convincing, form in a famous report by Hamilton, one of the founders of the United States, and one of the authors of *The Federalist*, which in my judgement is the best book on political science and its broad practical aspects written in the last thousand years. Hamilton's *Report of Manufacturers*, 1791, is partly a plea for protection of industry, in the early days of the United States, against unfair competition on the part of the more advanced British manufacturers. And I dare say that there was unfair competition from time to time, but the burden of his argument was a certain "fear of want of success in untried enterprises" [Hamilton, 1791, p. 203] in the communities in which manufacturing industry was of the kind which was developing in Great Britain and parts of continental Europe, but which was more advanced. And he made out a very powerful case, a case which was accepted by John Stuart Mill, although John Stuart Mill lived to regret the limited acceptance of his case by extreme protectionists in different parts of the world. It's a case which was accepted by Sidgwick and Marshall.

But Hamilton perhaps doesn't enter into the textbooks on the history of economic thought as he deserves to. The *outstanding* influence in this respect was a German of the name of List. List has exercised in the policy of various nations an influence I would say only surpassed by Adam Smith in his time and Karl Marx in our time.

He was born in 1789; he died in 1846. As a young man he got into trouble with the German government—remember, Germany was all split up in those days. And he betook himself to America where he was immensely impressed by the case which was being made out for the protection of infant industries in America, and he wrote widely on this subject. Eventually he returned to Germany. He played a part in the formation of

opinion favourable to the creation of a wider free trade area in Germany—
the beginning of the *Zollverein*—the tariff union—and at the same time he
systematised his views on the protection of infant industries in an attack on
Adam Smith entitled—it's translated into English, and you'll find it in the
library—*The National System of Political Economy* [1841].

And his attack on Adam Smith was, roughly speaking, threefold. First of
all, he attacked Adam Smith for putting the interests of the world as the
object of his political economy, rather than the interests of the nation.
Now, that's very doubtful. Adam Smith doubtless was cosmopolitan in
sympathy, but Adam Smith's attack on the mercantile system of wealth is
based on the view that the mercantile system of wealth was inimical to the
British nation. And what Adam Smith would have said if it had been
pointed out to him that sometimes the national interest and the world interest were in conflict is a matter of conjecture. It is not so conjectural
when you come to John Stuart Mill.

The second point that he made, which was also, I think, based on some
misreading of Adam Smith, was that Adam Smith mistook the true end of
political economy from a national point of view—that Adam Smith's
Wealth of Nations dealt with the increase of wealth and the ultimate subser-
vience of production to consumption in a broad sense, whereas *he*, List,
emphasised the importance of national economic power. Now again, this is
based, in my judgement, on a misreading of Adam Smith. Adam Smith's
second book, as you know, if you have even given half an ear to what I said
about Adam Smith, is devoted to accumulation, and what is accumulation
for but to increase, appropriately, national power? So that, analytically,
List, I think, considerably misses the point.

But his third point was that he admitted the case for national free trade
once the infant stage had been passed. He reproached the British Government for not going free trade, having fostered sufficiently, by the mercantile system and its present policy, the growth of industry in Great Britain.
And he felt that Great Britain was reaching a stage when free trade would
be in its national interest. And he generalised this, and he argued that once
a certain stage had been reached free trade was the order of the day, but
before then it was folly.

This book had enormous influence in America and in Germany, and it
has had a very considerable influence in some parts of the underdeveloped
world. Alas for intellectual influence, if you think of the United States of
America, long, long after the infants had grown into tremendous giants,
they still continued to be defended by the infant industry argument. However, that's another story. John Stuart Mill accepted the theoretical case for
the fostering of the beginnings of industry by some form of State assistance. He wrote to a friend that he greatly regretted the use that had been
made by tariff mongers, especially in Australia, of his argument, and that he
would now prefer to say that if the infant industry argument applied, that

it should be supported by subsidies rather than by protective tariffs. Well, that, I think, is all that I need say about the strictly economic side of economic nationalism at this stage.

The second school which I wish to draw your attention to is, so to speak, the historical school, which, in its way, in Germany at any rate, was tremendously the by-product of the change between the eighteenth- and the nineteenth-century outlook with which I began this section of the lecture.

The historical school, in a way, can be regarded, in its German manifestations at any rate, as a by-product of academic nationalism. And it manifested itself in various ways and gave rise, especially in law and in history, to notable intellectual achievements. Whether you regret the tendency of which they were part, as I do, or whether you regard them as inevitable, as many people do, or whether you regard them as positively an embellishment of human history, you must admit that the intellectual influence was notable.

It was notable in history. Very remarkable historical works were written, fastening attention on national history—the vicissitudes of national interest—rather than, if you think of the eighteenth century—Voltaire, Gibbon and so on—when the interest of history was much more the evolution of the human outlook.

It manifested itself secondly in jurisprudence. The emphasis was no longer on *the* law—natural law—but rather on national law—German law, British law or English law, Scottish law and so on.

And further it manifested itself in what is one of the very great achievements of the nineteenth century—in philology. People began to take very seriously differences between languages. In the Middle Ages, you know, the conversation of educated people was in Latin. Gradually, as society changed, the language in which the ordinary people—not scholars or servants of the State—communicated with one another became the ascendant. And you had the emergence of national literature, some of which is the most glorious product of the human race in that respect—Dante, Shakespeare, Racine. But academic interest fastened on differences between languages, and philologists had immense success in tracing the evolution of languages in different parts of the world.

The word *Aryan* is a dirty word because it was polluted by Hitler and the Nazis, but the Aryan group of languages, which was most studied in this particular connection, does show extraordinary uniformities of evolution. The growth of language—which had already attracted the attention of Adam Smith, who has a marvelous essay on language in general, which is reprinted usually as an appendix to his *Theory of Moral Sentiments* [1792]—is not organised by the State; no authoritarian body regulates the changes in the way in which people speak to one another, and yet it is susceptible of scientific study. And the Aryan group of languages, at any rate, was used in my boyhood when I studied this thing called Grimm's Law. Whether Grimm's Law has stood up to criticism in the past thirty years or so, I don't know, but the advances made there were interesting and important. In a sense, the contemplation of the evolution of language is almost as awe-inspiring as biological evolution or the evolution of the starry sky above us. But all that by way of background.

Now, don't think that I am slipping in a bit of nationalism at this moment. I would hate for you to think that, but I am bound to tell you as a dispassionate historian that a great deal of what was in the historical school of economics—and not all of it was bad—is to be found in the work of an English divine who held the position of Professor of Political Economy over the way, at King's College in the Strand, which, you know, was founded by the Duke of Wellington and his associates as a rival to University College. University College was founded by the philosophical radicals, the disciples of Bentham and James Mill, Grote and so on and so forth, and because it did not enforce conformity to the Church of England, it was called the "godless college," as a result of which—this is not the history of economic thought—University College has probably the most distinguished set of alumni of any college in this country—except perhaps Trinity College, Cambridge. Anybody could go to University College, but King's College in the Strand was set up as a counterblast to the godless college and it has always been particularly associated with theology.

And Richard Jones was a professor there. And he lived from 1790 to 1855, and he wrote an institutional study, *On the Distribution of Wealth* [1831], which was largely an analysis of the institution of landholding at different points of history and in different parts of the world. And it was, in a sense, a reproach to the wide-sweeping application of the details of Ricardian analysis without qualifications, as it was sometimes applied. His *Distribution of Wealth* was published in 1831. When he was dead, his *Literary Remains* [1859]—*Literary Remains*, as you know, is a Victorian title for collected essays (his are two unpublished essays)—were edited by no less a person than the very great historian and philosopher, the Master of Trinity, Whewell. And in Jones' inaugural lecture at King's College, which was reprinted in his *Literary Remains*,[1] he comes out into the open with his critique of the classical system. He argues that before you can generalise about the production and the distribution of wealth, you must look at the institutional framework. You must look at the law governing distribution and production in different parts of the world and in different parts of history.

And it would do you all good to have a look at Jones' inaugural lecture, which contains very much good sense and, in a more or less polite way, qualifications and disagreements with Ricardo and the Ricardians which any dispassionate reader must regard as being, at any rate, partially justified. And he led up to the text that political economy must found all maxims which pretend to be universal on comprehensive and laborious appeal to experience [Jones, 1859, pp. 568–69]. OK, but it didn't justify him in attacking the formation of hypotheses as such, and the deduction of the consequences of these hypotheses, which you *then* proceed, according to modern views, to test for their falsifiability or for their provisional applicability.

On the whole, I think that Jones is a person who must be respected, and his inaugural lecture contains nearly all of what one would respect in much more ambitious works of the historical school proper.

Now, I shan't get to the end of this today, but the historical school proper certainly flourished and was a manifestation of the *intense* nationalism which characterised universities and university teachers in central Europe during that period of history. Burke said—and he was very right—that no one can draw up an indictment against a nation, and I wouldn't like you to think that the rather disparaging remarks that I am going to make about the German historical school are made in any sense as a disparagement of the whole contribution of Germany to the tradition of Western thought. No one can call Emmanuel Kant infected by intense nationalism—the author not only of one of the most famous philosophical books in the whole of history, but the author of the *passionate* plea for international peace and international law and so on. And there were certainly during this period university teachers and philosophers and so on who took the other view, but it is true to say that, at any rate in its later stages, the German historical school was, I think, an unfortunate manifestation of the romantic nationalism characteristic of the period I'm talking about.

There are two stages in the development of the historical school. There is the first historical school, or the early historical school as it is called, whose leader probably must be regarded as being a man called Roscher, who was, in my opinion, a good economist for his time. And while in one or two lectures and prefaces he went more or less along the same grounds as Jones—I do not know whether he knew Jones—I think that Roscher is to be treated with the same respect as one would treat Jones. In point of fact, Roscher's *Principles of Political Economy* [1854]—I don't recommend those of you who don't read German or who read German with difficulty to tackle Roscher at this stage—Roscher's *Principles* was translated in America, so it is accessible in an English translation [1878].

The second man who is associated with the early historical school was a man called Knies, and he wrote extremely well on money and banking and the history of money and banking [1885]. And he also wrote rather more difficult discussions of method in the social sciences [1853]. His work in this respect is frightfully difficult. In my youth I read it all through, and it took quite a long time, but I am glad that I did it because both the work of Roscher and Knies are the subject of a famous essay by Max Weber[2] who, unquestionably, whether you agree with him or not, was the most powerful sociological mind of his period. He died in the early '20s of this century. You oughtn't to be mere economists; you ought to take a broader view of social studies than that. And anybody who takes social science seriously, even if in the end you disagree with a good deal of it, should make the acquaintance of Max Weber.

Well, Roscher and Knies were in some revolt against the British tradition of classical economics—especially Roscher, who was a good historian of economic thought, and who wrote a monograph on the seventeenth-century history of economic thought [1851]. Roscher incorporated a good deal of what he thought was valid in the classical economic tradition.

Then comes the later historical school, and I warn you here that although I have a friendly feeling for Roscher and Knies and treat them with respect, if not always with agreement, I am apt to be much less sympathetic to the later historical school which was dominated by the famous Schmoller.

If one talks about historicism, if you think for instance of Popper's famous book on *The Poverty of Historicism* [1960], insofar as Popper deals with the economic side of historicism, it is Schmoller that is the target. And Schmoller was an extremely powerful person. At one stage in the history of united Germany, it was difficult to get a Chair, and a Chair meant something in Germany in those days—Herr Professor Doktor von So-and-So. You only had, even if you were a British traveller, in my youth, to write that you were a "professor" in the hotel book in which you were registering to be treated as though you were royalty. As a German student said to me in those days—he had come to the London School of Economics—"When one meets one's professor in the street it is just an accident of time and place that one does not go on one's knees to him and present him with frankincense and myrrh." Well, all that has changed now. Since the war we call each other by Christian names and have, roughly speaking, human faces. But Schmoller was a powerful person [and he exercised immense control over appointments to Chairs in Germany in those days].[3] But what his views were I shall consider tomorrow.

NOTES

1. "An Introductory Lecture on Political Economy, Delivered at Kings College, London, February 27, 1833," in Jones (1859, pp. 539–79).

2. This essay is reprinted in Weber (1922).

3. See lecture 5, where Robbins gives this characterization of Schmoller's power over chair appointments.

E. Beginnings of Modern Analysis

The Historical School (cont.)—Precursors of Change: Cournot, von Thünen, and Rae

IN TODAY'S lecture, I shall continue with the remarks that I have to make on the historical school. I talked to you yesterday about Richard Jones. I then dwelt on the two stages of the German historical school, mentioning Roscher and Knies as representative of the earlier, more acceptable, attitude, and secondly Schmoller and his school, whose point of view, from my position, is not so acceptable.

Now the main distillation of the historical attitude can be summarised under three headings. First, they made an awful lot of fuss about the alleged assumptions of the classical school—in particular, the failure of the classical school to indicate the purpose of their interest. I have already discussed that in connection with List's attitude on economic nationalism. Secondly, they protested against the picture which they alleged emerged from the classical tradition. It was said not to be a picture of universal truth, that it neglected the institutional factor and the rate of mobility of capital and labour and so on and so forth. And thirdly, this all led up to an attack on the method of classical political economy, which was alleged to be pure deduction from simple postulates which were, of course, their history. And therefore, the Schmoller school urged that a new method was necessary—that, in order that you might say anything about economic phenomena, you must indulge in a laborious detailed study of the history of particular communities. And eventually perhaps, they promised, in the future there would emerge, not the kind of analysis which emerged from the classical preoccupation, but that you would be able to say something about the laws of economic development—the attitude which Popper [1960] has described as historicism.

Well now, how does this stand up to criticism? I have already said that I think that the attack on the assumptions of classical political economy was misplaced. I think certainly Adam Smith would have urged that the ideas attributed to him had not passed through his head, and the same I think can be said of the nineteenth-century classical economists.

The attack on the picture which was presented by the nineteenth-century classical economists, or some of them, is to some extent true. Adam Smith took some account of the institutional framework and its history. Ricardo and his followers, intensely interested as they were in certain problems arising against the background of the Smithian picture, left a good deal out, and from time to time I think that their ignoring of the institutional framework led them to exaggerate the application of some prescriptions which they laid down. It is not true to say that all of them were guilty of these omissions. Even Bentham, for instance, who perhaps for the history of thought can be classified with the classical economists, had an *Essay on the Influence of Time and Place* [1843] on social phenomena. And of course John Stuart Mill was very careful to underline the necessity of taking account of the institutional structure.

So far as the general attack on method was concerned, I am bound to say that I think it was rested on a complete misconception. It is certainly not true that all the classical economists ignore history and economic history. It is not even true of Ricardo, where, in his *Reply to Bosanquet* [1811], he shows himself a master, in his time, of empirical investigations.

But the historical school, in my judgement, had got the logic of scientific discovery wrong. Their emphasis on the priority of induction was surely misplaced. This is not to say that it is not essential that hypotheses should be tested eventually against their correspondence with fact, but it is to say that *no* science really approaches the confusion of experience without a principle of selection—a principle of selection which, in the last analysis, is traceable to consciously formulated hypotheses or unconsciously formulated principles of selection. The idea that you look, so to speak, at something called history with a mind entirely devoid of ideas—to start what Locke calls *tabula rasa*—is nonsense. And in consequence, I think that, so far as the Schmoller section of the historical school was concerned, the history was sterile. Schmoller and Schmoller's department and its followers produced interesting historical studies, but they produced no significant theory, no significant laws of development which would stand up to logical and historical analysis.

In my young days, when I used to mix a good deal with the Austrian economists, who were banished, as I shall explain in a moment, from the universe of Schmoller and company, they used to tell a fanciful story of Schmoller's student who addressed himself to the study of the fluctuations of the price of tinned meat in East Berlin in the years 1900 to 1905. And he produced a doctor's thesis of some hundreds of pages, illustrated with statistical tables and with graphs, and then, as a good doctor student, he produced a final short chapter on conclusions. And he said: "As a result of these investigations, we may venture tentatively to say that the supply of tinned meat in the eastern districts of Berlin in the years 1900 to 1905 was influenced by supply and demand."

But more seriously, the effect of the ascendancy of Schmoller was that, although at an earlier time German economists had produced notable additions to the body of general economics, the tradition more or less died out, save to some extent in Munich and in Vienna. And it is really safe to say that by 1914 the main body of faculties of economics in Germany were not producing anything which is of historical interest.

Now, if you think that that is a biased verdict deriving from an English-speaking background, I commend you to read Schneider's chapter in his *admirable* history of economic thought—*Geschichte der Wirtschaftstheorie* [1962]—which is, I am sorry to say, not translated into English—where you will find that he is as condemnatory as I am. What happened was that by revulsion, so to speak, there took place a controversy between the Austrian and the historical schools which received its permanent embodiment in the second great book of Carl Menger—his *Researches into Method* [1883], which have been translated into English [Menger, 1963] and which still have, I think, sociological and economic importance.

So far as the U.K. was concerned—I have talked to you about Jones—a very superior critic of the classical writings on the ground that they tended to neglect history and institutions was the Irish economist, Cliffe Leslie, whose *Essays in Political Economy* [1888] are quite worth your attention. Then there were the economic historians, such as William Cunningham, who wrote a three-volume history called *The Growth of English Industry and Commerce* [1890]. Cunningham was a pupil of Marshall, but for some reason or other he didn't altogether gather what Marshall was getting at. And he wrote an attack on Marshall's *Principles* which so misrepresented Marshall that Marshall, who didn't like controversy, was moved to write a rather biting attack. And I think, if you read in the early numbers of the *Economic Journal* the controversy between Cunningham [1892] and Marshall [1892b], there is no doubt that Marshall came out on top.

A more formidable figure than Cunningham, in my opinion, was Ashley, who I think you have to take more seriously than I personally would take Cunningham on matters of this sort. Ashley was a man of prejudice. When he was appointed to a Chair at Birmingham he refused to have it described as a Chair of Economics on the ground that the economic tradition against which he was in revolt had been so misleading, and his Chair was called the Chair of Commerce. But Ashley's [1901] history is still interesting reading, and Ashley's contribution to the methodological discussion is more interesting than Cunningham's.

On all this—the methodological controversy—there is an absolutely invaluable book by the father of the famous Keynes—not John Maynard Keynes, who was the great economist of my lifetime, but his father, John Neville Keynes, who wrote a very temperate book on *The Scope and Method of Political Economy* [1890] in which he desperately tried to hold the scales even and to do justice to the various schools of thought which could be classified under the title "historicism" and the more classical tradition in which he had grown up. And although it was published many years ago, it has recently been republished—I think in America. And it's beautifully written. It doesn't contain the witticisms and the imaginative perspectives of his son, but it's a classic of its kind. And from reading that, and reading the footnotes, you get a very good introduction to the so-called *Methodenstreit*, as the Germans call it—a controversy about method.

Now, enough of the incidental critics—the economic nationalists on one hand and the historical school on the other. I now want to return to the history of economic analysis in the form in which it has survived. I am not going to talk to you any more about the classical tradition, save insofar as it hitches up eventually with the so-called marginal revolution. But before I talk to you about the marginal revolution, which I shall be doing next week, I want to say a word or two about important precursors of modernism. I will leave out the meritorious precursors of marginal utility theory, because it will be more convenient for me to deal with that in the lecture in which I deal with Jevons, who was responsible for the beginnings of the marginal revolution over here. And there is no system in my selection here. I simply want to draw your attention to important contributions from various quarters.

And the first, and certainly one of the most important, is Cournot, who lived from 1807 to 1877—a French mathematician who was Rector, in his old age, of the distinguished French University of Grenoble. And his *Researches*, as all of you know, *into the Mathematical Principles of the Theory of Riches*—I am translating the French, because it is translated into English under the auspices of no less a person than Irving Fisher—which was published in 1838 is the first great work on mathematical economics.

You mustn't think that there was no mathematical economics before Cournot. Professor Theocharis, who was here in the '50s, wrote, ostensibly under my supervision, an early history of mathematical economics [1961], which, when he proposed it to me, I thought would lack content. But as usual in the graduate school, one learns a great deal more from one's students than one teaches them, and it was not long before Theocharis had taught me that he had chosen a very good subject, and his early work, which culminates in Cournot, on the history of attempts at mathematical economics, is thoroughly worthwhile the attention of specialists. But there were many worthy writers. And Whewell, whom I mentioned last time—the famous Master of Trinity and historian of science and logician and historian of moral philosophy—himself contributed to a society at Cambridge quite notable papers translating Ricardo into mathematics [1829].

But Cournot's book does put things on a new plane. It is astonishingly modern, and it contains, for those who take the trouble of reading it, many discoveries which have been claimed in certain quarters—I hope never at the School of Economics—to have been invented in the late '20s in other universities in this country.

It starts [Cournot, 1838, preface, pp. 1–5] with a most excellent rationale of mathematical economics. It does not claim very much. It just enables you to clear up your mind on certain matters and enables you to be more precise in a subject which deals with greater and less magnitudes than you could be otherwise.

And then it goes on to deal with the laws of demand [ibid., chap. 4, pp. 44–55], so called, and demand is exhibited for the first time in print—

his book came out in 1838—as a function of price. John Stuart Mill had already done it in his unpublished essay, which was only published, as the first essay in the *Unsettled Questions*, in 1844, but Cournot certainly deserves the credit of setting it out mathematically, with curves and with algebra.

He then proceeds to deal with market forms. And he deals first of all with monopoly [ibid., chap. 5, pp. 56–66], and, strange to say, the formula "marginal revenue equals marginal cost" in the monopoly equilibrium is there for anybody who has eyes to see it. It really wasn't invented at Oxford or Cambridge in the last half of the '20s. It's all in Marshall, of course, who acknowledged his general indebtedness to Cournot. It even—the monopoly equilibrium formula—is in a popular book—popularising Marshall— *Outlines of Political Economy* [1913] by Sidney Chapman, published before the war. There is some use in having a nodding acquaintance with the history of thought.

Well, he then goes on [Cournot, 1838, chap. 7, pp. 79–89] to break new ground. Having dealt with markets where the seller is one, he deals next with the duopoly problem—a market where the sellers are twofold. And he achieves, on certain specialised assumptions, a determinate solution. As you know, the theory of duopoly has been the subject of very expert examination in the 1930s and '40s and '50s, and it's very clear that the solution is only determinate when one introduces very special assumptions. But Cournot, without stating all the assumptions, got it right on the implicit assumption that he was making. And so Cournot proceeds until you get to the limiting case of mathematically pure competition [ibid., chap. 8, pp. 90–98], and he makes various contrasts between monopoly and pure competition.

And then finally, you should note his propositions regarding costs and monopoly—his proposition being that if you have increasing costs, which go on increasing until you get to the point of equilibrium, then whatever the situation at the beginning, duopolistic or competitive, it will lead to monopoly. This proposition disturbed Marshall, and led Marshall to give special attention to the problem of increasing costs and competition and to make the distinction between internal economies of scale which, if the market was small, would eventually lead to the Cournot position, and external economies, which might permit competition, in some form or other, to persist. Well, so much for Cournot.

I am dealing with them in this order because the two precursors of modern theory to whom Marshall expressed indebtedness, apart from Adam Smith and John Stuart Mill, were chiefly Cournot and von Thünen, an east German landowner who lived from 1783 to 1850. Von Thünen was passionately interested in the management of his agricultural estate. He had a thoroughly scientific approach to these matters, and he eventually embodied his reflections in two books. Both are called *The Isolated State*. They are really one book. Volume 1 was issued in 1826 and volume 2 in 1850, and a complete edition was issued in 1876, long after he was dead. And there is an English edition of the important parts, edited by Professor Peter Hall, published in 1966.

Well so far as part 1 is concerned, von Thünen is concerned with intensity of cultivation and the localisation of industry. And he devises a model where the market is in the centre of a series of concentric circles, and soil of uniform quality in each of the different circles, but differing as regards advantages of access to the market, is cultivated by agriculturists producing something called corn. And consequently, you get a very serious disquisition on the theory of rent, including rent of position and the influence of locality.

Part 2, to which he attached enormous importance, is quasi-mathematical, and the relevant chapter heading in part 2 runs—I am translating—"The Wage Is Equal to the Extra Product of the Last Labourer Who Is Employed in a Large Enterprise." And he elaborated his marginal productivity theory of wages and bridged a rather *simpliste* formula, which he was so proud of that he instructed that on his grave nothing was to be inserted except his name and his formula for the marginal productivity of wages.

You will also find marginal productivity, this time of capital, in the *Lectures*, published in 1834, of the man to whom I made allusion to when I was talking about the development of demand theory in international trade —Mountifort Longfield, *Lectures on Political Economy*, 1834. And in lecture 9 you find what is a very fair statement of a marginal productivity theory of capital.

But now among these precursors is a man who was *totally* neglected in his own day, but who, in my judgement, had one of the most astonishing minds that has applied itself to general economics—a man called John Rae. He was born in 1796 and died in 1872. He was uniformly unfortunate. His family went bankrupt before he had completed what must have been a brilliant career at the university. He emigrated to Canada, where he got an obscure job under a local government as a school teacher, and eventually—I guess he was a rather quarrelsome man—he quarrelled with the people there and lost his job. He went to the early days of the gold discoveries in California, where he nearly died of typhus fever and didn't discover any gold. And then he migrated to Hawaii, and he had a humble position as an inspector of health. He died utterly unknown—in America, at any rate—in Brooklyn in 1872. But in 1834 he wrote a book called *New Principles of Political Economy*, and this *New Principles* was in fact an attack on certain aspects of Adam Smith, particularly as regards the infant industry argument.

I did not mention Rae to you when I was talking about economic nationalism, because I knew that I was coming to him here in a wider context. But Rae makes out a far better case for the protection of infant industries than anybody else has ever done, and his strictures, some of which I think can be answered, on Adam Smith are thoroughly worth attention.

But much more important is Rae's contribution to general economic theory, especially capital theory. Now, his book, the *New Principles of Political Economy*, is one of the rarest. I don't think we possess the original here in the library; it may be at the Goldsmiths' library. I have often seen a copy at a club that I used to belong to, and have felt fantastically inclined to theft. Nobody had read it since it was published, but, being well brought up, I refrained. And it is now available, reprinted by Kelley in New York, and with a very, very scholarly biography of Rae by a man called James in the University of Toronto.

Now, Rae begins the more general part of his book, which is called "the Nature of Stocks," with a disquisition which very much anticipates Irving Fisher's *Nature of Capital and Income* [1906]. The important focus of economic analysis must be, I quote, "the course of events and the connexion of one with another" [Rae, 1834, p. 81]. The capacity to anticipate—I am not quoting now—the focus of economic calculation is what distinguishes men from animals, and the possibility of altering the course of events by deliberate conduct is vouchsafed to human beings if they choose to use their intellect. Well, so much for mere terminology.

Then there comes a certain amount of description of the formation and exhaustion of capital instruments. But he now ascends to a plane which no one had ascended to before in these terms, and the plane can best be described by the relevant chapter heading: "Every instrument"—capital instrument, that means—"may be arranged in some part of a series, of which the orders are determined, by the proportions existing between the labor expended in the formation of instruments, the capacity given to them, and the time elapsing from the period of formation to that of exhaustion" [ibid., p. 100]. And this is developed with copious arithmetical illustrations of instruments producing events equivalent to double their costs in short periods or medium periods or longer, and there is much ingenious analysis showing how more complicated returns can be recalculated so as to make them fit into such a series.

And then in the next chapter he formulates a sort of law of diminishing return to investment in terms of a delay of the doubling period: "The capacity"—I'm quoting—

> which any people can communicate to the materials they possess, by forming them into instruments, cannot be indefinitely increased, while their knowledge . . . remains stationary, without moving the instruments forward continually onwards in the series [ibid., p. 109; italics deleted]

that he has described. And he illustrates this with reference to different degrees of durability which could be imparted to houses:

> A dwelling might be slightly run up of wood, lath, mud, plaster, and paper, . . . like the unsubstantial villages, that Catherine of Russia saw in her progress through some parts of her dominions. [ibid., p. 110]

And he contrasts these villages with those

> of the same size, accommodation, and appearance, that might last for two or three centuries. . . . by employing stone, iron, and the most durable woods, and joining and compacting them together, with great nicety and accuracy. [ibid.]

Well, having elaborated an investment function, Rae then turns in another chapter to the grand question: To what extent will it be exploited? And the answer to this he finds in time preference, or, to use his own terminology, the effective desire of accumulation. And he says—I'm quoting:

> The formation of every instrument therefore, implies the sacrifice of some smaller present good, for the production of some greater future good. If, then, the production of that future greater good, be conceived to deserve the sacrifice of this present smaller good, the instrument will be formed, if not, it will not be formed. [ibid., p. 118]

And then he branches out into economic sociology and contrasts the history of different countries with different dispositions on the part of their inhabitants to accumulate—the Egyptians, who produced durable monuments, and other communities who never got beyond instruments very lacking in durability.

And even here Rae hasn't exhausted his originality. He then goes on to discuss the relation between liquidity preference and the rate of interest. Those of you who think that the discussion of the liquidity preference and the rate of interest only began in the '20s and the '30s should read your Rae: "Every man"—I'm quoting—

> must be more unwilling to run the risk of having a sum of money lying useless by him, by how much the greater the amount of the returns he could have by turning it to the formation of instruments. If then, in the society of which any man is a member, instruments are not far removed from the first orders of our series, when they soonest double the expenditure of their formation, he will rather risk the inconvenience of having too little money by him, than the loss of having a sum in his coffers long unemployed, which might have been converted into instruments yielding large returns. But if, in the society of which he is a member, instruments are far removed from the first orders of our series, he will be disposed to reserve a greater amount in the hopes of making more by some advantageous bargain, than he could by expending it on the formation of any instrument. [ibid., p. 178]

And this leads on to an analysis of the functions of money and credit and so on.

Now, poor Rae's book fell absolutely dead from the press. It is one of the most tragic examples in the history of our subject of an utterly first-class book being neglected. Senior read it and appreciated it, and John Stuart Mill read it—years after it was published—and admired it. And in his *Prin-*

ciples he commends it by saying that John Rae has done for the accumulation of capital what Malthus did for the multiplication of population. High praise, but this didn't reach poor Rae's ear, way out in the gold fields, and it was only when he was in Hawaii, I think, that somebody mentioned to him that his book had been praised by John Stuart Mill. And he wrote to John Stuart Mill, thanking him for his praise and confessing that he himself no longer possessed a copy of his book.

And that is not the end of the story, which I can tell you in thirty seconds. There was some mention of Rae in Böhm-Bawerk, and a Harvard economist called Mixter felt moved to read Rae and to reprint him. Mixter must be given a good mark for having perceived that here was something excellent, but he deserves the worst possible mark for having rearranged Rae according to *his* idea of what was important. And Rae would have been absolutely horrified to find his remarks about Adam Smith relegated to an appendix and republished under the grotesque heading—certainly grotesque for 1834—*The Sociological Theory of Capital* [Rae, 1905], which is enough to put most economists off. So that it is only in our own day that the University of Toronto has really done justice to Rae as regards proper publication. And Irving Fisher dedicated *The Rate of Interest* [1907], probably the most outstanding work on the real theory of interest published this century, "To the memory of John Rae who laid the foundations upon which I have endeavoured to build."

Well, so much for our important precursors. This clears the way for me to start with the marginal revolution next week.

The Marginal Revolution (I): Jevons

HAVING picked up various bits and pieces with regard to precursors, we come now to the section of my lectures which could be called the marginal revolution. I won't at this stage discuss whether it was a revolution or whether it was an orderly process of change or whether it was something in between. I think that it will be better for me to deal with that section of history, which will occupy me from now until the end of the lectures, bit by bit.

And I want for the lectures this week to deal with the innovations in the theory of value connected with the names of Jevons and Menger. But as always in these matters, the people who put the theory on the map—and it is exactly the same with, say, the Malthusian theory of population— had predecessors. And I am not going to spend very much time talking about the predecessors of the marginal utility theory of value, but I ought at any rate to mention two or three names and stress the importance of two others.

So far as this country is concerned, Jevons himself appeals to the name of Banfield, who wrote a book called *The Organisation of Industry* in 1844.[1] I doubt very much whether anybody reads it nowadays. He also appeals to the name of Richard Jennings, who wrote a book in 1855 called *Natural Elements of Political Economy*—a book about degrees of satisfaction. And there was an Oxford man, a clergyman called Lloyd, who wrote a lecture on the notion of value in 1833, which is reprinted in volume 1 of the supplement to the *Economic Journal* which appeared in dark blue covers in the interwar period. And that is, I think, quite a considerable intellectual achievement, but I don't intend to detain you with it.

Much more important than these names are two others. The first is a French engineer of the name of Dupuit—Jules Dupuit. He was a civil engineer who was led to consider the problems of public utilities charging tolls for bridges and so on. And he wrote, in 1844, an article "On the Measurement of the Utility of Public Works," and he followed that up in 1849 and in 1853 by supplementary articles. And you will find in the works of Dupuit declining (what we should call) marginal utility and, for good or for bad, the beginnings of the theory of consumer surplus. These have been reissued in our own day by the firm of Einaudi [Dupuit, 1933], in the time when it was influenced by the great Einaudi, who became President of Italy, and should therefore be tolerably familiar, and those of you who are graduates certainly should read them.

Then the second is a tragic name, a German called Gossen—H. H. Gossen. And in 1854 he wrote a book called, for those of you who understand German, *Entwicklung der Gesetze der menschlichen Verkehrs*—the development of the laws of human, what shall we say, commercial intercourse. And that is a very complete working out of the economic implications of the idea of declining marginal utility. I cannot recommend it to you as easy reading to embark on a reading of Gossen, which is available—it was reprinted by Hayek in the 1920s, and I should think that there are copies of it knocking about still—but to embark on it is to embark on wading through a sea of very, very long sentences, an absence of paragraphing, and so on. But it is a *most* impressive intellectual achievement, and it had the deplorable fate of being noticed by no one until by chance a colleague of Jevons at Manchester University drew Jevons' attention to it. And Jevons, who thought that he had invented the marginal utility theory of value, was amazed, and I think a little mortified, to find that Gossen had written it out even more systematically than he had. But, like the honest and great man that he was, he at once, in the second edition of his book, mentioned Gossen's name. And he communicated the fact to Walras, who had also independently discovered the application of the theory of value to the idea of declining marginal utility, and Walras, being also an honourable man—although a very irritable man, I am bound to say—wrote it up in a French journal.

Now, all that is rather fascinating intellectual history, but considerations of time lead me to concentrate my attention in these lectures on Jevons and Menger, the first Austrian economist, whom I shall deal with tomorrow. I shall delay dealing with Walras until later on, for reasons which I shall explain then. But make no mistake about it that, in spite of Dupuit and Gossen, not to mention these other obscure figures, it was the three names I have mentioned—Jevons, Menger and Walras—who put this aspect of the modern theory of value on the map.

Well now, let us deal with Jevons. And there is no reason why you shouldn't all read Jevons' book, *The Theory of Political Economy* [1871]. It is comparatively short. It is issued by a firm called Penguin, and it has a splendid introduction by Professor Collison Black, who is one of the great authorities on the history of economic thought, and there it is in a comparatively cheap edition [Jevons, 1970]. My edition was sent to me by Professor Collison Black, and therefore I can't tell you the price of it, but it can't be very much. Jevons is not so thorough in some respects as Menger (in one respect) and Walras (in others), but he is earlier, and he is much the most vivid and readable of the three.

Well, he was born in 1835; he died, as a result, I should think, of a heart attack—he was drowned—prematurely in 1882. His family lived in Liverpool and got into financial difficulties in 1848, and these difficulties continued. Jevons entered University College, London, and then in 1852 he accepted a job in Australia as Assayer of precious metals, gold in particular. As you all know, gold was discovered in Australia in the late 1840s and early 1850s, and Jevons, in order to relieve the financial difficulties of his family, accepted this post. And he had a vivid and interesting life as head of the Assay office of the Government which employed him. His letters and journals are now available in six volumes, edited by Professor Black [Jevons, 1972–81], and there is another one still to come. But there is a very good life and letters by Harriet Jevons, his wife, which she wrote in consultation with Foxwell and Wicksteed and others, and if you haven't time to read the Black complete edition of available letters, Harriet Jevons' *Letters and Journal of W. Stanley Jevons* [1886] is thoroughly worth reading. And make no mistake, that, although Jevons is very high up in the history of economic analysis, he is higher still as an all-round intellect in the social sciences: an expert in formal logic, an expert in scientific method, and he published various works on applied economics—the application of index numbers to the measurement of the value of money, the coal question, and so on and so forth.

He came back from Australia and took his M.A. at University College in 1862. He was made Professor at Owen's College, Manchester in 1866, moved down to University College in 1876, and was drowned in 1882.

His important works, from your point of view—not from the point of view of these lectures—are four. First, his *A Serious Fall in the Value of Gold* [1863], which employs index numbers and graphs to the measurement of the value of money. The second is his long book on *The Coal Question* in 1865 [Jevons, 1906], in which he discussed the eventual possibility of the exhaustion of coal supplies. The possibility has moved rather ahead. Nowadays when we talk about exhaustion of natural resources, we look at the exhaustion of oil and gas pretty quickly, but the amount of coal in this country, at doubtless increasing cost, will perhaps last, on estimates which are bound to be wrong, for another couple of hundred years at least. And thirdly, he wrote a very interesting elementary book on *Money and the Mechanism of Exchange* [Jevons, 1920]. Finally, he wrote, just before he died, a book on *The State in Relation to Labour* [1882].

He was one of those eminent figures in the late Victorian period who achieved excellence in many branches of knowledge. But now our concern is with *The Theory of Political Economy*. This has some antecedents. When he was still a student, in 1860, at University College, he wrote to a relative on 1 June: "During the last session I have worked a good deal at Pol. Economy; in the last few months I have fortunately struck out what I have no doubt is *the true theory of Economy*, so thorough-going and consistent, that I cannot now read other books on the subject without indignation."[2] He embodied his views on the subject already in 1860. I mention this because Keynes got this quite wrong in his life of Marshall. Keynes thought that Marshall was irritated with Jevons because he—Marshall—had thought out the same thing, roughly speaking, at the same time, and Jevons had rushed into print. But this was wrong. Jevons presented his views to the British Association in 1862, and they were reprinted in the *Journal of the Royal Statistical Society* in 1866. He published *The Theory of Political Economy* in 1871 and an important second edition, which contains an important long new preface signalising the discovery of Gossen and others, and providing the first bibliography of mathematical economics, in 1879.

Now, *The Theory of Political Economy* is not to be regarded as a system. It's an exposition of two important ideas. The first, which will occupy the greater part of this lecture, is the theory of value in relation to utility, and the second, for which he hasn't been given as much credit as he deserves, is a theory of capital. Keynes admired Jevons very, very much and wrote a splendid essay on Jevons, but in his famous biography of Marshall, published when Marshall died, Keynes does say, and it's worth remembering his inimitable prose: "Jevons saw the kettle boil and cried out with the delighted voice of a child. Marshall too had seen the kettle boil and sat down silently to build an engine" [Keynes, 1933/1972, p. 185]. Well, that's very clever, but it happens to be wrong.

The Theory of Political Economy is not immune from error, as we shall see. And it's certainly not the last word to be said on the theory of value, but it's a notable book and it's so well written. You can read almost every page of it, except perhaps the rather boring elaboration of the theory of value and the theory of exchange, with tremendous interest and even excitement. Knowing that I was going to talk about it today, I have read it again, for about the seventh or eighth time, over the weekend, and it inspired in me much the same excitement as when I first read it.

The introduction begins on Black's page 77. (The pages before 77 are occupied with prefaces and Black's essay on Jevons.) The introduction begins, in the second paragraph:

> Repeated reflection and inquiry have led me to the somewhat novel opinion, that *value depends entirely upon utility*. Prevailing opinions make labour rather than utility the origin of value; and there are even those who distinctly assert that labour is the *cause* of value.

—thinking about some classical economists—

> I show, on the contrary, that we have only to trace out carefully the natural laws of the variation of utility, as depending upon the quantity of commodity in our possession, in order to arrive at a satisfactory theory of exchange, of which the ordinary laws of supply and demand are a necessary consequence. [Jevons, 1970, p. 77]

Well, then he goes into an apology for the mathematical nature of the theory which he is going to develop. But it's fiddling mathematics, and indeed I think Marshall was probably right when he said that Jevons would have done well to leave the mathematics out. At the same time it's a splendid, although not so strained as Cournot's, apologia for the use, where relevant—and that needs to be said very, very strongly at this stage in the twentieth century, where relevant—of mathematics. He explains very vividly that economics deals with matters of greater and less, and therefore is implicitly mathematical from the beginning.

He also goes on to make a plea for econometrics, if you can call it that. He points out that there are abundant numerical data which should be taken account of by economists, and which should enable deeper insights to be reached into the laws of supply and demand.

And he goes on to say, which is quite important at this stage, that his theory of value makes no attempt to compare the amount of feeling in one mind with another. He doesn't, that is to say, argue that people are equal or unequal in capacity for satisfaction. His theory doesn't depend upon that. But that's perhaps another story.

Well now, Jevons' intellectual origin in this respect is obviously Benthamite. His second chapter is a short chapter on the "Theory of Pleasure and Pain." He quotes Bentham from the celebrated—which you have all looked at, I hope, in other connections—*Introduction to the Principles of Morals and Legislation*. He quotes from Bentham that feelings of pleasure and pain depend upon four circumstances: "intensity," "duration," "certainty" and "propinquity" [ibid., p. 94]. Well, those words explain themselves, and I don't think that we need dwell upon these very much.

He illustrates the intensity of satisfaction by a diagram [see figure 6] on which the intensity is measured here [on the vertical axis] and the quantity of the commodity is along here [the horizontal axis].

And he illustrates it first by rectangles each corresponding to a small quantity of the commodity in question, and then he draws another diagram in which he *assumes* that the quantity of the commodity varies continuously, and consequently the intensity can be represented by a single line.

Well then, chapter 3 comes to "Utility." Utility has its foundation in wants, and the utility of a commodity is not intrinsic. There is nothing—he does not say this—but there is nothing which has utility, but thinking makes it so. And having made that clear, he gets down to his main discovery, as he thinks. He distinguishes between *total* utility of a whole stock or a rate of flow and the *degree* with which total utility is changing. And after a few words on disutility and discommodity, in which he suggests that these concepts can be regarded simply as algebraic variations of what he said about utility, he then comes to what he would regard as the rational distribution of any commodity in its different uses, such that the final degree of utility in different uses are equal.

Now, notice his terminology. He is talking about "final degrees" and "rate of change" of total utility. Later writers have got into the habit, following an Austrian economist called Wieser, of talking about marginal utility. But strictly speaking, marginal utility and final degree of utility are not quite the same thing, because marginal utility applies rather to the last *unit* of a commodity, whereas of course final degree of utility, or mar-

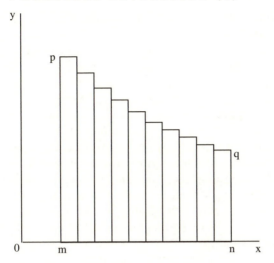

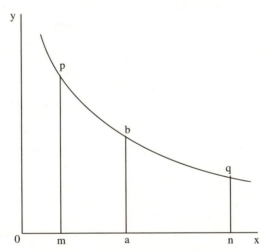

Figure 6. Jevons' Intensity of Satisfaction.
Source: Jevons, 1970, p. 96.

ginal degree of utility, simply refers to the rate at which the total utility is changing.

And then in this chapter he deals with the distribution of utility in time, and he there anticipates what was worked out much more thoroughly by the Austrians—the possible diminution of the appreciation of utility, either total or final degree, in time, as time gets more distant. This is obviously the same as Böhm-Bawerk's "diminished telescopic faculty," although there is more to say about that later on. And then finally in the same chapter he deals with the influence of uncertainty and the possibility of error.

Well, then, in his chapter 4, he applies the idea of diminishing final degree of utility to the theory of value. And he begins his chapter by insisting that value is not, like weight or length or any other similar kind of measurement, an intrinsic quality of commodities. Value is essentially, according to the Jevonian conception, a ratio of exchange between two unlike commodities. And he dwells at some length on the "Ambiguity of the term Value" [ibid., p. 127] in popular speech.

Well then, he gets down to the mechanics of this subject, and first of all he deals with the concept of markets. His concept of a market is an area of sale. And in the perfect market there is no conspiracy among the various buyers and sellers, and, at the same time, within the market there is instant knowledge of the values prevailing in isolated acts of exchange. He makes it perfectly clear that this is an ideal type—he does not use that terminology—that he proposes to operate with. After all—you can think of the London Stock Exchange or Wall Street—a few seconds or perhaps a minute or two may prevent knowledge spreading of the ratio at which money has been exchanged for securities in wide supply, and the various organised commodity markets in the world exhibit a similar degree of imperfection. But Jevons said that he's not going to take account of that degree of imperfection, and he regards the result of the absence of conspiracy, and the more or less instant knowledge of what goes on, as leading to what he calls the law of indifference in his ideal market, which simply means that the same price will prevail throughout the market.

Well, so far so good, but then he begins to elaborate his application of the theory of final degree of utility to a market in which two commodities are exchanged and in which the law of indifference prevails. And he only gets this partly right. He gets the main point right—that exchange will take place unless (to use a term that he doesn't use, but which is used by one of his disciples, Wicksteed) the position on the relative scale of any of the buyers and sellers in the market is exactly the same, in which case no exchange would take place. He explains that the exchange will take place one way or the other. An exchange will proceed while the party to the exchange can acquire, by means of exchange, something which is higher on his relative scale than on the relative scale of the person who possesses it, and vice versa. "The ratio of exchange"—and this is his great conclusion—"of any two commodities will be the reciprocal of the ratio of the final degrees of utility of the quantities of commodity available for consumption after the exchange is completed" [ibid., p. 139; italics deleted]—page 139 of the Black edition of *The Theory of Political Economy*.

But unfortunately, he doesn't realise that there is an *area* in which that equality of the ratios of final degrees of utility can be settled, depending upon the rates at which the first exchanges take place. Now, I am not here to teach you elementary modern economic analysis, but you all know this sort of diagram in which indifference curves denote points of indifference for two possible exchanges of x and y.

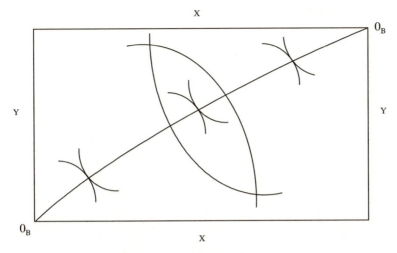

Figure 7. The Edgeworth Box.

And you also know that this curve between the indifference curves, which is called the contract curve, at which the condition of equality of marginal rates of substitution or whatever you like is satisfied again and again, and so on and so forth. This is the famous Edgeworth diagram, and Edgeworth points out that Jevons should have made this indeterminacy of the final rate of exchange along the contract curve clear. But his assumption of a law of indifference perhaps concealed from him the fact that only under conditions, not only of no conspiracy, but also of what Edgeworth [1881] called "recontract"—the people in the market go round to each of the other people in the market and make trial bargains which they can revoke when they have got perfect knowledge of the frame of mind of all people in the market—do we get a determinate solution. And in that case, of course, if you draw in aggregate demand and supply curves, you get a determinate position of perfect competition at the intersection of the aggregate demand and supply curves on the contract curve.

Well, he goes on and deals with complications. He mentions indivisibility of commodities, in which case you will not get this perfect fit; negative value; and he discusses in a very dubious way—you needn't worry very much when you are reading the book because he does not get it quite right—the gain by exchange. And he winds up with a plea for statistics of demand and supply in actual markets, and points out that among the political arithmeticians of the late seventeenth and early eighteenth centuries—Gregory King and Davenant—there were the beginnings of some statistics in regard to commodities such as wheat.

And then at the end of the chapter he sticks his neck out and says that he has discovered the origin of value: utility and scarcity. He dismisses labour. There are all sorts of things which had labour disposed on them in the

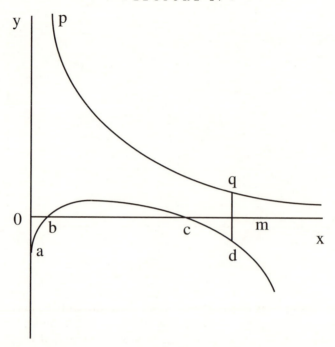

Figure 8. Jevons' Labour Diagram. *Source:* Jevons, 1970, p. 192.

past—rare books, coins and so on—but that's of no influence. Their value is determined by the circumstances which he has elaborated in this chapter. And he coins the phrase, which is so frequently used in all sorts of economic conversations nowadays: "In commerce bygones are for ever bygones" [Jevons, 1970, p. 186]. Past labour does not influence his conception of the theory of value.

But he then actually sets out a little table:

Cost of production determines supply;
Supply determines final degree of utility;
Final degree of utility determines value. [ibid., p. 187; italics deleted.]

Well, as Marshall said in reviewing *The Theory of Political Economy*, he was letting cost of production in, after all, by the back door. Future cost of production determines the supply which is going to be put on the market, and so the mutual determination of value on the demand side and the cost side is vindicated by his own words.

Well then—I shan't be able to talk about the theory of capital today; I'll do that in the first five minutes tomorrow—he goes on to deal with labour, and he invents a very famous diagram [see figure 8]. He measures along here [the horizontal axis] quantity of a commodity, and here [along the vertical axis] he measures final degree of utility, which is plus up to there [above the horizontal axis] and minus there [below it].

And so he draws a utility curve like that [line *pq*]. And then coming to labour, his thoughts are a lot more complex. Perhaps when you get up in the morning, you feel disinclined to work, and so your final degree of the first labour that you perform is minus, and then as you warm up, it may actually become a pleasure, and consequently the final degree of utility algebraically expressed is in the plus area, but eventually he thinks that it falls [line *ad*], and the equilibrium position is when the final degree of a commodity [*qm*] is equal to the final degree of disutility of labour [*md*] in that simple case.

But I think that time is up. I shall have to talk about the theory of rent and the theory of value tomorrow, but I don't think that that will involve a very great discontinuity.

Notes

1. See Banfield (1848).
2. Letter from W. S. Jevons to Herbert Jevons, 1 June 1860, in Jevons (1972–81, vol. 2, pp. 409–12, at 410).

The Marginal Revolution (II): Jevons and Menger

LAST TIME we began an examination of Jevons and discussed his theories of utility, exchange, and labour. Looking at my notes, I think I will not say anything about his chapter on rent. It is more or less Ricardian. It contains a diagram to represent rent as a curvilinear area after the payment of wages. So far as Jevons on rent is concerned, the most important thing is in the preface to the second edition, in which he points out that John Stuart Mill had realised that, where land has more than one use in agriculture, then the value of one use enters into the cost of the other. And Jevons very rightly says: If this applies to agriculture, why doesn't it apply all round? Jevons is very near the opportunity cost theory.

But I do want to say just a word or two about his theory of capital. While his theory of value has been quite sufficiently praised, having regard to the fact that part of it was incomplete, his theory of capital has not been sufficiently praised and was done some injustice to by Böhm-Bawerk.

It appears equally with the theory of value in his marvelous paper submitted to the British Association in 1862 [Jevons, 1866], and at the beginning of the chapter on capital in *The Theory of Political Economy* he emphasises the fact that his theory here is different from his theory of value, or from his theory of exchange, because exchange could only take place in the community, whereas capital would be useful to isolated man. I think that's a little artificial myself, because one of the ways of dealing with the economics of isolated man, which is a very good way into the pure theory of statical economics, is to regard the choice as to how he distributes the various scarce commodities at his disposal, and, if you like, his labour, as being acts of exchange.

But be that as it may, and Jevons makes a strong distinction between the theory of exchange and the theory of what he calls capitalisation, later on, in a letter to his sister in 1859, he says: "I think you do not duly appreciate the comparative importance of *preparation and performance*, or perhaps as I may illustrate it, of *Capital* and *Labour*."[1] In a letter to his brother in 1860 he says: "my definition of Capital and the law of the Interest of Capital are as far as I have seen quite new."[2] And in the last year of his life he wrote to Edgeworth saying: "you have not yet approached to a comprehension of my theory of capital as involving solely the element of time. . . . Indeed, as long as you speak of 'capital' instead of 'capitalisation,' I think you are pretty sure to go wrong."[3]

Well, at the end of the chapter on capital, he develops his views on this subject, and his views tend to be a rather special approach to the problem.

His conception of capital is resticted to wage goods which enable you "*to expend labour in advance*" [Jevons, 1970, p. 227] of the final product. And he illustrates this geometrically and there is an extensive discussion. He obviously anticipates the Austrian concept of the period of production, which has remained highly controversial even to this day, or nearly to this day. But assuming the problem of fixed capital to be elided in Jevons' treatment—and it's with the problem of fixed capital where you get all the difficulties arising, operating as he does with capital as fundamentally wage goods, used in advance of the final product—he reaches a very interesting formula for the rate of interest—namely, it is "*the rate of increase of the produce divided by the whole produce*" [Jevons, 1970, p. 241], which, if you look at it carefully, you can see is a primitive marginal productivity theory of capital.

Jevons was not absolutely the first to develop the marginal productivity theory of capital. In the concluding chapters of Longfield's [1834] very remarkable work on principles, which was published in the middle of the 1830s, he deals in a less precise way than Jevons with the same concept. You get in Longfield, anticipating Jevons in this respect, a marginal productivity theory of capital, and coupled with that of course, in both cases, the idea of diminishing marginal productivity if you take time into account.

And that's all I want to say about Jevons. Those of you who like intellectually rebellious views would derive pleasure from reading the last page and a half of his *Theory of Political Economy*, which is called "The Noxious Influence of Authority." Here, he *protests* that political economy has got bogged down because of the great authority of Ricardo and John Stuart Mill and the classical economists. But that's just a flourish, so to speak.

Well now, I want to devote the rest of this lecture to the beginnings of the Austrian theory—the second place in which the marginal revolution in theory began to take place in such a way as to put it on the map. As I said to you last time, there are all sorts of meritorious people who had complete or incomplete ideas of some aspects of the marginal revolution, but it was Jevons, the Austrians, and Walras who put the thing on the map and brought it about that serious-minded people, whether they agreed with it or disagreed with it, had to take it seriously.

So far as I am talking about the Austrians in these lectures, I mean the founder, Carl Menger, and his two brilliant disciples, Wieser and Böhm-Bawerk. Now, I don't think that we shall get to Wieser this time, but we may. At any rate, I want to concentrate on Menger, who I suspect is not so well known in your generation as Böhm-Bawerk and Wieser. Perhaps with the revival of interest in the Austrian school, due very largely to von Hayek's work, it may be that more people read Menger than did in my young days.

But there is no doubt that Menger is the fountain and the origin of Austrian views, at any rate as regards the theory of value, and therefore you ought to know a little bit about him. He lived from 1840 to 1921. He had his "habilitation"—his entitlement to teach—in 1872. In 1879 he was made Professor Ordinarius at Vienna, and he resigned his Chair quite early, in 1903, hoping—a hope which was frustrated—to complete his great book. As a matter of interest—nothing to do with economics—have any of you seen Kenneth MacMillan's latest three-act ballet "Mayerling"? Does the word "Mayerling" ring a bell in the minds of any of you? The suicide of the Crown Prince of the Austro-Hungarian Empire and his mistress, Countess Versera. Well, it is quite an exciting ballet, rather horrible, but with splendid choreography, and why I introduce it at this stage is because, strangely enough, Menger, who was a very, very sober man indeed, as you will learn, was actually the tutor to the unfortunate Crown Prince, who went more or less dotty and killed himself and his mistress.

Menger was a man of two outstanding works. He wrote a number of articles as well. He published the first volume of his *Principles, Grundsätze*, when he was only 31, in 1871. In 1883 he was, so to speak, blown off course in the writing of his *Principles*, incensed by the rise of the extreme historical school, which he thought was putting economic science in Germany completely on the wrong track, and he wrote his second great book—it is translated nowadays, so I can translate the German—*Inquiries into the Method of the Social Sciences and of Political Economy Particularly*. Well, I am not going to deal with the book on method. As I say, it was provoked by the doctrinaire pronouncements by Schmoller and the extreme methods of the historical school. Menger was not "anti" economic history, and indeed if you look at the original edition of the *Principles*—the *Grundsätze*—you will find that it is dedidated to Roscher, who was the senior member of the early historical school. Not that Menger agreed with Roscher in every respect, but he respected him, whereas I do not think that he respected Schmoller. And since Schmoller wrote an almost libellous review of his book on method, Menger was provoked into a much more lively pamphlet than his two great books, called *The Error of Historismus* [1884], which Schmoller publicly announced he had returned to the author without a review.

But the important thing from the point of view of this stage of the history of economic thought is the *Principles*, which was translated—it was a long time to wait—in 1950 by Professors Dingwall and Hoselitz [Menger, 1950]. As I say, I suspect that, even in English, it is comparatively little read, but there is *no* doubt that it is the fountain and origin of the Austrian school. Böhm-Bawerk and Wieser, who are much more famous names in the English-speaking world, were taught by Menger. I won't deceive you: Even in an English translation, Menger is pretty heavy going. He is not in any sense obscure, but he is very thorough, and if there is the slightest suspicion of a thing needing to be said twice, Menger certainly grasps it. He's in sharp contrast with Jevons: Jevons is vividly readable; Menger needs something of an effort. And again, preparing for this lecture, I read, not the German, which I have read before, but the English translation right through over the weekend, and I hasten to say that it is an impressive performance. Whatever one may think of the virtues of brevity, he goes very deep, and he's very thorough. Unfortunately he was blown off course by the controversy about method, and the *Principles* stopped short at volume 1, and thus we do not know Menger's views on many of the questions on which one would like to have his views.

A further contrast with Jevons is an entire difference of background. Jevons' *Theory of Political Economy* was avowedly derived from Jeremy Bentham's *Principles of Morals and Legislation* [1789]. There is *no suspicion* of Benthamite Utilitarianism in the Menger *Principles of Economics.* I don't think that Menger, although he had one of the best libraries in Europe, was altogether good on the classical economists—at any rate I have called him out before this in misreadings of Adam Smith. He defended him against the historical school, but he didn't get to the bottom of Adam Smith. It is difficult to say what his inspirations were. He was apparently ignorant of Cournot, and he was certainly ignorant of Gossen, in spite of his marvellous library. He obviously had read a number of relatively obscure, but rather down to earth, earlier German economists, particularly a man called Rau, but there is no mention of Cournot, Gossen or Dupuit in his work.

Well now, I want to take you through the book. Chapter 1 is headed— I'm giving you the English translation in each case—"The General Theory of the Good," and he sets forth at some length—some of you may think unnecessary length—the desiderata which need to be satisfied before anything can be called a "good." Notice that I am not saying "economic good," and he's not dealing with economic goods in that chapter. He's talking about *anything* which satisfied these desiderata. First of all, there must be a human need for the good. Secondly, there must be the properties necessary to satisfy that need. Thirdly, someone must have knowledge of this and fourthly, someone must have access to this [Menger, 1950, p. 53]. His conception of goods includes not only economic goods but free goods, and at the same time it includes, from this point of view, human abilities and rights to goods.

Well then, in this chapter, he discusses "The Causal Connections between Goods" [Menger, 1950, pp. 54–58] in a very broad sense, and he makes the first of his great distinctions (after all, all sorts of people had talked about goods and their utility before): He makes the distinction between goods of the first and goods of the second and higher orders. Goods of the first order are goods and services appropriate to consumption. Goods of higher orders are goods which in some ways or another are complementary to or are concerned with the production of goods of the first order. Well, the distinction is open to some question. In one of the footnotes which he retains, Marshall asks: Well, how would you classify a train which takes tourists to their destination—a service of the first order—and at the same time has some goods carriages which would, under the Mengerian classification, be goods of the second order? [Marshall, 1920/1961, pp. 64–65 at n. 3]. Well, well and good, but I suppose Menger would have said that some things were mixed.

But the distinction between goods of the first and goods of higher orders figures quite large in the Austrian theory, and goods of the higher orders are distinguished by the fact that they must be complementary to something. A good of a higher order doesn't exist by itself; it has to have another good or service of a higher order to be combined with in order that the productive process may take place in time. And consequently the utility of goods of the higher order, or the satisfaction-giving quality—let us avoid the word "utility" as much as we can in this connection—is *derived* from the goods of the first order, and, he goes on to say, may be derived after, and is necessarily derived after, a certain lapse of time—be it only a few seconds, in which you can boil an egg, or an oak tree which only reaches maturity after fifty or sixty or 100 years.

And the chapter concludes by paying some tribute to the division of labour. With the division of labour there are more and more goods, but this of course depends upon the existence of knowledge as to how to divide labour. Well that's all in chapter 1.

Chapter 2 deals with "Economy"—the activity of economising—"and *Economic* Goods" [emphasis added by Robbins]. And this chapter is important, I think, in that it is, at any rate, the *modern* origin of the conception of economics as concerned with that aspect of behaviour and institutions which arises because of scarcity. It is not true that scarcity only makes its appearance for the first time in Menger's book. It makes its appearance in Hume's *Treatise on Human Nature* [1882] as regards Hume's particular justification of the institution of property. And of course the nineteenth-century classical economists recognised all sorts of valuable objects, the value of which could only be attributed to their scarcity, their present quantity being incapable of further increase by the application of labour— Old Masters, the signatures of dead boxers, and so on and so forth.

Well, Menger goes on to say that the concern for human needs leads to some provision in advance, and requirements for goods of the first order derives directly from needs. And of course there is a certain amount of uncertainty as soon as you look forward in time and take account of future needs. Some needs are pretty certain to recur during your lifetime; other needs are contingent upon the growth of knowledge and changes in the environment and so on.

Well, this business of conservation to meet future needs, according to Menger, involves four aspects of behaviour: conservation of quantity, conservation of quality, choice between goods, and choice such as to secure the greatest result all round [Menger, 1950, pp. 95–96]. And he pauses to say that where scarcity is concerned, where economic goods are scarce in relation to the demand for them, there you have—and here he follows Hume—some rationale for property. And in common with Hume, although not recognising Hume, he makes a contrast with "*non-economic goods*," which may satisfy his criteria of "goods," but which do not satisfy the criteria of "scarce goods" [Menger, 1950, pp. 98–109; emphasis added]. And he dwells a little on the conception of needs in relation to quantity. He points out the well-known fact that water beside a stream is not scarce—if you lose a bucket of it, it doesn't matter, because you can have another bucket of it for the asking—whereas water in the desert may be very scarce indeed. And he reminds us that requirements for goods of higher orders depend upon the lower goods—the goods of the first order—being economic goods.

And he concludes the chapter with some warning about the conception of national wealth—adding together all sorts of values which arise from this subjective factor which may vary from person to person and from place to place.

Well then, in chapter 3 he comes to "The Theory of Value." And the economic activity which leads to the greatest result, the act of economising, obviously depends, in his exposition, on the subjective value which is put upon scarce goods. Value, he emphasises at tremendous length, is *not* an intrinsic quality of goods, but is dependent on the conception, whether truthful or imaginary, of the needs, and it arises only where economic goods are concerned. And he goes out of his way—as if he hadn't done it before—to emphasise the distinction between value and utility. Things which are not valuable, he emphasises again and again, can have utility. And so he comes to the analysis of the subjective factor, as the Austrians called it. Different satisfactions, different imaginary future satisfactions, have different importance, and of course there is an objective side to value—namely, the quantity of goods which are subjectively valued.

And now Menger illustrates his conception of economising in an enormous arithmetical table which I have very greatly simplified in those figures I put on the board. The contrast between Roman and Arabic figures is Menger's, but I have economised my time by not reproducing the whole of his table, because I think that the whole point of it can be produced in that this simple way.

The Roman I, II, III, IV, ad infinitum represents different qualitative kinds of goods, which are believed to be goods, and the Arabic figures— 10, 9, 8, 7, . . . —indicate the subjective orders of magnitude of the satisfactions which can be obtained by equal small quantities of the goods in question. And if you come to compare the table—which may puzzle you if you look at Menger and don't read very, very carefully, because the comparisons here under the different Roman headings depend upon equal amounts of expenditure being devoted to the small quantities of the differ-

I	II	III	IV	V	VI	VII	VIII	IX	X
10	9	8	7	6	5	4	3	2	1
9	8	7	6	5	4	3	2	1	0
8	7	6	5	4	3	2	1	0	
7	6	5	4	3	2	1	0		
6	5	4	3	2	1	0			
5	4	3	2	1	0				
4	3	2	1	0					
3	2	1	0						
2	1	0							
1	0								
0									

Figure 9. Menger's Magnitude of Satisfactions. *Source.* Menger, 1950, p. 127.

ent commodities—with Jevons, all this is just a little clumsy. But remember he was thinking this out for himself, and remember you are at the *beginning* of the Austrian theory of value.

And supposing that you have limited means, and you can't afford all the things in the table, you will distribute the equal quantities of expenditure in such a way as to *equalise* the subjective value of the things that you can afford. That is to say that, supposing you were not able to afford all the 7s, you would find yourself landing up with three examples of number I and two examples of number II and one example of number III. Now, that almost looks as though Menger was propounding a cardinal theory of subjective valuation, but I think one must give him the benefit of the doubt and regard his Arabic numbers as merely indicating orders.

Anyway, after page after page of this—all sober and impressively profound, even if repetitive—you reach the Austrian conception of the determination of value—namely, that the value of any commodity, in comparison with the value of some other commodity, is determined by *the least dependent use*. And he actually gives a little illustration of this. Suppose that Roman I indicates corn, and that first item under Roman I indicates units of corn devoted to food that keeps you alive, that the second item under Roman I represents a small quantity of corn devoted to, shall we say, making whisky, to cheer you up a little bit on your desert island, and that the third thing under Roman I might be devoted to the nourishment of some pet—the parrot who Robinson Crusoe taught to talk, for instance. Well now, supposing that he loses one of his units, he will rearrange his conception of dependent uses, and presumably the parrot will starve—well, if he was a teetotaler, of course, he might give up whisky.

You see, in completely different language, Menger has given you something equivalent—value depending on the least use—to the Jevonian theory. And he enlarges on this. He enlarges on the possibility again of error in anticipation, of changes in knowledge which affect the subjective valuation of the dependent uses, and he suggests that the values of goods of the higher order are in the end derived from the values of goods of the first order, and values of goods of the first order are derived from the least dependent use of the quantity in existence.

And he develops this at considerable length, and so far as goods of the higher order is concerned, he elaborates the possibility of substitution if there are changes in the quantity available—if you have more land and less labour, or less land and more labour, and so on. And the principle of substitution depends upon, eventually, the value of the least dependent use of the good of the first order which is derived from it. And he goes out of his way to challenge the right of land or labour or capital to need special treatment at this stage. At this stage he is content simply with his classification of goods—the first and goods of higher order.

Well then, chapter 4 is devoted to "The Theory of Exchange," and he illustrates by primitive arithmetical illustrations, which I don't think I need reproduce. He emphasises the purpose of exchange—namely, to enable each party to the exchange to achieve a greater dependent use with what remains after the exchange than he was able to achieve before.

And then in chapter 5 you have an elaborate—and in my judgement, for those of you who are trying to read the book, skippable—series of illustrations. The important thing is that he does realise that you have got to proceed from monopoly to competition and make different generalisations about different market situations.

Then in chapter 6 he comes back to the contrast between "Use Value and Exchange Value."

Chapter 7 deals with "The Theory of the Commodity"—and at first sight you wonder why on earth he is coming back to this, because, after all, you would think that it was capable of being inferred from what he has said before. But he dwells on the theory of the commodity—"commodity" being goods intended for sale, goods which are capable of entering into the market. And that is a preparation for a final chapter, which is the Mengerian theory of money in which—and he wrote on money elsewhere and with far greater elaboration—the main emphasis, after some historical account of the origin of money, the greater saleability of cattle in communities in which cattle was the chief money, and so on, through the history of coinage and so on and so forth, is the conception of money as the most saleable commodity of all. And that opens the door to all sorts of thoughts, which the breaking up of his meditations in volume 1, and his failure to complete volume 2, rendered very tantalising.

Now, that's all that I am going to say about Menger, and it's a very convenient point to stop, because nowhere here in direct connection with Menger have I talked at all about the cost of production. How does that fit into the Austrian theory? Well, I shall devote ten minutes to that in the first lecture next week.

NOTES

1. Letter from W. S. Jevons to Henrietta Jevons, 30 January 1859, in Jevons (1972–81, 2:358–63, at 359).

2. Letter from W. S. Jevons to Herbert Jevons, 1 June 1860, in Jevons (1972–81, 2:409–12, at 411).

3. Letter from W. S. Jevons to F. Y. Edgeworth, 26 December 1881, in Jevons (1972–81, 5:156).

The Marginal Revolution (III):
Costs (Wieser)—The Pricing of Factor Services (Wieser, Clark, Wicksteed)

IN MY last lecture I expatiated at some length on the views of Carl Menger in developing volume 1 of his *Principles of Economics*. I expatiated at some length because I think that in a great many histories of economic thought the contribution of Carl Menger is insufficiently recognised. Partly that is due to the heaviness, but not obscurity, of his style, and, it might be argued, its undue length. But partly, I think, it is due to the failure of casual readers to appreciate how deeply Menger thought on these very fundamental subjects. I personally would ascribe to Menger a more or less noncontroversial view of the part played by the scarcity of goods in conditioning economic behaviour and economic institutions in some way or other, and although there are many traces of references to scarcity from Hume onwards, it is Menger who perhaps insensibly has shaped the view which that conception occupies at the foundation of our subject.

Now, I am not going to say anything more about Menger, but you may have noticed that, in spite of all of this rather heavy-handed business of goods of the first and second order, complementarity and substitutability, and the derivation of their value from the value of goods of the first order, nothing is said about costs. Doubtless he intended to deal with that in volume 2, which he never managed to complete. But the Austrian theory of costs is extremely important, and it sprang from the reflections of one of the two most famous pupils of Menger—namely, von Wieser.

And he lived from 1851 to 1926. Incidently, he is also, I think, the first to use the word "marginal" utility—in German of course. Menger didn't use that phrase; he always talked about the least dependent use. Wieser first developed his views in a seminar paper under the presidency of the historical economist, Knies, whom I indicated to you as being one of the more considerable of the earlier historical school. And he then developed them in a work published in 1884 called—let me translate literally—*On the Origin and Leading Laws of Economic Values*. And he subsequently published a more comprehensive work, *Natural Value*, which was translated into English under the supervision of Professor Smart of Edinburgh in 1893. And the first of these books is in a sense, I think, the most important. For those of you who can read German, it happens to be the shortest.

Wieser asks the question: What part do costs of production play in this presentation of value, deriving from Menger, and what is the appropriate conception of costs? The short formulation is that, in the Austrian view, as presented by Wieser—but it spread to the Austrian school in general and has had a wider influence since—costs are the values which are foregone in devoting resources to this kind of production rather than to any other. Costs are, in a sense, the reflection of utilities elsewhere. And formulated in the way which I have explained it to you, it of course must ring a bell. It is the same thought which underlies the famous opportunity cost concept, which was formulated, with or without Austrian influence—I wouldn't know—by a comparatively obscure American economist in 1894 in the *Quarterly Journal of Economics* for that year—D. I. Green, "On Opportunity Cost."

Arising from Green's suggestions, this conception was elaborated at great length in an eccentric but learned work by Davenport—a famous American economist in my young days—entitled *Value and Distribution* [1908]. The British formulation of the same idea, which is beautifully clear and illuminating, is to be found in the relevant chapters of Wicksteed's *Common Sense of Political Economy* [1910]. Don't, for goodness sake, be put off by the title of Wicksteed's book. It is probably, in any language, the most detailed and thorough examination of the idea that value depends upon marginal utility.

Now, you should note at this point that, although we are talking of the origins of modern value theory, here there is a contrast between the Austrian theory and Jevons, not to say, later on, Marshall and Edgeworth. In that diagram which I put on the board just a minute or two before ending the exposition two lectures ago [figure 8], you had a utility curve and a disutility curve, most of which registered negative utilities and degrees of utility. And it is clear that, in the Jevonian conception, costs of production reflected the opposite, so to speak, of utility—the disutility, pain cost if you like—on the supply curve. And Marshall and Edgeworth, who, in his peculiar and highly individualistic way, was both a disciple of Jevons and of Marshall—the Jevonian influence is predominant in his famous work, *Mathematical Psychics* [1881], which is in the School of Economics series—Marshall and Edgeworth insisted that, land apart, the influences behind supply were flexible, and that you could have a supply schedule reflecting disutility of the cost elements as a function of price. It's not at all clear whether Marshall would have been sufficiently a classical economist to regard the size of the working population as a function of price. That is an obscure point. But what is clear is that he insisted, in his preliminary models at any rate, before he got on to institutional considerations, on regarding supply as influenced by disutility in the Jevonian method.

Now, there was a controversy about this. The Austrians, and particularly Wieser's famous companion Böhm-Bawerk, defended the Austrian assumption of fixity of ultimate supplies of factor services by the institutional consideration that the factor services were determined, so to speak, exogenously—that is to say, they were not determined inside the system that they were contemplating, but were influenced by all sorts of institutional considerations: legislation as regards hours, custom and so on and so forth. Well, this part of the controversy, I think, is an empirical question. But if you wish to pay tribute in a model to the flexibility of supply as a function of price, you can still exhibit it in the Austrian manner if you regard leisure as one of the goods which may be foregone in producing the commodity in question. I personally have put this forward in the past, and my friend Jack Viner criticised me, urging that there were other influences determining supply which couldn't easily be fitted into that construction. I think that some reply to Viner's criticism could be made by employing the theory of joint products in this respect, but that perhaps is a minor footnote.

Well, so much for the Austrian conception of value and cost of production. Now, I am leaving Walras until next week, for reasons which I hope will be obvious when I come to deal with him. But we now proceed to a further stage in the examination of the marginal revolution, so-called, by an explicit discussion of the history of the evolution of views with regard to the pricing of factor services of one kind or another.

So far, in discussing value and costs, although there have been references by Menger to the valuation of goods of higher order and their complementarity and their substitutability, this branch of the full model of value and distribution has not come under explicit examination. And it's here, of course, even more I think than in the theory of value of goods of the first order, that the marginal revolution element comes into its own. I say "element" because of course Marshall was right in urging that there was much less of a revolution, much more continuity of thought, than, let us say, Jevons, in his enthusiasm, and the Austrians, in their comparative ignorance of the minutiae of the British classical tradition, suggested. Even Menger, with his tremendous library and his undoubted erudition, got Adam Smith wrong on one quite important occasion.

Well now, let me start with the Austrians. There are hints, which I don't want to repeat, in Menger, but in this connection—the pricing of factor services—Wieser and Böhm-Bawerk are the most important, and they diverge. It is wrong to think that the marginal revolution, so-called, did not include a great many personal divergences on quite important matters. Wieser—and here you should have a look at his *Natural Value* [1893/ 1971, pp. 72–78]—poses the question of the pricing of factor services as being—and he borrowed this from the law—"a problem of imputation." The prices of the factor services were, in the last analysis, influenced by the marginal utility of goods of the first order and the costs which reflected the utilities foregone elsewhere.

But the process was one of imputation back. That was his terminology, and you do not get that explicitly emphasised in Menger. And it derives, as I've hinted, from jurisprudence. If you are considering, for instance, the guilt of a corpse found on your front doorstep one morning, and you establish the antecedents of the murder, of course you can go back into all sorts of circumstances—the financial entanglements of the murderer, his relations à la Freud and Jung, and so on and so forth (this boring, fashionable talk about his father and his mother and his grandparents and so on)—and all these, perhaps, if they are true, form part of a conception of the causation which, when you are making up your minds as regards the sociological and moral influences—boring subjects [inaudible wording]—are relevant. But from the point of view of jurisprudence, the question is: Who fired the gun? And the point of view of the pricing of factor services was the economic influences which were directly responsible for the pricing of the factor services.

And then Wieser, having expatiated at some length and with some good sense on this, believed that he had found the answer by simple algebraic equations involving no calculus. Thus, for instance, if he was considering the pricing of the service in a three-good community, the services involved being denoted by x, y and z, you could have three simultaneous equations [Wieser, 1893/1971, p. 88]:

$$x + y = 100,$$
$$2x + 3z = 290,$$
$$4y + 5z = 590.$$

And you work out the solution to that, if you like.[1]

But of course it does assume that prices are given—the prices for the ultimate commodities. The interdependence of things is not emphasised. And, of course, since he does not emphasise the substitution effect, about which Menger had thrown out broad hints, and which is *so* important in our conception of the circumstances determining value and distribution, the only way to deal with fixed technical coefficients—that is to say (if there be any soul in this room who doesn't understand that), complete and unavoidable fixity of the proportions in which the factor services are combined to produce a given good—in the end, as you learn from your Hicks on *The Theory of Wages* [1932] and so on and so forth, is to assume shifts between the quantities of the goods of the first order which they produce. You can't get shifts as regards substitution in the production process, but you can get shifts, according to the demand schedules, among the ultimate consumption goods which are concerned.

Edgeworth [1893?], when he reviewed Wieser's *Natural Value*, was pretty scornful of it. But Edgeworth—whom in my young days I knew slightly as a member of the Oxford Political Economy Club, at which he was the most charming conversationalist you could possibly imagine, bounding in splendid witty stories of his predecessors and of his contemporaries and so on and so forth—was a mixed-up character. His lectures were absolutely *no good at all*. They were so obscure. I think Roy Harrod was the only person who sat them out, and he told Roy on one occasion that he didn't in the least mind an empty lecture room, so long as he had a blackboard and a piece of chalk with which to work out his differential equations. He was over-deferential to Marshall, and he was, I think, pretty antagonistic to some, at any rate, of the Austrians and the continental economists. He was polite, and not so polite, in controversy. He was of a Spanish mother. His name was Francis Ysidro Edgeworth, and Marshall used to say, "Well, Francis is all right to get on with, but beware of Ysidro." But in modern times people, although not accepting Wieser's suggestion, have gone out of their way to give him credit for some anticipation of the techniques of linear programming. But that's another story.

Well now, Böhm-Bawerk had a different theory of prices and the factors of production. He followed a phrase of Menger's, which, being translated, is called "the loss principle," and the loss principle consisted in applying to the price of the ultimate commodity what would be lost if one of the factor services were withdrawn. Well, taken like that, it is very clear that you may, in simple cases, get a completely wrong answer. Let us suppose the services of a horse and cart, designed to take goods of the first order—turnips—to market. Remove the horse and there is no product at the market. Keep the services of the horse, but take the cart away, and there are no products on the market. Twice as much is imputed by the loss principle than the value of the product, so that does not work in all cases. But of course Böhm-Bawerk had an inkling of the idea, which was developed elsewhere, of marginal productivity analysis which operates with very small—in the limit, infinitesimally small—subtractions from the factor services. And that brings us to the main subject of this part of the history.

The early history I have already intimated to you. In Longfield's *Lectures* in the '30s—in his lecture 9, I think it is—the rate of profits is determined by cases in which the efficiency of capital is least [Longfield, 1834/1931, pp. 186–99]. Well, that's a more cautious way of putting it than Böhm-Bawerk's, but it gets nearer to marginal analysis. And as for von Thünen, in the second part of his *Die isolierte Staat—The Isolated State*—which was published in 1850, he applies this to labour, and he says that wages are equal to the extra product raised by the last of the labourers; I am translating very loosely from page 174 of the English translation (or at least I've got "2, page 174" in my notes, but I think that's the English translation) [von Thünen, 1966].

Well, these estimable people, Longfield and von Thünen, weren't taken much notice of, except von Thünen was taken *great* notice of by Marshall. Marshall was scrupulous in acknowledging the influences, and he *repudiated* the inference, which irritated him very much, that he had been influenced by the Austrians: "Böhm-Bawerk and Wieser were at school when I thought these things out," he wrote to somebody. But von Thünen and Cournot he rendered due tribute to. But I'll come to Marshall later on.

The popularisation in the English-speaking world of a full marginal productivity theory of the pricing of the factor services is due to a man whom I do not expect any of you read nowadays, but who was very famous in his day in America: John *Bates* Clark—not to be confused with his son, a much subtler intellect, John Maurice Clark, who was at Chicago, not necessarily intimately allied with what is called the Chicago School, but one of the famous figures at Chicago in my younger days. John Bates Clark must obviously have been a rather forceful and fine character. The tributes that were paid to him on his seventieth or eightieth birthday dwell on the nobility of his character and the forcefulness of his exposition and so on. An unkind critic could say that he was given to premature and facile generalisations. You can take your choice, and probably the truth is in between.

His first book, which was published in the 1880s, called *The Philosophy of Wealth* [1886], makes the claim—he makes the claim for it—that he discovered the marginal utility theory for himself. A very peculiar book; I don't recommend you reading it—it's not important for this part of the history. His wage theory was developed in a very famous article in the *Proceedings of the American Economic Association* in 1889, called "Possibility of a Scientific Law of Wages," and he generalised this in his famous book on *The Distribution of Wealth*, which was issued in 1899 [Clark, 1925]. And there is some interesting analysis there if you didn't build too much on it. He perceives the marginal element in the Ricardian analysis of rent, and, assuming the population to be constant, which he does—and he also assumes the capital to be constant—he suggests that the same marginal element in the Ricardian rent could be applied to a working population of fixed habits as regards wages.

And so far as capital is concerned, he it was who, carrying on from John Stuart Mill, who carried it over from Comte, made the rigid distinction between statical and dynamic analysis. And Marshall, who had corresponded in a friendly way with J. B. Clark, and always treated him with great respect, protested about this. He said, and this gives you a preliminary insight into Marshall: "I could no more write one book about my static state"—because J. B. Clark had promised that he would deal with dynamics in another book, which he did partially in his *Essentials of Economic Theory* [1918]—"and another about my dynamic state, than I could write one book about a yacht moving at three miles an hour through the water which was running against it and another about a yacht moving through the still water at five miles an hour."[2]

Well, Marshall wouldn't have liked this so much, but it is important as spreading the marginal idea as applied to the demand side. But Marshall always had reserves about the marginal analysis, especially as regards wages. He said that the marginal analysis there was not a complete theory of wages, although it enabled you to determine certain influences on the demand side—which is probably the good sense of the matter. But more about Marshall and Marshall's other reservations towards the end.

Coming back—not to Marshall's influence, because it began long before the 1890s and his *Principles of Economics*—in 1894, Wicksteed, obviously inspired by Jevons, published a very slim book, which was frightfully rare until we reprinted it, a famous book called *Co-ordination of the Laws of Distribution*, which aroused the most terrific controversy. You will get a very good account in Stigler's *Production and Distribution Theories* [1941] about the detail of Wicksteed's thought in this respect. He takes up the point—I don't think he got it from J. B. Clark—of the similar determination of rent and wages and different classes of land—the value of land and the value of labour—and he argues the general case for their determination by marginal productivity.

The book is quasi-mathematical, for which he apologises. He actually taught himself differential calculus in order to understand Jevons—and it seems that by skilled people his mathematics is thought to be rather clumsy and lengthy—and as a result of his mathematics he determines the further proposition that by adding up the marginal productivity of different factor services involved in any process, you exhausted the value of the product. And that implies, as he put it, a homogeneous production function—constant costs, linear and homogeneous. And he applies a famous mathematical theorem which is often associated in this connection in economics with Wicksteed's name—Euler's theorem.

Well, here the trouble began. Edgeworth, for obscure reasons, ridiculed Wicksteed, which he ought not to have done because Wicksteed was a very considerable figure. But I think that it was Wicksteed's derivation from the Austrians which invoked Wicksteed's [sic: Edgeworth's] sort of polite raillery. Pareto criticised Wicksteed on the ground that some technical coefficients were fixed and were certainly not capable of being dealt with his way. So, far as Walras was concerned, there was an *absolute outburst of gall* against Wicksteed. Walras pretended that the marginal productivity theory was actually implicit in his first edition and thenceforward. But in point of fact, he only mentioned it explicitly in his later editions, and you can take it from me that all the people who knew Wicksteed, who was a saintly character, would regard Wicksteed as *absolutely incapable* of plagiarism. If you read Walras' correspondence, the way that he talked about all this, I do not think it should lower your admiration of Walras as an innovator, but it should make you realise that he was rather a difficult character.

Well then, the mystery is a little deepened by the fact that Wicksteed actually, in *The Common Sense of Political Economy* [1910], although he goes on using marginal analysis, retracts the rigid demonstration of the *Coordination of the Laws of Distribution*. And a mystery hung about this retraction. People didn't know what it was due to. But in the '60s a letter from Wicksteed was discovered, in which he confessed that he had been shaken by Pareto's criticism.

Meanwhile, however, Wicksell—Knut Wicksell, the great Scandinavian economist—had shown that his retraction was unnecessary and that constant cost was not a necessary assumption of the adding up proposition. All that was needed—and this is worked out in the first chapters of Hicks' book on *Wages* [1932], in respect of which he is, I think, unnecessarily contrite about certain errors that it contained later on (the first two chapters are very useful in this respect)—all that's necessary, according to Wicksell, and as translated by Hicks, is that firms should be in equilibrium at their minimum cost level.

Now, coming back to Marshall, Marshall always insisted that this was not a complete theory of wages—that it only illuminated certain matters on the demand side. And you'll find that in the sixth book of Marshall [1920], which you have all read, let us hope, he hovers between using the words "marginal" and "marginal net" product, which makes it very clear that Marshall was aware of Pareto's assumptions and criticisms. But he didn't think it worthwhile going into this matter.

But now I must return to Clark and certain others. Clark claimed—and this is why I said that perhaps he was given to hasty and facile generalisations—Clark actually claimed in his book that if it could be shown that the pricing of factor services—labour and capital and all that—was determined by marginal productivity, *then* distribution could be regarded as just, which is a pretty tall order and really frightfully superficial. Imagine putting to a very intelligent but very low-paid wage earner the proposition that "Your wages are determined by marginal productivity and therefore are just." And this very intelligent but low-paid man might reply, saying, "I agree that I am rewarded according to the marginal value of my product to the employer, but you haven't dealt with the reasons why my marginal productivity is so low—the failure of my parents to obtain access to capital which would have made my marginal productivity higher, not to mention all the institutional obstacles which prevent my mobility being greater, and having a wider range of choice, and having access to places where the wages as determined by marginal productivity are higher." Well, I think that puts paid to J. B. Clark's simple proposition.

Don't think that I think that these problems are at all simple on the one side, or that I don't think that it is possible to have a grown-up talk about problems of this sort. All that I want you to realise at this hour is that in explaining the evolution of the *useful* conception of marginal productivity as illuminating *some* factors on the demand side *sometimes*, but it doesn't exhaust the matter, and it doesn't settle any ethical questions at all.

Well, I have caught up with my programme, and tomorrow I shall be proceeding to the unsolved problem of the rate of interest—not merely the marginal productivity of capital, but the really profound problem of the rate of interest. And as before I shall start with a general discussion of the problem and then go on to the Austrians and then go on to Fisher and modern theory.

NOTES

1. The solution of this system is $x = 40$, $y = 60$, $z = 70$; see Wieser (1893, p. 88).

2. Letter from Marshall to John Bates Clark, 15 December 1902, reprinted in Pigou (1925, p. 415).

Capital Theory: Böhm-Bawerk and Fisher

NOW, don't let me recapitulate what I was doing yesterday, save recalling, for those of you who weren't present, that I was dealing with the pricing of factor services—labour, quasi rents, rents, and so on. But all that, which is, so to speak, in the second division of Walrasian rows in his ultimate model, does not in the least solve the problem of the *rate* of interest, the capital value of existing instruments—if you like, the capitalisation of a *flow* of services in the future.

Well now, poor old J. B. Clark regarded this as settled by regarding capital in its broad sense as relatively fixed—fixed in the sense that Ricardian land was fixed. Or he sometimes regarded it as being, so to speak, self-renewing, and Knight and other estimable members of his school fell into that trap too. But that shouldn't satisfy us. It doesn't satisfy the problem of the rate at which future services of any kind are discounted to give a capital value, and it does not, incidentally, solve the problem of whether there is accumulation or decumulation. And this is one of the ticklish problems of economic theory, although I think that the side of it that I'm going to talk about today has been, roughly speaking, cleared up by modern developments. But it is complicated, and is not sufficiently cleared up, even to this day, by the fact that the value of money is not constant and that consequently the interest rate reckoned in different commodities is different. And I shall ignore all that as not being, so to speak, within the limits of the subject which I am engaged to lecture on.

Now, the discussion of causes determining the rate of interest goes right back into the past. And let me, in a very superficial way, get rid of misconceptions.

First of all, it is a misconception to suppose that the quantity of money, as such, determines the rate of interest. You will remember what Hume said about that. And although the proposition is well refuted by Hume and well tested by experience of great inflations—when the experience has been that as the quantity of money increased, so the rate of interest, anticipating further increases in the quantity of money, went up—this misconception continued to have some currency. You mustn't think that my remarks cover Keynes, whose formula was that the rate of interest was determined by the quantity of money and liquidity preference, because, as you all know, when Keynes talked about the quantity of money he was converting the money into wage units. He was talking about real money rather than money as such. Well, that's the first misconception.

The second misconception is—and I say this dogmatically, and those of you who are Marxians may think that this is all unjustified, I warn you—present in the Marxian theory, which regards the rate of profit and hence the rate of interest as determined by exploitation—the appropriation of surplus value by those who have the ownership of capital. Now, there is much more to be said about the Marxian theory than these dogmatic remarks will suggest. But any simple idea that the rate of capitalisation, which is a fundamental thing, is determined by the degree of exploitation is really refuted by, let's say, a simple example. Supposing a purely collectivist community plants an oak sapling, with a certain quantity of labour to dig the hole and so on. It will go seriously wrong in its anticipations of future capital value if it sticks to the quantity of labour expended at that time. An oak tree certainly doesn't reach its maturity until fifty or more years have passed, and in the meantime the anticipated value will have greatly appreciated from the value of the sapling. And you need not assume that any further labour has been disposed on the oak tree. So that a collectivist community which really based its allocation of resources on a pure labour theory of value would get some things grievously wrong.

Thirdly, there is a misconception relating to productivity. Some people, having regard to my example of the oak tree or similar examples, have said that the rate of interest depends upon *the rate of natural growth* of things which are capable of growing. Well, that is a pretty vague idea and involves all sorts of averaging and so on. But the whole point is, to return to the oak tree for a moment: What is its capital value, having regard to its price fifty years hence? The capital value *will depend on* the rate of interest, so that natural growth productivity theory stands the problem on its head, so to speak.

But now let us come to productivity in general, and let us be sophisticated and talk about marginal productivity. But the conception of a *rate* of the value of the services of instruments—or if people were bought and sold, of human services—depends essentially—the capital value depends essentially—upon which rate you use for capitalisation. Only in the market for free capital, as distinct from capital which has been invested in various ways, is there homogeneity between capital as a stock and the returns on the stock. But the explanation of the market for free capital involves further complications.

And then finally, what about the abstinence theory which Lassalle—I think it was Lassalle and not Marx—made such fun of, talking about the abstinence of the Rothschilds of his day, the austerity imposed on rich people in accumulating further, and so on and so forth? Well, the word "abstinence" was very, very mistaken. It was naive of Senior [1836] to put it that way. Marshall [1920/1961, pp. 233–34], who was *acutely* conscious of what people thought of his terminology, substituted the word "waiting"—waiting for a future return—and, as we shall see in a moment, Fisher [1907] adopted the splendid term *time preference*. Well, we shall see in a moment that time preference does enter in, but it is obviously incomplete. It is not a good theory of interest just to say that interest depends on time preference, or at least I say so. For instance, no less a person than Frank A. Fetter [1904]—not Frank Whitson Fetter, who is still alive—thought that he could present a pure time preference theory of interest, leaving productivity out of account altogether. But I don't think he was right.

Now let us turn to the history of the subject under the marginal revolution, and let me remind you first of what I said when I was talking about the neglected meritorious economists of the middle of the nineteenth century—what I said about John Rae, who, in his *New Principles of Political Economy* [1834, book 2, chaps. 4–8, pp. 100–197], a polemic against Adam Smith and in favour of the infant industry argument, developed marvelous chapters giving a more or less complete—not mathematical, but complete—general view of the broad factors influencing the real rate of interest. But I'm not going to go into that again.

The modern discussion starts with the second of Menger's great pupils (the first being Wieser), Böhm-Bawerk, whom I have spelled for you before and whose dates therefore I will give you simply: 1851 to 1914. If you want to read about Böhm-Bawerk, there is an extremely eulogistic review which I was acquainting myself with this morning. It's rather a long article in Schumpeter's *Ten Great Economists* [1956]. He has about fifty pages devoted to Böhm-Bawerk, and much as I admire Böhm-Bawerk, I think that Schumpeter's praise is just a spot excessive—but not all that. At any rate it is an interesting, stimulating article to read, as everything that Schumpeter wrote, except that laborious book on business cycles, was stimulating and thought provoking.

First of all, Böhm-Bawerk made Menger much more intelligible. He wrote a couple of articles, which have not been translated into English so far as I know, but which were reprinted by the London School of Economics—you can get them in German in that series—*Fundamentals of the Principles of Economic Worth—Grundzüge der Theorie des wirtschaftlichen Güterwerts* [1886]. But his fame depends upon his two volumes on *Capital and Interest* [1890], and there are English translations of the two volumes available, so there is no excuse for your not having a squint at them and paying some attention to the main part.

Well, the two volumes begin with an extensive history of all conceivable possible theories of interest before Böhm-Bawerk. It's a long book; I regard it as one of my useful merits that I read it in German. But there you have a classification of all conceivable theories which are each designated as wrong—abstinence theories, productivity theories, exploitation theories, use theories, miscellaneous theories and so on and so forth.

And I am bound to say that, in spite of the brilliance of the book and its occasional theoretical profundity (because Böhm-Bawerk is to be taken as being one of the great economists and anything that I have said about Schumpeter's exaggeration mustn't subtract from that tribute) yet I am bound to tell you that I think that the first volume of Böhm-Bawerk is a bit unfair on his predecessors. He doesn't give people the benefit of the doubt at any point, and after all, before the modern development of economics, people wrote rather loosely and took things for granted which we set out at boring length nowadays. And if you give some of the writers the credit for perceiving some of the things which eventually Böhm-Bawerk perceived, you get a rather different view of history. And I am bound to say that, although it is not nearly so extensive—it's sufficiently scholarly, but it's much shorter—I think the historical chapters of Cassel's *The Nature and Necessity of Interest* [1903], itself an important contribution to the subject, far fairer than Böhm-Bawerk.

So I'm not going to linger on that. But then his main contribution is volume 2, which is called *The Positive Theory of Capital* [1891]. And in its third edition, which he wrote when he had retired from being Austrian Minister of Finance and a great public figure and all that sort of thing—he was a universal chap, was Böhm-Bawerk—he wrote with twelve "excursions" replying to all sorts of criticisms, and those too are worth reading. But I'm not going to go into the excursions; I just want to give you the main outlines.

The Positive Theory of Capital is very extensive. There is a lot of talk about the capital concept at the beginning—the distinction between capital as a means of production and capital as a means of earning interest, and the question of whether you are to put consumption goods into the category of capital as a stock, or whether to leave them out, which he did. And he then goes on to deal with the theory of value à la Menger, making it much more vivid and precise than Menger, although not perhaps so philosophically profound. And it reproduces—and that's why I didn't recommend you to read the *Grundzüge*, which is in German in the London School of Economics series—he reproduces, more or less, with simplifications and elaborations, the Mengerian theory of value and his own theory of the pricing of the factors of production.

But eventually he screws himself up to the positive theory of capital and the rate of interest. And his general conception here is, I think, aesthetically marvellous. It's aesthetically marvellous because it fits into the Austrian theory and at the same time, the idiosyncrasies of the Austrian theory apart, it is a permanent analytical insight into this profoundly important problem.

The theory of the rate of interest, says Böhm-Bawerk, is essentially an explanation of the influences determining *exchange between present goods and future goods* [Böhm-Bawerk, 1891, pp. 237–48]. Now, one only has to enunciate that simple statement to realise what a profound and important perspective he had established. And you see it fits into the Austrian theory of dealing with all this central body of value and distribution problems, at any rate, within the theory of exchange and value.

Now, the question is—and he puts it this way, and this is a slight limitation of his view—of asking why the exchange, why the *agio*, as he calls it—the rate of exchange—is positive, why it tends to be in favour of the present. Now, as you know, there is no reason why, in certain circumstances, it shouldn't be the other way round, but perhaps Böhm-Bawerk could reply to that—that of course that was implicit in his mind, at any rate, although he did not deal with it in the foreground.

And then he gives his famous three grounds for a positive rate of interest. And he says, firstly, that in the present human environment present goods *are* more valuable than future goods, either because people have urgent need for them—are in distress of some sort—or because they entertain hopes of having more goods in the future and consequently being able to pay a positive rate of interest for the use of capital to obtain them [ibid., pp. 249–52].

And then his second ground is "deficient telescopic faculty—the systematic undervaluation of the future." I don't know who invented this phrase. I learned it from Hugh Dalton when I was a student here, and it may be that that stimulating and fertile mind (he was a great teacher, whatever you may think of him—he was Chancellor of the Exchequer later on in his life, trying to reduce the long-term rate of interest in a time of inflation from 3 percent to 2½ percent) invented the term *deficient telescopic faculty*, the systematic undervaluation of the future [ibid., pp. 253–59].

Now, there is a Russian economist—those of you who are devout Marxians will know his name; he was a very famous man—called Bukharin, who I deeply regret to say was done to death by Stalin. But Bukharin [1927] attacked Böhm-Bawerk on these first two grounds, and he explained it in terms of the environment. Böhm-Bawerk's *Positive Theory of Capital* was written in Vienna, and in the Vienna of those days, before the collapse of the Austro-Hungarian Empire, the prevalent atmosphere was high society—wine and women and display. And that explains the reliance on deficient telescopic faculty—the systematic undervaluation of the future and so on and so forth. I mention Bukharin. He was a brilliant man, insofar as his works have been translated into English, but he obviously was an entertaining person, and he had bright ideas even if rather superficial ones. I think this particular explanation of Böhm-Bawerk is pure nonsense, but it's an amusing nonsense. It lightens, so to speak, the systematic explanation, even at this level, of the rate of interest. But it's obviously not general. Even if there was a deficient telescopic faculty among the social group of Vienna, it did not explain the fact that through history the rate of interest in organised money markets has tended to be positive.

And then, returning to Böhm-Bawerk, he introduced what was at once a profound conception of the nature of advanced production and at the same time an oversimplification which made it slightly misleading. His third ground was the famous ground which has occupied so many articles in my middle age that I can't bear to think of the ones that I have left unread—the famous proposition, namely, that roundabout methods of production are more productive than direct methods of production [Böhm-Bawerk, 1891, pp. 260–72]. And I hasten to say that Böhm-Bawerk did not mean, as some people without a sense of humour have thought that he meant, that any roundabout method of production would be more productive—even the sort of methods of production that you used to get in my boyhood by a man called Heath Robinson, who, in order to explain the production of the simplest commodity, would erect a terrific apparatus of wheels and pulleys and indicators and so on, all of which was rather comic. But Böhm-Bawerk was quite clear with his proposition— and this wasn't what was wrong with it—that cleverly selected roundabout methods of production were more productive than direct methods of production.

Well now, some people have thought, and in my judgement not entirely without justification, that Böhm-Bawerk was really letting productivity in by the back door, having so to speak, with oaths and with curses turned any productivity theory out by the front door. He *denounced* it in the terrific passage of the first volume of *Capital and Interest* [1890, book 2]—page after page after page denouncing all productivity theories. Even he doesn't do justice to Jevons, who in many ways anticipated Böhm-Bawerk in this respect. But that's not, I think, a matter on which Böhm-Bawerk is open to final criticism. He may have thought, since he did describe the roundabout methods of capital-using production in greater vividness and with greater power than anybody had done before except Rae, that he'd got hold of a good idea—and he had.

It was when he started to talk about the average period of production, overall, that he became involved in theoretical traps. As those of you who know anything about advanced economic theory know, you do become involved in all sorts of theoretical traps as soon as you play about with averages. And certainly the average period of production hasn't stood up to criticism in recent years, and Professor Hayek, who used to be at the School of Economics, has wrote a book deeply influenced by Böhm-Bawerk [Hayek, 1931] in which, inter alia—it's a good book, although a frightfully difficult book to read—he shows that Böhm-Bawerk's conception of the average period of production, which he, Hayek, had begun by believing in, wouldn't altogether hold water and needed reformulation.

Well, Böhm-Bawerk's analysis was all very stimulating and, in its way, very profound. And it's much better stated, and in a much more stimulating way, by Knut Wicksell in the first volume of his principles [1934–35]. The first volume of his principles was translated here and appears in two volumes, the first of which deals with real economics and the second of which deals with monetary economics. And his original book, *Über Wert, Kapital und Rente* [1893], is also translated into English [Wicksell, 1954].

Wicksell has a beautiful simplification, and I'm not going to go into it, because you all ought to read Wicksell if you are self-respecting modern economists. He develops a theory of what he calls in German, *Kapitallose Produktion*—"production without capital"—and then he introduces the roundabout methods, and he shows how the time element which they necessarily involve contributes to the formation of the rate of interest. But Wicksell only managed to do this for circulating capital. He was one of the most candid men on earth, and he admitted that he had not ultimately solved the problem as regards fixed capital. And all sorts of people have messed about with the problem of fixed capital since then, including Hayek, and many people would say that there are approaches to the problem of fixed capital which modern theory hasn't solved.

I myself think that the first approximation, at any rate, is solved in that great work—the greatest work on *real* economics, as distinct from free economics and so on, to come out of America, at any rate, in the first fifty years of this century—Irving Fisher's *The Rate of Interest*, which was published in 1907. It was republished as *The Theory of Interest* in 1930, with alterations to meet various criticisms. And *The Theory of Interest* is incumbent on you all if you are taking your work seriously. And I think I have told you already that at a preternaturally young age Fisher had a very serious illness.[1] He was a most extraordinary person in many ways. He was an absolute crank as regards subjects of health: He didn't believe in the consumption of alcohol in any form, and he didn't believe in smoking. He was a brilliant writer; he wrote a book in favour of prohibition of all kinds of alcohol as a beverage, and he entitled it *Prohibition at Its Worst* [1926], so to *entice* people who believed in the anti-prohibition point of view into reading his book, which contained all sorts of statistics.

And he himself as a young man had a very serious illness, and he didn't believe in the consumption of alcohol in any form, and he didn't believe in smoking. I have been told of meetings of the American Economic Association [where Fisher attempted to enlist his professional colleagues in promoting his views]. These are meetings in which *trainloads* of Americans go to the skyscrapers in different capital cities of different states in the United States, and there you have learned papers read, and there is a sort of cattle market for junior economists being bid for by senior economists to improve their own departments. It does not work badly, you know. Let us not look down our noses at this system. There are two ways of looking at it, but it hasn't turned out awefully badly as regards the production of economists in the United States this century. [Well, in the 1920s, Fisher attempted to organise a panel at the American Economic Association meetings in which leading members of the profession would go on record as saying that prohibition was an *economic* blessing.][2]

Now, Fisher on capital. Let us start with his work by mentioning his *Mathematical Investigations in the Theory of Value and Prices* [1892], which anticipates the whole bag of tricks. He hadn't read Edgeworth, and long, long before Pareto he had got all modern stunts—indifference curves and integrability and non-integrability and so on and so forth. But that's modern economics and not history—at any rate germane to this literature.

He started by writing an article in 1896 on "Appreciation and Interest," and he deals with the relation between money rates of interest and real rates of interest. And then he published articles in the journals on the nature of capital and income,[3] and eventually he published this first part from this marvellous doctor's thesis—the best doctor's thesis in our subject—his *Nature of Capital and Income* [1906], summing up these articles, in which he distinguished between capital as essentially a stock of wealth, including, if you like, the potentialities of human beings, and income as a flow of ultimate experiences, in which he had been anticipated by Rae, to whom he paid ample tribute later on. And that in itself is a must book, especially for those of you who are interested in accountancy, because it really builds a bridge between accountancy and economic analysis.

But then comes *The Rate of Interest* [1907]. He follows Böhm-Bawerk in distinguishing the nature of the problem—an exchange between present income, so defined by him, and future income. And his theory is in a sense eclectic, but it's based in such a simple and convincing way that it stands on its own legs as *the* introduction to the modern theory of *real* interest (as distinct from all the monetary complications which we are not going into, in this lecture at any rate). And he starts [Fisher, 1907, chaps. 6, 7, and Appendix to chap. 7] with the subjective side—time preference—and in the simplest geometrical way. He takes these symbols of next year's income and this year's income, and you can imagine any point there indicating the combination of next year's income and this year's income. And thence you can imagine an indifference curve drawn connecting up different alternatives of time preference as regards this year and next year. And then, supposing the rate of interest is given, you can draw a straight line which is tangent to the indifference curve, and the angular difference of this from forty-five degrees, which is *equal* time preference between next year and this year, measures the actual rate of interest, whether positive or negative.

And then he goes on and he imagines that the individual will adjust—given the rate of interest prevailing and his income this year—his distribution of income between this year and next year according to his indifference system in this respect. But now he imagines—and again we have measuring [inaudible words]—an exchange between this year's income and next year's income, taking into account the rate of return over cost, which can be positive or negative, as the case may be. If there is an opportunity for investment, then the rate of return over cost will be positive, and, consequently, the individual, having regard to the rate of return in the capital market over cost, will have to take that into account in adjusting his time preference to it.

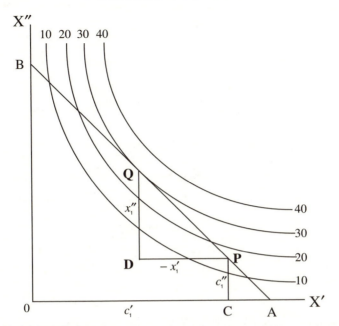

Figure 10. Fisher's Rate of Interest. *Source:* Fisher, 1907, p. 387.

Well, you can extend this geometrically, as my dear friend von Hayek does at very great length in this extremely difficult book of his [Hayek, 1931] and with very great ingenuity. And this is Fisher's "second approximation" to the rate of interest,[4] and of course he doesn't confine himself to geometrical representation. He goes on with the chaste use of mathematics. (The great mathematical economists, you know, always use mathematics rather chastely. They don't end up with conclusions which can't be put into economic terms.) And he extends this with many years ahead instead of exchange between two years, which permit of geometrical representation.

And then in the "third approximation" [chap. 11], he deals with risk and the different rates of interest which different degrees of risk involve. And so if any of you encounter, as I have encountered, someone who argues that before the last twenty years there was no treatment of capital markets in regard to the subjective reaction to risk in people of different temperaments and in different parts of the world, you can not only refer them back to Rae, which will perhaps show you to be just a bit of a pedant, flaunting your own expertise in the history of thought, but you can refer them to so obvious and widely read a book as Fisher's *Rate of Interest.*

Well, I hope that I've said enough to stimulate your dipping into Fisher at any rate. I know that you don't like me to recommend the reading of whole books.

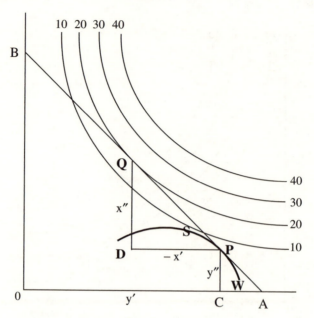

Figure 11. Fisher's Exchange between Present and Future Income.
Source: Fisher, 1907, p. 409.

Well, that's all I have to say about the theory of interest. In my next lecture we will deal with Walras and the school of Lausanne, and in the lecture after that with Marshall.

NOTES

1. The illness was tuberculosis.
2. In the lecture, Robbins launched into his general characterization of the American Economic Association meetings in midsentence and never returned to indicate the link between Fisher and these meetings. Professor William Barber has provided us with the Fisher story that Robbins likely intended to tell, and that we have inserted here.
3. See Fisher (1896b, 1897a,b, 1904).
4. See Fisher (1907, chap. 8 and appendix to chap. 8).

Walras—Pareto

NOW, at last, in discussing the marginal revolution, so called, I reach the subject of Walras. He lived from 1834 to 1910, and he was Professor at Lausanne until 1892. I'll say a few words about him later on, but unlike Menger, whose original contributions sprang from nowhere, so to speak—all that we know is that he read the standard German texts, but he doesn't mention von Thünen and he didn't know about Gossen—Walras had a rather distinguished ancestry. As regards Jevons, there is no doubt about Jevons' originality, but Jevons was more of a classical economist, outside the theory of value and capital, than he knew. But Walras goes back. There was always in France a tendency to take utility rather more seriously than the English classical school, who, following Adam Smith's lead, emphasised the so-called paradox of value. I don't know any method of tracing this history. I can only mention conspicuous names.

The first name is the name of Galiani, an Italian who spent a great deal of his time as a representative—I think it was to the Neapolitan Government—in Paris in the middle of the eighteenth century, mixed with intellectuals there a good deal, and who wrote a famous critique of the physiocrats—an essay on the theory of corn (grain, as he called it) [1770].[1] And in 1750 Galiani published a work on money [Galiani, 1751]. His essay on the theory of grains was considerably later than that and while it contains very interesting and well-written controversial points, it is not connected, I think, with the main history of economic theory. But Galiani's *Della Moneta* [1751] certainly got pretty near a utility theory of value which would stand up to criticism. And it's never been translated that I know of, but there is a French version of the important parts, published in our own day by Professor Bousquet, under the title *De la Monnaie*.

Well, there was Galiani, and then later on in the eighteenth century—did I give you Galiani's dates? It was 1728 to '87—Abbé de Condillac, who lived from 1714 to 1780, and who wrote notable books on philosophy and psychology, and published, in the same year as Adam Smith's *Wealth of Nations*, a *splendid* book, *Le commerce et le gouvernement* [1776]—"Commerce and Government." And for specialists—I don't say undergraduates—it's certainly worth reading. He was really a noted intellectual. And he wrote beautifully, and his argument develops in a truly French logical style. The whole thing is a pleasure to read. And he also dwelt upon utility and value but didn't quite get to the point.

And then there was Leon Walras' father, Auguste, who was, by way of being, a teacher of economics, and he lived from 1801 to 1866. And he wrote books which were entirely neglected, of which the most famous has been reprinted in our own day, with an introduction by Professor Le Duc. The most famous is *De la nature de la richesse* in 1831. And he got nearest of all to a utility theory of value, and he exhorted his son to continue the advancement of his interests. Well there you are. I don't recommend you to read Auguste Walras' book, which is estimable but I don't think frightfully distinguished. It is not as distinguished as Galiani or Condillac, who I certainly think is one of the important eighteenth-century writers.

Well now, Leon Walras—the subject of this lecture. He had a highly eccentric youth but I'll not attempt any account of it. Professor Jaffé, who has devoted his life of *supreme* scholarship to the work of Walras, has translated the main book of Walras, his *Elements of Pure Economics* [1874a; 1954], which is much more intelligible than the French, with all sorts of translator's notes and elucidations of obscure passages. I don't often recommend you to read translations when the original is accessible in French, but certainly, if you want to have a look at Walras' book, you should take Jaffé's translation. He has also devoted years to collecting Walras' correspondence with various eminent people. It's published by a Dutch firm. The Royal Economic Society had to be exhorted to make a contribution to this highly esoteric compilation. It's three volumes as thick as that and as tall as that, beautifully printed, with appropriate annotations to each letter. And Professor Jaffé is now devoting the declining years of his life, which I hope goes on, to writing a biography of Walras. And the early part of it, I fancy, will be rather piquant—nothing to do with economics.[2]

But eventually, on the strength of a paper which he read to a Swiss society on taxation, he was appointed a Professor at Lausanne in 1870, which Chair he held until 1892, when he handed it over to a scarcely less famous man—although I don't place him on the same plane as Walras—namely, Vilfredo Pareto, about whom I'll have a word to say in this lecture.

Walras is at once a pathetic, an admirable and a not frightfully likeable character. He was pathetic because with his great intellectual excellence, he was not recognised in France at all, and he never could get a Chair in France. He went to live at Lausanne, which was rather a nice place to live at. He was recognised in this country. He sent an offprint of his article [1874b] in 1874 to Jevons, who at once wrote to him a very handsome letter inquiring whether he—Walras—knew of Jevons' paper to the British Association 1862 and its publication in the *Journal of the Royal Statistical Society* in 1866, and whether he knew of Jevons' *Theory of Political Economy*, in which case, if he didn't, he—Jevons—would be pleased to send him a copy. And Walras replied in a very candid and admirable letter, acknowledging Jevons' slight priority in publication and explaining how his own ideas had developed, especially under the influence of his father, Auguste, and suggesting that he—Walras—should write some notice bringing Jevons to the attention of the French public.

This was before the bitterness had developed. He remained on good terms with Jevons. He eventually developed an animus against the British.

This I mentioned when I was dealing with the pricing of factor services, and I alluded to the *explosion* of wrath on the part of Walras, who thought that Wicksteed should have sent him a copy of his privately circulated memorandum, and that he should have acknowledged the hints that he had presumably got from Walras. And he wrote an absolutely disgraceful appendix to the third edition of his *Elements*, in which he accused Wicksteed of plagiarism, which anybody who knew of Wicksteed—in the senior generation in my young days, everyone knew him and respected him very much—knew he was quite incapable of. And indeed, if you read Wicksteed's writing, he is always careful to acknowledge his debts—unnecessary debts in some respects.

But Walras, by this time, had accumulated a store of grievances against Edgeworth, who had not, for not very intelligible reasons, printed a review by the Italian, Barone—a very *good* review—of Wicksteed's *Co-ordination of the Laws of Distribution*.[3] It is suspected that this was under the influence of Marshall, who was very choosy and very peculiar in regard to a good many other economists. No one can say that Marshall was not acquainted with them, unlike Pigou, who read all sorts of things, but who didn't read the history of economic thought, and who actually more or less boasted of it. He was sent a book by the *Economic Journal* on the history of the theory of value, and he said he had so much difficulty in keeping apace with contemporary economics that he didn't want to know about the theories of dead men—which explains quite a lot which happened in Cambridge in the '10s and '20s, before the fashion changed again.

Well, I think I have said enough to say that Walras was a peculiar man. But he certainly, as the compilation by Jaffé of the letters shows, hadn't anything to complain about of recognition elsewhere. The British had read him; the Americans read him; the Italians read him; the Dutch read him. These letters are absorbingly interesting to read on tiny little points, and on the general campaign which Walras initiated for the treatment of pure economics by mathematical form.

Well now, Walras is bracketed with Jevons and Menger for having discovered, independently, the connection of marginal utility with value. Walras does not use the term *marginal utility* any more than Menger did. Menger talked about the least dependent use, and Walras talks about rarity (in French—it's never been adopted elsewhere). But the reason I didn't deal with Walras when I was talking about value—Jevons and Menger—was that, although Walras deserves full credit for thinking this out for himself (because he did solve the problem which had not been solved by Galiani or by Condillac or by his father—he *did* make explicit the marginal element), Walras is important for more than that. He's important for having propounded a *complete system* of more or less statical economics, the nature of which I shall proceed to unfold. And although this was not generally recognised—his correspondence was with a select few, although widely spread—it has in our own time been taken up. And Schumpeter, whose opinion I don't agree with because Walras has been right at the top of those who have propounded a system of pure economics, ascribes primary importance to Walras' development of the marginal utility concept [Schumpeter, 1956, p. 77]. But this is a personal question and I'm not going to argue it. He is much more important for his system than he is for having discovered the significance of declining marginal utility.

Well, his book begins [Walras, 1954, preface and part 1, pp. 35–80] with a disentanglement of pure and applied economics, and I ought to say—because I am not going to say anything about it at all—that it is a mistake to regard him as limited to pure economics. There are two books of essays on applied economics and on public economics, but they have perhaps never received the attention that they deserve. Professor Hutchison, in his interesting chapter on Walras [1953, chap. 13], mentions them and summarises the chief purport of Walras' political opinions and attitude toward applied economics. But that's not my subject today. His book on pure economics disentangles pure and applied economics and all that. I think that we can take that as read.

Then he goes on to emphasise that pure economics must be mathematical—just as Jevons had done, but more vividly. And he pays tribute to Cournot, whose book he had read. But Cournot's book, which is mainly partial equilibrium analysis, starts, as I told you, from monopoly and then widens out to pure competition, whereas Walras, throughout his book, deals with purely competitive conditions.

And then, after these preliminaries, he plunges into analysis. And it is very significant that he begins with an elucidation, algebraic and geometrical, of the laws of supply and demand [Walras, 1954, part 2, lessons 5, 6, pp. 83–106]. He exhibits supply and demand as functions of price. He draws them geometrically, and he has differential equations to go on to develop them. The only thing that it need be said—and I don't think that with such an intelligent audience I need draw them on the board—is that you should always remember that a good many continental economists adopt the reverse labelling of the axes. With the English-speaking world, variations of price are measured on the vertical axis and quantity on the horizontal axis. But Walras measures quantity on the vertical axis and price on the horizontal axis. It doesn't make the slightest difference to the logic, but it's a bit puzzling if you don't realise that that is what he's up to.

The only thing that I think that I need to mention in connection with his elucidation, at considerable length, of the laws of supply and demand, is that, quite independently of Marshall, he did indicate that there might be more than one point of stable equilibrium. You all know the picture, don't you, in which a supply curve cuts a demand curve from downwards—that's all right—and then it cuts it from upwards—and that is an unstable position—and then it turns round again and cuts it from down below—and that's another position of equilibrium. That is regarded in a good many of the textbooks as a refinement. It has been the subject, in an elaborate way, of investigations by modern economists on whether the total system of Walrasian equations is determinate or not. But that, I think, is modern theory.

After having dealt with supply and demand, he deals with the market [ibid., part 2, lessons 6, 7, pp. 92–114]. And he abstracts from error, and he imagines a gathering in which people are gathered together and, in Gallic fashion, so to speak, they *cry aloud* the prices that they are prepared to buy and sell at. Now, Edgeworth, who had so many piercing insights and really was a considerable economist, makes great to-do about Walras' imperfect description of perfect competition. And Edgeworth, whose construction I alluded to a lecture or two ago, had a very elaborate description of the conditions of the perfect market, and among these conditions was the possibility of re-contract. I always think that there is a slight sociological joke to be made about this. Edgeworth was considering a market frequented by rather dull and perhaps well-behaved people, who went round quietly inquiring what prices their vis-à-vis would be prepared to do business at. But they didn't finalise the contract. They went around and inquired all round the market, and then, when the process of re-contract had been finished, you had a determinate price. Well, I don't see, really, from the commonsense point of view, a pennyworth of difference, except national habits, between the Walrasian market and the Edgeworthian market.

Well, then he goes on—and this is interesting—to derive his demand curves from marginal utility [ibid., part 2, lesson 8, pp. 115–31]. There is a long discussion of extensive and intensive utility, and then he lays it down that as quantity increases utility falls.

And then he proceeds to exchange [ibid., part 2, lessons 9, 10, pp. 132–49], and he formulates what Wieser [1893] calls Gossen's second law—namely, that exchange will continue until the marginal significance to each participant in the market is proportionate to price. Not that there is some sort of collective jelling of utility in the market. The utility is an entirely individual matter; it is just the order in which the different commodities are ranked on the subjective scales, to use Austrian terminology. So that he has reached the point which Jevons reached in his chapter on the theory of exchange, although Jevons, unlike Walras, did not completely realise that, unless he had made the conditions of pure competition completely rigid, as Edgeworth did, and as I think that Walras intended to do, his equation of exchange left price indeterminate between certain limits.

Well, all that is in the paper which Walras [1874b] forwarded to Jevons, which was published slightly after Jevons' *Theory of Political Economy*. In the first edition of the *Élements*—*Éléments d'économie politique pure*—which was published in 1874, he extends this analysis in subsequent lessons. His chapters are headed lessons 1, 2, 3, up to 40 or so. He extends this analysis, still on the plane of commodity value, to many commodities [Walras, 1954, part 3, pp. 151–207], and he makes demand a function, not only of the price of one commodity, but of the prices of all the commodities which come within his range of valuation.

And that characteristic of making the demand function multiple, in that sense, is characteristic of the followers of Walras—the so-called school of Lausanne. And they are always bellyaching about the English-speaking economists—especially Marshall—who focused on partial equilibrium analysis instead of going the whole hog and going to general equilibrium analysis. And they were their own worst enemies in that respect. It certainly is an intellectual step forward to realise that there is this multiple functional dependency, but no one who has ever attacked particular problems has tried to make demand a function of n commodities. If he has tried to go outside the commodity market particularly in question, and of course many people have done that, then the n commodities—this is a favourite device of John Hicks—are amalgamated into one commodity, so that you simply have two commodities to deal with.

The thing is theoretically interesting, but certainly Marshall, who knew all about this, as I shall explain tomorrow, brushed it aside. Marshall wanted to get down to something which explained the real world, and although the Walrasian system does in a sense pose, in their simplest form, certain problems of the real world, it is, I would say—and this is my judgement; others might take a different view—the emphasis all the time on general equilibrium that cut Walras and his followers off from the rest of the professional economists, for the most part, and it was to the *detriment* of both groups.

But the Walrasian system does not stop here. He then extends his analysis to production [ibid., part 4, pp. 209–63], and this is what all the row was about. In the first two editions of his *Élements*, he dealt with the pricing of productive services on the assumption of what we should call fixed technical coefficients. That is to say, the production of any one commodity involves the combination in fixed ratios of the factor services concerned. And so, in order that you may get a determinate system of factor service prices, the adjustment has to take place via the incentive of the profitability of producing the ultimate consumer's goods. And unless all the ratios are the same, in which case the problem of pricing would be indeterminate, there are some reasons for supposing that—in any case in certain conditions—the device of varying fixed technical coefficients will get you somewhere. And then, having dealt with that, and in the third edition having reproached Wicksteed for having inferred what was only implicit in his system in the first editions, he introduced, explicitly, variable technical coefficients. And marginal productivity therefore came into his third and final system [ibid., part 8, lesson 36, pp. 382–92].

And not content with that, he went on to deal—you'll notice that I have cribbed from Walras in the order in which I have developed the last few lectures—he then went on to capital value outright—the problem of capitalisation [ibid., part 5, pp. 265–312]. His treatment there was subject to some criticism by Wicksell, who felt that he dealt only with fixed capital. Various attempts have been made to show that Wicksell was not entirely correct in the criticism that he made, and Wicksell finally admitted that there was more in Walras than that. But I am far from thinking that the Walrasian theory of capitalisation is really a satisfactory one.

But then, finally, he turns to money [ibid., part 6, pp. 313–74]. And there, in the early editions of his work, he just postulated that money was a unit of account in which prices could be expressed. But eventually, in a separate paper, and then in subsequent editions of the *Élements,* he developed the idea of the "desire balance," the *encaisse désirée* [ibid., part 6, lesson 29, p. 321]. And he developed the idea, independently of all who preceded him, of the Cambridge approach to the quantity theory of money—the Cambridge approach of the '20s.

Well, you can see why I left Walras until the end. His fame rests on the amplitude of his conception, on the completeness of his system, whether in detail he was right or wrong as regards a statical system. Jevons didn't do that. Menger didn't do that. Walras did do that, and in the '30s of this century his systematic treatment came into much greater vogue.

Now, Walras founded a school, of whom the most famous was Vilfredo Pareto, who succeeded him in the Chair at Lausanne, who lived from 1848 to 1923, and who published a *Cours* [1896–97]—(A very rare book this. Any of you pick it up? Don't sell it.)—in 1896, which is compounded of the system that he had inherited from Walras, plus a little bit of his own terminology. And then in 1906 there appeared in Italian, and in 1909 there appeared in French, a *Manual of Political Economy* [Pareto, 1927], which I gather has in the United States been translated into English [Pareto, 1971], but Professor Jaffé [1972] reviewed it in such a critical way that I myself haven't looked at it. He thinks that they haven't got the translation right and that all sorts of nuances are upset.

Well now, Pareto was the leader of the school of Lausanne after Walras had given up his solitary Chair. And Pareto made a much greater noise during his lifetime than Walras. Pareto was essentially Walrasian. He eliminated certain elements of Walrasian analysis which he thought to be unnecessary. In the end, learning from Edgeworth, he introduced indifference curves. Really don't forget that it was Edgeworth who introduced indifference curves—it was not Pareto. He claimed that in that way he was eliminating any talk of the subjective factor; he could deal with indifference curves as deriving from observation. God knows what observations you would have to make in order to find any large set of indifference curves. He also repudiated the idea of measurable utility. The choices which the indifference curves denoted were, in his opinion, not cardinal choices, but ordinal. They could be arranged in an order, but you could not attach an exact numerical value to them.

Pareto also invented a new word in the course of his elimination of utility. He thought utility carried with it certain tinges of psychological doctrines which he repudiated, and consequently he suggested the word "ophelimity," which is a completely neutral word and which hasn't been used much since. If you come across it, you can simply regard it as Pareto's name for what is usually in the textbooks called utility, although you ought to follow explanations that "utility" begs all sorts of questions.

Pareto of course is also famous for an excursion into applied economics which is still under discussion—Pareto's curve. Some people actually called it Pareto's Law, such that if you arrange the numbers of the population and the recipients of income, and you turn these into logarithms, then you get a curve which is remarkably stable as between different communities, at any rate in the middle regions. But God forbid that I should get involved in the controversy which still goes on there.

There were minor members of the school of Lausanne, whose works are much easier to read than either Pareto or Walras. On Walras the best is by a man called Antonelli, *Économie pure* [1914]—it's in French. And then there are several books written after Pareto's book had appeared, the best of which is by Zawadzki [1914]—not the present Professor, but I suppose some relative of the present Professor—which was published in 1914, and by a man called Osorio [1913], a Portugese mathematician. And there are many others. I was looking at half a shelf of them before I came away from home this morning. They all follow more or less the same plan. They demonstrate at great length the argument that economics must be mathematical. They then give a certain amount of history—at any rate the post-Paretian ones—a certain amount of history of earlier attempts at mathematical economics. And then they go on to explain the Walrasian system, and then the modifications that Pareto introduced into it.

Well, I see my time is up. I am quite sure that devout Paretians would think that I haven't given enough time to Pareto, but I propose tomorrow to leave the marginal revolutionaries, who said that they had stood the classical economists on their heads—which in a sense they had—and get into Marshall, who, while knowing all these tricks, detected much more of a continuity.

NOTES

1. Galiani, *Dialogues sur le commerce des blés* (1770), translated as *Dialogues on the Grain Trade*.

2. This biography was never completed.

3. As Robbins (1970, p. 196 at n.1) has noted, this review by Barone "at once corrected imperfections in Wicksteed and gave due credit to Walras for the way in which he had posed the problem" of marginal productivity.

Marshall

ACCORDING to my reckoning we are getting to the end of these lectures. There is another lecture on Wednesday, when I shall deal with the semi-modern development of monetary theory and fluctuations, but today I want to deal with Alfred Marshall.

Now, all the other leading participants in the so-called marginal revolution were very unkind to classical political economy as developed from Hume and Adam Smith and the nineteenth-century people. Their complaints were of various degrees of plausibility. Jevons was opposed to that wrong-headed man [i.e., Smith] and his equally wrong-headed disciple, John Stuart Mill, but this was, after all, only in regard to the elementary theory of value, and, to some extent, capital, although he didn't make any allusion in that respect. As regards wages, the cost of production and rent, Jevons, although much more vivid than many of the classical economists—not more than Adam Smith or Ricardo—was more or less classical. Menger refers deferentially to Adam Smith from time to time in his writings, but in spite of his immense library he obviously hadn't read very much of the classical literature. And as regards the central doctrine of Adam Smith's theory of production—that the co-ordination of the economy and its division of labour took place through the market and was not, in that sense, consciously planned—Menger was positively wrong. He goes out of his way to blame Adam Smith for that. I thought I had discovered that myself, but I notice, looking at Hutchison's [1973] contribution to a very useful book on Menger, edited by Sir John Hicks and one of the Austrian economists, he makes the same point. Walras certainly didn't know very much about classical political economy as it developed in this country, and he certainly thought that his theory dispensed with all that.

But now we come to Marshall, who emphasised much greater continuity. And perhaps it might be said that he was excessively *modest* about his own contribution, which was pretty considerable. Now, there is a very good paper on Marshall which is reproduced in Gherity's [1965] collection of essays, and which appeared in the *Economic Journal* for the centenary of Marshall's birth, by Shove [1942]—Gerald Shove—who was one of the most distinguished of the generation of Cambridge economists after Pigou: Shove, Robertson and, last but not least, Keynes, who was, so to speak, in between Robertson and Shove—and Lavington, whom I shall mention next time.

Well, I don't know how many of you have read Marshall. I am not sure to what extent I shall bore you in devoting a whole lecture chiefly to his *Principles*. But he is an important figure. As regards the history of economic thought since the eighteenth century, it is really a case of Adam Smith—Ricardo—John Stuart Mill—Marshall. And he had, for many years, a tremendous influence in the English-speaking world. Whether that influence was entirely for the good is a question I shall discuss a little later on.

Now, I won't give you details of his life. He was born in 1842 and died in 1924. He had a very sedate academic life. He was a brilliant mathematician at Cambridge and then taught in a modest way. He went to be head of Bristol University, then shifted to Oxford for a brief period, and was appointed Professor at Cambridge, which post he held until he retired in favour of Pigou.

And his chief works are as follows. First, the chapters in the *Pure Theory of Foreign Trade—The Pure Theory of Domestic Values* [1879], which are reprinted by the London School of Economics. And then there was a book which he wrote with his wife, Mary Marshall, to whom he owed so much of the tranquility of his career and the worship by which he was surrounded, *The Economics of Industry* in 1879 [Marshall and Marshall, 1881]. And in the end—this is the shabby side of Marshall—he was rather ashamed of it and more or less repudiated it, which was very ungallant. And it is in fact an extremely good representative of the most advanced economic thought of its day. True, it was superseded by the *Principles*—if I had time I could tell you the stories about this repudiation, but I'll restrain myself.

After the publication of that, he worked away at *Principles*, and published them in 1890. And they ran into eight editions during his lifetime, and, since then—and those of you who are graduates would be recommended to *consult* it (I don't say to buy, because it's rather expensive)—the two-volume Variorum edition [1961] of the *Principles*, which is edited by Mr Guillebaud, now recently defunct. But the good thing about Guillebaud's edition is that, owing to the skill of Macmillan's, the pagination is the same as the eighth edition, and volume 2 is devoted to Guillebaud's reproduction of the variations and comments from various angles on Marshall's slight changes of view and the things that he left out. Guillebaud was well qualified to do this; he was actually Marshall's nephew.

And then, confusingly enough, in 1892 Marshall published a book called the *Economics of Industry*, which is the same title as the title of the book that he wrote with Mary Marshall. But it's entirely different. The book that he wrote with Mary Marshall is rather exciting to read, and the *Economics of Industry*, which is a boiled-down, allegedly popular version of the *Principles*, is terribly dry reading. Marshall hadn't got the capacity for a popular boil-down, and I don't recommend you to read it at all, *except* that it does contain one chapter which is not in the *Principles*—namely, Marshall's thoughts about trade unionism and its effect on distribution.

And that is the locus classicus of the Cambridge treatment of that very important subject, and it is by far the most interesting and brightest chapter in the book.

Well then, poor old Marshall laboured on, and, in 1919, having read widely and corresponded with all sorts of people and taken part in the Royal Commission on Labour and so on, he produced the second volume of his great work dealing with economics, *Industry and Trade* [1923], which I think is still worth reading. It's true that Keynes says in his remarkable essay on Marshall [1933/1972, pp. 161–231] that it deals with the state of industry about the early twentieth century. To some extent it was out of date when it was published, in its realistic details. But it is, I venture to say, a good book, and a good many contemporary courses on applied economics would be gingered up in excellence if those who gave the courses had some reference to Marshall's opinions from time to time.

And finally, when he was old and doddery, in 1923, he published a book called *Money, Credit, and Commerce*. And that is a very varied book. It contains a reproduction of his almost pathbreaking treatment of international trade, published originally at Sidgwick's suggestion in 1879, because private copies of it were being shown around, and Sidgwick thought that Marshall might not get the credit for his ingenious apparatus of curves and all that he said about it. Part of *Money, Credit, and Commerce* contains a reproduction of the early work, largely in the Appendix, and part of it consists of rather banal platitudes—the sort of thing that you would expect a man of Marshall's age to give utterance to if he was going downhill—and in my opinion is not worth reading at all.

And then when he was dead, his *Official Papers* [1926] were published by the Royal Economic Society, and they contain some of the most important things that he ever wrote on applied economics: on money, Indian finance and—this is a value judgement—what I should think the good sense of international trade policy.

In the last few years, Professor Whitaker, who used to be at Bristol, has raked through the early Marshall writings at the Marshall Library and has published a book called *The Early Economic Writings of Alfred Marshall* [Marshall, 1975], which is worthwhile reading for those of you who are going to be professional economists or those of you who are doing doctors' theses and so on. It throws some light on Marshall's own recollection of the dates when he thought out on his own marginal utility theory and all that, but I don't think that it's essential reading.

Shove, in this essay in the *Economic Journal* in 1942, says quite bluntly that the origin of Marshall's *Principles* was the translation of Ricardo and Mill into algebra and geometry. I don't think there is any doubt at all that Shove is *right*, that the chief inspirations were Ricardo and Mill, and of course, in the background, Adam Smith. Marshall himself in the eighth edition continues to pay tribute to Cournot and von Thünen. For some reason which I don't understand, he left Dupuit out, probably not wishing to load a book which he intended for grown-up reading on the part of laymen with too many footnotes.

Also, when you are thinking about his origins you must remember that Marshall, although he didn't agree with them completely, was in some sense *terrified* of the German historical school. All sorts of dull places in the *Principles* are qualifications put *in* lest he should be attacked by members of the German historical school. He was attacked, as I think that I told you, by Cunningham [1892], and was so aroused that he actually replied [Marshall, 1892b]—usually he did not reply to criticism, unfortunately— and he got much the better of it.

Marshall was an all-rounder. I am going to talk mostly about his contributions to pure economic analysis, but Marshall was himself a talented economic historian. He was immensely interested in economic development, and he even went so far as to say in the preface to his *Principles* that "The Mecca of the economist"—I'm quoting—"lies in economic biology rather than in economic dynamics" [Marshall, 1920/1961, p. xiv].

Well now, let me first of all deal very briefly with certain misapprehensions of his system. It used to be said that his system was a synthesis of the classical economics and the modern. And in a sense that's analytically correct, but historically I think it is true that Marshall's claims, however inaccurate Whitaker may have shown them to be, to have thought out his characteristic contributions to other than the classical heritage which he borrowed from Ricardo, was original.

But of course, analytically, his work—and this is where I begin, so to speak—is much more than a synthesis of his contemporaries and the classicals. He contributed in his own way, which was masterly, extremely important principles: the principle of substitution, which he certainly developed independently of Menger and applied in a way that Menger didn't need to apply in his unpublished volumes; the elasticity of demand—you can discover in the dark abyss of time anticipations of elasticity, but *measurement* of elasticity, that is Marshall; period analysis, which we shall come to; and external and internal economies and the working out of the theory of the firm. All these are to be found in Marshall's *Principles*; all these, there is every reason to suppose, originated in the course of his thinking. And of course outside the *Principles*, there are important contributions to the theory of money, the theory of international trade, not to mention very important observations on industrial organisation and so on and so forth in *Industry and Trade*.

The second misapprehension is one which I find peculiarly irritating. The School of Lausanne, to whom I devoted yesterday's lecture, are always spluttering about the restriction of the British School under the influence of Marshall to partial equilibrium analysis. *Nonsense*! If you look at Marshall's "Mathematical Appendix" [ibid., pp. 838–58], you can see that he understood perfectly well the generalisations which Walras and his school were elaborating. But as a trained mathematician, he felt that there were more important things for him to do, and insofar as he was interested in applied economics, well, partial equilibrium was obviously the instrument to hand. But how *anybody* who had read chapters 1 and 2 of book 6 of Marshall, which takes a broad view of the economic system, as foreshadowed in book 5 and books 3 and 4, could arrive at such a misapprehension beats my understanding. I think the Lausanne School did themselves harm by insisting that they, and they only, were the proprietors of general equilibrium analysis. It was a pity. We should have been spared a great many misunderstandings if there had been mutual understanding between the early modern writers on this subject up to my boyhood.

Why was Marshall so much less formal than the School of Lausanne? I won't dwell on his attitude to the Austrian School, which perhaps was temperamental, and to some extent, as regards Wieser and Böhm-Bawerk, doctrinal. At any rate, Marshall's rather ambiguous temperament developed an irritation when his work was represented as deriving from theirs. But he was *less formal* than the others for various reasons which I think are worth dwelling on. I am assuming in this very elusive lecture, that you all—undergraduates as well as graduates—will *read*, at any rate, the main parts of Marshall. You're not much of an economist if you don't.

Well first of all, there is a rather ambiguous reason. He wanted to be read. He wanted to be read just as Adam Smith was read—by people of good general education. And I used to belong to the Reform Club, which has a very famous library which was intitiated by Francis Place, whose name some of you may have heard of. And the economics section of the Reform Club library did pretty good on the pamphlet literature and on the nineteenth-century literature in general, but it stops, roughly speaking, with Marshall. Economics, as it developed in the nineteenth century, was *not* a subject which was a part of the obligatory reading of a well-educated gentleman. And Marshall wanted to get to the well-educated gentleman as well as professional economists, of whom there were very few in his time. And so he tended to put his assumptions and his qualifications in footnotes and in the appendix. And speaking as one who began to study economics in the early 1920s, or a little before then, and was enormously confused by the controversies of the day, and at that time enormously irritated by friends at Cambridge who said, "It's all in Marshall," I have now come to the conclusion that *it is* mostly in Marshall. But how much intellectual agony and bloody sweat one would have been spared if Marshall had been just a little more explicitly formal.

Well, that was the ambiguous reason. The second reason is that he thought that stationary equilibrium, which is what his contemporaries were elucidating for the most part, was too easy. And he was interested not in these—for him, a mathematics wrangler at Cambridge—comparatively easy differential equations, which gave a complete system of stationary equilibrium; he was interested in change, and an economic system which was in process of change. And he says in his Appendix: "It would be possible"—and he obviously has Walras in mind, although he didn't like provoking controversy and didn't mention many of his contemporaries—"It would be possible to extend the scope of such systems of equations"—that is the "Mathematical Appendix" in the *Principles*—"and to increase their detail, until they embraced within themselves the whole of the demand side of the problem of distribution." Notice the careful qualification: not the supply side of distribution—he didn't believe in that at all.

> But while a mathematical illustration of the mode of action of a definite set of causes may be complete in itself, and strictly accurate within its clearly defined limits, it is otherwise with any attempt to grasp the whole of a complex problem of real life, or even any considerable part of it, in a series of equations. For many important considerations, especially those connected with the manifold influences of the element of time, do not lend themselves easily to mathematical expression: they must either be omitted altogether, or clipped and pruned till they resemble the conventional birds and animals of decorative art. And hence arises a tendency towards assigning wrong proportions to economic forces; those elements being most emphasized which lend themselves most easily to analytical methods. [ibid., p. 850]

That is on page 850 of the eighth edition—or Guillebaud's volume 1—of the *Principles*. Now, in my extreme old age, I agree with Marshall, and in consequence I dare say that my name will be mud with all sorts of much more eminent contemporaries than I pretend to be. But I do see his point.

Thirdly, he wanted realistic applications of his theories. And here there is a definite proof of the fact that he *ignored* complications which have been made an awful lot of since. He says: "Prof. Edgeworth's plan of representing U and V"—the utility of the two commodities—"as general functions of x and y has great attractions to the mathematician" [ibid., p. 845]. Walras only regarded his equations as functions of price—the prices of different articles which were available in the market. It was Pareto who made utility depend upon your possession of the different articles. But it was Edgeworth who invented it, and Marshall says that "Edgeworth's plan . . . has great attractions to the mathematician; but it seems less adapted to express the every-day facts of economic life than that of regarding, as Jevons did, the marginal utilities of apples as functions of x simply" [ibid.]. Marshall *wanted* to see statistical applications of his theory of demand. Whether he was right or wrong in that particular respect is an open question, but Marshall was impatient with the theoretical refinements which would prevent him getting down to rough quantitative approximations.

Well now, for the content. I will go very rapidly here, because I assume that you have read them.

The first part of book 5 [ibid., pp. 323ff.], which deals, incidentally, with partial equilibrium analysis, deals with market value—the exchange of given stocks of commodities, having regard, of course, to the utility of the stock possessors as well as their prospective utilities to buyers. Marshall deals with barter in an Appendix [ibid., appendix F, pp. 791–93]. And instead of the complicated recontract arrangement for markets of Edgeworth, or Walras' auction, Marshall adopts a mathematical trick which is perfectly satisfactory for his point of view. He assumes, when he's discussing the formation of the price of a particular commodity, that as a first approximation the marginal utility of money income—he calls it the marginal utility of money, but that's confusing—is constant [ibid., pp. 334–36]. Now, as those of you who have done any geometrical economics know, that if you assume the marginal utility of money to be constant, then the contract curve—to use Edgeworthian terminology—degenerates into a straight line parallel with the money axis, and, whatever the initial moves in the market, the eventual price is determinate.

He goes out of his way to say that the assumption that the marginal utility of income is constant does not apply in the theory of distribution, and he particularly, in his theory of wages, bases his theory, whether rightly or wrongly, on the assumption that the marginal utility of money is *not* constant for one side of the labour market. There are some very interesting early articles by Sir John Hicks on that matter—both the early chapters in his *Theory of Wages* [1932] and other articles in the journals. Marshall's theory of consumer surplus depends upon the assumption that marginal utility of income is constant, and if you assume variations in the marginal utility of income, then you need a more complicated theory of consumer surplus—a matter which again has been elucidated chiefly by Sir John Hicks.

Now book 5 proceeds to deal with value and production, with rates of flow rather than with stocks. And he devotes a great deal of attention in this connection to the theory of the firm—to a combination of factor services of one kind and another, substitution at the margin, the scale of the firm, and the relation of the firm with industry. He takes up the point of Cournot, that where you have diminishing costs which go on to the bitter end, then there is a tendency, eventually, to complete monopoly [Marshall, 1920/1961, p. 459 at n.1]. And Marshall, looking round at the industry of his day, could think of all sorts of firms which had diminishing costs, but where the tendency to monopoly was not very strong. And consequently he was led to introduce the difference between internal economies of the firm and *external* economies of the *industry*. And so long as there were the external economies, you could have diminishing costs without a tendency to monopoly [ibid., pp. 284–86, 314–18].

There is a certain unreality about Marshall's theory of the firm there—not because it's wrong, but because it is so incomplete. The theory of external economies perhaps applies to firms in some lines of production, but the general concept of external economies depends upon the division of labour. It's much better represented, although not in this terminology, in Adam Smith, revived by Allyn Young's article on "Increasing Returns and Economic Progress" [1928]. External economies characteristically arise by the disintegration of firms—witness the history of the motor industry, for instance. So Marshall is incomplete there, but what he suggested has given rise to very interesting developments.

And secondly, in his dealing with production, there is the all-important period analysis [Marshall, 1920/1961, book 5, chap. 5, pp. 363–80]. Now, this is not entirely new. Of course, you get some little hint of period analysis in the classical economists. But Marshall made it his own. The short-period theory of value and price, given production, was a period in which factor services had no time in which either to move into the industry, if it was unusually profitable, or to move out of the industry if it was unusually unprofitable. Whereas the long period in Marshall, which in a way linked up with the theories of the stationary state in the classical economists, is when the factor services have time to sort themselves out by wastage and the direction of new capital and mobility.

Well now, let's contrast Marshall with the classics at this point. Demand and utility, Marshall shares with other participants in the marginal revolution, introducing all sorts of new elements. And the Marshallian analysis makes it very, very clear that you've got to take account of demand and utility save when you are considering constant costs, and even then demand settles the point at which quantity will be determinate—if not price.

So far as demand for services is concerned, Marshall is always careful to insist that marginal productivity is not a complete theory of distribution, and he uses the term *marginal productivity* sometimes and sometimes "marginal net product."[1] It is very clear that he was quite aware of the joint productive combination in which the technical coefficients were fixed rather than varied.

As regards the classical theory of rent, Marshall tended to be conservative [ibid., book 6, chaps. 9, 10]. John Stuart Mill and Jevons had pointed out that rent did enter into cost of production when there was a factor which had more than one use in space or time or industry. Marshall was very unwilling to say that land cost entered into cost of production, although he said it was "*wisest not* to say" that it didn't enter into cost of production.[2]

But as regards Marshall's period analysis on the distribution side, although deriving a great deal as regards the supply side—as distinct from the demand side—from the classical economists, far more than the other moderns did, it's not clear whether Marshall wanted to introduce the quantity of working population as a function of price. But he certainly wanted to introduce a flexible supply schedule into his consideration of distribution, which some of the moderns didn't want to in their stationary state.

But he also introduced, as regards period analysis, his important conception of quasi-rent [ibid., p. 74]. Now, what does "quasi-rent" mean? In Marshall there is no doubt—and he invented the theory: It was the whole return to a manmade instrument of production—the whole return, not the difference between the actual return and the long-period equilibrium return. And the genesis was that the classical economists had been inclined to urge—with the exception of John Stuart Mill—that, in the long period, interest and profits were determined on the cost side. Then came along a man called Macleod, who had bright ideas but a very poor way of expressing them. And he said that the profits or losses which are made on machines are due to the fact that the machine is there, and profits or losses are price determined rather than price determining.[3]

Well, Marshall recognised the cogency of Macleod's definition, and he solved the difficulty by his period analysis. In the short period, the whole return to manmade instruments of production—the quasi-rent—was, as the classical economists had thought rent to be, not entering into cost of production, but to be determined, like rent, on the demand side. But in the long period, when things had time to sort themselves out, other things being equal, Marshall felt that quasi-rents tended to approximate to the rate of interest (plus various allowances which can easily be thrown in, but need not be at this stage), and quasi-rents in the long period were more like interest. In the short period they were more like rent and in the long period they were more like interest—hence the term *quasi-rents*. [ibid., p. 421].

You can't exaggerate the importance of Marshall's period analysis in this respect, and if you go forward, in a way that I'm not going to go forward in these lectures, to modern theory, you can certainly regard the more formal parts of Keynes' *General Theory* as being the general application of Marshall's period analysis to macroeconomic problems. Of course, in the course of his informal remarks, Keynes made many remarks which more properly belong in the field of true dynamics, which traces the path which the system moves through as it proceeds from one position to another. But the formal Keynesian theory is Marshallian time analysis applied to the macroeconomic problems.

As regards Marshall on money, I will say something next week. As regards Marshall on international trade, it's all in his *Pure Theory*, which those of you who don't find geometry too difficult could easily read in an evening. And I leave you to it.

NOTES

1. See Marshall (1920/1961, book 6).
2. Letter from Marshall to Edgeworth, 28 August 1902, reprinted in Pigou (1925, pp. 435–38, at 436). See also Marshall (1961, 2:439).
3. See Marshall (1920/1961, appendix 1, p. 821) and letter from Marshall to J. B. Clark, 11 November 1902, reprinted in Pigou (1925, pp. 413–14).

Money: Fisher, Marshall, Wicksell

I SHALL devote the greater part of this lecture, which is the last of the series, to clearing up various ambiguities connected with the place of money in the marginal revolution and in that part of early modern economic theory that I'm concerned with. If there is time, I will say a few bibliographical words on literature on fluctuation theory, but I am not quite sure that I shall reach that point and in any case it is very marginal.

Now, the main point that I wish to bring out is that, in the course of the development which one has loosely called the marginal revolution, matters were made more precise as regards the way in which money fitted in. But at the same time, you must realise that there was then, and there is now, two modes of approach to the theory of money. Both, in my judgement, can be called the quantity theory of money, but the approaches are different.

Let me begin with a continuation of the praise which I have given to Irving Fisher as one of the most notable contributors to economic thought of the period before 1914. He lived longer than that and continued to make contributions, but his main contributions, in my judgement, come before that time.

Fisher's contribution here is contained in the famous third treatise with which he occupied the years before 1912. I am not thinking about the *Mathematical Investigations in the Theory of Value and Prices* [1892], that marvelous doctor's thesis, and I'm not thinking here of a monograph, *Appreciation and Interest* [1896], which I shall be alluding to later. But the three famous treatises are: *The Nature of Capital and Income* [1906], which I have touched upon; *The Rate of Interest* [1907], on which I've expatiated at rather greater length; and the famous *Purchasing Power of Money* [1925], which must certainly be regarded as the standard example of the first approach to the quantity theory of money that I had in mind when I said that there were two approaches. It is a massive exposition of what I think is probably the majority approach through history to the theory of the value of money—that which deals with the quantity of money, however defined, and its rapidity or velocity of circulation. And Fisher put this into elementary symbols. The famous symbol is $MV=PT$, or, enlarging it a little bit, to take account of credit instruments: $MV + M'V'=PT$. Now, there is no doubt that Fisher is quite immune from the charge that these formulae are tautologies. He recognised that they were tautologies if left at that, but his book was devoted to the causes of changes in M and M' and

V and V'. It was not confined to an equation which simply looks at the same things twice but from a different angle.

Well, his formulation and his investigations have given rise to multitudinous developments in the age since he published his book, and I would say that it's still continued, probably, to be the leading approach in the United States of America. The most modern exponent of that approach is, of course, Friedman—and his various disciples.

But there is another way of putting the quantity theory of money—the so-called Cambridge cash balance approach. I say "so-called" because one can find anticipations of this approach as far back as Petty. You will find a very good exposition in very simple language of this approach in Nassau Senior's tract on *The Value of Money* [1829b], which remained unpublished through his life and until the London School of Economics published it round about the beginning of the 1930s.

All the same, I think that the term *Cambridge* is not altogether misapplied in this connection. Keynes [1933/1972, pp. 161–231], in his biographical essay on Marshall, one of the best biographical essays, both from the literary point of view and from the economic point of view, which has ever been written, produces an extract from an early manuscript of Marshall's. The full manuscript is reprinted in this extremely expensive book, which has been fathered to some extent by the Royal Economic Society, and consists of a selection of the early unpublished writings of Alfred Marshall [Marshall, 1975], edited in a large way by Profesor Whitaker who used to be at Bristol and is now at the University of Virginia. And this is a very interesting book. This that I hold in my hand is only the first volume. As I think I said last time, it casts some doubt on Marshall's recollection of the dates at which he made his original discoveries or developments pertaining to the marginal revolution. But there is doubt about the date of this extract. It's inscribed in what appears to be Marshall's hand, "Theory of Money, manuscript about 1871" [Marshall, 1871].

And this is Marshall at his very best, I think, and I propose to read you a long extract:

> The value of all commodities is determined by an equation of supply and demand: this is the ordinary method of expressing the following fact:—for every particular amount of the commodity there is some price at which it can on the average be supplied and there is some price at which each particular amount can on the average be got rid of. The amount which is actually sold on the average is that for which the price at which it can be on the average so supplied is exactly equal to the price at which it can be on the average got rid of. We here have the causes which determine prices expressed in terms of the desires of individuals. . . . We have seen that the willingness of a seller to sell at any price depended upon his expectations of . . . being able to put it to some use himself; that accordingly if we considered the average conditions of a period

very long as compared with the time required for the production of a commodity on a scale sufficiently large, the prices at which those sellers who are only just willing to sell are induced to do it is such as to cover the cost of production of that portion of the commodity which, on the supposition that the given amount is to be produced, is at the greatest expense. . . . But when we come to the theory of money

—I've missed out a bit about the demand for money, because that comes in later—

we are told that its value depends upon its amount together with the rapidity of circulation, and although from this account we should naturally be led to infer the presence of some other regulating conditions—although, on reading an exposition of the theory *in extenso* as it is given for instance in Mill, we find these conditions distinctly enunciated—we do not find

—and this is the reason why I personally incline to the Cambridge approach—

we do not find a clear statement of that balancing of advantages which in the ultimate analysis must be found to determine the magnitude of every quantity which rests upon the will of man. If we seek for this we shall find that "the rapidity of circulation" is not the most convenient thing to be made the basis of our investigations. We shall show that it may be more conveniently deduced from other considerations and indeed, that it may be best applied in illustrating instead of in enunciating. [ibid., pp. 165–66]

Well, he then goes on to develop his theory, and since this was not published until Keynes published it, I propose to review the theory as he enunciated it to the Committee on Indian Currency which sat in the late 1890s. He did enunciate it earlier in his "Evidence Before the Gold and Silver Commission" [Marshall, 1887] which sat in the 1880s, but the clearest enunciation, I think, is at the beginning of his examination by the Committee on Indian Currency [Marshall, 1899]: "[Chairman:] You are Professor of Political Economy at the University of Cambridge?—Yes." Then there is a little modest bit in which he says that he has been trying to make up his mind about what currency arrangements are best for India.

But, on being informed that the scope of the Committee's inquiry extended beyond questions of practical administration, and raised some broad issues of economic principle, and that I might be excused from expressing opinions on questions that required much knowledge of India, and might confine my evidence to the general relations of currency and trade, I have ventured to accept the invitation with which the Committee have honoured me.

[Chairman:] Then, in questioning you, we will confine ourselves to the limits which you yourself have laid down. I will ask you first, what do you consider to be the relation between the volume of currency and the general level of prices in a country?

[Answer:] I hold that prices vary directly with the volume of currency, if other things are equal; but other things are constantly changing. This so-called "quantity theory of the value of money" is true in just the same way as it is true that the day's temperature varies with the length of the day, other things being equal; but other things are seldom equal. This theory has been the cause of much controversy; but it has never been seriously denied by anyone who has taken it as a whole, and has not stopped short, omitting the words "other things being equal." The fact is

—and here we come to the background of the Cambridge doctrine—

that in every state of society there is some fraction of their income which people find it worth while to keep in the form of currency; it may be a fifth, or a tenth, or a twentieth. A large command of resources in the form of currency renders their business easy and smooth, and puts them at an advantage in bargaining; but, on the other hand, it locks up in a barren form resources that might yield an income of gratification if invested, say, in extra furniture; or a money income, if invested in extra machinery or cattle. In a primitive state of society, even in one as far advanced as that of India,

—India of those days—

only the rich care to have much of their resources in the form of currency. In England, all but the very poor keep a good deal; the lower middle classes keep a relatively very large quantity; while the very rich who pay all their tradesmen by cheques use relatively little. But, whatever the state of society, there is a certain volume of their resources which people of different classes taken one with another care to keep in the form of currency; and, if everything else remains the same, then there is this direct relation between the volume of currency and the level of prices. . . . Of course, the less the proportion of their resources which people care to keep in the form of currency, the lower will be the aggregate value of the currency, that is, the higher will prices be with a given volume of the currency. [ibid., pp. 267–68]

Well, there you have the basis of the Cambridge cash balance tradition. You find it very authoritatively stated in two works: in Pigou, in his *Essays in Applied Economics* [1923]—page 174, "The Exchange Value of Legal-Tender Money"—and you find it in an even more famous form in the opening chapters of Keynes' *Tract on Monetary Reform* [1923]. You will find it in Robertson's elementary textbook on *Money* [1922], and you will find it in that much-neglected book, Lavington's *English Capital Market* [1921].

Now, Marshall and his disciples—those who derived from him—were not the only ones who approached the qualifications of a crude quantity theory of money by a cash balance approach. As we saw last week, Walras rounded off his system in the third and fourth editions of his book, and in a monograph on the theory of money [Walras, 1886], by a similar device which made what he called the *encaisse désirée*—the amount of money which people desired to hold—a function of the value of money.

In the second generation of the Austrian school, the great teacher of Haberler, Machlup, Hayek, Morgenstern—most of the famous names that you associate with the third generation of the Austrian school—von Mises, in his first book, *Theorie des Geldes und der Umlaufsmittel—The Theory of Money and the Means of Circulation* [1912; 1934]—probably provides a more detailed linking up of the cash balance approach with the general marginal utility theory as developed by the Austrians than is to be found anywhere else in the literature.

Now, Mises is a very controversial figure in regard, let us say, to his views on methodology and in regard to his views on the possibility of calculation in a pure collectivist state. These are highly controversial matters on which reasonable people take more than one view, even at this distance of time, and Mises probably owes his reputation to the more controversial of his views. But *The Theory of Money*—it was translated in the London School of Economics and used to be a standard textbook here—is not controversial in that sense, although of course all the matters connected with money and macroeconomics have their controversial fringe, even at the present day. But Mises on money is certainly worth the attention, especially those of you who are graduates and aspire to be teachers.

Finally, I must say a word for the first professor of economics in this institution: my teacher, Edwin Cannan. Cannan has a bad name among your generation because he made one theoretical mistake. He denied the possibility of the creation of additional purchasing power by properly regulated banks. This was, as it was called in my day, a "cloakroom" theory of banking. And it must be said that a great many bankers for a hundred years before Cannan simply found that the cloakroom theory of banking put into academic form what they had been professing to do themselves. But of course he was wrong. I think that one would have to say that quite definitely—that there are conditions under which all banks acting together can produce an enlargement of the effective money supply, and central banks can also, in various ways.

But Cannan deserves much more credit for his scholarship than I think he enjoys at the moment. His edition of the *Wealth of Nations* [Smith, 1776] is a model to us all although some said it's superseded by the Glasgow edition now, and his general history of economic thought [1929] is stimulating and scholarly. Also, his general introduction to economics, called *Wealth* [1919], though it contains controversial sections, is packed with acute analysis and plain and simple wisdom. But coming back to the theory of money, Cannan, at the British Association in the early 1920s, read a paper called "The Application of the Theoretical Apparatus of Supply & Demand for Units of Currency" [1921], and in that article, with great skill, he applied the apparatus and reached a version of the cash balance approach himself.

Now, you see the difference between your day and my young days in the following story. I became a junior lecturer at the School when this sort of thing was still very controversial. It was a frightful headache for students because the other professor of money and banking, Foxwell, believed that banks *could* create credit, and we used to argue on such fundamental questions—wrongly, I think now—what answers should we give to examination questions. Well, I might say that my experience is that if you give an intelligent answer controverting the examiner, he is more likely to mark you up than if you echo his opinions. But you may not believe that; it's based on reading—alas, it was the least productive part of one's academic life—thousands and thousands of examination papers in conjunction with people of opposite views. I used to examine, in the 1930s, in the final examinations here, with Maurice Dobb, who was a member of the Communist party. We differed completely in our views about the future of society; we *very, very seldom*, when independently marking the papers and bringing our marks together, disagreed about the order. And if we disagreed, five minutes' friendly elucidation of some point which one or the other thought that the other one had overlooked was enough to clear up the disparity. I don't remember in all that time examining with Maurice Dobb, either at London or at Cambridge, having to call in a third examiner because we couldn't agree. But this is another matter.

I got to know Cannan quite well, and one day he said to me—I was at Oxford at the time; he lived at Oxford and I used to go to tea with him there—"You know, someone was telling me that my quantity theory of money is all in Marshall, and I looked it up in the evidence that he gave to these two committees, and there it was." Now, I think that that state of affairs has completely ceased; it would not be possible for a professor at London to be ignorant of what had been the oral tradition of Cambridge. It was only written out at Cambridge, round about Cannan's time, by Pigou towards the end of the 1910s, and by Keynes at the beginning of the 1920s. But Marshall had said this in a private note in 1871. He had said it to the Gold and Silver Commission in the 1880s and to the Committee on Indian Currency in the 1890s, and his pupils sustained the oral tradition. Well, I hope that things are a little better now.

Now let's go on to developments. I have, I think, mentioned to you, in connection with the marginal revolution generally, the name of Wicksell. And Wicksell is a name which I think deserves to be put among the greatest names of the marginal revolution—Jevons, Menger, Böhm-Bawerk, Wieser, Walras and Marshall. He was an eclectic: He gathered from all sources and settled down to economics rather late in life. But his book *Über Wert, Kapital und Rente—Value, Capital and Rent* [1893; 1954]—is probably the best synthesis of Walras and the Austrian School and the British School which was published at an early period. And his *Lectures*, which were translated also here at the School of Economics, are in many ways, in my judgement, *by far* the best introduction to economics as it was in the first twenty-five years of this century.

Well, I don't want to go over his contributions to the theory of capital and to the theory of distribution and so on and so forth, but I want to say just a little more about his marvellous book, the substance of which is reproduced in volume 2 of the *Lectures* [1934–35]: *Geldzins und Güterpreise*, which has been translated by Professor Richard Kahn as *Interest and Prices* [Wicksell, 1936] and is published by the Royal Economic Society. Whether it's in print or not, I'm not absolutely sure.

He recognises both modes of approach to the quantity theory of money, sets them forth beautifully, and shows how they are two different modes of approach which are to some extent a matter of taste. But he has reserves about the quantity theory of money, however approached, up to the date of his writing of the book. He doesn't question the quantity theory of money if there is no credit. And he goes into the velocity question and all that sort of thing—the cash balance approach—perfectly satisfactorily. But opposing the idea of a purely metallic money to a pure credit system, such as we live under at the moment, he is led to wonder whether statements of the quantity theory—which he still thinks is important—have not missed out an important causal element.

If you state the quantity theory, either in cash balance terms or in velocity terms, according to Wicksell, and do not include the money rate of interest, then a pure credit system is indeterminate—a conclusion which is also reached by Hawtrey in his famous book *Currency and Credit* [1919], which came a little later. And thus Wicksell, in this book on interest and money, is led to rediscover the classical proposition—Thornton's proposition, the proposition even admitted by Ricardo—that the demand for loans is dependent on the rate of interest, and *that* in turn depends upon the profitability of real investment.

And so he conceives a natural rate of investment; a normal rate of interest, determined in the mode in which it had been explained by Böhm-Bawerk and simplified and popularised and made more sophisticated by Wicksell himself; and a money rate of interest which was determined by banking policy. And he felt that the volume of credit could be controlled by money interest rates, and that if there were a disparity between money rates of interest and real rates of interest or profitability, then if the money rate was above the natural rate there would be a tendency to deflation, which might be cumulative, and if it were below the normal rate, then there would be a tendency, which might be cumulative, to inflation.

This was the pure theory of the subject. Coming closer to reality, and dealing with a banking system which had some sort of connection with convertible metal, he felt that the cumulative processes would be arrested sooner or later, but he urged—and he urged very, very strongly—that it was for the central banks, keeping their eye on the long-term profitability of investment, to keep money relatively stable.

Now, at this point Wicksell made a mistake. He felt that if the money rate of interest and the natural rate of interest were to coincide continually, then the value of money would be stable. But there would be other influences affecting the value of money, and that was an over-simplification. But the broad common sense of the matter—that either by deliberate control of the volume of a credit money or by influencing the rate of interest, the value of money can be kept reasonably stable—that, I think, was an important step in the history of thought. It was developed further in Cambridge in the 1920s, following some discovery of Wicksell: by Keynes, who was a little influenced by Wicksell—not as much as Wicksell thought he ought to be—and by Hawtrey, who although he was a Cambridge man, was not a Cambridge economist. He was a Treasury economist. He died only the other day at a preternaturally long life—into his 90s. His famous book is *Currency and Credit* [1919], which, with Robertson's *Banking Policy and the Price Level* [1926] and Keynes' *Treatise on Money* [1930] and *General Theory* [1936], must be regarded as being, on this side of the Atlantic in the English-speaking world, the source of the tremendous discussion and investigation of money which has taken place since my period.

Now finally—I shan't have time to ennumerate all the literature relating to fluctuations; you must regard it as being left out of these lectures, just as I left out the classical theory of taxation—finally—again, rediscovery of Thornton—Marshall, in his evidence to these commissions and in the first edition of his *Principles*, shows clearly the effect on interest rates by *changes* in the value of money, and he shows how, if the value of money is falling, then people who lend at stable money rates of interest are getting a rate of interest which may be zero or may be negative, as has happened in this country for many years past. And the rate of interest is now, with the money rates as high as they are, roughly speaking, zero, having regard to the present rate of inflation.

But the main figure here, I think, is not Marshall. Marshall pays ample tribute to Fisher, although Fisher comes a little later. Fisher wrote another marvellous monograph before he wrote his three treatises, *Appreciation and Interest*, 1896. And there he investigates a problem which was very much agitated in connection with the parallelism which existed in the world at that time between different kinds of metallic money: pure gold systems on one hand, pure silver systems on the other, and mixed systems—bimetalism—on the other. And he shows, first of all, how you can measure interest rates in *any* couple of commodities. And he approached his exposition on this rather complicated question in terms of just two or three commodities—corn and wool. And supposing 100 bushels of corn are equivalent to 100 pounds of wool today, and, regarding the rate of interest as being an exchange between present and future, supposing that in a year's time 104 bushels of corn exchange for 104 pounds of wool next year, the corn rate of return and the wool rate of return are the same. But now supposing corn appreciates in terms of wool. Say it's 1.01 wool the price of a bushel of corn, so that the price of 104 bushels is equal to 104 multiplied by 1.01, which is 105.04. So the corn rate is 4 percent and the wool rate is 5.04 percent.

Well then, Fisher goes on to show that all this happens, and that you can have divergencies between gold and silver rates while people don't tumble to what's going on. But when they realise that there are divergent rates in the different metals, *then* there will be a tendency to switch into the metal which gives the highest return if there is no obstacle. And similarly with paper money. If there had been no exchange control in the last thirty years, few of us would have preferred to be paid in sterling. It was Abraham Lincoln who said that you can fool some of the people some of the time, but you can't fool all the people all the time.

Well, that must be the end. I commend you to read—in the lamentable situation in which those of you who are British are, by reason of the mismanagement of British currency in the last quarter century—I commend you all to read Fisher's *Appreciation and Interest.*

And that's the end, and I thank you all for your patience in listening to my imperfect and informal exposition and statements of epiperiphery.[1] [Applause]

I always have maintained that the present generation of students is much nicer than we were in the 1920s. Goodbye.

NOTE

1. Robbins voice trailed off at the end of this sentence, making it difficult to understand the final word he spoke—which, on the tape recording, sounds like "epiphery." As we are unable to find this word in the *Oxford English Dictionary*, we have chosen to assume that Robbins stumbled over the word "epiperiphery," although he could also have meant to say "epiphany," both words having similar connotations in the present context.

The Further Evolution of the Subject

LIONEL ROBBINS' lectures on the history of economic thought were those of a master of the field. Still, they were Robbins' lectures and not those of someone else. The history of economic thought does not write itself; it is written by historians and others, each of whom have more or less unique perspectives on the subject. These perspectives govern what is included, what is excluded, the weights assigned to various topics, and both the broad outlines and the details of the story told.

We want, in this supplementary chapter, to give an account of the history of economic thought from the point at which Robbins left it. We cannot necessarily provide the account which Robbins would have given, had he been writing today. For one thing, neither of us are him; for another, he changed his mind on a number of important interpretive matters—and he might have made further changes that we cannot anticipate.

We can get some idea of what Robbins might have dealt with by examining what he did in fact deal with for the period covered in the lectures. One obvious matter is that, in one respect at least, the history did write itself. Robbins covered the ancient Greeks; the Scholastics; a variety of writers in the century or so before Cantillon, the Physiocrats, and Smith; the major figures of English Classical Political Economy; Saint-Simon and Marx; the Historical School; some anticipators of marginal analysis; the English and Continental marginalists; Marshall; and several early twentieth-century writers on monetary economics. There are several points to be made. First, these individuals and groups did exist and had to be discussed; by almost any reckoning they are central to the history of economics during their periods. Second, Robbins' focus tended strongly to be on value and distribution theory. Third, notwithstanding that focus, the materials compelled Robbins to deal with other questions: Not only money, international trade, and the foundations of economic development and growth (for example), but also the role of moral systems, the theory of property, the economic role of government, the organization and control of the economic system, systemic evolution, and the critique of the modern economic system.

We are faced with several tensions. First, we have Robbins the mainstream neoclassicist and Robbins the promulgator of the definition of economics as the study of how scarce resources that have alternative uses are allocated among those alternative uses. Robbins would have strongly tended to concentrate on the further development of the theory of value and distribution, especially insofar as these became the theory of the allocation of resources through the price mechanism in more or less competitive markets, i.e., microeconomics. He would have resonated affirmatively with and likely concentrated on neoclassical economics as the theory of resource allocation, markets, the pure logic of choice, constrained maximization, and so on. His coverage likely would have been broader than the neoclassical paradigm of a given, abstract, pure, a-institutional conceptual economy; the neoclassical research protocol of requiring the production of unique determinate optimal equilibrium solutions; and the correlative making of those assumptions, such as given, fixed preferences and utility or profit maximization, necessary to produce such solutions. These would have been included, and even would have tended to centrality, but likely also included would be other ways of doing neoclassical economics, some static partial equilibrium in the Marshallian mode, some quest for explanations of phenomena using some version of market demand-supply analysis, and so on.

Second, notice that the story told by Marshall is a British and Continental story. The only U.S. economist to figure into Robbins' story is Irving Fisher (Friedrich List hardly counts). With some important exceptions, and especially after World War II, the history of mainstream neoclassical economics is primarily a U.S. story.

Third, the practice of both economics as a whole and of each of the schools which came to comprise economics in the twentieth century has been heterogeneous. Neoclassicism came to dominate, especially after World War II, but at all times what has passed for both mainstream orthodoxy and heterodoxy alike has taken variegated forms.

Fourth, the number of economists, and thus the practice of economics, have multiplied enormously during the twentieth century. Consider the following: Volume I of the *Index of Economic Journals* covers the period 1886–1924, almost forty years. The pages dedicated to the classified index of journal articles were numbered 1–156. The pages devoted to the index of authors were numbered 157–270. The pages given to the listing of journals were numbered xvii–xx. The three totals were 156, 114, and 4 pages, respectively. In Volume VIII, now entitled *Index of Economic Articles*, covering both journals and collected volumes for the year 1966 alone, for example, the comparable totals were 232, 193, and 5. The comparable numbers for Volume XXXVI (in two volumes), are 1,300, 882, and 30. Accordingly, the domain constituting economic thought and its history became enormously wider and more complex and variegated as the twentieth century progressed.

Fifth, Robbins would likely have followed the practice, still widely common, of not discussing "contemporary" economics. Wherever the cut-off point, one reason is apparent: the historian is too close to contemporary work and authors to have a suitable objective perspective.

So, the questions arise: What attention would Robbins have given to diversity within neoclassical economics? Would he have paid much attention to the pre-Hicks/pre-Samuelson development of neoclassicism? Would he have concentrated on British, or British and Continental, writers? Would he have dealt separately with the evolving Austrian School? How would he have treated, if he treated them at all, the evolving socialist tradition, U.S. institutionalism, Neo-Ricardian economics, and so on? How would he have treated Hicksian and post-Hicks general equilibrium economics, especially in relation to Marshall? What would he have said about Joan Robinson and John Maynard Keynes, and about post-Keynesian economics (U.S. and/or English-Italian variants)? Would some of the answers be different if he had lectured on these topics during, say, 1997–1998 (Robbins, who was born in 1898, died in 1984) rather than during 1979–1981?

We think it fair to say, as already suggested, that Robbins probably would have concentrated on selected figures in the neoclassical mainstream, with some more or less marginal attention to a few selected others; and on the main topics of neoclassical interest—price theory, capital theory, monetary theory, and the like.

With the foregoing considerations held in abeyance, let us outline the development of economics during the twentieth century as we see it, with an eye to some broad dimensions of an innovating neoclassical economics, to what Robbins might well have concentrated upon, and to what else was to be found in the practice of economics.

1. Aspects of the Development of Neoclassical Economics

The broad framework of neoclassical microeconomics was laid down in Alfred Marshall's *Principles of Economics*. It centers on the analysis of price and quantity in more or less competitive markets, the respective economic characteristics of the factors of production, the respective roles of households and firms in generating demands and supplies, the role of time with regard to the differing periods taken for certain factors and forces to come to fruition, and, inter alia, the implications of the foregoing for the remuneration of the factors of production. Large social questions, such as the relations of capital and labor, the nature and sources of economic progress, and the overall organization of the economy, were neither omitted nor given central prominence. Marshall took an instrumentalist position, creating various concepts to be used together as an engine of analysis, not treating them as a self-subsistent, true specification of the economy. He was in part a synthesizer, for example, combining marginal utility and cost of production theories of value, his creative role residing in part in his conversion of value theory into price theory, and including therein his period analysis of time. But Marshall neither could cover everything of interest in (what later came to be called) microeconomics, nor could he preclude further, even divisive, analyses of topics whose historic conflicts he may have tried to paper over.

On the demand side of the market-price mechanism, later economists took up the question of whether utility was ordinal or cardinal. Solutions to the question were sought in the use of indifference curves and in revealed preference. The question was at least partly reformulated when economists came to define the objects of purchase and sale in terms of social-psychological characteristics rather than as specific commodities. In time, the specification of economic problems as matters of constrained maximization led to the conventional use of utility functions of various degrees of specificity. In time also, economists, increasingly aided by psychologists, reformulated the idea of "rationality," suggesting its variegated complexities and the roles of social factors and learning.

On the supply side, economists tended to work with models of pure competition. But they also took up and developed models of noncompetitive conditions: theories of monopoly, duopoly, oligopoly, imperfect competition and monopolistic competition. Increasingly central to these theories was the role of economies of scale. Economists also continued to work with profit maximization as the goal of firms. But some economists explored the modeling of firms with differently specified objective functions, such as market share, bounded rationality, managerial lifetime earnings, and the value of equity securities. Similarly, most economists most of the time assumed something approaching perfect certainty on the part of economic actors; but some pursued the implications of uncertainty, for example, along the lines of subjective probabilities. Various, quite different conceptions of "cost" were juxtaposed to each other, with varying implications. Complex theories of production were worked out. Firms were treated sometimes as passive responders to market forces and at other times as active agents of change. Industries were typically treated as producers of essentially homogeneous or near-homogeneous commodities, but sometimes as groups of producers of commodities with high cross-elasticity of substitution.

Just as Marshall's theory of price (value) was more technical and complex than that of most earlier economists, soon the newer theories were becoming even more technical and more complex. The work of economists was also becoming more mathematical and quantitative, i.e., econometric and formalist.

This increasing technicality and complexity, perhaps even greater sophistication, certainly great conflict, was seen in other, related fields of economic theory. These included the following: 1) welfare economics, with a fundamental tension between Pigovian and Paretian conceptions of welfare maximization; 2) theories of instability, various and conflicting, yet all in opposition to Say's Law, which was typically held to rule out business cycles of any importance; 3) theories of growth and of dynamics, which varied among themselves and which, further, had to ground and differentiate themselves from the dominant neoclassical statics; 4) continuation and revision of the Walrasian-Paretian general equilibrium theory (treated by Robbins in lecture 21); 5) theories of capital and of interest, differing as to their nature and rationale as well as to the mode of their determination; 6) theories of the distribution of income, including differences over both what distribution theory was to explain and the substance of theory; 7) moreover, alongside a generalized marginal productivity theory (in one form or another) were individual theories of wages, interest, rent, and profit.

A number of issues in monetary economics were controversial (as some remain). These include the definition of money as between specie and paper and as between currency and bank credit, the relation of debt to money both in general and in relation to demand deposit balances, the nature and role of reserves, the multiple expansion and contraction process, the definition of money supply, the nature and role of commercial banks and the central bank in the creation and management of money, the respective roles of money substitutes and of nonbank financial intermediaries and other institutions, and, inter alia, the goals of monetary policy and the relation of the monetary and banking system to the larger polity and society.

For all the varied specification and conflicting theories, there nevertheless emerged a canonical neoclassical corpus of theory, one increasingly attached, in one way or another, to a notion of a pure abstract a-institutional conceptual economy and to a research protocol seeking unique determinate optimal equilibrium solutions.

2. SOME ECONOMISTS ON WHOM ROBBINS MIGHT HAVE FOCUSED

On the basis of Robbins' essay, "The Evolution of Modern Economic Theory," first delivered in 1960 and published in 1970 in a book of that title, one can surmise that he likely would have lectured, in one way or another, on the following topics: the extension and refinement of post-Marshallian neoclassical economics (theories of demand, the firm, the market, and international trade), the Keynesian revolution and its aftermath, and formal dynamic theory.

Much of Robbins' lectures dealt with specific individuals as such. Some lectures treated general topics—discussion of individuals conducted so as to illustrate larger themes. Accordingly, one can imagine Robbins devoting one or more lectures to a wide-ranging and deeply nuanced survey of the development of neoclassical economics in the twentieth century, more or less along the lines and topics sketched in Part 1, supra, and in the first paragraph of Part 2. One lecture might have been on the development of price theory per se; another on the development of the general theory of markets; and still others on statics and dynamics, capital theory, distribution theory, monetary theory, macroeconomics, economic growth, and so on, perhaps including the theory of economic policy (the theory of the economic role of government). But one suspects that Robbins might well have focused on a number of prominent individuals whose work was directly important, though in some cases as representative of a group working in an important area. Remembering that Robbins did lecture on John Bates Clark, Carl Menger, Friedrich von Wieser, Philip Wicksteed, Eugen von Böhm-Bawerk, Irving Fisher, Leon Walras, Vilfredo Pareto, and Alfred Marshall, some possibilities include the following, in no particular order of importance.

Frank H. Knight: Knight's theory of risk, uncertainty and profit attempted to explain the existence of profits under perfect competition on the basis of unpredictable and unmeasurable, hence uninsurable, change, or uncertainty. He contradicted the Austrian theories of a period of production and of the rate of return on capital as due to waiting, emphasizing problems of measurement and causation. His theory of social cost anticipated the Paretian-Coasian analysis, emphasizing the possibility of market solutions to externality problems. He greatly enriched the conceptual foundations of microeconomic theory. Much of the second half of his career was devoted to the philosophy of economics, the general theory of socioeconomic organization, and the general theory of economic policy, all of which tended to focus on the relationships of knowledge (or what is taken for knowledge) and social action, especially the limits to deliberative social engineering. Many of Knight's interests and ideological orientation were shared by Robbins.

Dennis H. Robertson and Ralph G. Hawtrey: Both men studied monetary economics and developed theories of the business cycle and policy that were earlier than and different from those of John Maynard Keynes. Hawtrey emphasized the monetary nature of the business cycle and the key role of monetary policy in its control, centering on the demand for monetary balances and the discount rate of the central bank. He gradually lessened his view that government expenditures crowded out private investment spending but never became a convert to Keynesian macroeconomics. Robertson was both a collaborator and critic of Keynes. He studied both monetary and non-monetary causes of business cycles and initiated the modern period analysis and the analysis of the relationships between saving and investment. He criticized some of the elements of Keynes' model, especially the relationships of saving and investment to income and the liquidity-preference theory of money. He remained more of a traditional monetary theorist while making major contributions to modern macroeconomics.

Joseph A. Schumpeter: One of the more flamboyant economists, Schumpeter made important contributions to the theories of price, economic development, business cycles, and, somewhat in the manner of Max Weber, the general social theory of capitalist economic systems. He combined a grasp of equilibrium theory, social formations, and socioeconomic evolution which made one recall the earlier work along these lines by Weber and Pareto. He emphasized the key roles of the entrepreneur, innovation, the initial monopoly profits from innovation, and the price mechanism. He developed a multi-cycle model of instability and his own analysis of the transformation of capitalism into socialism. His was probably the broadest and most heterogeneous paradigm of any mainstream twentieth-century orthodox economist. Schumpeter shared with Robbins a deep interest in and mastery of the history of economic thought.

John Maynard Keynes: Keynes and Robbins, the former more radical and the latter more conservative (in the sense of eighteenth- and nineteenth-century liberalism), were for many years more or less rival candidates for the "position" of Great Britain's leading economist public intellectual. Keynes, not quite single-handedly, created the self-conscious field of macroeconomics, providing theories of both the determination of the aggregate level of income and of its instability, focusing on the determinants of that spending which generates new output. He also helped, for many people, to transform monetary theory and policy, as well as to provide new lines of reasoning with regard to the roles of fiscal policy, wage rates, saving in relation to investment, interest rates, and so on. His general model of the determination of income and its instability and control contradicted many long-held notions. Having started as a monetary theorist who envisioned an active role for monetary policy, Keynes switched his focus from the price level to the level of income and from the quantity of money to the level of spending and its multitudinous causes, including the new focus on fiscal policy.

Friedrich A. von Hayek: Hayek made fundamental contributions to Austrian and general neoclassical economics in such areas as prices and production, capital theory, subjectivism, and the general theory of markets, especially in regard to knowledge and ignorance. Hayek emphasized the role of the price mechanism and, therefore, of prices in a variety of areas: the accumulation of capital, business cycles, the limits of socialist calculation, and the marshalling of diffused knowledge in the formation of spontaneous order. Like Knight, Hayek increasingly turned from technical economic theory to questions of general social theory, focusing on the role of the price mechanism and markets, the relation of knowledge to forms of social action, the theory of spontaneous order, the principle of unintended and unexpected consequences, and the relationships between common law, legislation, and liberty. In the process, he worked out both positive and normative aspects of a general theory of what he considered a free economy and society. Hayek, a colleague and friend of Robbins' at LSE, was analytically and ideologically the opposite of Keynes.

Ragnar Frisch and Jan Tinbergen: Frisch was a wide-ranging thinker but is best known for his pioneering work in the econometrics of production and macroeconomic performance, and also, though less so, in the theory and practice of economic planning. Tinbergen also produced a wide range of theoretical and econometric studies, likewise in the areas of production and planning but also in macroeconomics and labor economics. The work of both men was highly technical but both also wrote about nontechnical aspects of economic policy. Both men were actively engaged in the planning of economic policy in their native countries, Norway and The Netherlands, respectively.

Roy F. Harrod: Harrod wrote principally on the theories of competitive and noncompetitive markets, international trade, business cycles and general macroeconomics, and what can be seen as either (or both) economic dynamics and economic growth theory. He was a dedicated practitioner of high theory, typically working at the level of the neoclassical model of a pure a-institutional abstract conceptual economy. This is illustrated by his model of growth, later combined with that of Evsey Domar, which traces the rate of growth to the relationship between saving-income and capital-output ratios. Yet he was very active in the realm of economic policy. Harrod was a major supporter of Keynes's revolution in macroeconomics; he was also Keynes's first biographer.

John R. Hicks: Hicks wrote on a wide range of topics; his influence on how economists do economics was comparable to that of Keynes and Paul Samuelson. His most influential work is in general equilibrium theory, macroeconomics, the theory of wages, capital theory, and economic dynamics, but he also wrote on the theory of economic history, causation, and methodological topics.

Paul A. Samuelson: Samuelson is undoubtedly the single most important economist of the twentieth century. He wrote in almost every field of economics, including the theories of capital, consumer behavior, growth, welfare economics, public expenditure theory, international trade theory, macroeconomics, fiscal policy and so on. His deepest influences reside in his treatment of economic problems as matters of constrained maximization; the mathematization of economic theory; and his Neoclassical Synthesis, his combination of neoclassical microeconomics and Keynesian macroeconomics, a key factor in the absorption of Keynesian economics in the United States and elsewhere.

Simon Kuznets and Richard Stone: Both Kuznets and Stone made fundamental contributions to national income accounting and its analysis. Stone pursued the econometric investigation of a host of important substantive topics, for example the measurement of consumption, but also the theory and problems of measurement per se. Kuznets studied cyclical and other types of economic change and developed an approach to economic growth which was both technologically proficient and socially, demographically, and historically rich.

Milton Friedman: Friedman is best known for his reformulation and econometric treatment of the quantity theory of money, his permanent-income theory of the consumption function, his own approach to macroeconomics, and, among other things, a host of contributions to microeconomics, including the theory of utility. His monetarist counterrevolution against Keynes' (and Keynesian) macroeconomics, juxtaposed to Samuelson's Neoclassical Synthesis, was a major feature of both professional and public discussion for at least three decades after World War II.

Among other possible candidates for Robbins are Arthur Cecil Pigou and Joan Robinson. Pigou developed the technical articulation of an approach to welfare economics which began, in large part, with Henry Sidgwick and Alfred Marshall. Pigou also contributed to most, if not all of the then-dominant fields of economics, including labor, public finance, business cycles, and so on. Robinson achieved early stature with her theory of imperfect competition and its geometric techniques. Robinson being English, Robbins would most likely have elected to discuss her work rather than that of her close theoretical rival, the American, Edward H. Chamberlin. But Robbins would not have been comfortable lecturing on much of her subsequent work, which denigrated neoclassical economics and originated and/or affirmed various strands of quite heterodox, if not (to Robbins) radical, lines of reasoning. Robinson was a founder of European post-Keynesian economics, with ideas quite at variance with neoclassical economics in such fields as distribution, macroeconomics, and production.

Robbins might well have lectured on the Austrian school, or the Austrian-Chicago schools, perhaps focusing on Hayek and Friedman and perhaps on the socialist-calculation debate. It is less likely that he would have lectured at length on the econometric revolution, though surely he would have done more than call it to the students' attention. He might well have devoted lectures to the theories of economic development and of economic policy as well as to the new welfare economics, subjects on which he published several books, and to varieties of neoclassical practice.

It is also possible that Robbins might have chosen to lecture on one or more of the specialized fields that crystalized and/or proliferated in the twentieth century, although he was not equally deeply conversant with all of them. These include: international economics, labor economics, public finance, demographic economics, industrial organization, technological change, urban and regional economics, the economics of finance, and economic growth and development. And he might well have determined to lecture specifically on the practice and doctrines of two of the fields to which he was a foremost contributor: the history of economic thought and the methodology of economics.

Whether Robbins might have included, and how he would have treated, certain late twentieth-century developments remains uncertain. We have reference to game theory, rational expectations economics, transaction cost economics, real business cycle theory, public choice theory, new institutional economics, new classical economics, new Keynesian economics, experimental economics, economic psychology, and so on.

3. What Else Is to Be Found

Much of what is suggested as possibilities in Part 2 comprises the main core of neoclassical economics—the school which Robbins was clearly inclined to identify with economics as an intellectual discipline. But there has been more to economics than neoclassical economics, more than what is outlined above. It is unlikely that Robbins would have devoted lectures to these other schools and topics, though some references may well have been made in passing.

These include the following, also in no particular order of importance:

1. varieties of Marxian and other socialist and radical economics
2. post-Keynesian economics, in either its British-Italian and/or American forms, and neo-Ricardian economics
3. varieties of the old American institutional and evolutionary economics of Thorstein Veblen, John R. Commons, Walton Hamilton, Wesley C. Mitchell, and others
4. varieties of economic history
5. theories of planning
6. the initial stages of concentrated theoretical and empirical analysis of technology and economic organization, and, inter alia,
7. varieties of general-economic-systems theorizing.

One would have been surprised if Robbins had elected to lecture, for example, on John R. Commons, Thorstein Veblen, John Kenneth Galbraith, Gunnar Myrdal, Nicholas Kaldor, Michal Kalecki, Paul Sweezy, Maurice Dobb, or, among others, Piero Sraffa.

The point is that none, or very little, of the foregoing comported with Robbins' view of what economics and the history of economic thought were all about. Thus it is that the history of economic thought does not write itself. Whatever Robbins might have gone on to discuss, he would have been contributing to the social construction of our image of the history of economic thought.

Steven G. Medema
and
Warren J. Samuels

Bibliography
General Histories of Economic Theory

Backhouse, Roger. *A History of Modern Economic Analysis*. New York: Blackwell, 1985.
Blaug, Mark. *Economic Theory in Retrospect*. 5th ed. New York: Cambridge University Press, 1995.

Dasgupta, A. K. *Epochs of Economic Theory.* New York: Blackwell, 1985.

Done, Takuo. *History of Economic Theory: A Critical Introduction.* Brookfield: Elgar, 1994.

Ekelund, Robert B., Jr, and Robert F. Herbert. *A History of Economic Theory and Method.* 3rd ed. New York: McGraw-Hill, 1990.

Negishi,Takashi. *History of Economic Theory.* New York: North Holland, 1989.

Niehans, Jürg. *A History of Economic Theory: Classic Contributions, 1720–1980.* Baltimore: Johns Hopkins University Press, 1990.

Some Economists on Whom Robbins Might Have Focused

MILTON FRIEDMAN

with Simon Kuznets, *Income from Independent Professional Practice*, New York: NBER, 1945.

Essays in Positive Economics, Chicago: University of Chicago Press, 1953.

A Theory of the Consumption Function, Cambridge: Harvard University Press, 1957.

A Program for Monetary Stability, New York: Fordham University Press, 1959.

Capitalism and Freedom, Chicago: University of Chicago Press, 1962.

with Anna J. Schwartz, *A Monetary History of the United States, 1867–1960*, Princeton: Princeton University Press, 1963.

The Optimum Quantity of Money and Other Essays, Chicago: Aldine, 1969.

RAGNAR FRISCH

Theory of Production, Dordrecht: Reidel, 1965.

Economic Planning Studies, Dordrecht: Reidel, 1976.

ROY F. HARROD

The Trade Cycle, London: Macmillan, 1936.

Towards a Dynamic Economics, London: Macmillan, 1948.

Life of John Maynard Keynes, London: Macmillan, 1951.

Economic Dynamics, London: Macmillan, 1975.

RALPH G. HAWTREY

Currency and Credit, London: Macmillan, 1919.

Economic Aspects of Sovereignty, London: Longmans, 1930.

The Art of Central Banking, London: Macmillan, 1932.

A Century of Bank Rate, London: Longmans, 1938.

Capital and Employment, London: Longmans, 1939.

Bretton Woods: For Better or Worse, London: Longmans, 1946.

Incomes and Money, London: Longmans, 1967.

FRIEDRICH A. VON HAYEK

Prices and Production, New York: Macmillan, 1931.

The Pure Theory of Capital, New York: Routledge & Kegan Paul, 1941.

Individualism and Economic Order, London: Routledge & Kegan Paul, 1949.

The Constitution of Liberty, New York: Routledge & Kegan Paul, 1960.

The Sensory Order, Chicago: University of Chicago Press, 1963.
Studies in Philosophy, Politics and Economics, New York: Routledge & Kegan Paul, 1967.
Law, Legislation and Liberty, 3 vols., New York: Routledge & Kegan Paul, 1973, 1976, 1979.
New Studies in Philosophy, Politics, Economics and the History of Ideas, New York: Routledge & Kegan Paul, 1978.
Money, Capital and Fluctuations, New York: Routledge & Kegan Paul, 1984.
The Fatal Conceit, Chicago: University of Chicago Press, 1988.

JOHN R. HICKS

Theory of Wages, London: Macmillan, 1932.
Value and Capital, Oxford: Oxford University Press, 1939.
The Social Framework, Oxford: Oxford University Press, 1942.
Capital and Growth, Oxford: Oxford University Press, 1965.
Critical Essays in Monetary Theory, Oxford: Oxford University Press, 1967.
The Crisis in Keynesian Economics, Oxford: Basil Blackwell, 1975.
Collected Essays in Economic Theory, 3 vols., Oxford: Basil Blackwell, 1981, 1982, 1983.

JOHN MAYNARD KEYNES

A Treatise on Money, 2 vols., London: Macmillan, 1930.
The General Theory of Employment, Interest and Money, London: Macmillan, 1936.
The Collected Writings of John Maynard Keynes, 30 vols., London: Macmillan, 1971–1983.

FRANK H. KNIGHT

Risk, Uncertainty and Profit, London: London School of Economics, 1921.
The Ethics of Competition, Chicago: University of Chicago Press, 1935.
Freedom and Reform, New York: Harper, 1947.
On the History and Method of Economics, Chicago: University of Chicago Press, 1956.
Intelligence and Democratic Action, Cambridge: Harvard University Press, 1960.

SIMON KUZNETS

Secular Movements in Production and Prices, Boston: Houghton Mifflin, 1930.
with Milton Friedman, *Income from Independent Professional Practice*, New York: NBER, 1945.
National Product since 1869, New York: NBER, 1946.
National Income: A Summary of Findings, New York: NBER, 1946.
Modern Economic Growth, New Haven: Yale University Press, 1966.
Economic Growth of Nations, Cambridge: Harvard University Press, 1971.
Population, Capital and Growth: Selected Essays, New York: W. W. Norton, 1973.
Growth, Population, and Income Distribution: Selected Essays, New York: W. W. Norton, 1979.

ARTHUR CECIL PIGOU

Principles and Methods of Industrial Peace, New York: Macmillan, 1905.
Unemployment, New York: Holt, 1914.
The Economics of Welfare, London: Macmillan, 1920.
The Political Economy of War, London: Macmillan, 1921.
Industrial Fluctuations, London: Macmillan, 1927.
A Study in Public Finance, London: Macmillan, 1928.
The Theory of Unemployment, London: Macmillan, 1933.
The Economics of Stationary States, London: Macmillan, 1935.
Socialism versus Capitalism, London: Macmillan, 1937.
Employment and Equilibrium, London: Macmillan, 1941.
Income: An Introduction to Economics, London: Macmillan, 1946.
The Veil of Money, London: Macmillan, 1949.
Essays in Economics, London: Macmillan, 1952.

DENNIS H. ROBERTSON

A Study of Industrial Fluctuations, London: P. S. King, 1915.
Banking Policy and the Price Level, London: P. S. King, 1926.
Utility and All That, London: George Allen, 1950.
Essays in Monetary Theory, London: P. S. King, 1940.

JOAN ROBINSON

Economics of Imperfect Competition, London: Macmillan, 1933.
Essays in the Theory of Employment, London: Macmillan, 1937.
An Essay on Marxian Economics, London: Macmillan, 1942.
Accumulation of Capital, London: Macmillan, 1956.
Economic Philosophy, London: C. A. Watts, 1962.
Aspects of Development and Underdevelopment, Cambridge: Cambridge University Press, 1979.
Collected Economic Papers, 5 vols., Oxford: Basil Blackwell, 1951–1973.

PAUL A. SAMUELSON

Foundations of Economic Analysis, Cambridge: Harvard University Press, 1947.
Economics, 1st ed., New York: McGraw-Hill, 1948.
Collected Scientific Papers, 4 vols., Cambridge: MIT Press, 1966–1977.

JOSEPH A. SCHUMPETER

Theory of Economic Development, Cambridge: Harvard University Press, 1934 (1912).
Business Cycles, 2 vols., New York: McGraw-Hill, 1939.
Capitalism, Socialism and Democracy, New York: Harper, 1942.
History of Economic Analysis, New York: Oxford University Press, 1954.

RICHARD STONE

with James E. Meade, *National Income and Expenditure*, Oxford: Oxford University Press, 1944.

The Role of Measurement in Economics, Cambridge: Cambridge University Press, 1951.
with J.A.C. Brown, *A Computable Model of Economic Growth,* London: Chapman & Hall, 1962.
Mathematics in the Social Sciences and Other Essays, London: Chapman & Hall, 1966.
Mathematical Models of the Economy and Other Essays, London: Chapman & Hall, 1970.

JAN TINBERGEN

Statistical Testing of Business Cycle Theories, 2 vols., Geneva: League of Nations, 1939.
On the Theory of Economic Policy, Amsterdam: North-Holland, 1952.
Economic Policy: Principles and Design, Amsterdam: North-Holland, 1956.
Income Distribution, Amsterdam: North-Holland, 1975.

What Else Is to Be Found

JOHN R. COMMONS

Trade Unions and Labor Problems, Boston: Ginn, 1905.
Industrial Government, New York: Macmillan, 1921.
The Legal Foundations of Capitalism, New York: Macmillan, 1924.
Institutional Economics, New York: Macmillan, 1934.
The Economics of Collective Action, Madison: University of Wisconsin Press, 1950.

MAURICE DOBB

Political Economy and Capital: Some Essays in Economic Tradition, London: Routledge & Kegan Paul, 1937.
Studies in the Development of Capitalism, London: Routledge & Kegan Paul, 1946.
On Economic Theory and Socialism, London: Routledge & Kegan Paul, 1955.
Welfare Economics and the Economics of Socialism, Cambridge: Cambridge University Press, 1969.
Theories of Value and Distribution since Adam Smith, Cambridge: Cambridge University Press, 1973.

JOHN KENNETH GALBRAITH

American Capitalism, Boston: Houghton Mifflin, 1952.
The Affluent Society, Boston: Houghton Mifflin, 1955.
The New Industrial State, Boston: Houghton Mifflin, 1967.
Economics and the Public Purpose, Boston: Houghton Mifflin, 1973.

NICHOLAS KALDOR

Collected Economic Essays, 8 vols., London: Duckworth, 1960–1980.
The Scourge of Monetarism, Oxford: Oxford University Press, 1982.
Economics without Equilibrium, New York: M. E. Sharpe, 1985.

MICHAL KALECKI

Essays in the Theory of Economic Fluctuations, London: Allen & Unwin, 1939.
Studies in Economic Dynamics, London: Allen & Unwin, 1943.
Theory of Economic Dynamics: An Essay on Cyclical and Long-run Changes in Capitalist Economy, London: Allen & Unwin, 1954.
Studies in the Theory of Business Cycles, 1933–1939, Oxford: Basil Blackwell, 1966.
Selected Essays on the Dynamics of the Capitalist Economy, 1933–1970, Cambridge: Cambridge University Press, 1971.
Selected Essays on the Economic Growth of the Socialist and the Mixed Economy, Cambridge: Cambridge University Press, 1972.

GUNNAR MYRDAL

Monetary Equilibrium, London: Hodge, 1939.
An American Dilemma: The Negro Problem and Modern Democracy, New York: Harper, 1944.
The Political Element in the Development of Economic Theory, London: Routledge & Kegan Paul, 1953.
Economic Theory and Underdeveloped Regions, London: Duckworth, 1957.
Value in Social Theory, London: Routledge & Kegan Paul, 1958.
Beyond the Welfare State, New Haven: Yale University Press, 1960.
Challenge to Affluence, New York: Pantheon, 1963.
Asian Drama: An Inquiry into the Poverty of Nations, New York: Twentieth Century Fund, 1968.
Objectivity in Social Research, New York: Pantheon, 1969.
Against the Stream, New York: Pantheon, 1972.

PIERO SRAFFA

The Works and Correspondence of David Ricardo, 11 vols., Cambridge: Cambridge University Press, 1951–1973.
Production of Commodities by Means of Commodities, Cambridge: Cambridge University Press, 1962.

PAUL M. SWEEZY

The Theory of Capitalist Development: Principles of Marxian Political Economy, New York: Monthly Review Press, 1942.
with Paul A. Baran, *Monopoly Capital: An Essay on the American Economic and Social Order*, New York: Monthly Review Press, 1966.
Modern Capitalism and Other Essays, New York: Monthly Review Press, 1972.

THORSTEIN VEBLEN

The Theory of the Leisure Class, New York: Macmillan, 1899.
The Theory of Business Enterprise, New York: Charles Scribner's Sons, 1904.
The Instinct of Workmanship, New York: Huebsch, 1914.
Imperial Germany and the Industrial Revolution, New York: Macmillan, 1915.
An Inquiry into the Nature of Peace and the Terms of Its Perpetuation, New York: Macmillan, 1917.

The Higher Learning in America: A Memorandum on the Conduct of Universities by Businessmen, New York: Huebsch, 1918.

The Vested Interests and the Common Man, New York: Huebsch, 1919.

The Place of Science in Modern Civilization, New York: Huebsch, 1919.

The Engineers and the Price System, New York: Huebsch, 1921.

Absentee Ownership and Business Enterprise in Recent Times, New York: Huebsch, 1923.

ROBBINS' READING LIST

History of Economic Thought
Lectures by Lord Robbins

I. Bibliography

The following list is intended as a guide to reading for students preparing themselves for the paper in the History of Economic Thought in the B.Sc. Econ. Part II, the B.A. in Economics and Philosophy, or the one year M.Sc. Econ. option of that designation. It clearly includes *very many* more works than the undergraduate, or even the graduate, student will be capable of reading in the time available while he is preparing himself for examination. *But it is not intended as a list of prescribed reading*: it is prepared rather as a guide to a field within which reading will be profitable—a select library from which to choose. Each student must make his own choice within this field according to his own interest and capacity for assimilation.

The sovereign maxim for success in this branch of studies is to concentrate on the study of original texts. Most short histories of economic thought of the text book variety, with their facile generalisations and slick classifications, are to be avoided. There is a great deal of second-rate work in this field which is of no use to anybody, least of all the beginner. There are, as indicated below, valuable secondary authorities which, at a certain stage, may be consulted with great profit. And the student who knows nothing of the field may well begin with reading Blaug's *Economics in Retrospect* in itself a work of great intellectual excellence. But no secondary authority is a real substitute for contact with the original texts. Books about books are chiefly useful for those who know the books they are about.

Accordingly, in what follows, the original texts are separated from commentaries.

Texts

(A) ANTICIPATIONS

For the literature prior to the publication of ADAM SMITH's *Wealth of Nations*, MONROE's *Early Economic Thought* (Harvard University Press) contains a most valuable collection of extracts from the leading writers from Aristotle onwards. Compilations of *short* extracts are to be avoided: they are an encouragement to superficiality and poor scholarship. But MONROE's compilation does not fall into this class. The extracts given are long extracts or whole works and the fact that they are bound in one volume rather than printed in a series of separate books or pamphlets is simply a matter of convenience to the student.

For further work on this period the collection of *Scarce Tracts* edited by MCCULLOCH and printed by the London Political Economy Club or Lord Overstone are invaluable. They comprise:—

Early Tracts on Commerce
Old and Scarce Tracts on Money

Select Tracts on Paper Currency, etc.
Select Tracts on the National Debt
Select Tracts on Commerce
Miscellaneous Economic Tracts

The originals are scarce. But the collection of *Early Tracts on Commerce* has been republished by the Economic History Society and a reprint of the entire set has recently appeared in America.

Some of the gaps in these collections are filled in W. A. SHAW's *Select Tracts, etc., Illustrative of English Monetary History*.

Another series of pamphlets and tracts chiefly appertaining to this period, but also including Classical works, is the famous series published by Johns Hopkins University, Baltimore, *A Reprint of Economic Tracts*. Many of these are still in print; all should be accessible in good university libraries. They have valuable introductions and notes.

A useful collection is also to be found in *Écrits notables sur la monnaie de Copernic á Davanzati*, edited by J. LEBRANCHU (Alcan, 1934).

HULL's *Economic Writings of Sir William Petty* is a valuable edition of the works of the first Englishman to bring a truly scientific mind to the subject. Particularly important are the *Treatise on Taxes* and the *Quantulumcunque Concerning Money*.

Needless to say, the undergraduate is not expected to read all the tracts and pamphlets reprinted in these collections. In the end he must make his own selection. But he should certainly read *all* the extracts in MONROE; *The Discourse of the Commonwealth* by W.S. (This is not reprinted in any of the English series mentioned above; it is included by LE BRANCHU but is published by the Cambridge University Press, edited by MISS LAMOND); and JOHN LOCKE's *Some Considerations of Lowering the Interest and Raising the Value of Money* and *Further Considerations*, etc. In contrast, a graduate aspiring to Professional competence is not excused for not reading everything as time goes on. But even he must make a selection to start with; and the lectures may afford some guide in this connection.

(B) FRENCH AND OTHER NON-BRITISH EIGHTEENTH-CENTURY THOUGHT

Under this heading knowledge of two works is essential:

CANTILLON, *Essai sur la nature du commerce*, edited by by HENRY HIGGS, with the original text and a parallel translation, published by the Royal Economic Society. A modern French edition by SAUVEY is also available.

QUESNAY, *Tableau économique*, edited by KUCZYNSKI and MEEK (Royal Economic Society). This is also reprinted with an invaluable commentary by MEEK in his *Economics of Physiocracy*. It is reproduced without comment by MONROE.

In addition to these, MERCIER DE LA RIVIÈRE, *L'ordre naturel*, and DUPONT DE NEMOURS, *Origins et progres d'une science nouvelle*, are also useful. (Both are reprinted in the series *Économistes et reformateurs sociaux de la France*.)

TURGOT's *Réflections sur la formation et distribution des richesses* (of which there are translations in the Harvard *Economic Reprints* and in MEEK's *Turgot: Progress Sociology and Economics*) has some connection with Physiocracy but stands out in its own right as an important contribution. CONDILLAC's *Le commerce et le gouvernement* is thoroughly worth reading.

GALIANI's *Della Moneta* is one of the most remarkable works in economics of the eighteenth century. The most significant sections are available in a French translation entitled *De la monnaie* by BOUSQUET and CRISAFALLI.

Sir James STEWART, *An Inquiry into the Principles of Political Economy*. An abridged edition of this rare work has been edited by Dr. Skinner.

MEEK's *Precursors of Adam Smith* 1750–1775 has useful extracts both from French and British eighteenth-century thought.

(C) BRITISH CLASSICAL ECONOMISTS AND J. B. SAY

Here the reading of three works is obligatory: HUME's *Economic Essays* (These may be consulted in GREEN & GROSE's edition of HUME's *Essays* or in HUME's *Writings on Economics* edited by ROTWEIN), ADAM SMITH's *Wealth of Nations* and RICARDO's *Principles*. Unless they are thoroughly mastered, any further work in this period is likely to be ill-founded.

The best edition of the *Wealth of Nations* now is that edited by Campbell, Skinner and Todd in the *Glasgow Edition of Adam Smith's Works*, but CANNAN's edition is still very useful and can be obtained fairly cheaply in the Modern Library Edition published in America or in a paperback published by Methuen.

PUFENDORF's *The Law of Nature and Natives* and Francis HUTCHESON's *System of Moral Philosophy* will be found useful as a background to the economic thought of Adam Smith.

There is a cheap edition of RICARDO's *Principles* in the Everyman Library but the standard edition is in Volume I of DR. SRAFFA's great edition of the *Works of Ricardo* (published by the Royal Economic Society). Students who take the study of Ricardo seriously will certainly find it worth while to read also Ricardo's main economic essays which are to be found in Volume III and IV of DR. SRAFFA's edition: and the letters reprinted in Volumes VII–X cast an invaluable light on various aspects of the thought of the age.

Beyond this, the following works are of significance and are all worth consulting, though it is not suggested that the undergraduate will find time to read more than a selection from the list:

J. E. CAIRNES, *Scope and Logical Method of Political Economy, Some Leading Principles of Political Economy*.

MALTHUS, *Essay on Population*. The First Edition re-published by the Royal Economic Society should be read. But care should be taken to become acquainted with the substance of the important doctrinal changes in the Second Edition. His *Political Economy* (LSE Reprint) is also significant for detailed study of the history of thought.

JAMES MILL, *Selected Economic Writings*, edited by Winch.

JOHN STUART MILL, *Principles of Political Economy*. The Toronto Edition contains the best text and commentary. *Essays on Economics and Society* (Toronto 1967) includes the papers originally issued under the title *Unsettled Questions of Political Economy*. *The Unsettled Questions* is also reprinted in the LSE *Series of Reprints of Scarce Works*, etc.

J. B. SAY, *Traité d'économie politique*. (An English translation exists.) The student should not be deterred from reading this either by what he has heard of "Say's Law" in some quarters or by the fact that the Say tradition had for many years an inhibiting influence on the development of economics in France.

SENIOR, *Political Economy* (a reprint was published in 1938 by Allen and Unwin) and the three sets of *Lectures* reprinted in the LSE *Reprints*.

THORNTON, *Paper Credit* (Hayek's edition). The best single work on Money before the XXth century.

TOOKE, *An Inquiry into the Currency Principle* (LSE Reprints).

FULLARTON, *On the Regulation of Currencies.* This latter is the best statement of the position of the so-called Banking School.

TORRENS, *Letters on Commercial Policy* (LSE *Reprints*), and *Sir Robert Peel's Act of 1844*, 3rd edition. (The second of these is by far the ablest statement of position of the so-called Currency School.)

The Bullion Report, edited by CANNAN under the title *The Paper Pound.* (This has recently been reprinted by Cass.)

(D) SOCIALIST THOUGHT

Some attention should be paid to nineteenth-century socialist thought in so far as this is concerned with economic questions. A survey of part of the field is to be found in ANTON MENGER's *Right to the Whole Produce of Labour*, edited by FOXWELL, especially the long preface by FOXWELL. Some of the works there referred to, GRAY's *Essay on Human Happiness*, and BRAY's *Labour's Wrongs and Labour's Remedies*, are published in the LSE *Reprints*. A selection of the writings of ST. SIMON, edited by MARKHAM, is published by BLACKWELL and the pivotal *Exposition du Doctrine de St. Simon* by BAZARD and ENFANTIN is edited by BOUGLE and HALEVY in the series *Économistes et reformateurs sociaux de la France.*

For MARXIAN theory, Volume I of *Capital* is the "locus classicus" of the better known Marxian doctrines, but a thorough knowledge of the system can only be obtained by much more extensive reading, including Volumes II and III of *Capital* and the earlier *Critique of Political Economy* and *Theorien über den Mehrwert* of which selections are translated by Bonner and Burns in *Theories of Surplus Value.*

(E) ECONOMIC NATIONALISM AND THE HISTORICAL SCHOOL

Both these sources of criticism of the English Classical School should be known. On Economic Nationalism, HAMILTON's *Report of Manufacturers* reprinted by Columbia University Press, 1936 and LIST's *System of National Economy* (trans. Lloyd) are the standard texts.

The criticism of the Classical System by the so-called Historical School is mostly to be found in German works, conspicuously the works of ROSCHER, HILDERBRAND, KNIES and SCHMOLLER. English works taking something of the same point of view and certainly more agreeable reading are R. JONES, *An Introductory Lecture* printed in his *Literary Remains*, edited by WHEWELL, 1859, and CLIFFE LESLIE, *Essays on Political and Moral Philosophy.* See also W. BAGEHOT's *Postulates of English Political Economy.* A balanced review of the main issues involved is to be found in J. M. KEYNES' *Scope and Method of Political Economy.*

(F) PRECURSORS OF MODERN ANALYSIS

There are a number of isolated works appearing at different dates in the middle of the nineteenth century which in significant ways anticipate the theoretical work which was to come later. Among the more important are:

COURNOT, *Recherches sur les principes mathématiques de la théorie des richesses*, 1938. (This has been translated and edited by IRVING FISHER, New York, 1927. It is the origin of modern theories of the Demand Function and Monopoly.)

LONGFIELD, *Lectures on Political Economy*, 1834. (LSE *Reprints.*) This antici-pates marginal productivity theories of distribution, as does:

VON THÜNEN, *Die isolierte Staat*, 1826. (Reprinted Jena, 1921.) This is also the *locus classicus* of early location theory. A translation of parts of this work has been edited by PROFESSOR HALL (Pergamon Press).

RAE, J., *New Principles of Political Economy*, 1834. This is known chiefly for its presentation of a time preference theory of interest. But it is almost equally impor-tant on inventions and as a general critique of Adam Smith. It was republished and re-arranged by C. W. MIXTER in 1905 under the inappropriate title, *The Sociologi-cal Theory of Capital*, but it is now available in faithful reprints by Kelley and the Toronto University Press, the latter with an introductory volume of biographical details and unplublished letters and essays edited by DR. WARREN JAMES.

HERMANN, F., *Staatswirtschaftliche Untersuchungen.*

GOSSEN, N. H., *Entwicklung der Gesetze der menschlichen Verkehr*, 1854. (Re-published with an introduction by F. A. HAYEK.) The first systematic marginal util-ity theory of value.

MANGOLDT, H. VON, *Der Untermehmergewinn*, 1855. This anticipates modern profit theory.

(G) ECONOMIC ANALYSIS SINCE 1870

Coming to the history of more modern economic analysis, it should be noted that the fundamentals of the so-called revolution of the seventies were laid down in JEVON's *Theory of Political Economy*, WALRAS' *Elements*, and MENGER's *Grundsätze der Volkswirtschaftslehre*. Walras has been translated by PROFESSOR JAFFE and pub-lished by the the Royal Economic Society and Messrs. Allen and Unwin, Menger by DINGWALL and HOSELITZ and published by the Free Press, Glencoe, Illinois. *The Letters and Journals of W. Stanley Jevons* by his wife or, more extensively, in the edition by Professor Collison Black, and the *Correspondence of Leon Walras*, edited by W. JAFFE are well worth reading as throwing further light on the authors concerned.

So far as the English literature is concerned, important developments are to be found in F. Y. EDGEWORTH's *Mathematical Psychics* and WICKSTEED's *Essay on the Co-ordination of the Laws of Distribution*. The *Papers Relating to Political Economy* of the former writer and the *Commonsense of Political Economy* by the latter should also be consulted.

Developments of the so-called Austrian theories are to be found in FRIEDRICH WIESER's *Über den Ursprung und die Hauptgesetze des wirtschaftlichen Wertes* and his *Natural Value*, and BÖHM-BAWERK's *Capital and Interest*.

For developments springing from Walras, PARETO's *Manual* is representative; while a combination of Austrian and Walrasian and Classical influence is to be found in WICKSELL's *Lectures* and his *Interest and Prices*.

For American developments, J. B. CLARK's *Distribution of Wealth*; the early works of IRVING FISHER, *The Nature of Capital and Income*, *The Rate of Interest* and the *Mathematical Investigations of the Theory of Value and Price*, and F. A. FETTER's *Economic Principles*, Volume 1, are essential reading.

Above all, however, A. MARSHALL's *Principles of Economics* should be read thor-oughly. It should be studied in the eighth edition or the variorum edition edited by GUILLEBAUD, published by the Royal Economic Society. This book is a bridge be-

tween the History of Economic Thought and Modern Analysis, and in devoting
thorough attention to it, the student kills at least two birds with one stone. The
student would be well advised to read the life and correspondence of MARSHALL as
set forth in *Memorials of Alfred Marshall*, edited by PIGOU. MARSHALL's evidence
before the *Gold and Silver Commission* and the Committee on Indian Currency,
reprinted in *Official Papers* by the Royal Economic Society is worth consulting
by those interested in the history of monetary theory; and his papers on the *Pure
Theory of the International Domestic Value* (LSE *Reprints*) contain the main beginnings of modern geometrical economics. A collection of the *Early Economic Writings of Alfred Marshall*, edited by J. M. WHITAKER, is interesting as some correc-
tion of Marshall's recollections in old age.

    Precursors in Mathematical Economics by BAUMOL and GOLDFELD in the LSE
Series of *Reprints* is an anthology of contributions to this field from Bernoulli to
the present day, chosen and presented in a way which puts it in a class by itself as
regards value to the student.

Commentaries

By far the most comprehensive general survey of the field is SCHUMPETER's *History
of Economic Analysis*. This, however, is very long and students are not recommended to attempt it at an early stage. Beginners who wish for a rapid survey of the
field should read SCHUMPETER's *Shorter History*, of which an English translation is
available under the title *Economic Doctrine and Method*. *Economics in Retrospect* by
Mark Blaug is an excellent introduction to the period since the middle of the eighteenth century; it contains extensive bibliographies and is probably the most useful
single work of this kind for the student to consult. JAMES BONAR's *Philosophy and
Political Economy* is a useful survey of the field indicated by its title. O. H. TAYLOR's
History of Economic Thought is a readable and profound study of the mainstreams
of development; it deals explicitly with ideology as well as analysis. H. M.
ROBERTSON's *Aspects of the Rise of Economic Individualism* is an examination of
erroneous views of the history of ideology. A survey of the general field, proceeding
subject by subject rather than author by author, is to be found in EDWIN CANNAN's
Review of Economic Theory. SCHNEIDER, *Geschichte der Wirtschaftstheories* is valuable, particularly in regard to XIXth century continental authors.

    Collections of Essays covering various parts of the field are to be found in
BOWLEY's *Studies in the History of Economic Theory before 1870*; *Essays in Economic
Thought* edited by SPENGLER and ALLEN; *The Development of Economic Theory* edited by SPIEGEL and *Economic Thought: A Historical Anthology* edited by GHERITY.
STIGLER's *Essays in the History of Economic Thought* are very strongly recommended. ROBBINS, *The Evolution of Modern Economic Theory* and his *Theory of Economic Development in the History of Economic Thought* may be consulted.

    Special sections of the field are covered as follows:—

    BARRY GORDON *Economic Analysis before Adam Smith* (This title is somewhat
misleading; the history ends at 1623!)

    The Economic Thought of Plato and Aristotle, by the relevant section of
SCHUMPETER's *History*, Part II, Chapter 2. See also BARKER's *The Political Thought
of Plato and Aristotle*.

    Medieval Economic Thought in SCHUMPETER's *History*, Part II, Chapter 3;
ASHLEY's *Economic History*, Part 1, Chapter III, Part 2, Chapter VI; MAX BEER's
Early British Economics (this also covers some of the following period), and

T. DIVINE's *Interest: A Historical and Analytical Study*. DE ROOVER's *San Bernadino of Siena and Saint Antonino of Florence* is a fundamental corrective to some earlier conceptions of this period. GRICE-HUTCHINSON's *School of Salamanca* and *Early Economic Thought in Spain* are pioneering essays in a significant area.

The so-called mercantile period, by ELI HECKSCHER's *Mercantilism*. LIPSON's *Economic History*, and FURNISS' *The Position of the Labourer in a System of Nationalism*, E. A. J. JOHNSON's *Predecessors of Adam Smith*, ROSCHER's *Zur Geschichte des englischen Volkswirtschaftslehre*, *Revisions in Mercantilism* edited by D. C. COLEMAN, P. J. THOMAS's *Mercantilism and the East India Trade*. KNORR's *British Colonial Theories 1570–1850* covers both the mercantile and the classical period.

DE ROOVER in his *Gresham and the Foreign Exchanges* should be consulted on the discussion of problems of external monetary policy in the sixteenth century. *Tudor Economic Documents* edited TAWNEY and POWER, *Vol. III* reprints the report of the *Royal Commission on the Exchanges of 1564* and TAWNEY's Introduction to THOMAS WILSON's *Discourse upon Usury* deserves to be read.

Useful studies of the late seventeenth and early eighteenth century literature are to be found in LETWIN's *Origins of Scientific Economics*.

KAREN IVERSON VAUGHN's *John Locke: Economist and Social Scientist* is the only work known to me which is solely devoted to this aspect of the work of this important philosopher.

SEN's *Economics of Sir James Stewart* gives a sympathetic account of the works of this somewhat neglected eighteenth century writer.

The Physiocratic literature, by HENRY HIGGS' *The Physiocrats*, ONCKEN's *Geschichte der Nationalökonomie*, Volume 1, and WEULERSSE, *Le mouvement physiocratic en France*; SCHELLE, *Dupont de Nemours et l'école physiocratic*; MEEK, *Economics of Physiocracy*.

Classical Economic Theory. The best general conspectus is O'BRIEN's *The Classical Economists*; CANNAN, *Theories of Production and Distribution*; TAUSSIG, *Wages and Capital*, are excellent supplements.

The following may be consulted on special authors: *Essays on Adam Smith* edited by SKINNER and WILSON; SAMUEL HOLLANDER, *The Economics of Adam Smith*; *The Economics of David Ricardo*; SHOUP, *Ricardo on Taxation*; BOWLEY, *Nassau Senior and Classical Economics*; ROBBINS, *Robert Torrens and the Evolution of Classical Economics*; MEEK, *Studies in the Labour Theory of Value*; RAUNDER, *Samuel Bailey and the Classical Theory of Value*; O'BRIEN, *McCulloch: A Study in Classical Economics*—see also his introduction to the reprint of McCulloch's *Treatise on Taxation* (Scottish Economic Classics); PEDRO SCHWARTZ, *The New Political Economy of J. S. Mill*; SOWELL, *Say's Law*.

Classical Political Economy, by LESLIE STEPHEN, *The English Utilitarians*; E. HALEVY, *The Philosophical Radicals*; ROBBINS, *The Theory of Economic Policy in English Classical Political Economy* and his *Political Economy: Past and Present*; D. WINCH, *Classical Political Economy and Colonies*; BLACK, *Economic Thought and the Irish Question 1817–1870*.

The history of population theories, STRANGELAND, *Pre-Malthusian Theories of Population*; SPENGLER, *French Predecessors of Malthus*; McCLEARY, *The Malthusian Population Theory*. (This contains a reprint of the important correspondence with Senior.)

Marxian socialism by BÖHM-BAWERK, *Karl Marx and the Close of His System* and JOAN ROBINSON, *An Essay in Marxian Economics*. MORISHIMA, *Marx's Economics*,

W. J. BAUMOL, *On the Folklore of Marxism* (*Proceedings of the American Philosophical Society, Volume 123 Number 2, 1979*).

General Socialist Theory by A. GRAY, *The Socialist Traditions*; SWEEZY, *The Theory of Capitalist Development.*

The Austrian School of WILLIAM SMART, *An Introduction to the Theory of Value*; and *Carl Menger and the Austrian School of Economics* edited by HICKS and WEBB.

The history of theories of international trade by JACOB VINER, *Studies in the Theory of International Trade.* This is valuable too for the history of general monetary theory.

The history of monetary and banking theory by A. MARGET, *The Theory of Prices,* Volumes I and II; LLOYD MINT's *History of Banking Theory*; HORSEFIELD, *British Monetary Experiments 1650–1700*; D. VICKERS, *Studies in the Theory of Money*; CHARLES RIST, *Histoire des doctrines relatives au-crédit et à la monnaie*, LIEPMANN, *Der Kampf um die Gestaltung der englischcen Wahrungsverfassung 1819–1844*; CORRY, *Money Saving and Investment in English Economics, 1800–1850*, and FETTER, *Development of British Monetary Orthodoxy, 1791–1895.*

The history of interest theories, by CASSEL, *Nature and Necessity of Interest*; BÖHM-BAWERK, *Capital and Interest*, Volume I, is much more extensive than Cassel but his judgements, although interesting, are very one-sided and often palpably unfair; and G. S. L. TUCKER, *Progress and Profits in British Economic Thought.*

The history of fluctuation theory, by ROBERT LINK, *English Theories of Economic Fluctuation*, and BERGMAN, *Geschichte der Nationalökonomische Krisen-Theorien.*

The early history of mathematical economics, by THEOCHARIS, *Early Developments in Mathematical Economics.*

An excellent survey of developments of modern economic theory between JEVONS and WICKSTEED is given by GEORGE STIGLER, *Theories of Production and Distribution.* T. W. HUTCHINSON, *A Review of Economic Doctrines, 1870–1929*, is also a standard work; see also his thought-provoking *On Revolution and Progress in Economic Knowledge.* CARL UHR, *Economic Doctrines of Knut Wicksell* is a useful survey.

SCHUMPETER, *Ten Great Economists*, and KEYNES, *Studies in Biography*, provide sidelights on the evolution of recent theory—the latter happens also to be one of the masterpieces of modern prose. RECKTENWALD, *Political Economy: An Historical Perspective* provides interesting biographical and critical studies.

JAMES A. GHERITY's *Economic Thought, a Historical Anthology*; JOSEPH SPENGLER's *Essays in Economic Thought, Aristotle to Marshall*, and H. W. SPIEGEL's *Development of Economic Thought* are useful collections of essays on outstanding figures or schools.

The journal HISTORY OF POLITICAL ECONOMY, published by Duke University is very worth consulting.

II. OUTLINE OF THE COURSE

The following list of names and subjects gives a rough indication of the course which the lectures will follow. There is no guarantee that it will be exactly adhered to.

(A) ANTICIPATIONS

(i) Introduction. Plato

(ii) Aristotle and Early Scholasticism

(iii) Scholasticism (continued)
(iv) Pamphleteers—Money (Oresme Bodin "W.S.")
(v) Pamphleteers—Mercantilism (Serra, Malynes, Mun)
(vi) Petty
(vii) Child and Locke (Interest)
(viii) Locke and Lowndes on the Standard. North.[1]

(B) EMERGENCE OF SYSTEMS
(ix) Cantillon
(x) Physiocracy
(xi) Physiocracy (continued)
(xii) Turgot and Galiani
(xiii) Locke and Hume on Property
(xiv) Hume on Money, Interest and Trade
(xv) Precursors of Adam Smith and General Survey of His Intentions.
(xvi) *The Wealth of Nations*—Analytical
(xvii) *The Wealth of Nations*—Analytical
(xviii) *The Wealth of Nations*—Policy[2]

(C) XIXTH CENTURY CLASSICISM
(xix) General Review: Malthus on Population
(xx) Value and Distribution—Historical Origin
(xxi) Value and Distribution—Analytical
(xxii) Value and Distribution—Analytical
(xxiii) Money and Banking—Historical Background[3]
(xxiv) Money and Banking—Analytical[3]
(xxv) Overall Equilibrium
(xxvi) International Trade
(xxvii) John Stuart Mill
(xxviii) Say and Hermann[4]

(D) OTHER MID-XIXTH CENTURY THOUGHT
(xxix) Marx
(xxx) List and the Historical School

(E) BEGINNINGS OF MODERN ANALYSIS
(xxxi) Precursors of Change (Cournot, Von Thünen)
(xxxii) Precursors of Change (continued) Rae. Decline of Classical
   Influence. Anticipations of Marginalism.
(xxxiii) The Marginal Revolution: Jevons—Edgeworth
(xxxiv) The Marginal Revolution: Menger and Wieser (Costs)
(xxxv) The Marginal Revolution: The Price of Services
   (Austrians, Clark, Wicksteed)
(xxxvi) Capital Theory: Jevons, Böhm-Bawerk and Fisher
(xxxvii) Walras—Pareto—Hicks and Allen
(xxxviii) Marshall
(xxxix) Money: Fisher, Marshall, Pigou, Keynes, Mises, Hawtrey,
   Robertson
(xl) Fluctuations: Jevons, Juglas, Spiethoff, Hawtrey, Robertson[4]

Students unacquainted with LSE traditions should realise that contrary to contemporary mythology the majority of University teachers positively welcome questions and criticism. I am always happy to talk after the lectures and to arrange for meetings at other times.

August 1981

NOTES

1. Lecture not given. Some of this material is in lectures 7 and 8.
2. Lecture given in two parts.
3. Lecture not recorded.
4. Lecture not given.

Robbins' Writings in the History of Economic Thought

BOOKS

1935. *An Essay on the Nature and Significance of Economic Science*. London: Macmillan, 1932. 2d edition. London: Macmillan, 1935. 3d edition. London: Macmillan, 1984.

1932. "Introduction." In Philip H. Wicksteed, *The Co-ordination of the Laws of Distribution*. Edited by Lionel Robbins. London: London School of Economics Reprints of Scarce Tracts on Economics and Political Science No. 12. Revised edition, with an introduction by Ian Steedman. Aldershot: Edward Elgar, 1992.

1933. "Introduction." In Philip H. Wicksteed, *The Commonsense of Political Economy and Selected Papers and Reviews on Economic Theory*, edited by Lionel Robbins, 1–9. London: George Routledge & Sons. Reprinted as "Robbins on Wicksteed." In *The Development of Economic Thought: Great Economists in Perspective*, edited by Henry William Spiegel, 700–17. New York: Science Editions, 1952. Also reprinted as "Philip Wicksteed as an Economist." In *The Evolution of Modern Economic Theory and Other Papers on the History of Economic Thought*, 189–209. London: Macmillan and Chicago: Aldine, 1970.

1935. "Introduction." In Knut Wicksell, *Lectures on Political Economy*, translated by E. Classen, vii–xix. London: George Routledge & Sons. Reprinted as "Wicksell's *Lectures on Political Economy*." In *The Evolution of Modern Economic Theory and Other Papers on the History of Economic Thought*, 210–22. London: Macmillan and Chicago: Aldine, 1970.

1952. *The Theory of Economic Policy in English Classical Political Economy*. London: Macmillan. 2d edition. London: Macmillan, 1978.

1958. *Robert Torrens and the Evolution of Classical Economics*. London: Macmillan.

1958. "Introduction." In R. Torrens, *Letters on Commercial Policy* (1833). Reprinted as the London School of Economics Reprints of Scarce Works on Political Economy No. 14, v–x. London: LSE. Reprinted as "Torrens's *Letters on Commercial Policy*." In *The Evolution of Modern Economic Theory and Other Papers on the History of Economic Thought*, 92–96. London: Macmillan and Chicago: Aldine, 1970.

1968. *The Theory of Economic Development in the History of Economic Thought being the Chichele Lectures for 1966, revised and extended*. London: Macmillan.

1970. *The Evolution of Modern Economic Theory and Other Papers on the History of Economic Thought*. London: Macmillan and Chicago: Aldine.

1976. *Political Economy: Past and Present, A Review of Leading Theories of Economic Policy*. London: Macmillan.

ARTICLES IN JOURNALS

1930. "The Economic Works of Phillip Wicksteed." *Economica* 10 (1930): 245–58. Provides the basis of the Introduction in Robbins (1933). Also published as

"The Economic Works." In C. H. Herford, *Philip Henry Wicksteed, His Life and Work,* 228–47. London and Toronto: J. M. Dent & Sons, 1931.

1935. "A Student's Recollections of Edwin Cannan." *Economic Journal* 45: 393–98.

1936. "The Place of Jevons in the History of Economic Thought." *Manchester School* 7: 1–17. Reprinted in *Economic Thought: A Historical Anthology,* edited by J. A. Gherity, 328–45. New York: Random House, 1965. Also reprinted as "The Place of Jevons in the History of Economic Thought." In *The Evolution of Modern Economic Theory and Other Papers on the History of Economic Thought,* 169–88. London: Macmillan and Chicago: Aldine, 1970.

1938. "Live and Dead Issues in the Methodology of Economics." *Economica* n.s. 5: 342–52.

1955. "Schumpeter's History of Economic Analysis." *Quarterly Journal of Economics* 69: 1–22. Reprinted as "Schumpeter on the History of Economic Analysis." In *The Evolution of Modern Economic Theory and Other Papers on the History of Economic Thought,* 47–72. London: Macmillan and Chicago: Aldine, 1970.

1956. "A Letter from David Ricardo." *Economica* n.s. 23: 172–74.

1957. "Packe on Mill." *Economica,* n.s. 24: 250–59. Reprinted as "The Life of John Stuart Mill." In *The Evolution of Modern Economic Theory and Other Papers on the History of Economic Thought,* 97–110. London: Macmillan and Chicago: Aldine, 1970.

1967. "Malthus as an Economist." *Economic Journal* 77: 256–61. Reprinted as "Malthus in Perspective." In *The Evolution of Modern Economic Theory and Other Papers on the History of Economic Thought,* 85–91. London: Macmillan and Chicago: Aldine, 1970.

1981. "Economics and Political Economy." Richard T. Ely Lecture. *American Economic Review* 71, Supplement: 1–10. Reprinted as "Economics and Political Economy." In *An Essay on the Nature and Significance of Economic Science,* 11–33. 3d edition. London: Macmillan, 1984.

1982. "The place of Jevons in the History of Economic Thought." *Manchester School* 50: 310–25.

PAMPHLETS AND REPORTS

1965. *Bentham in the Twentieth Century: An Address to the Assembly of Faculties, University College, London on 16 June 1964.* London: Athlone Press. Reprinted as "Bentham in the Twentieth Century." In *The Evolution of Modern Economic Theory and Other Papers on the History of Economic Thought,* 73–84. London: Macmillan and Chicago: Aldine, 1970.

1970. *Jacob Viner (1892–1970): A Tribute.* Princeton: Princeton University Press.

CHAPTERS IN BOOKS

1930. "Introduction." In Harold E. Batson, *A Select Bibliography of Modern Economic Theory 1870–1929,* vii–ix. London: Routledge & Kegan Paul.

1949. "Cannan, Edwin." In *Dictionary of National Biography,* Supplement 1931–1940, edited by L. G. W. Legg, 141–43. London: Oxford University Press. Reprinted as "A Biographical Note on Edwin Cannan." In *The Evolution of Modern*

Economic Theory and Other Papers on the History of Economic Thought, 229–33. London: Macmillan and Chicago: Aldine, 1970.

1961. "Foreword." In Reghinos D. Theocharis, *Early Developments in Mathematical Economics,* v–vi. London: Macmillan.

1962. "The Economic Functions of the State in English Classical Political Economy." In *Private Wants and Public Needs: Issues Surrounding the Size and Scope of Government Expenditure,* edited by Edmund S. Phelps, 94–101. New York: Norton. An abridged version of sections 1–3 of Lecture 2, "The Economic Functions of the State." In *The Theory of Economic Policy in English Classical Political Economy,* 34–46. London: Macmillan, 1962.

1966. "Foreword." In *The Travel Diaries of Thomas Robert Malthus* edited by Patricia James, vii–ix. Cambridge: Cambridge University Press.

1967. "Introduction." In *The Collected Works of John Stuart Mill, Vols. IV and V: Essays on Economics and Society,* edited by J. M. Robson, vii–xii. Toronto: University of Toronto Press. Reprinted as "Mill's Essays on Economics and Society." In *The Evolution of Modern Economic Theory and Other Papers on the History of Economic Thought,* 118–63. London: Macmillan and Chicago: Aldine, 1970.

1975. "Foreword." In David Seckler, *Thorstein Veblen and the Institutionalists: A Study in the Social Philosophy of Economics,* ix–xi. London: Macmillan.

1978. "Economists and Trade Unions, 1776–1977." In *Trade Unions: Public Goods or Public "Bads"?* IEA Readings No. 17. London: Institute of Economic Affairs: 5–16 and 19–20.

REVIEWS IN JOURNALS

1927. "Review of *The Tables Turned: A Lecture and Dialogue on Adam Smith and the Classical Economists,* by James Bonar."*Economica* 7 (December): 391–92.

1929. "Review of *A Review of Economic Theory,* by Edwin Cannan." *Economic Journal* 39 (September): 409–14.

1930. "Review of *Industrial Efficiency and Social Economy,* by Nassau W. Senior (edited by S. Leon Levi)." *Economic Journal* 40 (June): 272–75.

1932. "Review of *A Catalogue of the Library of Adam Smith,* by James Bonar." *Economica* 12 (August): 365.

1940. "Review of *Karl Marx: His Life and Environment,* by I. Berlin." *Economica* n.s. 7 (February): 93–94.

1957. "Review of *On the History and Method of Economics—Selected Essays,* by Frank H. Knight." *American Economic Review* 47 (June): 397–99.

1960. "Review of *Lectures on Economic Principles,* by Sir Dennis H. Robertson." *Economica,* n.s. 27 (February): 71–74. Reprinted as "Robertson's *Lectures on Economic Principles.*" In *The Evolution of Modern Economic Theory and Other Papers on the History of Economic Thought,* 248–52. London: Macmillan and Chicago: Aldine, 1970.

1960. "Review of '*Papers on Economic Theory* by Knut Wicksell, edited with an Introduction by Erik Lindahl' and '*The Life of Knut Wicksell* by Torsten Gardlund, translated by Nancy Adler.' " *Economica* n.s. 27 (May): 173–77. Reprinted as "New Light on Knut Wicksell." In *The Evolution of Modern Economic Theory and Other Papers on the History of Economic Thought,* 223–28. London: Macmillan and Chicago: Aldine, 1970.

1960. "Review of *The Saint Simonians, Mill and Carlyle: A Preface to Modern Thought,* by K. D. Pankhurst." *Economica* n.s. 27 (August): 278–79.

1961. "Review of *Ricardo on Taxation,* by C. S. Shoup." *Economica* n.s. 28 (August): 326–28.

1962. "Review of *John Millar of Glasgow, 1735–1801: His Life and Thought and His Contributions to Sociological Analysis,* by William C. Lehmann." *Economica* n.s. 29 (February): 96–97.

1962. "Review of *The Early Draft of John Stuart Mill's Autobiography,* edited by Jack Stillinger." *Economica* n.s. 29 (May): 202–4. Reprinted as Annex (i) to "The Life of John Stuart Mill." In *The Evolution of Modern Economic Theory and Other Papers on the History of Economic Thought,* 110–13. London: Macmillan and Chicago: Aldine, 1970.

1962. "Review of *Progress and Profits in British Economic Thought, 1650–1850,* by G. S. L. Tucker."*Economic Journal* 72: 374–76.

1963. "Review of *Jeremy Bentham: An Odyssey of Ideas, 1748–1792,* by Mary P. Mack." *Economica* n.s. 30 (May): 196–97.

1965. "Review of *The Collected Works of John Stuart Mill, Vols. XII–XIII: The Earlier Letters of John Stuart Mill, 1812–1845,* edited by Francis E. Mineka." *Economica* n.s. 32 (November): 458–60. Reprinted as Annex (ii) to "The Life of John Stuart Mill." In *The Evolution of Modern Economic Theory and Other Papers on the History of Economic Thought,* 113–17. London: Macmillan and Chicago: Aldine, 1970.

1966. "Review of *The Collected Works of John Stuart Mill, Vols. II–III: Principles of Political Economy with Some of Their Applications to Social Philosophy,* edited by J. M. Robson." *Economica* n.s. 33 (February): 92–94. Reprinted as "Mill's *Principles of Political Economy.*" In *The Evolution of Modern Economic Theory and Other Papers on the History of Economic Thought,* 164–68. London: Macmillan and Chicago: Aldine, 1970.

1966. "Review of *Economics of Physiocracy: Essays and Translations,* by Ronald L. Meek." *Economica* n.s. 33 (February): 94–96.

1966. "Review of *A History of Marginal Utility Theory,* by Emil Kauder." *Economica* n.s. 33 (August): 347–48.

1966. "Review of *Life of Adam Smith,* by John Rae, with introduction by Jacob Viner." *Economica* n.s. 33 (August): 348–49.

1967. "Review of *On the Logic of the Moral Sciences,* by John Stuart Mill, and edited by Henry M. Magid." *Economica* n.s. 34 (February): 90.

1967. "Review of *John Rae, Political Economist: An Account of His Life and a Compilation of His Main Writings,* edited by R. Warren James." *Economica* n.s. 34 (August): 335–37.

1969. "Review of *Economic Theory in Retrospect,* by Mark Blaug." 2d edition. *Economica* n.s. 36 (November), 442–43.

1970. "Review of *The Improvement of Mankind: The Social and Political Thought of John Stuart Mill,* by John M. Robson." *Economica* n.s. 37 (May): 194–95.

1970. "Review of *The Collected Works of John Stuart Mill, Vol. X: Essays on Ethics, Religion and Society,* edited by J. M. Robson." *Economica* n.s. 37 (November): 422–24.

1971. "Review of *J. R. McCulloch: A Study in Classic Economics,* by D. P. O'Brien." *Economica* n.s. 38 (August): 321–22.

1973. "Review of *Essays in Biography: Volume X of the Collected Writings of John Maynard Keynes.*" *Economic Journal* 83 (June): 530–31.

1974. "Review of *The Collected Works of John Stuart Mill, Vols. XIV–XVII: The Later Letters of John Stuart Mill, 1849–1873,* edited by Francis E. Mineka and Dwight N. Lindley." *Economica* n.s. 41 (August): 336–38.

1976. "Review of *The Collected Works of John Stuart Mill, Vols. VII–VIII: A System of Logic Ratiocinative and Inductive,* edited by J. M. Robson." *Economica* n.s. 43 (November): 446–47.

1977. "Review of *The Early Economic Writings of Alfred Marshall (1867–1890),* edited by J. K. Whitaker." *Economica* n.s. 44 (February): 91–92.

1978. "Review of *The Economic Advisory Council, 1930–1939: A Study in Economic Advice during Depression and Recovery,* by Susan Howson and Donald Winch." *Journal of Economic Literature* 16 (March): 114–15.

1979. "Review of *The Collected Works of John Stuart Mill, Vols. XVIII and XIX: Essays on Politics and Society,* edited by J. M. Robson." *Economica* n.s. 46 (February): 89–90.

1980. "Review of *Population Malthus: His Life and Times,* by Patricia James." *Economica* n.s. 47 (November): 471.

1980. "Review of *Religious Thought and Economic Society, Four Chapters of an Unfinished Work by Jacob Viner,* edited by Jacques Melitz and Donald Winch." *Economica* n.s. 47 (November): 489–90.

1980. "Review of *The Collected Works of John Stuart Mill, Vol. XI: Essays on Philosophy and the Classics,* edited by J. M. Robson." *Economica* n.s. 47 (November): 490–91.

REVIEWS IN THE POPULAR PRESS

1951. "Review of *The Life of John Maynard Keynes,* by Roy F. Harrod." *The Times,* 26 January, 7f–g. Reprinted as "Harrod on Keynes." In *The Evolution of Modern Economic Theory and Other Papers on the History of Economic Thought,* 243–47. London: Macmillan and Chicago: Aldine, 1970.

1972. "Review of *The Correspondence of Lord Overstone,* edited by D. P. O'Brien." *Financial Times,* 6 January, 20.

1975. "Review of *The Classical Economists* by D. P. O'Brien and *Classical Economics Reconsidered* by T. Sowell." *Times Literary Supplement,* 1 August.

• R E F E R E N C E S •

Antonelli, Étienne. *Principes d'Économie pure. La théorie de l'échange sous le régime de la libre concurrence.* Paris: Rivière, 1914.

Aquinas, St. Thomas. *Summa Theologica.* In *Early Economic Thought: Selections from Economic Literature Prior to Adam Smith,* edited by Arthur E. Monroe, 51–77. Cambridge, Mass.: Harvard University Press, 1948.

Aristotle. *The Nichomachean Ethics of Aristotle.* Translated with an analysis and critical notes by James Edward Cowell Welldon. London: Macmillan, 1892.

———. "Politics—Ethics." In *Early Economic Thought: Selections from Economic Literature Prior to Adam Smith,* edited by Arthur E. Monroe, 1–29. Cambridge, Mass.: Harvard University Press, 1948.

———. *Topica.* Translated by E. S. Forster. Cambridge: Mass.: Harvard University Press, 1960.

Ashley, William James. *An Introduction to English Economic History and Theory.* London: Longmans, Green, 1901.

Bain, Alexander. *John Stuart Mill; A Criticism: With Personal Recollections.* London: Longmans, Green, 1882.

Bainfield Thomas Charles. *The Organization of Industry.* 2d ed. London: Longman, Brown, 1848.

Barone, Enrico. *Grundzüge der theoretischen Nationalökonomie. Übersetzt und mit einem Anhang versehen von Hans Staehle Bonn.* Bonn: Schroeder, 1927.

Barton, John. *Condition of the Labouring Classes of Society by John Barton* (1817). A Reprint of the Economic Tracts edited by Jacob H. Hollander. Baltimore: Johns Hopkins University Press, 1934.

Baumol, William J. "Say's (at Least) Eight Laws, or What Say and James Mill May Really Have Meant." *Economica* 44 (May 1977): 145–62.

Becker, Gary S., and William J. Baumol. "The Classical Monetary Theory: The Outcome of the Discussion." *Economica,* n.s. 19 (November 1952): 355–76.

Bentham, Jeremy. *An Introduction to the Principles of Morals and Legislation.* 1st ed. London: T. Payne and Son, 1789.

———. *Manual of Political Economy* (1793–95). In *The Works of Jeremy Bentham,* Vol. 3, edited by John Bowring, 31–84. Edinburgh: William Tait, 1843.

———. *Rationale of Judicial Evidence, Specially Applied to English Practice.* 5 vols. London: Hunt and Clarke, 1827.

———. *Essay on the Influence of Time and Place in Matters of Legislation* (1843). In *The Works of Jeremy Bentham,* edited by John Bowring, 1:169–94. Edinburgh: William Tait, 1843.

Bodin, Jean. *Jean Bodin's Reply to the Paradoxes of Malestroit Concerning the Dearness of All Things and the Remedy Therefor* (1568). In *Early Economic Thought: Selections from Economic Literature Prior to Adam Smith,* edited by Arthur E. Monroe, 121–41. Cambridge, Mass.: Harvard University Press, 1948.

——— *Les six livres de la République* (1576). Abridged and translated by M. J. Tooley as *Six Books of the Commonwealth.* Oxford: Basil Blackwell, n.d. (c. 1952).

Böhm-Bawerk, Eugen von. *Grundzüge der Theorie des Wirtschaftlichen Güterwerts* (1886). L.S.E. Reprints of Scarce Tracts in Economics No. 11. London: London School of Economics.

——. *Capital and Interest: A Critical History of Economical Theory.* Translated with a preface and analysis by William Smart. London: Macmillan, 1890.

——. *The Positive Theory of Capital.* Translated by William Smart. London: Macmillan, 1891.

Boisguilbert, Pierre le Pesant. *Le détail de la France.* 1707.

Bowley, Marian. "Utility, the Paradox of Value and 'All That' and Classical Economics." In *Studies in the History of Economic Theory before 1870,* edited by M. Bowley, 133–57. London: Macmillan, 1973.

Bukharin, N. I. *Economic Theory of the Leisure Class.* New York: International Publishers, 1927.

Cairnes, John Elliot. *The Slave Power; Its Character, Career and Probable Designs: Being an Attempt to Explain the Real Issues Involved in the American Contest.* 2d ed. London: Macmillan, 1863.

——. *Essays in Political Economy: Theoretical and Applied.* London: Macmillan, 1873.

——. *Some Leading Principles of Political Economy Newly Expounded.* London: Macmillan, 1874.

Cannan, Edwin. *Wealth: A Brief Explanation of the Causes of Economic Welfare.* 2d ed. London: P. S. King, 1919.

——. "The Application of the Theoretical Apparatus of Supply & Demand for Units of Currency." *Economic Journal* 31 (December 1921): 453–61.

——. *A History of the Theories of Production and Distribution in English Political Economy from 1776 to 1848.* 3d ed. London: King, 1924.

——. *Wealth: A Brief Explanation of the Causes of Economic Welfare.* 3d ed. London: P. S. King, 1928.

——. *A Review of Economic Theory.* London: King, 1929.

——. *A History of the Theories of Production and Distribution in English Political Economy from 1776 to 1848.* 3d ed. London: Staples Publishing, 1953.

Cantillon, Richard. *Essai sur la nature du commerce en général* (1755). Edited with an English translation and other material by Henry Higgs. London: Macmillan for the Royal Economic Society, 1931.

——. *Essai sur la nature du commerce en général.* Texte de l'édition originale de 1755, avec des études et commentaires par Alfred Sauvy, Amintore Fanfani, Joseph J. Spengler, Lois Salleron. Paris: Institute National d'Études Démographiques, 1952.

——. *Essai de la nature du commerce en général.* Texte manuscrit de la Bibliothèque municipale de Rouen. Avec le teste de l'édition originale de 1755 et une étude bibliographique par Takumi Tsuda. Economic Research Series No. 18, the Institute of Economic Research, Hitotsubashi University. Tokyo: Kinokuniya Bookstore, 1979.

Cassel, Gustav. *The Nature and Necessity of Interest.* London: Macmillan, 1903.

Chalmers, Thomas. *On Political Economy in Connexion with the Moral State and Moral Prospects of Society.* 2d ed. Glasgow: William Collins, 1832.

Chamberlin, Edward Hastings. *The Theory of Monopolistic Competition.* Cambridge, Mass.: Harvard University Press, 1933.

Chapman, Sydney J. *Outlines of Political Economy.* 2d ed. London: Longmans, Green, 1913.

Child, Sir Josiah. *Brief Observations concerning Trade and Interest of Money* (1668). In *Josiah Child, Selected Works 1668–1697.* Republished from originals in the Goldsmiths' Library of Economic Literature, the University of London. Farnborough: Gregg Press, 1968.

———. *A New Discourse of Trade.* London: Sam. Crouch, 1693. In *Josiah Child: Selected Works, 1668–1697.* Republished from originals in the Goldsmiths' Library of Economic Literature, the University of London. Farnborough: Gregg Press, 1968.

Clark, John Bates. *The Philosophy of Wealth: Economic Principles Newly Formulated.* Boston: Ginn and Company, 1886.

———. "Possibility of a Scientific Law of Wages." *Publications of the American Economic Association* 4 (March 1889).

———. *The Essentials of Economic Theory as Applied to Modern Problems of Industry and Public Policy.* New York: Macmillan, 1918.

———. *The Distribution of Wealth: A Theory of Wages, Interest and Profits.* London: Macmillan, 1925.

Coleman, Donald Cuthbert, ed. *Revisions in Mercantilitsm.* London: Methuen, 1969.

Condillac, Étienne Bonnot de. *Le commerce et le gouvernement.* Amsterdam: Jombert and Cellot, 1776.

Cournot, Antoine Augustin. *Researches into the Mathematical Principles of the Theory of Wealth* (1838). Translated by Nathaniel T. Bacon. With an essay on Cournot and mathematical economics and a bibliography of mathematical economics by Irving Fisher. New York: Macmillan, 1927.

Cranston, Maurice. *John Locke: A Biography.* London: Longmans, Green, 1957.

Culpepper, Sir Thomas. *A Tract Against Usurie, Presented to the High Court of Parliament* (1621). London. Reprinted in *Josiah Child, Brief Observations Concerning Trade, And Interest of Money.* London: Calvert & Mortlock, 1668. In *Josiah Child: Selected Works, 1668–1697.* Farnborough: Gregg Press, 1968.

Cunningham, William. *The Growth of English Industry and Commerce.* 3 vols. Cambridge: Cambridge University Press, 1890.

———. "The Perversion of Economic History." *Economic Journal* 2 (September 1892): 491–506.

Davenport, Herbert Joseph. *Value and Distribution: A Critical and Constructive Study.* Chicago: University of Chicago Press, 1908.

de Roover, Raymond. "The Concept of the Just Price: Theory and Economic Policy." *Journal of Economic History* 18 (1958): 418–34. Reprinted in *Economic Thought: A Historical Anthology,* edited by James A. Gherity, 23–41. New York: Random House, 1965.

———. *San Bernardino of Siena and Sant' Antonino of Florence: The Two Great Economic Thinkers of the Middle Ages.* Boston: Baker Library, Harvard Graduate School of Business Administration, 1967.

Dewar, Mary. "The Authorship of the 'Discourse of the Commonweal.'" *Economic History Review* 19 (August 1966): 388–400.

Divine, Thomas F. *Interest: A Historical and Analytical Study in Economics and Modern Ethics.* Milwaukee, Wis.: Marquette University Press, 1959.

Dryden, John. "To My Honored Friend, Dr. Charleton" (1663). In *The Works of John Dryden*, edited by Edward Niles Hooker and H. T. Swedenberg Jr., 43–44. Berkeley: University of California Press, 1961.

Dumoulin, Charles (Carolus Molinaeus). *A Treatise on Contracts and Usury* (1546). In *Early Economic Thought: Selections from Economic Literature Prior to Adam Smith*, edited by Arthur E. Monroe, 103–20. Cambridge, Mass.: Harvard University Press, 1948.

Dupuit, Jules. "On the Measurement of the Utility of Public Works." *Annales des Ponts et Chaussées*, 2d series, 8 (1844). Reprinted in *Readings in Welfare Economics*, edited by Kenneth J. Arrow and Tibor Scitovsky, 255–83. Homewood, Ill.: Richard D. Irwin for the American Economic Association.

———. *De l'utilité et de sa mesure: Écrits choisis et republiées par Mario Bernardi* Turin: La Riforma Sociale, 1933.

Dutot, Charles Ferrare de. *Reflexions politiques sur les finances, et le commerce*. The Hague: Vaillant & Nicolas Prevost, 1738.

Edgeworth, Francis Ysidro. *Mathematical Psychics: An Essay on the Application of Mathematics to the Moral Sciences* (1881). L.S.E. Reprints of Scarce Tracts No. 10. London: London School of Economics, 1932.

———. "Review of *Natural Value*, by Professor Friedrich von Wieser" (1893?). In F. Y. Edgeworth, *Papers Relating to Political Economy*, 3:50–58. New York: Burt Franklin, 1925.

———. "The Laws of Increasing and Diminishing Returns." *Economic Journal* (1911). Reprinted in F. Y. Edgeworth, *Papers Relating to Political Economy*, 1:61–99. New York: Burt Franklin, 1925.

Fanfani, Amintore. *Storia Economica*. Torino: Unione Tipografico-Editrice Torinese, 1961.

Fetter, Frank A. *The Relations between Rent and Interest*. New York: Macmillan, 1904.

Fisher, Irving. *Mathematical Investigations in the Theory of Value and Prices* (1892). Transactions of the Connecticut Academy of Arts and Sciences. Reprint. New Haven: Yale University Press, 1925.

———. *Appreciation and Interest*. New York: Macmillan for the American Economic Association, 1896a.

———. "What Is Capital?" *Economic Journal* 6 (December 1896b): 509–34.

———. "The Senses of Capital." *Economic Journal* 7 (June 1897a): 199–213.

———. "The Role of Capital in Economic Theory." *Economic Journal* 7 (December 1897b): 511–37.

———. "Precedents for Defining Capital." *Quarterly Journal of Economics* 18 (May 1904): 386–408.

———. *The Nature of Capital and Income*. New York: Macmillan, 1906.

———. *The Rate of Interest: Its Nature, Determination and Relation to Economic Phenomena*. New York: Macmillan, 1907.

———. *The Purchasing Power of Money: Its Determination and Relation to Credit Interest and Crises*. Assisted by Harry G. Brown. New and revised edition. New York: Macmillan, 1925.

———. *Prohibition at Its Worst*. New York: Macmillan, 1926.

———. *The Theory of Interest as Determined by Impatience to Spend Income and Opportunity to Invest It*. New York: Macmillan, 1930.

Fitzmaurice, Lord Edmond. *The Life of Sir William Petty: 1623–1687*. London: John Murray, 1895.

Fourier, Charles. *Selections from the Works of Fourier*. Translated by Julia Franklin. London: Swan Sonnenschein, 1901. Reprinted as *Design for Utopia: Selected Writings of Charles Fourier*, with a new forward by Frank E. Manual. New York: Schocken Books, 1971.

Galiani, Ferdinando. *De la monnaie* (1751). Introduction and notes by G. H. Bousquet and J. Crisafulli. Paris: Marcel Rivière, 1955.

———. *Dialogues sur le commerce des blés*. 1770.

Gherity, James A. *Economic Thought: A Historical Anthology*. New York: Random House, 1965.

Godwin, William. *An Enquiry concerning Political Justice, and its Influence on General Virtue and Happiness*. London: G. G. J. and J. Robinson, 1793.

Gossen, Hermann Heinrich. *Entwicklung der Gesetze des menschlichen Verkehrs und der daraus fliessenden Regeln für menschliches Handeln* (1854). Auflage mit einem Vorwort von Dr. F. A. Hayek. Berlin: Prager, 1927.

Green, David I. "Pain-Cost and Opportunity-Cost." *Quarterly Journal of Economics* 8 (January 1894): 218–29.

Grice-Hutchinson, Marjorie. *Early Economic Thought in Spain, 1177–1740*. London: George Allen & Unwin, 1978.

Hamilton, Alexander. *Report on Manufacturers, Communicated to the House of Representatives December 5, 1791* (1791). In Alexander Hamilton, *Papers on Public Credit, Commerce, and Finance*, edited by Samuel McKee Jr., 175–276. New York: Columbia University Press, 1934.

Hawtrey, Ralph George. *Currency and Credit*. London: Longmans, Green, 1919.

———. *Currency and Credit*. 4th ed. London: Longmans, Green, 1950.

Hayek, Friedrich A. *Prices and Production*. London: Routledge, 1931.

Heckscher, Eli F. *Mercantilism*. Translated by Mendel Shapiro. London: George Allen & Unwin, 1935.

Hewins, William Albert Samuel. *English Trade and Finance. Chiefly in the Seventeenth Century*. London: Methuen, 1892.

Hicks, Sir John R. *The Theory of Wages*. London: Macmillan, 1932.

Hicks, J. R., and W. Weber, eds. *Carl Menger and the Austrian School of Economics*. Oxford: Clarendon Press, 1973.

Hollander, Jacob H. *David Ricardo: A Centenary Estimate*. Baltimore: Johns Hopkins University Press, 1910.

Hollander, Samuel. *The Economics of Adam Smith*. Toronto: University of Toronto Press, 1973.

———. *The Economics of David Ricardo*. Toronto: University of Toronto Press, 1979.

Hollander, Samuel, and Sir John Hicks. "Mr. Ricardo and the Moderns." *Quarterly Journal of Economics* 91 (August 1977): 351–69.

Hornick, Philipp Wilhelm von. *Austria Over All If Only She Will* (1684). In *Early Economic Thought: Selections from Economic Literature Prior to Adam Smith*, edited by Arthur E. Monroe, 221–43. Cambridge, Mass.: Harvard University Press, 1948.

Horsefield, J. Keith. *British Monetary Experiments 1650–1710*. London: G. Bell and Sons, London School of Economics, 1960.

Hume, David. *A Treatise on Human Nature* (1739–40). Edited, with preliminary dissertations and notes, by T. H. Green and T. H. Grose. London: Longmans Green, 1882.

———. *An Enquiry Concerning Human Understanding, and Other Essays* (1748). Edited by Ernest C. Mossner. New York: Washington Square Press, 1963.

———. *An Enquiry Concerning the Principles of Morals* (1751). In David Hume, *Essays Moral, Political, and Literary*, edited, with preliminary dissertations and notes, by T. H. Green and T. H. Grose, 2:167–287. London: Longmans, Green, 1907.

———. "My Own Life" (1776). In David Hume, *Essays Moral, Political, and Literary*, edited, with preliminary dissertations and notes, by T. H. Green and T. H. Grose, 1:1–8. London: Longmans, Green, 1907.

———. *Essays Moral, Political, and Literary.* Edited, with preliminary dissertations and notes, by T. H. Green and T. H. Grose. London: Longmans, Green, 1907.

———. *The Letters of David Hume.* Edited by J. Y. T. Greig. Oxford: Clarendon Press, 1932.

———. *New Letters.* Edited by Raymond Klibansky and Ernest C. Mossner. Oxford: Clarendon Press, 1954.

———. *Writings on Economics.* Edited and introduced by Eugene Rotwein. London: Nelson, 1955.

Hutcheson, Francis. *An Essay on the Original of our Ideas of Beauty and Virtue; in two treatises.* 3d ed. London: J. and J. Knapton, 1729.

———. *A System of Moral Philosophy, in Three Books* (1755). Glasgow and London: R. and A. Foulis. Reprinted in Francis Hutcheson, *Collected Works*, vols. 5–6. New York: G. Olms, 1990.

Hutchison, Terence W. *A Review of Economic Doctrines, 1870–1929.* Oxford: Clarendon Press, 1953.

———. "Review of *An Inquiry into the Principles of Political Economy*, by James Steuart, edited by A. S. Skinner (1966 reissue)." *Economic Journal* (1967): 645–47.

———. "Some Themes from *Investigations into Method*." In *Carl Menger and the Austrian School of Economics*, edited by J. R. Hicks and W. Weber, 1–37. Oxford: Clarendon Press, 1973.

Jaffé, William. "Pareto Translated: A Review Article." *Journal of Economic Literature* 10 (December 1972): 1190–1201.

Jennings, Richard. *Natural Elements of Political Economy.* London: Longman, Brown, 1855.

Jevons, W. Stanley. *A Serious Fall in the Value of Gold Ascertained, and Its Social Effects Set Forth.* London: Edward Stanford, 1863.

———. "Brief Account of a General Mathematical Theory of Political Economy." *Journal of the Royal Statistical Society* 29 (June 1866): 282–87.

———. *The Theory of Political Economy.* London and New York: Macmillan, 1871.

———. *The Theory of Political Economy.* 2d ed., revised with new preface and appendices. London and New York: Macmillan, 1879.

———. "Richard Cantillon and the Nationality of Political Economy." *Contemporary Review* (January 1881). Reprinted in Richard Cantillon, *Essai sur la nature du commerce en général*, edited with an English translation and other material by Henry Higgs, 331–60. London: Macmillan for the Royal Economic Society, 1931.

Jevons, W. Stanley. *The State in Relation to Labour*. London: Macmillan, 1882.

————. *Letters and Journal of W. Stanley Jevons*. Edited by Harriet A. Jevons. London: Macmillan, 1886.

————. *The Coal Question: An Inquiry Concerning the Progress of the Nation, and the Probable Exhaustion of Our Coal-mines*. 3d ed. Edited by A. W. Flux. London: Macmillan, 1906.

————. *Money and the Mechanism of Exchange*. 24th ed. London: Kegan Paul, Trench, Trubner, 1920.

————. *The Theory of Political Economy*. Edited by R. D. Collison Black. Harmondsworth: Penguin, 1970.

————. *Papers and Correspondence of William Stanley Jevons*. 6 vols. Edited by R. D. Collison Black et al. London and New York: Macmillan and Augustus M. Kelley, 1972–81.

Jones, Richard. *An Essay on the Distribution of Wealth, and on the Sources of Taxation* (1831). New York: Kelley and Millman, 1956.

————. *Literary Remains, Consisting of Lectures and Tracts on Political Economy of the Late Rev. Richard Jones*. Edited by the Rev. William Whewell. London: John Murray, 1859.

Joplin, Thomas. *An Illustration of Mr. Joplin's Views on Currency, and Plan for Improvement; Together with Observations Applicable to the Present State of the Money-market; in a Series of Letters*. London: Baldwin, Cradock, and Joy, 1825.

Kaldor, Nicholas. *An Expenditure Tax*. London: Allen & Unwin, 1955.

Keynes, John Maynard. *A Tract on Monetary Reform*. London: Macmillan, 1923.

————. *The End of Laissez-Faire*. London: Leonard and Virginia Woolf at the Hogarth Press, 1926. Reprinted in *Essays in Persuasion, The Collected Writings of John Maynard Keynes*, 9: 272–94. London: Macmillan for the Royal Economic Society, 1972.

————. *A Treatise on Money*. London: Macmillan, 1930.

————. *Essays in Biography*. London: Macmillan, 1933. Reprinted in *The Collected Writings of John Maynard Keynes*, vol. 10. London: Macmillan for the Royal Economic Society, 1972.

————. *The General Theory of Employment Interest and Money*. London: Macmillan, 1936.

Keynes, John Neville. *The Scope and Method of Political Economy*. London: Macmillan, 1890.

Knies, Karl Gustav Adolf. *Die Politische Oekonomie vom Standpunkt der Geschichtlichen Methode*. Braunschweig: C. A. Schwetschke, 1853.

————. *Das Geld: Darlegung der Grundlehren von dem Gelde, insbesondere der wirtschaftlichen und der rechtsgiltigen Functionen des Geldes, mit einer Erörterung über das Kapital und die Übertragung der Nutzungen*. Zweite verbesserte und vermehrte Auflage. Berlin: Weidmannsche, 1885.

Kraus, Oskar. "Die aristotelische Werttheorie in ihren Beziehungen zu den Lehren der modernen Psychologenschule." *Zeitschrift für die gesamte Staatswissenschaft* 61 (1905): 573–92.

La Bruyere, Jean de. *The Characters* (1698). London: John Bullard, 1699. Reprinted with an introduction by Denys C. Potts. London: Oxford University Press, 1963.

Langenstein, Heinrich von. *Tractus bipartitus de contractibus emptionis et venditionis*. Part 1, cap. 12. Published in Johannes Gerson, *Opera omnia*, 4. Cologne, fol. 191, 1484.

Lauderdale, James Maitland, 8th Earl of. *An Inquiry into the Nature and Origin of Public Wealth, and into the Means and Causes of Its Increase*. Edinburgh: For Archibald Constable, 1804.

Lavington, Frederick. *The English Capital Market*. London: Methuen, 1921.

Law, John. *Money and Trade Considered* (1705). Glasgow: R. & A. Foulis, 1750.

Le Branchu, Jean-Yves. *Écrits notables sur la monnaie XVIe siècle de Copernic à Davanzati*. Paris: Félix Alcan, 1934.

Leslie, Thomas Edward Cliffe. *Essays in Political Economy*. 2d ed. Dublin: Hodges, Figgis, 1888.

Letwin, William. *The Origins of Scientific Economics: English Economic Thought 1660–1776*. London: Methuen, 1963.

List, Friedrich. *The National System of Political Economy* (1841). Translated by Sampson S. Lloyd. New edition. Introduction by J. Shield Nicholson. London: Longmans, Green, 1904.

Lloyd, W. F. *Lecture on the Notion of Value* (1833). Reprinted in R. F. Harrod, "An Early Exposition of 'Final Utility': W. F. Lloyd's Lecture on 'The Notion of Value' (1833) Reprinted." *Economic History* (Supplement to the *Economic Journal*) 1 (May 1927): 168–83.

Locke, John. *Two Treatises of Government* (1690). In *The Works of John Locke,* 9th ed., vol. 4, 207–485. London: T. Longman, B. Law, 1794.

———. *Some Considerations of the Consequences of the Lowering of Interest, and Raising the Value of Money* (1691). In *The Works of John Locke,* 9th ed., vol. 4, 1–116. London: T. Longman, B. Law, 1794. Reprinted in William Letwin, *The Origins of Scientific Economics: English Economic Thought 1660–1776*, appendix 5, 273–300. London: Methuen, 1963.

———. *Further Considerations Concerning Raising the Value of Money* (1695). In *The Works of John Locke,* 9th ed., 4:131–206. London: T. Longman, B. Law, 1794.

———. *The Works of John Locke.* 9 Vols. 9th ed. London: T. Longman, B. Law, 1794.

Longfield, Mountifort. *Lectures on Political Economy: Delivered in Trinity and Michaelmas Terms, 1833*. Dublin: Richard Milliken and Son, 1834. Reprinted in L.S.E. Reprints of Scarce Tracts No. 8. London: London School of Economics, 1931.

———. *Three Lectures on Commerce, and One on Absenteeism, Delivered in Michaelmas Term, 1834, before the University of Dublin*. Dublin: Milliken and Son, 1835. Reprinted in L.S.E. Reprints of Scarce Works, No. 4. London: London School of Economics. 1938.

Lowndes, William. *A Report Containing an Essay for the Amendment of the Silver Coins*. London: Charles Bill, and the Executrix of Thomas Newcomb, 1695.

Machiavelli, Niccolo. *The Prince and The Discourses*. With an introduction by Max Lerner. New York: Modern Library, 1950.

Malestroict, Jehan Cherruyt de. *Paradoxes inédites du Seigneur de Malestroit touchant les monnoyes* (1566). Turin: Giulio Einaudi, 1937.

Malthus, Thomas Robert. *First Essay on Population* (1798). With notes by James Bonar. London: Royal Economic Society and Macmillan, 1926.

Malthus, Thomas Robert. *An Essay on the Principle of Population: Or, a View of Its Past and Present Effects on Human Happiness; with an Inquiry into Our Prospects Respecting the Future Removal or Mitigation of the Evils Which It Occasions.* A new (second) edition, very much enlarged. London: J. Johnson, 1803.

———. *Observations on the Effects of the Corn Laws, and of a Rise or Fall in the Price of Corn on the Agriculture and General Wealth of the Country.* London: John Murray, 1814. Republished as *A Reprint of Economic Tracts*, edited by Jacob H. Hollander. Baltimore: Johns Hopkins University Press, 1932.

———. *An Inquiry into the Nature and Progress of Rent, and the Principles by Which It Is Regulated.* London: John Murray, 1815.

———. *Principles of Political Economy Considered with a View to Their Practical Application.* London: John Murray, 1820.

———. "Population" (1823). In *Supplement to the Fourth, Fifth, and Sixth Editions of the Encyclopaedia Britannica.* Reprinted as *A Summary View of the Principle of Population.* London: John Murray, 1830.

———. *The Travel Diaries of Thomas Robert Malthus.* Edited by Patricia James. Cambridge: Cambridge University Press for the Royal Economic Society, 1966.

Malynes, Gerard de. *A treatise of the Canker of England's Common wealth* (1601). In *Tudor Economic Documents*, edited by Richard H. Tawney and Eileen Power, 386–404. London: Longmans, 1951.

———. *The Maintenance of Free Trade.* London: William Shefford, 1622. Reprints of Economic Classics. New York: Augustus M. Kelley, 1971.

———. *Lex mercatoria.* 3d ed. London: T. Basset, R. Chiswell, M. Horne, and E. Smith, 1686.

Mandeville, Bernard de. *The Grumbling Hive, or, Knaves Turn'd Honest,* 1705.

———. *The Fable of the Bees: or, private vices, publick benefits.* 6th ed. London: J. Tonson, 1732.

———. *The Fable of the Bees: or, private vices, publick benefits.* With a commentary critical, historical, and explanatory by F. B. Kaye. Oxford: Clarendon Press, 1924.

Marshall, Alfred. *Theory of Money—Manuscript about 1871* (1871). In *The Early Economic Writings of Alfred Marshall, 1867–1890*, edited and introduced by J. K. Whitaker, 1:164–76. London: Macmillan for the Royal Economic Society, 1975.

———. *The Pure Theory of Foreign Trade. The Pure Theory of Domestic Values* (1879). L.S.E. Series of Reprints of Scarce Tracts No.1. London: London School of Economics, 1930.

———. "Memoranda and Evidence before the Gold and Silver Commission" (1887). In *Official Papers by Alfred Marshall*, edited by J. M. Keynes, 17–195. London: Macmillan, 1926.

———. *Principles of Economics.* London: Macmillan, 1890.

———. *Elements of Economics in Industry* (1892a). London: Macmillan, 1920.

———. "A Reply to 'The Perversion of Economic History' by Dr. Cunningham." *Economic Journal* 2 (1892b): 507–19.

———. "Evidence before the Indian Currency Committee" (1899). In *Official Papers by Alfred Marshall*, edited by J. M. Keynes, 263–326. London: Macmillan, 1926.

———. *Principles of Economics.* 8th ed. London: Macmillan, 1920.

———. *Industry and Trade.* 4th ed. London: Macmillan, 1923a.

———. *Money, Credit, and Commerce.* London: Macmillan, 1923b.

Marshall, Alfred. *Official Papers by Alfred Marshall*. Edited by J. M. Keynes. London: Macmillan, 1926.

———. *Principles of Economics*. 9th (variorum) edition with annotations by C. W. Guillebaud. London: Macmillan for the Royal Economics Society, 1961.

———. *The Early Economic Writings of Alfred Marshall, 1867–1890*. 2 vols. Edited and introduced by J. K. Whitaker. London: Macmillan for the Royal Economic Society, 1975.

Marshall, Alfred, and Mary Paley Marshall. *The Economics of Industry*. 2d ed. London: Macmillan, 1881.

Marx, Karl. *A Contribution to the Critique of Political Economy* (1859). Translated from the second German edition by N. I. Stone. Chicago: Charles H. Kerr, 1911.

———. *Capital. A Critique of Political Economy* (1867). Translated from the third German edition by Samuel Moore and Edward Aveling and edited by Frederick Engels. Revised and amplified according to the fourth German edition by Ernest Untermann. Chicago: Charles H. Kerr, 1918.

———. *Theories of Surplus Value: Selections*. Translated by G. A. Bonner and Emile Burnes. New York: International Publishers, 1952.

Massie, Joseph. *An Essay on the Governing Causes of the Natural Rate of Interest; wherein the sentiments of Sir William Petty and Mr. Locke, on that head, are considered*. London: W. Owen, 1750.

McCulloch, J. R., ed. *A Select Collection of Early English Tracts on Commerce* (1859). Reprinted for the Economic History Society as *Early English Tracts on Commerce*. Cambridge: Cambridge University Press, 1952.

Meek, Ronald Lindley. *The Economics of Physiocracy: Essays and Translations*. London: George Allen and Unwin, 1962.

Melon, Jean Francois. *A Political Essay on Commerce*. Translated by David Bindon. Dublin: T. Woodward, 1739.

Menger, Anton. *The Right to the Whole Produce of Labour*. Translated by M. E. Tanner with and introduction and bibliography by H. S. Foxwell. London: Macmillan, 1899.

Menger, Carl. *Grundsätze der Volkswirtschaftslehre* (1871). Zweite Auflage mit einem Geleitwort von Richard Schüller aus dem Nachlass herausgegeben von Karl Menger. Vienna and Leipzig, 1923.

———. *Untersuchüngen über die Methode der Socialwissenschaften und der politischen Oekonomie insbesondere*. Berlin: Duncker & Humbolt, 1883. Translated as Menger (1950).

———. *Die Irrtümer des Historismus in der deutschen Nationalökonomie*. Vienna: Alfred Hölder, 1884.

———. *The Collected Works*. L.S.E. Reprints of Scarce Tracts Nos. 17, 18, 19, and 20. London: London School of Economics, 1933–36.

———. *Principles of Economics*. Translated and edited by James Dingwall and Bert F. Hoselitz. With an introduction by Frank H. Knight. Glencoe, Ill.: Free Press, 1950.

———. *Problems of Economics and Sociology*. Edited and with an introduction by Louis Schnieder. Translated by Francis Nock. Urbana: University of Illinois Press, 1963.

Mill, James. *Commerce Defended*. London: C. and R. Baldwin, 1808.

———. *Elements of Political Economy*. 3d ed. London: Baldwin, Cradock, and Joy,

1826. Reprinted in *James Mill: Selected Economic Writings*, edited by Donald Winch, 203–366. Chicago: University of Chicago Press, 1966.

Mill, John Stuart. *Essays on Some Unsettled Questions of Political Economy*. London: John W. Parker, 1844.

———. *Principles of Political Economy with Some of Their Applications to Social Philosophy*. London: John W. Parker, 1848.

———. *On Liberty*. London: John W. Parker, 1859.

———. *Considerations on Representative Government*. London: Parker, Son and Bourn, 1861.

———. "Thornton on Labour and Its Claims." *Fortnightly Review*, n.s. 5 (May 1869): 505–18; (June 1869): 680–700. Reprinted in J. S. Mill, *Collected Works*, 5:631–68. Toronto: University of Toronto Press, 1967.

———. *The Subjection of Women*. 3d ed. London: Longmans, Green, Reader, and Dyer, 1870.

———. *Principles of Political Economy*. 7th ed. London: Longmans, Green, 1871.

———. *Autobiography*. London: Longmans, Green, Reader, and Dyer, 1873.

———. *Utilitarianism*. 6th ed. London: Longmans, Green, 1877.

———. *Early Essays of J. S. Mill*. Selected from the original sources by J. W. M. Gibbs. Bohn's Library. London: G. Bell & Sons, 1897.

———. *Lettres inédites de John Stuart Mill a Auguste Comte*. Publiées avec les réponses de Comte et une introduction par L. Lévy-Bruhl. Paris: Germer Bailliére et Cie, Felix Alcan, 1899.

———. *Principles of Political Economy with Some of Their Applications to Social Philosophy*. Edited with an introduction by W. J. Ashley. London: Longmans, Green, 1909.

———. *On Bentham and Coleridge*. With and introduction by F. R. Leavis. London: Chatto and Windus, 1950.

———. *Principles of Political Economy*. 2 vols. Reprinted as vols. 2–3 in J. S. Mill, *Collected Works*. Toronto: University of Toronto Press, 1965.

———. *Collected Works*. 14 vols. Toronto: University of Toronto Press, 1965–77.

———. *Essays on Economics and Society*. In J. S. Mill, *Collected Works*, vols. 4–5. Toronto: University of Toronto Press, 1967.

Mirabeau, Victor Riquetti, Marquis de. *Philosophie rurale ou économique générale et politique de l'agriculture, réduite à l'ordre immuable des loix physiques & morales, qui assurent la prospérité des empires*. Amsterdam: Les Libraires Associés, 1764.

———. *L'ami des hommes ou traité de la population*. Avec une préface et une notice biographique par M. Rouxel. Paris: Guillaumin, 1883.

Mises, Ludwig von. *Theorie des Geldes und der Umlaufsmittel* (1912). Munich and Leipzig: Duncker & Humblot, 1924.

———. *The Theory of Money and Credit*. Translated by H. E. Batson. London: Jonathan Cape, 1934.

Misselden, Edward. *Free Trade; or, The Meanes to Make Trade Flourish Wherein the Causes of the Decay of Trade in this Kingdom are discovered* (1622). Reprints of Economic Classics. New York: Augustus M. Kelley, 1971.

———. *The Circle of Commerce or the Ballance of Trade* (1623). Reprints of Economic Classics. New York: Augustus M. Kelley, 1971.

Monroe, Arthur Eli. *Early Economic Thought: Selections from Economic Literature Prior to Adam Smith*. Cambridge, Mass.: Harvard University Press, 1948.

Montesquieu, Charles de. *De l'esprit des lois* (1748). Translated as *The Spirit of the Laws*, translated and edited by Anne M. Cohler, Basia Carolyn Miller, and Harold Samuel Stone. Cambridge: Cambridge University Press, 1989.

Mossner, Ernest Campbell. *The Life of David Hume*. London: Nelson, 1954.

Mun, Thomas. *A Discourse of Trade from England unto the East-Indies* (1621). Reproduced from the first edition. New York: Facsimile Text Society, 1930.

————. *England's Treasure by Forraign Trade* (1664). Reprinted from the first edition. Oxford: Published for the Economic History Society by Basil Blackwell, 1928.

Newman, John Henry. *Apologia pro Vita Sua*. London: Longmans Green, 1864.

North, Sir Dudley. *Discourses upon Trade* (1691). A Reprint of Economic Tracts, edited by Jacob H. Hollander. Baltimore: Johns Hopkins University Press, 1907.

O'Brien, Denis P. *J. R. McCulloch: A Study in Classical Economics*. London: George Allen & Unwin, 1970.

Oresme, Nicholas (1360). *Traictie de la première invention des monnoies* (1360). Reprinted in part in *Early Economic Thought: Selections from Economic Literature Prior to Adam Smith*, edited by Arthur E. Monroe, 79–102. Cambridge, Mass.: Harvard University Press, 1948.

————. *The De Moneta of Nicholas Oresme and English Mint Documents*. Translated with introduction and notes by Charles Johnson. London: Thomas Nelson and Sons, 1956.

Osorio, Antonio. *Théorie mathématique de l'échange*. Paris: Giard and Briere, 1913.

Owen, Robert. *A New View of Society and Other Writings*. London: J. M. Dent, 1949.

Pareto, Vilfredo. *Cours d'économic politique professé a l'Université de Lausanne*. 2 vols. Lausanne: F. Rouge, 1896–97.

————. *Manuel d'économie politique*. Translated by Alfred Bonnet. Paris: Marcel Giard, 1927.

————. *Manual of Political Economy*. New York: Augustus M. Kelley, 1971.

Pattison, Mark. *Memoirs*. London: Macmillan, 1885.

Pentey, A. J. *Old Worlds for New: A Study of the Post-Industrial State*. London: G. Allen and Unwin, 1917.

Petty, Sir William. *A Treatise of Taxes and Contributions* (1662). In *The Economic Writing of Sir William Petty*, edited by Charles Henry Hull, 1:1–97. Cambridge: Cambridge University Press, 1899.

————. *Verbum Sapienti* (1664). In *The Economic Writing of Sir William Petty*, edited by Charles Henry Hull, 1:99–120. Cambridge: Cambridge University Press, 1899.

————. *The Political Anatomy of Ireland* (1672). In *The Economic Writings of Sir William Petty*, edited by Charles Henry Hull, 1:121–231. Cambridge: Cambridge University Press, 1899.

————. *Political Arithmetick* (1676). In *The Economic Writing of Sir William Petty*, edited by Charles Henry Hull, 1:233–313. Cambridge: Cambridge University Press, 1899.

————. *Quantulumcunque Concerning Money* (1682). In *The Economic Writing of Sir William Petty*, edited by Charles Henry Hull, 2:437–48. Cambridge: Cambridge University Press, 1899.

————. *The Economic Writing of Sir William Petty*, 2 vols. Edited by Charles Henry Hull. Cambridge: Cambridge University Press, 1899.

Pigou, Arthur Cecil. *Essays in Applied Economics.* London: P. S. King, 1923.

————. *Memorials of Alfred Marshall.* London: Macmillan, 1925. Reprint. New York: Augustus M. Kelley, 1966.

Place, Francis. *Illustrations and Proofs of the Principle of Population.* London: Longman, Hurst, 1822.

Plato. *Laws.* In *The Dialogues of Plato,* vol. 4, 4th ed., translated by B. Jowett. Oxford: Oxford University Press, 1953a.

————. *Republic.* In *The Dialogues of Plato,* vol. 2, 4th ed., translated by B. Jowett. Oxford: Oxford University Press, 1953b.

Pope, Alexander. "The Rape of the Lock" (1792). In *The Works of Alexander Pope,* edited by Rev. Whitwell Elwin, 2:113–93. New York: Gordian Press, 1967.

Popper, Sir Karl R. *The Open Society and Its Enemies.* London: Routledge, 1952.

————. *The Poverty of Historicism.* London: Routledge & Kegan Paul, 1960.

Postlethwayt, Malachy. *Great Britain's True System.* London: A. Millar, 1757a.

————. *The Universal Dictionary of Trade and Commerce.* 2d ed. London: John Knapton, 1757b.

Quesnay, Francois. *Tableau économique* (1758). Edited by Margeruite Kuczynski and Ronald Meek. London and New York: Macmillan and Augustus M. Kelley for the Royal Economic Society, 1972.

————. *Oeuvres économiques et philosophiques de ... fondateur du système physiocratique.* Frankfurt: Joseph Baer and Paris: Jules Peelman, 1888.

————. *Francois Quesnay et la physiocratie.* Paris: Institut National d'Études Demographiques Presses, Universitaires de France, 1958.

Rae, John. *Statement of Some New Principles on the Subject of Political Economy* (1834). Reprinted as volume 2 of R. Warren James, *John Rae: Political Economist.* Toronto: University of Toronto Press, 1965.

————. *The Sociological Theory of Capital, Being a Complete Reprint of the New Principles of Political Economy, 1834.* Edited, with biographical sketch and notes, by Charles Whitney Mixter. New York: Macmillan, 1905.

————. *Life of Adam Smith.* London: Macmillan, 1895.

Ricardo, David. *The High Price of Bullion.* London: John Murray, 1810. Reprinted in *The Works and Correspondence of David Ricardo,* edited by Piero Sraffa, 3:47–127. Cambridge: Cambridge University Press, 1951.

————. *Reply to Mr. Bosanquet's "Practical Observations" on the Report of the Bullion Committee.* London: John Murray, 1811. Reprinted in *The Works and Correspondence of David Ricardo,* edited by Piero Sraffa, 3:155–256. Cambridge: Cambridge University Press, 1951.

————. *An Essay on the Influence of a Low Price of Corn on the Profits of Stock.* London: John Murray, 1815.

————. *On the Principles of Political Economy and Taxation.* London: John Murray, 1817.

————. *On the Principles of Political Economy and Taxation,* 3d ed. London: John Murray, 1821. Reprinted in *The Works and Correspondences of David Ricardo,* edited by Piero Sraffa, vol. 1. Cambridge: University Press for the Royal Economic Society, 1951.

————. *Notes on Malthus' "Principles of Political Economy."* Edited with an introduction and notes by Jacob H. Hollander and T. E. Gregory. Baltimore: Johns Hopkins University Press, 1928. Reprinted in *The Works and Correspondence of*

David Ricardo, edited by Piero Sraffa, vol. 2. Cambridge: Cambridge University Press, 1951.

———. *The Works and Correspondences of David Ricardo.* Edited by Piero Sraffa. Cambridge: Cambridge University Press for the Royal Economic Society, 1951–73.

Robbins, Lord. "Philip Wicksteed as an Economist" (1970). In Lionel Robbins, *The Evolution of Modern Economic Theory,* 189–209. Chicago: Aldine, 1970.

Robertson, Sir Dennis Holme. *Money.* Introduction by J. M. Keynes. London: Nisbet and Cambridge University Press, 1922.

———. *Banking Policy and the Price Level: An Essay in the Theory of the Trade Cycle.* London: P. S. King, 1926.

Roscher, Wilhelm G. F. (1851), *Zur Geschichte der englischen Volkswirthschaftslehre.* Aus dem III. Bande der Abhandlungen der Königlich Sächsischen Gesellschaft der Wissenschaften. Leipzig: Weidmannsche, 1851.

———. *Geschichte der National–Oekonomik in Deutschland.* Munich: R. Oldenbourg, 1874.

——— *Principles of Political Economy.* From the thirteenth (1877) German edition, translated by John J. Lalor, A.M. Chicago: Callaghand, 1878.

Saint-Simon, Claude Henri de Rouvroy. *Doctrine de Saint-Simon: exposition premiére année* (1829). Nouvelle édition publiée avec introduction et notes par C. Bouglé et Elie Halévy. Paris: Marcel Rivière, 1924.

———. *Henri Comte de Saint-Simon (1760–1825).* Selected writings. Edited and translated with an introduction by F. M. H. Markham. Oxford: Basil Blackwell, 1952.

Samuelson, Paul A. *Economics: An Introductory Analysis.* New York: McGraw-Hill, 1948.

San Bernardino. *De Evangelio Aeterno (The Eternal Gospel).* Spires, 1484.

Sant' Antonino. *Summa Theologica.* Basel, 1511.

Say, Jean-Baptiste. *Traité d'économie politique,* 2 vols. 3d ed. Paris: Deterville, 1817.

——— (1821), *A Treatise on Political Economy.* 2 vols. Translated from the fourth edition by C. R. Prinsep. London: Longman, Hurst, 1821.

Schmoller, Gustav von. *The Mercantile System and Its Historical Significance: Illustrated Chiefly from Prussian History.* New York: Macmillan, 1902. Reprint. New York: Augustus M. Kelley, 1967.

Schneider, Erich. *Einführung in die Wirtschaftstheorie. IV Teil. Ausgewählte Kapitel der Geschichte der Wirtschaftstheorie.* Tübingen: Mohr, 1962.

Schumpeter, Joseph A. *History of Economic Analysis.* New York: Oxford University Press, 1954.

———. *Ten Great Economists from Marx to Keynes.* London: George Allen and Unwin, 1956.

Schwartz, Pedro. *The New Political Economy of J. S. Mill.* First edition in English. London: London School of Economics, 1972.

Scott, William Robert. *Adam Smith as Student and Professor.* Glasgow: Jackson, Son and Co., Publishers to the University, 1937.

Senior, Nassau W. *Three Lectures on the Transmission of the Precious Metals from Country to Country, and the Mercantile Theory of Wealth, Delivered before the University of Oxford in June, 1827* (1827). L.S.E. Reprints of Scarce Tracts No. 3. London: London School of Economics, c. 1930.

Senior, Nassau W. *Three Lectures on the Cost of Obtaining Money, and on Some Effects of Private and Government Paper Money; Delivered before the University of Oxford, in Trinity Term, 1829* (1829a). L.S.E. Reprints of Scarce Tracts No. 5. London: London School of Economics, c. 1930.

————. *Three Lectures on the Value of Money; Delivered before the University of Oxford, in 1829* (1829b). L.S.E. Reprints of Scarce Tracts No. 4. London: London School of Economics, 1931.

————. *A Letter to Lord Howick, on a Legal Provision for the Irish Poor, Commutation of Tithes, and a Provision for the Irish Roman Catholic Clergy.* London: John Murray, 1831.

————. *An Outline of the Science of Political Economy* (1836). London: George Allen & Unwin, 1938.

————. "Free Trade and Retaliation." *Edinburgh Review* 157 (July 1843).

Serra, Antonio. *A Brief Treatise on the Causes which can make Gold and Silver Plentiful in Kingdoms where there are no Mines* (1613). In *Early Economic Thought: Selections from Economic Literature Prior to Adam Smith*, edited by Arthur E. Monroe, 143–67. Cambridge, Mass.: Harvard University Press, 1948.

Shoup, Carl S. *Ricardo on Taxation.* New York: Columbia University Press, 1960.

Shove, Gerald F. "The Place of Alfred Marshall's Principles in the Development of Economic Theory." *Economic Journal* 52 (December 1942): 294–329. Reprinted in *Economic Thought: A Historical Anthology*, edited by James A. Gherity, 432–70. New York: Random House, 1965.

Smith, Adam. *The Theory of Moral Sentiments* (1759). 7th ed. London: A. Strahan; and T. Cadell, 1792.

————. *An Inquiry into the Nature and Causes of the Wealth of Nations* (1776). Edited with introduction, notes, marginal summary, and enlarged index by Edwin Cannan. 3d ed. London: Methuen, 1922.

————. *An Inquiry into the Nature and Causes of the Wealth of Nations.* Glasgow edition, edited by R. H. Campbell and A. S. Skinner. Oxford: Clarendon Press, 1976.

————. *Lectures on Jurisprudence.* Edited by R. L. Meek, D. D. Raphael, and P. G. Stein. Oxford: Clarendon Press, 1978.

Spence, William. *Britain Independent of Commerce.* 4th ed. London: W. Savage for T. Cadell and W. Davies, 1808.

Sraffa, Piero. "The Laws of Returns under Competitive Conditions." *Economic Journal* 36 (December 1926): 535–50.

Stangeland, Charles Emil (1904), *Pre-Malthusian Doctrines of Population: A Study in the History of Economic Theory.* New York: Columbia University Press, 1904.

Steuart, Sir James Denham. *An Inquiry into the Principles of Political Economy* (1767). 2 vols. Edited with an introduction by Andrew S. Skinner. Edinburgh: Oliver and Boyd for the Scottish Economic Society, 1966.

Stewart, Dugald. *Biographical memoirs, of Adam Smith, LL.D. of William Robertson, D.D. and Thomas Reid, D.D. read before the Royal Society of Edinburgh.* Edinburgh: For W. Creech, Bell and Bradfute, 1811.

Stigler, George J. *Production and Distribution Theories.* New York: Macmillan, 1941.

————. "Ricardo and the 93 Per Cent Labor Theory of Value." *American Economic Review* 48 (June 1958): 357–67. Reprinted in George J. Stigler, *Essays in the History of Economics*, 326–42. Chicago: University of Chicago Press, 1965.

Stigler, George J. *Essays in the History of Economics*. Chicago: University of Chicago Press, 1965.

Taussig, Frank William. *Wages and Capital*. New York: Appleton, 1897. Reprinted in L.S.E. Reprint of Scarce Tracts No. 13. London: London School of Economics, 1932.

———. "Wages and Prices in Relation to International Trade." *Quarterly Journal of Economics* 20 (1906): 497–522.

———. *International Trade*. New York: Macmillan, 1927.

Tawney, Richard Henry *Religion and the Rise of Capitalism*. London: John Murray, 1926.

Tawney, Richard Henry, and Eileen Power, eds. *Tudor Economic Documents: Being Select Documents Illustrating the Economic and Social History of Tudor England*. London: Longmans, 1951.

Taylor, William Leslie. *Francis Hutcheson and David Hume as Predecessors of Adam Smith*. Durham, N.C.: Duke University Press, 1965.

Theocharis, Reghinos D. *Early Developments in Mathematical Economics*. London: Macmillan, 1961.

Thornton, Henry. *An Enquiry into the Nature and Effects of the Paper Credit of Great Britain*. London: J. Hatchard, 1802.

———. *Substance of Two Speeches of Henry Thornton, Esq. in the Debate in the House of Commons, on the Report of the Bullion Committee, on the 7th and 14th of May, 1811*. London: J. Hatchard, 1811.

———. *An Enquiry into the Nature and Effects of the Paper Credit of Great Britain (1802). Together with His Evidence Given before the Committees of Secrecy of the Two Houses of Parliament in the Bank of England, March and April, 1797, Some Manuscript Notes, and His Speeches on the Bullion Report, May 1811*. Edited with an introduction by Friedrich A. von Hayek. London: George Allen & Unwin, 1939.

Thornton, William Thomas. *On Labour: Its Wrongful Claims and Rightful Dues. Its Actual Present and Possible Future*. London: Macmillan, 1869.

Thünen, Johann Heinrich von. *Von Thünen's Isolated State: An English edition of Der Isolierte Staat*. Translated by Carla M. Wartenberg. Edited with an introduction by Peter Hall. Oxford: Pergamon Press, 1966.

Torrens, Robert. *The Economists Refuted*. London: S. A. and H. Oddy, 1808.

———. *An Essay on the External Corn Trade*. London: J. Hatchard, 1815.

———. *Letters on Commercial Policy* (1833). With an introduction by Lionel Robbins. L.S.E. Reprints of Scarce Works No. 14. London: London School of Economics, 1958.

———. *The Budget: On commercial and Colonial Policy*. London: Smith, Elder, 1844.

———. *The Principles and Practical Operation of Sir Robert Peel's Bill of 1844 Explained, and Defended against the Objections of Tooke, Fullarton, and Wilson*. London: Longman, Brown, 1848.

Tucker, Graham Shardalow Lee. *Progress and Profits in British Economic Thought, 1650–1850*. Cambridge: Cambridge University Press, 1960.

Turgot, Anne Robert Jacques. *Reflections on the formation and distribution of Wealth* (1770). In *Turgot on Progress, Sociology and Economics*, translated, edited, and with an introduction by Ronald L. Meek, 119–82. Cambridge: Cambridge University Press, 1973.

Vauban, Sébastien le Prestre de. *Projet d'une dixme.* Translated as *An Essay for a General Tax.* 2d ed. London: John Matthews for Geo. Strahan, 1710.

Vickers, Douglas. *Studies in the Theory of Money 1690–1776.* London: Peter Owen, 1960.

Viner, Jacob. *Studies in the Theory of International Trade.* London: Allen and Unwin, 1937.

Voltaire. *The Man of Forty Crowns* (*L'homme aux quarante écus*) (1768). In *The Works of Voltaire,* translated by William K. Fleming, 2:244–308. New York: E. R. DuMont, 1901.

Wakefield, Edward Gibbon. *A View of the Art of Colonization, with Present Reference to the British Empire; in Letters between a Statesman and a Colonist.* London: John W. Parker, 1849.

Walras, Auguste. *De la nature de la richesse et de l'origine de la valeur augmenté de notes inédites de Jean-Baptiste Say* (1831). Reprinted with an introduction by Gaston Leduc. Paris: Félix Alcan, 1938.

Walras, Leon. *Éléments d'économie politique pure ou théorie de la richesse sociale.* Lausanne, Paris, Bale: L. Corbaz, 1874a.

———. "Principe d'une théorie mathématique de l'échange." *Journal des Économistes,* 3d series, 34 (1874b), 5–21.

———. *Théorie de la monnaie.* Paris: Bureau des Revues, 1886.

———. *Elements of Pure Economics or the Theory of Social Wealth.* Translated by William Jaffé. London: George Allen and Unwin, 1954.

———. *Correspondence of Léon Walras and Related Papers.* 3 vols. Edited by William Jaffé. Amsterdam: North-Holland, 1965.

Weber, Max. "Roscher und Kneis und die logischen Probleme der historischen Nationalökomie." In *Gesammelte Aufsätze zur Wissenschaftslehre,* 1–145. Tübingen: Mohr, 1922.

West, Sir Edward. *An Essay on the Application of Capital to Land, with Observations Shewing the Impolicy of any Great Restriction of the Importation of Corn, and That the Bounty of 1688 Did Not Lower the Price of It.* London: T. Underwood, 1815. Reprinted as A Reprint of Economic Tracts, edited by Jacob H. Hollander. Baltimore: Johns Hopkins University Press, 1934.

Whewell, William. *On the Mathematical Exposition of Some Doctrines of Political Economy.* From the Transactions of the Cambridge Philosophy Society. Cambridge: J. Smith, Printer to the University, 1829. Republished from the originals in the Goldsmiths' Library of Economic Literature, University of London. Farnborough: Gregg International Publishers, 1968.

Wicksell, Knut. *Über Wert, Kapital und Rente nach den neueren Nationalökonomischen Theorien* (1893). L.S.E. Reprints of Scarce Tracts No. 15. London: London School of Economics, 1933.

———. *Interest and Prices. (Geldzins und Güterpreise): A Study of the Causes Regulating the Value of Money.* Translated by R. F. Kahn with an introduction by Professor Bertil Ohlin. London: Macmillan for the Royal Economic Society, 1936.

———. *Lectures on Political Economy.* Translated by E. Classen and edited with an introduction by Lionel Robbins. London: George Routledge, 1934–35.

———. *Value, Capital and Rent.* Translated by S. H. Frowein and with a foreword by Professor G. L. S. Shackle. London: George Allen and Unwin, 1954.

Wicksteed, Philip H. *An Essay on the Co-ordination of the Laws of Distribution.*

London: Macmillan, 1894. L.S.E. Reprints of Scarce Tracts No. 12. London: London School of Economics, 1932.

———. *The Common Sense of Political Economy Including a Study of the Human Basis of Economic Law.* London: Macmillan, 1910.

Wieser, Friedrich von. *Über den Ursprung und die Hauptgesetze des Wirthschaftlichen Werthes.* Vienna: Alfred Hölder, 1884.

———. *Natural Value.* Edited by William Smart. Translated by Christian A. Malloch. London: Macmillan, 1893. Reprint. New York: Augustus M. Kelley, 1971.

Wilson, Thomas. *A Discourse Upon Usury by way of Dialogue and Orations, for the better Variety and more Delight of all Those that shall read this Treatise* (1572). With an historical introduction by R. H. Tawney. London: G. Bell and Sons, 1925.

Wordsworth, William. "The Prelude" (1805). In *The Poetical Works of Wordsworth,* 124–222. Boston: Houghton Mifflin, 1982.

———. "French Revolution" (1809). In *The Poetical Works of Wordsworth,* 340. Boston: Houghton Mifflin, 1982.

W. S. *A Discourse of the Common Weal of this Realm of England* (1581). Edited by Elizabeth Lamond. First printed in 1581 and commonly attributed to W.S. Cambridge: Cambridge University Press, 1929.

Xenophon. *On the Means of Improving the Revenue of the State of Athens.* In *Early Economic Thought: Selections from Economic Literature Prior to Adam Smith,* edited by Arthur E. Monroe, 31–49. Cambridge, Mass.: Harvard University Press, 1948.

Young, Allyn Abbott. "Increasing Returns and Economic Progress." *Economic Journal* 38 (December 1928): 527–42.

Young, Arthur. *Travels during the Years 1787, 1788, & 1789; undertaken for particularly with a view of ascertaining the cultivation, wealth, resources, and financial prosperity of the Kingdom of France.* 2 vols. 2d ed. London: Richardson, 1794.

Zawadzki, Wladyslaw Marian. *Les mathématiques Appliquées a l'économie politique.* Paris: Rivière, 1914.